IMAGINE A NATION

IMAGINE A NATION

Six Persian Poets in Search of a Homeland

Hamid Dabashi

I.B. TAURIS
LONDON · NEW YORK · OXFORD · NEW DELHI · SYDNEY

I.B. TAURIS

Bloomsbury Publishing Plc, 50 Bedford Square, London, WC1B 3DP, UK
Bloomsbury Publishing Inc, 1359 Broadway, New York, NY 10018, USA
Bloomsbury Publishing Ireland, 29 Earlsfort Terrace, Dublin 2, D02 AY28, Ireland

BLOOMSBURY, I.B. TAURIS and the I.B. Tauris logo are trademarks
of Bloomsbury Publishing Plc

First published in Great Britain 2025

Copyright © Hamid Dabashi, 2025

Hamid Dabashi has asserted his rights under the Copyright, Designs and
Patents Act, 1988, to be identified as Author of this work.

Cover design: Adriana Brioso
Cover image: *Landscape with Houses*, oil on canvas 24 3/8 x 35 3/8in. (62 x 90cm.) Painted
circa early 1970s by Sohrab Sepehri (1928–80).

All rights reserved. No part of this publication may be: i) reproduced or transmitted in any form, electronic or mechanical, including photocopying, recording or by means of any information storage or retrieval system without prior permission in writing from the publishers; or ii) used or reproduced in any way for the training, development or operation of artificial intelligence (AI) technologies, including generative AI technologies. The rights holders expressly reserve this publication from the text and data mining exception as per Article 4(3) of the Digital Single Market Directive (EU) 2019/790.

Bloomsbury Publishing Plc does not have any control over, or responsibility for, any third-party websites referred to in this book. All internet addresses given in this book were correct at the time of going to press. The author and publisher regret any inconvenience caused if addresses have changed or sites have ceased to exist, but can accept no responsibility for any such changes.

A catalogue record for this book is available from the British Library.

A catalog record for this book is available from the Library of Congress.

ISBN: HB: 978-0-7556-5563-2
PB: 978-0-7556-5562-5
ePDF: 978-0-7556-5565-6
eBook: 978-0-7556-5564-9

Typeset by RefineCatch Limited, Bungay, Suffolk
Printed and bound in Great Britain

For product safety related questions contact productsafety@bloomsbury.com.

To find out more about our authors and books visit www.bloomsbury.com
and sign up for our newsletters.

For

Mahmoud Omidsalar
Saïd Amir Arjomand
Fatemeh Keshavarz
Hamid Naficy
Ali Mirsepassi
Peyman Vahabzadeh
Nasrin Rahimieh
Hamid Keshmirshekan
Firoozeh Kashani-Sabet . . . and
Asef Bayat

The Last of the "Mohicans!"

CONTENTS

Introduction
IMAGINE A NATION   1

Chapter 1
NIMA YUSHIJ: THE ARCHETYPAL EVENT   33

Chapter 2
MEHDI AKHAVAN-E SALES: REMEMBRANCE OF THINGS PAST   63

Chapter 3
AHMAD SHAMLOU: THE TROUBADOUR OF A HOMELAND TO COME   89

Chapter 4
FOROUGH FARROKHZAD: THE POETICS OF THE PRESENT   115

Chapter 5
SOHRAB SEPEHRI: A METAPOETIC OF PRESENCE   151

Chapter 6
ESMAIL KHO'I: THE VOICE FROM NOWHEREVILLE   183

Conclusion
SIX PERSIAN POETS IN SEARCH OF A HOMELAND   207

Notes   223
Index   249

Introduction

IMAGINE A NATION

I am convinced, and I know this for a fact, that millions of Iranians like me know by heart more lines of poetry, classical and contemporary, than they do the sacred verses of the Qur'an. This is not to utter a blasphemy. This is just to share a fact—a fact that must not be abused and read as a sign of the colonial category code-named "secularity." I know countless verses of the Qur'an by heart, too. And there are times when they come to my mind naturally, effortlessly, confidently, happily. One of the most soothing (at the same time ecstatic) moments of my life has always been to listen to the Qur'anic recitations by the legendary Egyptian Qari Abdul Basit Abd us-Samad (1927–88). There are times when I get lost reading the original Arabic and then following the glorious Persian translations of the Qur'an, whispering them reverently to myself. And then there is Persian poetry. There is no contradiction in that. But when reciting verses of the Qur'an, we know we are in the presence of the sacred, the sublime, the supreme, the awesome. We have a more intimate, more immediate, more maternal (so I have always thought) facility with Persian poetry. It is as if we are sharing a happy moment with our mothers—or memories of our mothers. Reading or reciting the Qur'an is like listening to your fearful father: authoritative, oracular, prophetic. And yet: there are moments when, while reciting Persian poetry, you suddenly sense the presence of the sacred, too—although this time in a material and more palpable way, as if Mother Earth were now talking to you. Here is Nima Yushij's "Till the Morning Dawns" (March 1951):

Ta sobh-daman dar in shab-e garm . . .

Till the morning dawns
In this hot night—
I have lit a light
For I am building a wall
In this house of the blind!

A blind man points
To what I have built and finds faults with it:
While another blind man

Demands an explanation:
What is this, what is that?

This is how I place one brick on another
In this house of the blind—
So when the hot sun rises tomorrow
I will have built them a shady cover!

I have lit a light
Till the morning dawns
In this hot night—
For I am building an ever-solid wall
In this house of the blind![1]

I write this book on six Persian poets—definitive to the formation of a nation, my nation, the gathering of a people, my people—at the most iconic moment of its history, when from the scattered and distant relics of their memorial past they came together to craft a homeland in a world that was rapidly changing around them. These poets came together to imagine a nation, knowingly or unknowingly, with the power of their poetic imagination, definitive to the minds and souls of a people, now forming a new nation remembering their ancient past, invested in their most celebrated lyrical visionaries: at once poetic, political, potent, and unfolding like a melodious chess game! Six Persian poets in search of a homeland: the idea for this book came to me years ago, when I first read the English translation of Luigi Pirandello's *Six Characters in Search of an Author* (1921). I was aware of Pirandello's absurdist meta-theatrical play because of a legendary performance of it back in the 1960s, directed by the renowned Iranian dramatist Pari Sabari (1932–2024) and featuring the prominent poet Forough Farrokhzad in a lead role. The play was known to me for decades—even though it was not the absurdist or self-conscious cast of the play but its ironic and mimetic twist of characters looking for an author to complete their stories that reminded me of a similar scenario one might propose to be at work among (now I counted) six seminal Persian poets of Iran ("Persian" meaning the language in which they wrote their poems) in the twentieth century, as well as of the cumulative effects of their poetry, as they were inadvertently, but intuitively, looking for a conception of their homeland that would house and hold them all together. "Homeland" here is more an emotive universe, a place in the world, than the mere landscape of an ancient terrain on any old or new map. That search, so I thought, was emblematic of a larger collective consciousness that defined the entire nation, which they now poetically perceived, posited, defined, ennobled, and embraced.

I was born and raised to this poetic legacy, from the 1950s to the 1970s, when this poetry was well underway, and met a few of these poets in person: Ahmad Shamlou I met both in Iran and in the US when he visited, as I did Mehdi Akhavan-e Sales in London, and Esmail Kho'i both in London and in the US. The rest I knew so well through their prose and poetry, and I had read them so early and closely in my life, as if they had been members of my own family. I am not alone in this feeling of poetic legacy and intimacy. Most Iranians of my generation have a similar sentiment towards these six poets, among whom they, of course, have their favorites. I do not have any favorite among them. I love them all equally and dearly. I cannot think and read any one of them without thinking and recalling the rest of them. My project in this book is something that transcends them individually yet is rooted in the poetic oeuvre that they have left behind. One of the most striking things that I noticed when I had just come to the US and eventually moved into the English language was how exceptional, extraordinary, and rare the poetic occasion was at a general social level. The America to which I had moved had, of course, a rainbow of glorious poets: T. S. Eliot, Ezra Pound, Sylvia Plath, Langston Hughes, and Maya Angelou were already known to me when I arrived in the mid-1970s. But these poets stood apart from daily life, a rarity, and it was something of an elitist luxury to know, read, and recite them. This was not the case with these Iranian poets. They were part of our quotidian lives, definitive to our daily diction, and normative to our moral memory of our lives.

These six poets were almost entirely the products and crowning achievements of the twentieth century—or, more specifically, the outcome of the Constitutional Revolution of 1906–11, when a new poetic diction emerged from the harsh and hard political battles against an absolutist monarchy. Only Nima Yushij (1897–1960), the spiritual father of them all, was born late in the nineteenth century, and only the last of them, Esmail Kho'i (1938–2021), lived into the twenty-first century. One of them, Forough Farrokhzad (1934–67), died very young in an automobile accident. They were therefore definitive to the formative years of an entire century in which Iran emerged from the waning years of the Qajar dynasty (1789–1926) and the waxing years of the Pahlavi era (1926–79), before it was toppled by a massive revolution which the Islamists took over to establish an Islamic Republic. Four of these poets—Sohrab Sepehri (1928–80), Mehdi Akhavan-e Sales (1929–90), Ahmad Shamlou (1925–2000), and Esmail Kho'i—lived to see the rise of the Islamic Republic to supplant the Pahlavis, but only one of them, Kho'i, took full advantage of his departure from Iran and exile in England to leave a record of a bitter, angry, and hateful encounter with the Islamist regime.

Six poets in search of a homeland—imagining a nation: they gained and lost with a lasting memory that will leave no state at peace to lay a total claim to this "nation-state." That is the story I wish to share.

Periodizing Contemporary Persian Poetry

So when and where are we? We are in the Iran of the twentieth century. In what language is this poetry composed, read, recited, studied, discussed, and celebrated? Persian. Who is ruling in Iran in this period? We move from late in the Qajar period (1789–1926), all through the Pahlavi dynasty (1926–79), well into the early decades of the Islamic Republic that began soon after the revolution of 1977–9. From the Constitutional Revolution of 1906–11 onwards, well into the revolutionary momentum of the mid-1970s, a renewed rise and effervescence of Persian poetry became the solid site of the nation's moral imagination, political aspirations, and above all an aesthetic intuition of self-transcendence. Poetry is not a pastime, a luxury, an elitist preoccupation, or a rarity among the privileged few. It is potent, political, vastly popular, and, in fact, the very cast of a people's political and moral imagination.

Let me dwell for a moment further on the issue of historical period and periodization of this body of poetry, which I am about to present in greater detail. Let us divide the history of Persian poetry into two very broad periods: classical and contemporary, with the Constitutional Revolution of 1906–11 as the hard dividing borderline between these two general frameworks. Because in this book my thinking is directed at detecting and outlining an internal temporal dynamics evident in these poets' works themselves, and because I intend to make a philosophical point of poetic time and narrative, as well as of the New Poetry as an Event, I will intentionally avoid the deeply troubled terms "modern," "modernism," or "modernity," except in a decidedly critical cast from the vantage point of their colonial consequences and darker shadows.[2] The poets I consider in this book have been habitually, uncritically, and invariably considered to be "modern" or even "modernists."[3] I have in my own earlier writings worked through this concept by marking it as "colonial modernity." In this study, I wish to interrupt that unexamined attribution altogether. Iran, like the rest of the colonized world, received the European project of capitalist modernity through the terror of colonialism. For this critical choice I therefore have multiple reasons, mostly theoretical and philosophical, but also historical. To present only one piece of evidence, I ask my readers to consider a seminal book by the leading Iranian poet and literary critic Mohammad Reza Shafi'i-Kadkani, *Advar-e She'r-e Farsi/Periods of Persian Poetry*—which is a collection of lectures he initially delivered at Tehran University in the 1960s and 1970s, subsequently collected and published in 1980 and revised in 2001.[4] As you see, there is no word meaning "modern," "modernity," or "modernism" in the title, while the subtitle of the book does clarify the period: *Az Mashrutiyyat ta Soqut-e Saltant/From Constitutionalism to the Collapse of the Monarchy*. This means from around 1906–11 to 1977–9. This book is a solid document of how the Iranian literati as best represented by Shafi'i-Kadkani have periodized their own contemporary era in terms entirely internal to their national and cultural history. This book is a collection of lectures that Shafi'i-Kadkani over the years delivered to his students at Tehran University, meaning that generations of Iranian literary students and now scholars have been educated and cultivated in these terms. There is no indication of anything called "modern" or "modernist" in Shafi'i-Kadkani's articulation of this body of poetry—and rightly so. People can read, write, think, engage in literary criticism, and so on without any need for the word "modern" or any of its cognates. At best, we might therefore consider neutral terms such as "classical/*moteqaddem*" and "contemporary/*mote'akhkher* or *mo'aser*" to designate a periodization based on both temporal and stylistic measures.

The enduring trouble with much of the scholarship on Persian literary or cultural history in English or French, or any other European language, is a systematic ignorance of or disregard for the scholarship of Iranian scholars in their own national language. A watered-down fusion of old-fashioned Orientalism and now Area (Security) Studies has actively formed, informed, and deformed the field, rarely infused with any critical attention to cliché terms such as "modern," or, even worse, "tradition and modernity."[5] The word and idea of "modern" is categorically troublesome because we must immediately realize that its application to any non-European context is so deeply flawed, unless immediately coupled with the predatory consequences of European colonialism. Modernity was capitalist modernity, and that capitalism had a nasty, dark, and murderous colonial shadow. Europeans are perfectly entitled to do and be and speculate as much "modernity" as they want. But not Indians, Chinese, Africans, Latin Americans, Asians from any corner of the continent, and, of course, Iranians—unless they immediately add the factor of colonialism. Terms such as "multiple modernities" or "alternative modernities" are all serious attempts to come to terms with these issues, but to no conclusive effect to abandon the solid critical stance *vis-à-vis* the project of Eurocentric capitalist modernity.[6] Generations of scholars have falsely applied these terms to non-European contexts without a moment of critical reflection.[7] In this study, I wish to stay away from the word "modern" or identify the poets I study as "modernist," for it robs them all of their poetic distance to and political angle on the colonial consequences of European capitalist modernity that had come *at them* violently and not *to them* naturally. A critical stand *vis-à-vis* the project of European modernity, as the eminent Argentinian scholar Walter Mignolo and others have long held, is definitive to any decolonial project as the *modus operandi* of any postcolonial and decolonial knowledge production.

In this pioneering study on Persian poetry of his own time, Shafi'i-Kadkani has divided the contemporary period into seven distinct stages: (1) before the Constitutional period; (2) the Constitutional period; (3) Reza Shah's period; (4) from Shahrivar 1320 to the coup of 28 Mordad 1332 on the Persian calendar; (5) from the coup of 1332 to 1340; (6) from 1340 to 1349 and the rise of armed struggles; and finally, (7) from 1349 to Bahman 1357.[8] I have intentionally left these dates and references in their original Persian calendar insignia, before I convert them to the Gregorian calendar and explain what this periodization means.[9] In the common Christian calendar, the Constitutional period is between 1906 and 1911, when a massive national uprising swept the country and ultimately toppled the absolutist monarchy of the Qajar dynasty (1789–1926). This is a crucial event that Shafi'i-Kadkani has used as a landmark episode to consider the poetry before, during, and after that cataclysmic event. Reza Shah's period established the Pahlavi dynasty (1926–79), and Shafi'i-Kadkani has paid particular attention to the first Pahlavi monarch between 1925 and 1941—when a relative period of freedom was instantly crushed by Reza Shah's petty dictatorship during the Second World War. Then comes the period of the second and final Pahlavi monarch, Mohammad Reza Shah (reigned 1941–79), who came to power after his father's abdication, forced by the Allied Forces in 1941 (because he was too sympathetic to Hitler and the Nazis) and lasted until the 1953 US and UK military coup against the democratically elected premiership of Mohammad Mosaddegh, when the

Shah fled the country and was brought back to power by the combined treacheries of the American CIA and the British MI6—in a perfect show of "military modernity." The following period between the coup of 1953 and 1961 marks a time of political stagnation, followed by the decade between 1961 and 1970 when a new poetic urge took shape. Finally comes the crucial decade of the 1970s before the 1979 revolution, when Persian poetry assumed a potent political ferocity with its active celebration of armed rebellion.[10] For each of these seven episodes, Shafi'i-Kadkani has offered ample examples from the most significant poets of those eras.

In this periodization, Shafi'i-Kadkani has considered the pre-Constitutional period, meaning the declining decades of the Qajar dynasty, as "ground zero" as he has put it, and the normative scale against which the rest of his periodization follows. For this period of stagnant poetic production, he has used Marx's famous expression about Hegel—that history happens twice, once as tragedy and then as farce. Prominent figures of this period, such as Soroush Esfahani and Amir Mo'ezi, become caricatures of the previous masters.[11] These are all cliché poets of the classical genre of panegyrics in praise of kings and princes, where we see that the poet is woefully ignorant of changes happening in the world about them. Shafi'i-Kadkani has used the periodization of the "*Qorun-e Vosta*/Middle Ages" for this period—one of the few knee-jerk phrases borrowed from European historical narratives—without pausing to wonder if it is in any way applicable to Iranian or Islamic political or cultural history. What he has meant by that term is that the period is decadent; therefore, the term is used more as a negative adjective rather than any serious attention to what the "Middle Ages" actually mean. Shafi'i-Kadkani then proceeds to the Constitutional period proper, the years between 1906 and 1911, in particular, with poets such as Iraj Mirza, Mohammad Taghi Bahar, Ali Akbar Dehkhoda, Aref Qazvini, Mirzadeh Eshqi, Abolqasem Lahoti, and Farrokhi Yazdi as definitive to this era.[12] This period is defined by potent social criticism and a healthy dose of bourgeois nationalism, where the French Revolution of 1789 and the Industrial Revolution before and after that in Europe had already defined terms such as "freedom" and "democracy," which Iranian poets now adopted into their poetic dictions. Equally paramount in this period was the rise of socialist realism, including close and critical attention to issues of women's rights, particularly their public education. In this period, we also see attention to "the West" and its technology. A closer reading of these passages reveals that Shafi'i-Kadkani has actually confused and conflated Christianity and Biblical allusions with "the West." For example, he has marked Forough Farrokhzad's phrase "Sib-ra Chidim/We Picked the Apple" as a "Western" allusion to the myth of creation, whereas it is Biblical and therefore Jewish and Christian, to which the poet had access through Persian translations of the Bible.[13] Altogether, Shafi'i-Kadkani has sported too much of a reverential and uncritical take towards "the West" in this periodization.

Shafi'i-Kadkani then turns to the Reza Shah period, when for about twenty years, roughly between the early 1920s, when he came to power, and into the mid-1940s, when the Allied Forces made him abdicate, a number of seminal poets such as Farrokhi Yazdi and Abolqasem Lahoti are joined with the emerging figure of Nima Yushij to define the heyday of the first Pahlavi monarch. We are now in the thicket of Reza Shah's militant dictatorship and court-sponsored "modernization" project, when the previous gestations of anticolonial nationalism degenerated into state-affiliated "Aryan" chauvinism. At the same time, the socialist realism of the previous era was fading away, and a more bourgeois ideology of nationalism began to define the state. Shafi'i-Kadkani has here marked a kind of romanticism emerging in Nima's poetry that he believes to be influenced by a French version of it.[14] Formally, poetry was now maturing in anticipated and unanticipated directions. Soon after this period and with the Allied occupation of Iran, Reza Shah abdicated and fled the country, and his son Mohammad Reza Shah succeeded him to rule weakly until the CIA-MI6 military coup of 1953, when the leading poets of the period included Nima Yushij, Ahmad Shamlou, Siavash Kasra'i, and Nader Naderpour—chief among them he has identified Nima and his "romanticism" now turning into social symbolism, as Shafi'i-Kadkani has called it, where socialist ideas expanded in specifically poetic forms. Nima's signature poem, "Morgh-e Amin/Amen-saying Bird" is from this period. Shafi'i-Kadkani has also noted how the Russian poet Vladmir Mayakovsky (1893–1930) and the Turkish poet Nazım Hikmet (1902–63) were being translated into Persian and influenced poets such as Ahmad Shamlou.[15] The period that followed, from 1953 into the 1960s, saw poets like Mehdi Akhavan-e Sales and Ahmad Shamlou among the leading figures, marked best perhaps by Akhavan's now legendary poem "Zemestan/Winter" capturing the cold and brutal air of the post-1953 coup period. At this point, Shafi'i-Kadkani has positioned Forough Farrokhzad's early poems, where the abstract figure of the beloved becomes humanly particular. Next, he turns to the crucial decade of the 1970s, when Akhavan-e Sales, Shamlou, Farrokhzad, and Sepehri emerged as the iconic figures of their time. Here Shafi'i-Kadkani has also included Shamlou's attention to the Spanish poet Federico García Lorca (1898–1936) as particularly important for poets such as Shamlou. Shafi'i-Kadkani has considered the armed rebellion of the Siahkal incident of February 8, 1971, as a key moment that eventually led to the downfall of the Pahlavis, when poets such as Ahmad Shamlou and Esmail Kho'i were openly celebrating the armed struggle.[16] As one can see from Shafi'i-Kadkani's detailed periodization here, the six poets who are the subject of my study in this book surely fall into the context of his learned, judicious, and embracing thinking about contemporary Iranian history.

All this may appear too politically deterministic in Shafi'i-Kadkani's periodization of his contemporary Persian poetry, but towards the end of his book he shifts gears and proceeds to create a chart for the aesthetic evaluation of a poetic disposition predicated on what he has called the "*zat*/quintessence" of their poetry. This chart, which he developed in 1970 during his lectures to his students, features a two-directional horizontal and a two-directional vertical set of axes. Vertically a poet is rooted in an emotive universe going down and aesthetic sublimation going up, while at the same time horizontally poets navigate their cultural roots in one direction and popular reception in the other.[17] There are, in short, four navigational points that Shafi'i-Kadkani has placed around the *zat-e sha'er*, a poet's poetic quintessence, so that a poet like the twelfth-century Khaqani (*circa* 1120–91), for example, was not so popular, while a century later Sa'di was quite popular, as he also commanded a significant mythical culture (Iranian, Islamic, and Christian). Rumi meanwhile had the most solid command over an emotive universe, which a poet like Onsori, for example, did not; as for the poet's emotional depth, it is contingent on their formal aspects, such as music, diction, and imagination. Here Shafi'i-Kadkani has placed some poets in comparison to others and suggested that this chart could be used to divide the history of Persian poetry into various periods, or else categorize poets within a more limited period. He has then cast this chart on the contemporary Persian poetry of his own time, which he has now summarized into four periods: the first period is just before the Constitutional Revolution (which is the worst), followed by the Constitutional period, which is good as far as popularity is concerned, and also because it partakes in "the civilized world of Europe."[18] Poems by Ali Akbar Dehkhoda, Mohammad Taqi Bahar, and Adib Pishehvari are the examples provided here.

Shafi'i-Kadkani then comes to the third period, from the British-sponsored 1920 coup on behalf of Reza Shah to his forced abdication in 1941. Here, too, he has given importance to European culture as the main source of cultural influence.[19] From there he moves on to the contemporary era, meaning from 1941 onwards. Here, he has given three different designations for the kind of poetry under his investigation: *She'r-e Emruz*/Contemporary Poetry, *She'r-e No*/New Poetry, and *She'r-e Azad*/Free Poetry (again, notice that there is no mention of modern, modernism, or modernity). As evidence of this European influence, he has cited the Biblical references in Ahmad Shamlou's poetry, while immediately pointing to others such as Akhavan-e Sales and Sohrab Sepehri, who paid attention to Zoroastrian and Buddhist ideas. Again, his occasional fixation with "Europe" is the weakest and most uncritical part of this otherwise excellent periodization. Shamlou's attention to Christian iconographies was in part because his wife and collaborator Ayda Sarkisian was Armenian and had a profound impact on his poetry as a muse—yet the Armenian Church is not "the West." It is among the oldest Christian churches in Central Asia and Anatolia! Akhavan, Nima, and Shamlou are the best examples that Shafi'i-Kadkani has offered as evidence for this period. He has faulted them, however, for not having a wider readership. None of them is like Khayyam, Hafez, or Rumi (entirely oblivious to the historical interval of canonization of these classical poets on various levels). He has concluded: the Pre-Constitutional period is "non-dimensional; the Constitutional is one-dimensional; and his own contemporaries were three-dimensional." He has only considered such classical poets as Khayyam, Rumi, and Hafez as having been four-dimensional in his fourfold model.[20] He might indeed be correct in this assessment based on his own fourfold chart, but even there he has categorically disregarded the longevity of the process of canonization of classical poets that has resulted in the popularity of their legacies—a canonization process in which the European reception of these classical poets has played a significant role.[21]

Why Only These Six Poets?

I have detailed Shafi'i-Kadkani's learned and reliable periodization, despite the fact that I have some issues with it, in order to frame my own thinking in the context of a serious Iranian literary scholar writing in Persian, rather than of those trapped inside any brand of Area Studies fields with their irremeably Eurocentric limitations and frames of reference. In this book I intend to invite my readers to meet a number of bold and brilliant poets and help them see through the power of their words into the visions of their homeland. We need to remain solidly rooted in that homeland and allow it to teach us a new way of thinking. In short, I am teaching theoretical English prose how to read Persian poetry! As for my readers, they may be anyone who, by force of the colonial conquest of the globe, reads my work anywhere in Asia, Africa, Europe, the US, or Latin America, and for whom English might be their first, second, or third language.

Who are these six poets who are the subject of this book, and what is their significance? All these six seminal figures do appear in Shafi'i-Kadkani's periodization, although my take on them casts them in an entirely different light, with an internal dynamic to their poetic temporality beyond any politically anchored periodization. I believe that they have formed, framed, and posited their own poetic time and narrative—which I wish to decipher in this book. We just need to unpack and decode the matrix that they have collectively posited. These six poets are, in order of their seniority: Nima Yushij (1895–1960), a pioneering figure casting an *archetypal* light on what was soon to be called New Poetry/*She'r-e No*; Ahmad Shamlou (1925–2000), who was perhaps the most widely loved and admired poet of his and our time, with a clear and bold vision of his homeland's emotive *future*; Mehdi Akhavan-e Sales (1929–2000), who in his poetry had a deeply-rooted penchant for a distant, almost mythic *past*; Sohrab Sepehri (1928–80), who had the most mystic and mythic fixation with the *presence* of things in the world; Forough Farrokhzad (1934–67), who in her poetry brought the focal point of her generation to the *present* they all needed to feel, fathom, and understand; and, finally, Esmail Kho'i (1938–2021), who as a Marxist revolutionary poet had to leave his homeland after the Islamist take-over of the Iranian revolution of 1977–9 and lived the rest of his life in exile, where he changed the temporal cast of his poetic time into decidedly spatial terms in search of what he called *Bidar-koja*, or *Nowhereville*. As evident in my way of identifying them, in these six poets I detect, articulate, and argue a temporal disposition definitive to the cast of their poetry, in the following terms: archetypal (Nima), retrieval (Akhavan), futural (Shamlou), presentist (Farrokhzad), presential (Sepehri), and finally exilic (Kho'i). If we were to consider *She'r-e No*/New Poetry as an epistemic Event, then these six poets would form the temporal disputation of a poetic narrative definitive to that Event, set in a self-propelling Transubstantial Motion.

There is nothing magical about the number six, or about these six particular poets, except for the temporal matrix definitive to their respective poetry in which I locate and read them. Any number of other equally important poets can be added to them, notably Parvin E'tesami (1907–41), Simin Behbahani (1927–2014), Houshang Ebtehaj (1928–2022), Nader Naderpour (1922–2000), or Fereydoun Moshiri

(1926–2000)—chief among many others. My emphasis on these six poets is because of the simple fact that they form an epistemic whole, a visionary trope, a temporal matrix that is central to my thinking about them in this book. Any number of other poets can be added to them, but none of these six poets will be questioned in any formation of the most prominent and influential of their age. This book, as a result, is not a survey or an exhaustive account of Persian poetry in recent Iranian history. Rather, this book has a particular and potent theoretical point to make, a critical axe to grind, a visionary perspective to elucidate and share. Beyond these six poets, other poets were important and popular and consummately readable. But they did not add or subtract anything from what these six poets had collectively done, entailed, and performed. Before these six poets, everything that happened in the course of the Constitutional period's poetry was in anticipation of them, and everything else that happened after them was redundant, for the Persian poetry of their time and tenor had completed and ended, their paradigm exhausted and their "verb" fully conjugated—that is my contention, and with them so also concluded a vision of their homeland which they had archetypally articulated. Within that matrix, there was nothing more left to be said. They had said it all. After the Iranian revolution of 1977–9 and in the context of the Islamic Republic, any number of other widely read and admired poets did re-emerge, chief among them perhaps Qeysar Aminpour and Ali Moallem Damghani. But none of them, gifted and sometime even as widely popular as they were, added to or subtracted anything from what these six poets had already done. The episteme was complete, and the paradigm was exhausted. There was nothing left to be said in that particular paradigm.

After these six poets, the effervescent creative soul of the Event abandoned their gathering and moved away from the Persian poetry of the time and eventually metamorphosed into Iranian cinema and sublimated itself into other, more global, more visually palpable terms.[22] Iranian cinema, we might say, was the visual sublimation of Persian poetry of this period. This book therefore is something of a poetic prequel to my work on Iranian cinema over the past few decades. This is the poetry that informed and enabled that cinema, and in the figure of Forough Farrokhzad, one of these six poets whom I intend to examine here closely, we are witness to the transmutation of that poetic urge from a poet to a filmmaker, from a piece of paper to a visionary camera, which she used to make her one and only cinematic masterpiece, *The House Is Black* (1962). In my work on Iranian cinema, I have already articulated a similar paradigmatic matrix among twelve filmmakers, from Forough Farrokhzad to Jafar Panahi, including major signposts such as Abbas Kiarostami, Amir Naderi, Dariush Mehrju'i, and Bahram Beiza'i.[23] In this book I have a similar paradigmatic idea in mind, although this time it is cast onto six seminal poets, forming a formidable assemblage.

Poetics and Politics

Imagine a Nation: these six poets (all writing their poetry in the sublime gestation of a Persian diction that they literally invented) have been emotively definitive to the formation of Iran as a nation overcoming its colonial disposition, like no other poet, artist, novelist, filmmaker, or musician could have ever made a similar claim on the collective consciousness of a people. These six poets did, of course, not grow out of nowhere and were deeply rooted in the Iranian political and cultural history of the nineteenth and twentieth centuries. To be sure, there were other forms of cultural and literary expression—such as a potent and critical journalism, or global travel narratives, or political essays, and eventually drama, film, and fiction—which were equally important in certain other ways.[24] But from the Constitutional Revolution of 1906–11 onwards, Persian poetry in a potent and contemporary thrust began to recast the whole idea of *mellat*/nation or *vatan*/Homeland onto a new visionary platform. Poets and songwriters such as Aref Qazvini, Iraj Mirza, Mirzadeh Eshqi, or Farrokhi Yazdi were definitive to the Constitutional era that preceded the time of these six poets. In many ways, what these six poets did was predicated on the pioneering works of the generation that had come before them and sang the songs of freedom from tyranny and colonialism in the course of the Constitutional Revolution. But based on such solid grounds, these six poets were singing their songs in far more confident, purposeful, formally defiant, engaged, and emancipatory terms. Without them, the idea of Iran as a "nation" or a "homeland" and Iranians as a people, defined and readied to meet domestic tyranny and foreign domination alike, would have been emotively vacuous and politically shuttered in haphazard, hesitant, and uncertain political terms. With them, the idea of Iran as a nation assumed far more cogent, creative, contemporary, and potent currency. They were so unconsciously rooted in and breathed in and out the air of their homeland that they took it for granted, and precisely in those unconscious terms, Iran as a nation found its historic bearings in their poetry. In their poetic imagination, these poets fathomed the nation that they and we all could call home/land.

Imagining a nation beyond what was physically there and historically evident, but emotively lacking and morally befuddled in the face of European colonial modernity, was, of course, a profoundly political act, deeply rooted in a poetic verve which it needed to re-imagine and recast anew. That proposition places these six poets, and the genealogy of their morals, as it were, in the heart of the political destiny of their homeland, irrespective of their different and differing politics.[25] That fact, in turn, raises the crucial question of the dialectics between poetry and politics. Is poetry not too sublime for politics? Is politics not too mundane for poetry? It is the interface between poetry and politics, between the aesthetic imagination of poets and the moral imperatives of a people, which gives a rich and fertile ground for political poetry. The task at hand is to detect, uncover, and map out the landscape of that fertile ground. The only way for our speculations about Iran, and about these six Persian poets, to make sense to the outside world is to be placed in that outside world. It was when I first watched the young American poet Amanda Gorman deliver her by now legendary poem "The Hill We Climb" (2021) during the inauguration of President Joe Biden on January 21, 2021, and soon after the Trump-instigated raids on Capitol Hill on January 6 of that year, that it dawned on me I was being late and this book I was about to write had been brewing in me for a very long time—it was time that I should deliver it. The young Amanda Gorman's poem was revelatory and spoke to me in a potent language, echoed in the Persian of these six poets:

> When the day comes we ask ourselves,
> where can we find light in this never-ending shade?
> The loss we carry,
> a sea we must wade.
> We've braved the belly of the beast,
> We've learned that quiet isn't always peace,
> and the norms and notions of what just is
> isn't always just-ice.[26]

To me, resonating in the magnificent voice of a young African-American poet was the very soul of these Iranian poets whom I now wish to share with a larger audience. So farthest removed from a vague, vacuous, and superfluous notion of 'French romanticism' having anything to do with these Iranian poets, it is in the actual, potent, defiantly political force of an African-American poet in which I hear the resonances of their collective voices across time and space. Amanda Gorman's poem was, of course, immediately reminiscent of the best of Langston Hughes—who was familiar to me via Ahmad Shamlou's references to him long before I came to the US and before I had read him in his English original form. Here, in the Persian echoes of their English diction, politics and poetry had come together in the most vigorous and harmonious ways to define the poetry of these six seminal figures in casting the history of Iran as a postcolonial nation. From Hughes to Gorman, through Audre Lorde and Maya Angelou, a whole history of African-American poetry has had its counterparts around the globe, including the Iran of these seminal figures in my time. Close to half a century away from my homeland and now calling the language of Amanda Gorman home, the fusion of the Persian of Forough Farrokhzad and the English of Audre Lorde, or the echoes of Shamlou and Hughes in each other, had crafted a particularly potent fusion in my mind, with which I began to think about these six Persian poets of my formative, youthful, and politically most purposeful years. The very alphabet of thinking politics for my generation was formed by these poets.

A key issue at the very outset of this book certainly is the question for whom I am writing, whom I am addressing and trying to convince of the totality of the Persian poetry of these six poets. Who is my interlocutor? If I am to imagine an interlocutor sitting in front of me as I share and explain the stories of these six Persian poets, it would not be anyone in the failed and foregone field of "Area Studies." I have nothing to tell or teach them. My interlocutor would be the gifted young American poet Amanda Gorman. I write this book for her and as if she was sitting in front of me or taking one of my courses at Columbia University, and for countless students in the US and around the world—American, Iranian, Arab, and so on—who have heard her voice. I wish to convince Amanda Gorman and her generation inside and outside of the US that these Persian poets demand their attention—and if I succeed, I might also be able to convince Amanda Gorman that her precious words and sublime sentiments were wasted on Joe Biden and Kamala Harris and the rest of those politicians whom she addressed before reciting her poem "The Hill We Climb." It is now easier to speak of these six Persian poets in the past tense to Amanda Gorman's present sentiments, because all these poets are now part of a history mostly unknown to her generation. The same way in which Iranian cinema ended with the death of Kiarostami in 2016, Persian poetry of this particular constellation ended with the death of Ahmad Shamlou in 2000. To be sure, Esmail Kho'i lived until 2021 and was still quite productive in London, even composing some poems in English. But he had exited Iran in the aftermath of the revolution in the early 1980s and lived in London, or in "Nowhereville," as he called it for the rest of his life. With that exit also parted the soul of that poetic imagination that had begun with Nima and risen to a crescendo in five other poets, who had heard his voice as a calling to echo a revelation that they had heard him sing. There was politics to their poetry, and a poetics to their politics, which I want to tease out and lay bare for Amanda Gorman's generation to see and to hear, and to transcend the banality of evil of those sitting behind her when she recited her glorious poem for the first time:

> We, the successors of a country and a time where a skinny Black girl descended from slaves and raised by a single mother can dream of becoming president, only to find herself reciting for one . . .[27]

What Was New about Persian New Poetry/She'r-e No?

In one of his swift, almost telegraphic, off-the-cuff, short essays that he wrote as review of a recent collection of lyrical poetry, Ahmad Shamlou, a leading poet of his time, titled his musings, "Sayeh-ye Kodam Omr?/The Shadow of Which Life?" (1965). This title was a play on the title of the book he was reviewing, *Sayeh Omr/ Shadow of Life*, by another leading poet, Rahi Mo'ayyeri (1909–78).[28] This was a severely critical essay on this book, unabashedly objecting to the way in which the form of the *ghazal* had been abused for a kind of lyricism that was now so out of touch with the current realities. The *ghazal*, so Shamlou insisted, was for the age of caravans, not the era of cars and airplanes. The *ghazal* was no longer the poetic form of our time, which evidently required a different kind of poetry. To make his point, Shamlou presented a quick translation of Bertolt Brecht's poem "To Those Who Follow in Our Wake" (1939) as evidence to support his argument:[29]

> Truly, I live in dark times!
> An artless word is foolish. A smooth forehead
> Points to insensitivity. He who laughs
> Has not yet received
> The terrible news.

What times are these, in which
A conversation about trees is almost a crime
For in doing so we maintain our silence about so much wrongdoing!
And he who walks quietly across the street,
Passes out of the reach of his friends
Who are in danger?[30]

Evident in the review is a sense of temporal urgency. The world around us changed, and that world needed a new and corresponding poetic diction. Lyricism of the sort that Rahi Mo'ayyeri was offering would not cut it in this world. It was outdated, outmoded, unable to speak to our urgent realties. That poetry, which Shamlou himself best represented and championed, was now called *Sh'er-e No*/New Poetry.

Persian New Poetry, pioneered by Nima Yushij, was in the making in earnest from the 1930s to the 1970s, although rooted in earlier experimentations around the period of the Constitutional Revolution. This new gestation of Persian poetry was, of course, not the only poetry that was so enmeshed with its contemporary politics, or that had a politically anchored aesthetic imagination. This is a common feature of most anticolonial poetry, or the poetry of people who have been traumatized by the abuse of power otherwise, a poetry formed under political duress. In Europe and the US, too, politics and poetry have been cohabiting in iconic moments of their histories. William Wordsworth's "London, 1802," Percy Shelley's "England in 1819," W. B. Yeats's "Easter 1916," Langston Hughes's "I, Too" (1926), W. H. Auden's "September 1, 1939," and Nikki Giovanni's "Rosa Parks" (2002) all carry their signature dates with them and are some of the most iconic hallmarks of political poetry in the English language. In the US, in addition to the overwhelming presence of African-American poetry, there exists a wide-ranging spectrum of Native American, Chicano, Asian-American, and South Asian-American domains of similarly political poetry. In their midst, however, poet rappers such as Tupac Shakur, or political Hip Hop, Gangster Rap, and Underground Rap have their signature political poignancy. Closer to Iran, my generation grew up with the poetry of Mahmoud Darwish from Palestine, Nazım Hikmet from Turkey, Faiz Ahmed Faiz from Pakistan, Vladimir Mayakovsky from Russia, and then all the way to Pablo Neruda from Chile, Langston Hughes from the US, W. B. Yeats from Ireland, and the combined power of the poetries of Aimé Césaire, Léopold Sédar Senghor, and Chinua Achebe from Africa, or Amiri Baraka and Audre Lorde in the US, chief among many others.[31] We read our own political poetry in the context and bosom of a much larger and much more global frame of reference of the world about which we cared. Consider these two stanzas of Ahmad Shamlou's poem, "La'nat/Curse" (1956), for example:

Dar tamam-e shab cheraghi nist . . .

There is no light throughout the night
Throughout the city
Not a cry!

> Oh you fearful, dark, foreboding gods:
> Do not open the doors
> Of your dark rotten paradise to me:
> Until I raise high Satan's lantern,
> At the entrance of every hidden torture chamber
> In this tyrannosaur's paradise of yours—
> Until I curse ever so lasting
> With the light of a hundred thousand suns
> These endless, timeless magic-ridden nights![32]

As we read it, the political pain of the entire world (not just Iran) becomes evident in it. At the same time, the Persian New Poetry was equally rooted in the bold and brilliant legacy of our classical poets, who also were political but in different settings, and mostly in dynastic and imperial contexts and not in the framework of "the nation," an idea that emerged in earnest in the course of the Constitutional Revolution of 1906-11. The critical editions of the divans of classical poets that were now prepared and made widely available to these poets and their audiences were equally crucial in generating a *gestalt* view of Persian poetry beyond time and space. That constellation of classical poets now assumed definitive new readings and flaunted their contemporary significance. Some of these contemporary poets even produced their own versions of these classical poets—chief among them perhaps was Ahmad Shamlou, who had a deeply affective voice so that his recitation of classical poems on audio cassettes and LP records made him and those poets widely popular. Shamlou also edited and published his own version of Hafez's *ghazal*s, which, albeit quite controversial among our classicist literati, still gave a current relevance to the poetry of Hafez. Despite these classical roots, with Nima Yushij something entirely new happened in the very cast of Persian poetic diction, and the radical transformation of politics assumed an equally iconoclastic poetic form. The very form of Nimaic poetry was political. Over the course of the twentieth century, we as a nation faced a new colonial and postcolonial politics, and that confrontation demanded and produced a new poetic potency. This dynamic was the signature definition of the Persian New Poetry.

In this study, I am less concerned with the specific politics of these poets (who was more "radical" or more "liberal" than of the others—for these entirely American terms do not very much apply to them anyway) than with the evident politics of their poetry, with their collective search, *ipso facto* poetically political and as such entirely unbeknownst or subconscious to themselves, for the idea of a homeland large and caring and embracing enough to hold them all together. This very search made them nomadic subjects, notably unknowing to themselves.[33] All these poets were located on the borderline between the classical Persian poetry they had inherited, the radically defiant aspirations of the time in which they lived, and the worldly context of their self-consciousness. They were conversant with all these factors, but singularly under the sway of no particular force among them. Above all, they were poets: in direct, unmitigated, and bold communion with their inner emotive universes—universes that they made idiomatic to our lived experiences.

The certainty of this precarity accented their nomadic soul, marked their wandering habitat—with which they made their poetic parlance equally mobile, supple, light, transient, and itinerant. We, their readers, as we read them, memorized their stanzas, recited them to each other, fell in love with each other, married, and named our children after them, lived their poetics personally, passionately, politically.

One final word before I move forward to the next turn: like millions of other Iranians of my generation, I was born and raised to this New Poetry. In my moral and intellectual imagination, I am its product. These six poets were the collective pantheon of the moral imagination of an entire generation of which I am an aging member. The "Fifty-seveners" (*Panjah-hafti-ha*)—as the reactionary expat monarchists now call us with contempt, for having launched a revolution, so they gather, that toppled their monarchy and brought about an Islamist regime which they rightly despise and which we had not anticipated—voted for, or never even dreamed to rise to terrorize our revolutionary aspirations. These poets, these names—Nima, Shamlou, Akhavan, Forough, Sepehri, and Kho'i—as we always affectionately referred to them—were the poetic DNA, as it were, of our moral, political, and aesthetic imagination. They made our politics poetic, as they made our poetic imagination deeply and irreversibly political. We were blessed and cursed by that dialectic, entirely unbeknownst to ourselves. That generation has now become historical, archival, fading in memories. With this book, I wish to craft a sustained recollection of that fact, of that (now) lasting memory. As I reread these poets and write this book, I feel that I am also excavating the inner layers of my own soul, the soul of the nation to which I belong, the genealogy of morals of an entire generation of Fifty-seveners. This poetry was so very new that now, almost a century old, it still smells of the gentle aroma of its birth: cutting its umbilical cord from classical prosody, feeling at home in the post-classical age, bearing witness to the brutalities of the world it now mirrored, crafting a past, a present, a presence, and a future for the people who looked up to its visions of the sublime and the beautiful, the just and the judicious.

"What Are Poets for in a Destitute Time?"

If we were to pull back from the specificity of the Persian poetry of our own time for a moment and look at the matter from a distance, we see that the bond and the bend between poetry and politics (translated into the precarity of the knowing subject) forming a philosophical disposition of its own is not limited to any particular poetic tradition. Following the German philosopher Martin Heidegger's reflections on poetry in general and the poetry of Friedrich Hölderlin and Rainer Maria Rilke in particular, philosophical meditations on poetry found a serious and renewed epistemic shift. Such philosophical meditations, however, have had a much longer history that begins with Aristotle's treatise on *Poetics* (*circa* 335 BCE) and travels East and West of Greece. Since Aristotle, the two interrelated subjects of poetics and politics have preoccupied generations of philosophers and poets alike. Aristotle's *Poetics* had a lasting influence on Persian and Arabic sources on the subject. Al-Farabi (*circa* 870–950) expanded Aristotle's treatise and explored the link between logical and poetic thinking. In his seminal Persian treatise, *Asas al-Iqtibas*, Nasir al-Din al-Tusi (1201–74) followed through and provided the Persian thinking world with equally serious reflections on the place of poetry in philosophical contexts.[34] When it comes to thinking poetically, we need not choose among Greek, Arabic, Persian, or German sources. They all circumambulate similar if not identical themes.

Heidegger, however, speaking to the urgencies of our own time, had a particularly potent impact on how we perceive poetry philosophically today. "Poets," he has surmised, "are the mortals who, singing earnestly of the wine-good, sense the trace of the fugitive gods, stay on the gods' tracks, and trace for their kindred mortals the way toward the turning."[35] These god-terms, potently philosophically and non-denominational, and perforce irreducibly poetic, speak to the more compelling forces at work in the European history of Heidegger's time and the colonial shadows that it cast around the globe. Heidegger becomes more specific: "Rilke's poem thinks of man as the being who is ventured into a willing, the being who, without as yet experiencing it, is willed in the will to will. Willing is the way, man can go with the venture in such a way as to set himself up as the end and goal of everything. Thus is man more venturous than plant or beast. Accordingly, he also is in danger differently from them."[36] I have had multiple occasions in my previous work to turn that "will to power" into the "will to resist power"—which is a far more accurate designation of the nature and function of the art and poetry of those brutalized by European colonial modernity. That will to resist power is beyond the philosophical reach of Heidegger and marks the limits of that philosophical reach, where the destitute time of our poetry speaks in a language unlearned by European Orientalists.

In that post/colonial context, both enabled and disempowered by the colonial gaze at one and the same time, one of my main propositions in this book is to argue how in the Persian poetic context proper, classical and contemporary, the encounter between poetry and politics has resulted in a simulacrum of a metaphysics of its own transcendence, predicated on the philosophical tradition of *alam al-mithal*, or the *mundus imaginalis* (as the French scholar Henry Corbin has translated the term theorized by the Persian philosopher Shahab al-Din Yahya Suhrawardi).[37] The cliché concerns about poetry becoming too political, or not political enough, turns into a moot question about these poets I consider here. Each one of these poets was a paramount example of poetic virtuosity, and each one of them was also political in the most potent sense, but—and there is the rub—their poetry was not reducible to their politics, and their politics was not independent of their poetry. Where their poetics and politics met, which I would identify as the realm of *alam al-mithal/mundus imaginalis*, dwelled in the realm of parabolic poetics where that simulacrum of the metaphysics of the sublime and the beautiful takes shape. That *mundus imaginalis*, evident in both classical and contemporary poetry, clears our path away from the pitfalls of European colonial modernity and its inevitable alienating effect on our reading of the poetics of the colonized world under the alienating concept of "modernization" and all its other cognates. Consider the following stanza from Sohrab Sepehri's poem "Niyayesh/ Prayer" (1977):

Nur ra peymudim . . .

We traveled through the light,
Traversed the desert of gold—
We picked the myth,
And cast it aside wilted—
By the sand dune:
A sun full of shade gently caressed us—
We paused
By the wide river of mystery—
We cut the throats of dreams.
A cloud appeared, and we closed our eyes—
Darkness split, we saw Venus, and we ascended the summit.
A thunder descended
And took us to prayers:
Shaking we cried, crying we laughed.
A thunderstorm pounded, we were sympathetic to each other.
Darkness left, we raised our head to the blue sky, worthy of skies—
We abandoned the shades to valleys:
Planted smiles at the depth of nothingness.[38]

This is a poetic meditation entirely *sui generis*, rooted in Sepehri's own *mundus imaginalis*, his poetic intuition of transcendence. Its sense of the sacred is safeguarded inside itself, irreducible to Islamic, Christian, Buddhist, or any other kind of ready-made metaphysics of the sublime. We therefore need to resist by any means necessary to assimilating these poetic impulses backwards into any received or perceived "religious tradition" and read them as the poetry of a "Muslim" poet— or by a "secular" poet. These terms all collapse into a superior sense of the sacred. Sepehri was a Muslim, and he was a poet. But he was not a Muslim poet. The urgencies of his time and space were of an entirely different genealogy—which he crafted from the sacred certitude of his own poetic imagination.

There is therefore a theoretical adjustment necessary when we turn our attention to classical texts on Persian or Arabic poetics, to see how today they enable a poetic thinking even beyond their own particular circumstances. Critical thinkers past and present have been deeply preoccupied trying to understand what good poetry is and how it is that it makes such a profound impact on its audiences. In the history of Persian poetics in particular, Muhammad ibn Umar al-Raduyani's *Tarjoman al-Balaghah* (*circa* mid-eleventh century), Kaykavus ibn Voshmgir's *Qabus-nameh* (1080), Rashid al-Din Vatvat's (*circa* 1088–1183) *Hada'eq al-Sehr fi Dagha'eq al-She'r*, Nezami Aruzi Samarqandi's *Chahar Maqaleh* (1155), Shams Qais Razi's *Al-Mo'jam fi Ma'a'ir Ash'ar al-Ajam* (circa 1230s), Nasir al-Din al-Tusi's (1201–74) *Asas al-Iqtibas*, Mohammad ibn Mahmoud

Amoli's *Nafa'is al-Fonun fi 'Ara'is al-'Uyun* (*circa* mid-fourteenth century), and Dolatshah Samarqandi's (*circa* 1438–1507) *Tazkireh al-Sho'ara* are chief among countless other seminal texts reflecting on, meditating, and theorizing the nature of poetry. We should consider a much more critical interest in this body of literature than just an antiquarian or archival frame of reference when reading them.

This body of critical literature is at once site-specific to Persian poetry and yet conversant with a similar archive of work in Arabic—although the Persian domain begins to spread eastward into Central Asia and farther into the Indian subcontinent to form what would later be called "the Persianate World," a term that began innocuously but has now assumed ominous Iranophobic overtones.[39] The result is an embedded poetic multi-lingualism and aesthetic pluralism that extends from the shores of the Mediterranean to the mountains of the Himalayas, from the deepest steppes of Central Asia to the coastal shores of East Africa and the Indian Ocean.[40] Who was a good poet and why, what was an excellent poem and why, what were the best uses of metaphor, simile, metonymy, or rhyme and rhythm? From Ibn al-Mu'taz in the ninth century, over Abd al-Qahir al-Jorjani in the eleventh, to Shams Qais-e Razi and Mohammad ibn Mahmoud Amoli in subsequent generations, a rich and robust body of critical thinking about poetry was coterminous with the effervescent compendia of the Persian and Arabic poetry which they investigated. These texts have been the subject of extensive scholarship written by Orientalists and post-Orientalists. Picking any of these texts to read in the context of the rich and robust body of Persian New Poetry requires a frame of reference far more critical than merely an archival, historical, or genealogical one, as perhaps best evident in the monumental works of Abdolhossein Zarrinkub and Mohammad Reza Shafi'i-Kadkani—Iranian literary scholars who are writing in Persian and are therefore barely known, let alone carefully studied, by those in the US- and European-based "Area Studies" fields.

Thinking Poetically in This World

Persian New Poetry is a solid occasion of *thinking poetically* in the world—a project that remains to be fully deciphered, theorized, and delivered in its prospective promises. Over the last half century there has been considerable attention paid to New Poetry, but except for the extraordinary work done in Persian, the rest is mostly (though not entirely) in terms of translation and explication of the original poems into English, French, or other European languages and very little in terms of what this potent thrust of poetic legacy actually means, except for a cliché appeal to "modernity" (that Persian literary modernism was French modernism in translation), without any critical stance towards its colonial pedigree. Simply calling this poetry "modern" or "modernist" has, in fact, robbed it of its innate and potential significance in terms internal to its own idiomaticities. In Persian, of course, we have had some important critical work on this body of poetry, more rooted in the actual lived experiences of these poets and their work, beginning with perhaps the most famous essay of Jalal Al-e Ahmad, "Pir-e Mard Chashm-e Ma Bud/The Old Man Was Our Eyes" (1961), about Nima Yushij and his poetry, or Mehdi Akhavan-e Sales' equally important essays, "Bed'at-ha va Baday'-e Nima Yushij/The Innovations and Novelties of Nima Yushij" (1978), as well as his "Ata va Laqa-ye Nima/The Pros and Cons of Nima" (1982). In Persian and mostly in Iran we also have critical and authoritative editions of the collected works of these poets produced by caring and competent scholars, except for Forough Farrokhzad's, whose work has been the subject of an excessive and constant censorship by the Islamist regime that rules Iran. But the original prints of her work are still very much available in both print and digital format in major university libraries and private homes. (I have in my own library her entire collection in first-edition prints, which I brought with me from Iran in 1976, when I came to the US.) This body of work, both the original poems and the critical apparatus around them, form the nucleus of a spectrum of poetic thinking in terms particular to this poetry.

The English translators of New Poetry have given a significant contribution to non-Persian speakers, so that they are now able to read this body of poetry in the language most accessible to them. The indefatigable translator of masterpieces of Persian poetry, Dick Davis, has recently published *The Mirror of My Heart: A Thousand Years of Persian Poetry by Women* (2021)—an extraordinary compendium introducing Persian poets to the English-speaking world.[41] Forough Farrokhzad is by far the most widely translated poet among this group of six poets. An excellent recent example of critical reflections on her poetry would be Dominic Parviz Brookshaw and Nasrin Rahimieh's edited volume *Forough Farrokhzad, Poet of Modern Iran: Iconic Woman and Feminine Pioneer of New Persian Poetry* (2023), which includes a number of probing essays on the eminent Persian poet. An earlier volume, *Forough Farrokhzad: A Quarter Century Later* (1988), compiled and edited by Michael Craig Hillmann, was also a pioneering collection of essays on the same poet. This collection contains one of my earliest essays on Forough Farrokhzad, "Forough Farrokhzad and the Formative Forces of Iranian Culture."[42] We also have books such as Michael Hillmann's *A Lonely Woman: Forough Farrokhzad and Her Poetry* (1985) or Farzaneh Milani's *Forough Farrokhzad: A Literary Biography with Unpublished Letters* (2016), which has attended to her biography from a limited bourgeois-liberal feminist perspective and with very little to no attention to what her poetry actually means.[43] Ahmad Karimi Hakkak's *Recasting Persian Poetry: Scenarios of Poetic Modernity in Iran* (2012) remains a solid piece of scholarship, bringing the earliest debates concerning the structural transformations of Persian poetry to wider attention, but, again, its significance mostly lies in having capably translated some serious tracts with minimal but still useful critical commentary—albeit, again, basically in terms of the European and Eurocentric project of modernity, with which the author exhibits no critical engagement. In 2004, the Beirut-based literary journal *al-Adab* published a special issue devoted to Persian New Poetry. These have all constituted significant but limited steps towards thinking poetically in terms embedded and yet to be realized in this body of works, which we have collectively received as *She'r-e No*/New Poetry. With occasional

French, Italian, German, or Arabic translations, this English encounter with *She'r-e No* has been the most widely available venue for a general readership's engagement with Persian New Poetry.

Deeply appreciative of the work that these fine translators and scholars have performed, my project in this book is in an entirely different register and direction. I prefer to do my own translations of poems from the Persian originals as I plough away thinking with and through them in terms enabled by their inner logic and poetics. These fine and competent translators have read these poets in abstraction. I read them purposefully, towards the formation of a paradigm which I propose they formed. In this book, and for entirely theoretical reasons, for the first time I bring together these six seminal poets around a central idea and set them in their social and historical context in order to read them in terms at once aesthetic and political, yet entirely rooted in the poetic effervescence of their oeuvre. These poets are helping me make a case, a theoretical case, of nation-building as a poetic project. The whole purpose of the idea is to allow these poets to reveal their poetic dwelling in their world—that is, the world they crafted for the rest of us to inhabit.

To do so, our point of departure is, of course, perforce the Constitutional period (1906–11), when poets and critical thinkers such as Taqi Raf'at (*circa* 1889–1920) and Malek al-Sho'ara Bahar (1886–1951) were busy debating the emerging formal changes in Persian poetry in heated discussions, at a time when Shams Kasma'i (1883–1929) and Nima Yushij (1897–1960) were pivoting towards far more radical prospects and horizons. Ahmad Karimi Hakkak, a veteran student of this field, has published a book, *Recasting Persian Poetry: Scenarios of Poetic Modernity in Iran* (2012), in which he has translated these debates into English and added his own thoughts. In our own time, two major literary scholars, Abdolhossein Zarrinkub and Mohammad Reza Shafi'i-Kadkani, have contributed significant work recasting our reading of classical and contemporary poetry in classical contexts. Zarrinkub's two-volume opus, *Naqd-e Adabi/Literary Criticism* (1959), among his other books, is a solid review of the history of literary criticism in a global context, with obvious detailed attention to Arabic and Persian sources. Shafi'i-Kadkani's *Sovar-e Khayal dar She'r-e Farsi/Imaginative Images in Persian Poetry* (1971) and *Musiqi-ye She'r/Music in Poetry* (1989), among his other voluminous works, are particularly important to see how poetic thinking is performed in Persian. These are among the most serious works written in Persian— but there are a number of other, more recent works. In this context, the monumental work of Yahya Aryanpour, the three-volume opus *Az Saba to Nima* (1971) and its sequel *Az Nima to Ruzegar Ma* (1993), have mapped out the detailed passageway from classical to contemporary prose and poetry. In one of my earliest works, "The Poetics of Politics: Commitment in Modern Persian Literature" (1985), I have sought to pinpoint the contours of this interface between poetics and politics.[44] Central to that encounter remains a poetics of self-transcendence that poets of this period had crafted, such as here in the opening stanza of Forough Farrokhzad's signature poem "Iman Biavarim beh Aghaz-e Fasl-e Sard/Let Us Believe in the Beginning of the Cold Season" (1963):

Va in manam
Zani tanha . . .

And this is I
A solitary woman
At the beginning of a cold season—
At the beginning of grasping the polluted essence of this earth—
And the simple and sad discontent of the sky,
And the impotence of these hands as if made of cement . . .[45]

Dwelling in such moments is the *modus operandi* of thinking poetically—submitting to the poetic Event. These moments now happen more in reading the poems themselves, rather than in their learned "histories" or the imaginal dynamics at work to make them a particular kind of poetry, although much serious work has been done precisely in those historical terms. More recent studies of Persian poetry have introduced more cogent contemporary issues that have enriched our reading of the body of work over the last century. Among the notable examples of these works are Mohammad Shams Langeroodi's *Tarikh-e Tahlili-e She'r-e No/The Analytical History of New Poetry* (Tehran, 1991), Parviz Natel Khanlari's *Past-o-Boland-e She'r-e No/The Ups and Downs of New Poetry* (1988); Gholamhossein Youssefi's *Cheshmeh Roshan/The Enlightened Spring* (1990), and Mohammad Este'lami's *Barresi Adabiyat-e Emruz-e Iran/A Study of Contemporary Iranian Literature* (1977). Again, please note that not a single one of these classic titles has any use for the term "modern" or its derivatives, which is a refrain (something of a nervous tic) of "Area Studies" scholarship done in English and French and such. Meanwhile, works such as Mohammad Ali Sepanlu's *Chahar Sha'er-e Azadi: Josteju dar Sargozasht va Athar-e Aref, Eshqi, Bahar, Farrokhi Yazdi/Four Poets of Freedom: A Study of the Lives and Works of Aref, Eshqi, Bahar, and Farrokhi Yazdi* (1998) have specifically concentrated on the relationship between politics and poetry during the Constitutional period. English translations of some of these poets have given the translators added occasions to reflect on these poems with insightful introductions and commentary. Ahmad Karimi-Hakkak's translated volume *An Anthology of Modern Persian Poetry* (1978), as well as Nahid Mozaffari and Ahmad Karimi Hakkak's edited volume *Strange Times, My Dear: The PEN Anthology of Contemporary Iranian Literature* (2013), are prime examples of such translations. Other excellent translations with probing commentaries have been published by competent translators, such as Sholeh Wolpe's translations of Forough Farrokhzad and other poets. Geoffrey Squires's most recent volume, *The New Verse: A Selection of Modern Persian Poetry* (2021), has brought the sensibilities of an Irish poet to Persian New Poetry.[46]

Most of the sources in English and other European languages are solid indications that thinking poetically has enriched the world of those who gather around these poets, yet remain aloof from the Persian sources doing the same, which are either ignored or else have remained mostly unknown. The spatial and temporal distance, even in the age of the Internet, has created a thick and tall wall between a young scholar in Europe or the US picking up a book by Forough Farrokhzad and reading and writing on it, and those who do the same in Persian in Forough Farrokhzad's own homeland. Be that as it may, these publications, including the English translations of the original Persian poems, are all active indices of a sustained course of critical attention to the nature and function of poetry in its larger social and political frames of reference. Most of the initial works were, of course, written in Persian and published in Iran, but increasingly a significant body of literature has also been produced in English, French, Italian, and so on—signs of a generation of mostly (but not entirely) Iranians who have left their homeland and now claimed English, French, or German as their adapted intellectual diction. More than a century after Nima published his poem "Afsaneh/ Myth" (1921), both the initial effervescence of the kind of poetry that he inaugurated and the kind of poetic thinking that he and his followers have occasioned, the original Persian language of this body of poetic work remains the solid site of thinking poetically with them. Much but not all of the work written in English or other European languages has been mostly expository, in which there is a sense that we are explaining this body of poetry to a foreigner, a stranger, an inquisition, a "doctor of poetry" asking us to explain this poetry to them. That was and remains a fictional (mostly male, mostly white) interlocutor. We have long since overcome and abandoned that expository mode of discourse. It is time to dwell on the poems themselves and root them even deeper in the fertile soil from which they blossomed—and the audience whom this mode of thinking poetically will need (Amanda Gorman at large) will emerge on its own. At the end of the day, poetry is untranslatable. No poetry worth its name can be rendered into any other language. Only a distant aroma of the original may at best be carried over to the language into which a poem is translated. The original poems therefore are fruitful sites of thinking poetically with and through them, in any and all languages, where any "translation" is there solely to facilitate that thinking.

The Poetry of the Sublime as the Politics of Despair

The historical circumstances of the rise of these six poets, from the Constitutional Revolution of 1906–11 to the triumphalist rise of Islamist ideologues that led to the violent imposition of the Islamic Republic in 1979, culminated in the bitter exile of the last of them, Esmail Kho'i, to Europe, where he finally settled for the rest of his life in England and where I met him on multiple occasions. Definitive to this historic formation was the fusion of the interrelated themes of lyricism and politics, eroticism and militancy, which came together to define the poetic disposition of the age. The result was the casting of a lyrical politics—of the paradoxical fusion of love and violence—at the very subconscious roots of the nation.[47]

The six poets I read closely in this book were definitive to the formative consciousness of my generation, born and raised in the aftermath of the CIA-MI6 coup of 1953. The founding father of this movement was Nima Yushij, who died in

1966, when I was a young teenager in high school and had already started reading, reciting, memorizing, and writing compositions on his poetry. When a year later, in 1967, Forough Farrokhzad died in a tragic automobile accident, I remember the moment well for the traumatic impact it had on my female cousins, Sharifeh and Fattaneh Parvizi, as it did on an entire segment of the younger generation who knew and loved her poetry. My cousin Sharifeh had been the first person ever to read and recite her poetry for us and to interpret its significance. Sohrab Sepehri died in 1980, when I had already left Iran for the US, but during my frequent visits to Ebrahim Golestan's home in Sussex, I developed a close affinity for the collection of his paintings that Golestan owned and also arranged for a few to be purchased by members of my family. Akhavan-e Sales I met in person in Golestan's home, in the company of Esmail Kho'i, whom he deeply loved and admired. Ahmad Shamlou I met in person both in Iran, when I was an undergraduate student and ran into him in a bookstore, and then in the US, during one of his frequent visits to US campuses. Esmail Kho'i I met many times both in the UK and the US and developed a closer friendship with him. He and I were among the regular guests at Golestan's home in Sussex.

This I share because today, when I read learned scholarly essays on any one of these poets by a younger generation that has never known them in person or been in their close proximity, they have a totally abstract, alien, and remote significance, a subject of the younger generation's academic pursuit and scholarly curiosities. I read these pieces of scholarship and am happy to see that a new generation of enthusiastic scholars and translators are interested in this body of poetry. However, at the same time, there is a profound element of alienating historicity about their prose. They are insightful and eager, but they lack any sense of the existential immediacy that resonates about this body of work, where they were, and when they were being produced for their immediate audiences. I knew Golestan well, and I know Amir Naderi even closer, and they both knew Farrokhzad; members of my own family knew Al-e Ahmad, who knew Nima closely, and so on. That sense of immediacy does not give me a privileged position to read and interpret these poets with any sense of authority. I remain just one among millions of their other readers and admirers and translators. But it does give me a sense of urgency to convey my critical intimacy with their poetry in the body of the critical scholarship evident in this book.

I read this body of scholarship, delighted to see how a new generation of scholars have picked up these poets and are reading them closely, competently, and with significant insights. But at the same time, my take on this constellation of poets is somewhat different. For one thing, I have always read and taken these poets together, as a constellation, forming a formidable episteme, a matrix, a paradigm. But in English and other European languages, Forough Farrokhzad has received inordinate attention, in part for legitimate reason and in part for the vacuous "feminist" sentiments of bourgeois liberal vintage. To me, however, she makes better sense, as do all the others, in the company of the other poets with whom she shared a common universe. To be sure, this is in hindsight when we have the ability to look back at them collectively, without, of course, compromising their particularity—or, to put it more accurately, perhaps taking their particularity to a collective gathering, an assemblage (Gilles Deleuze and Félix Guattari), where they help others make more sense than they would on their own.

The basic schema, or the central argument, around which I narrate the rest of my contentions in this book, is therefore quite simple: I am reading these twentieth-century Persian poets together, as the constituent forces of a matrix of poetic imagining of a nation, along a temporal matrix that morally and imaginatively sublimated and transcended their particular time and space: Nima Yushij was the archetypal voice that inaugurated this thematic constellation and temporal take on this epistemic event called New Poetry, while Mehdi Akhavan-e Sales was more inclined to celebrate the past with heroic nostalgia, and Shamlou was always forward-looking and the poet of a future yet to come. Forough Farrokhzad and Sohrab Sepehri, meanwhile, were the poets of the present and the presential—and with Esmail Kho'i forced into exile, the entire episteme comes to a closure. We might therefore consider Ahmad Shamlou's iconic poem "Bon-bast/Cul-de-sac" (1979) the dead-end with which Nimaic poetry also ends. At its heights, in the decades between the 1940s and the 1970s, this poetic adventure constituted an Event, where the temporal take on contemporary history assumed poetic diction, and through which a "Transubstantial Motion" was unleashed, as the sixteenth-century Iranian philosopher Mulla Sadra would have called it. The conception of the nation that this matrix entails is therefore poetically contingent, which means that in and of itself it cannot be coopted by any state ideology, for it is by definition anticolonial, decolonial, and postcolonial all at the same time.

The archetypal, temporal, and poetic schema I propose here is therefore in interface with the traumatic constitution of a nation—a homeland to which these poets belonged and cast its temporal particularity as a spatial fore-structure for the emerging nation to dwell. The idea of "Iran" as a homeland, rooted as it has always been in its long and enduring historical and literary metaphors, had now assumed a defiantly anticolonial, postcolonial, and decolonial impetus during the Constitutional period, roughly between the Tobacco Revolt of 1891–2 and the height of the Constitutional Revolution of 1906–11. With rebellious poets such as Mirzadeh Eshqi, Mohammad Taqi Bahar, Parvin E'tesami, Aref Qazvini, Iraj Mirza, Shams Kasma'i, and the like building the poetic groundwork for the rise of Nimaic poetry, revolution was now fully afoot. The multiple genres of this period, in which poetry is located, included a vast tapestry of travelogues, politically potent critical prose, the budding seeds of drama, and revolutionary journalism. When today we read a precious little poem by Esmail Kho'i from the 1960s, "Tarh/Sketch" (1961), we should hear how the sense and sensibility of this entire history has accumulated and come down to a Haiku-like moment, when the poet dwells on a drop of rain:

Shadi ye yek qatreh baran ...

Happiness of a drop of rain—
And the sorrow of that drop in the swamp.[48]

At least two centuries of a dramatic contemporaneity, fiercely living in the moment, has come together to make that little poem possible: from birth to death, from joy to despair. There is a self-assured universality in those two lines that allows us to compare it to the Japanese haiku without a moment of hesitation, which in and of itself is rooted in a long and sustained history of moral and political imagination that has occasioned this poetic intuition of self-transcendence. This poetry of the sublime was the soul and summation of the politics of despair that had occasioned it.

An Epistemic Shift: Poetically Narrating the Nation

With Nima Yushij, as a poetic event, we are witness to a major epistemic shift in the formal and formative power of Persian poetry. With the publication of Nima's "Afsaneh/Myth" (1921), but particularly from the 1930s through to the 1960s, a new poetic thinking was announced, practised, and performed. For about half a century, from the 1920s to the late 1960s, Nima and the generation of poets he enabled, emancipated, and empowered were busy casting a new mold for the Persian poetic diction and thereby the Iranian postcolonial subject—poetically postulated.[49] Persian New Poetry read and wrote and sounded like inventing a new language for the newly liberated nation, from the scattered memories of that nation in its most distant moral, material, and imaginative roots. In my previous work on Nima and other poets, I have been concerned with the constitution of the national subject—a subject that was now politically postulated in the nation. Here, however, my concern is with the interface between the emerging postcolonial nation and the poetic narration of that nation, which was initially probed by Homi Bhabha working solely in and with English material. The decolonial project that perforce works through the power and audacity of languages outside the colonial contours of English puts us on an entirely different stand. At the very outset, Bhabha has shared with his readers that the title of his essay, "DissemiNation," owes something to the wit and wisdom of Jacques Derrida, but more to "my own experience of migration."[50] To be sure, he has shared that experience with millions of others from around the world. Let's read him more closely:

> I have lived that moment of the scattering of the people that in other times and other places, in the nations of others, becomes a time of gathering. Gatherings of exiles and emigres and refugees; gathering on the edge of "foreign" cultures; gathering at the frontiers; gatherings in the ghettos or cafés of city centers; gathering in the half-life, half-light of foreign tongues, or in the uncanny fluency of another's language; gathering the signs of approval and acceptance, degrees, discourses, disciplines; gathering the memories of under-development, of other worlds lived retroactively; gathering the past in a ritual of revival; gathering the present. Also the gathering of people in the diaspora: indentured, migrant, interned; the gathering of incriminatory statistics, educational performance, legal statutes, immigration status—the genealogy of that lonely figure that John

Berger named the seventh man. The gathering of clouds from which the Palestinian poet Mahmoud Darwish asks "where should the birds fly after the last sky"?[51]

The trouble with this passage is its bemoaning of fragmentation—and conversely the fetishization of origin, of a sense of departure without any prospect of return. It yearns for a belonging yet to come, yet to happen, but that would not ever happen. The sense of nationhood about which I write through these poems is far more confidently rooted and stated in the poetic potency of the moral and epistemic legacy that these poets have reclaimed and staged. There is no state ideology that can be built on this poetry. The nation which it envisions, enables, and empowers transcends all such state ideologies. Imagining a nation was therefore a poetically posited polity that could never be fully materialized in political or ideological terms. The nation was conceived poetically much sooner than it was later, or could ever be, politically. Four poets of the Constitutional period are usually considered definitive to a revolutionary conception of the nation: Aref Qazvini, Mirzadeh Eshqi, Mohammad Taqi Bahar, and Farrokhi Yazdi.[52] To these four must be added two more—Iraj Mirza and Parvin E'tesami—in order to give the idea of the nation its satirical and moral effervescence. The case of these seminal Persian poets whom I examine here posits the proposition that the formation of the nation is poetically contingent—that the nation is perforce an imagined community, as Benedict Anderson has suggested, although his idea should be balanced by the key question that Partha Chatterjee has posed about who does that imagining. As Chatterjee has put it:

> I have one central objection to Anderson's argument. If nationalisms in the rest of the world have to choose their imagined community from certain "modular" forms already made available to them by Europe and the Americas, what do they have left to imagine? History, it would seem, has decreed that we in the postcolonial world shall only be perpetual consumers of modernity. Europe and the Americas, the only true subjects of history, have thought out on our behalf not only the script of colonial enlightenment and exploitation, but also that of our anticolonial resistance and postcolonial misery. Even our imaginations must remain forever colonized.[53]

The answer, of course, is obvious and evident in Chatterjee's own question: our imagination is not colonized, nor even theorized, and these poets are the solid evidence that from Anderson to Bhabha, there is much to be learned from the lived histories of nations, from India, over Iran and the Arab world, all the way to the rest of Asia, Africa, and Latin America, until we reach the gates of the British "Foreign Office." I, as just one among many other ideas, propose the prospect of this poetic contingency by way of making the idea of the nation allegorically contingent, variable, transformative, metamorphic.

But what does that exactly mean? The idea of the nation arrives on the colonial edges of capitalist modernity already contingent and compromised by the vagaries of a conceptual imbalance between its ideological European centers and its non-European colonial edges. That colonial interplay and indeterminacy is made allegorically contingent by a coterie of fresh and powerful poetic voices that updates and resurfaces itself in a potent encounter with colonial modernity—"modernity" here standing squarely as codification of the Eurocentric disempowerment of the colonized. Reza Shah and his entire Pahlavi dynasty were agents of a "modernizing" dictatorship. Nima was not a "modernist" poet. The colonizing project of European modernism does not have the moral and philosophical capacity for an anticolonial poetic of defiance. Period. Homi Bhabha's project is therefore more vacuous than ambitious by grasshopping from Asia over Africa to Latin America, with no particular linguistic, literary, aesthetic, or poetic competence to explore any one of them in any serious detail. He is just a "postcolonial theorist"—whatever that may mean—about an English literature specialist. These nations thus lose their particularities when manhandled by the English professor. In this book, I go exactly in the opposite direction, by focusing on just one particular moment of a national aesthetic imaginary that was and remains at once anticolonial and decolonial. Homi Bhabha's "postcoloniality" compliments Thomas Babington Macaulay's colonialism.

Is nation narrated, imagined, or both at one and the same time? Nimaic poetry broke up with classical prosody in one and the same breath when it conceived and imagined a decolonized nation. This project was poetically perceived and thus remained always allegorically potent. The case of Iranian nationhood has a very specific poeticism definitive to and driven into it. It became an allegory of itself by virtue of the fragments of a rich and empowering past, which it recovered for and wove into a poetic future. As Nima and his followers broke rank with classical Persian prosody, in both their poetry and their poetics, they also assumed the mantle of their authority in a bold and daring pose. Central to this poetic project is not a political polity but a poetic polis, a *mundus imaginalis*. Democracy is therefore not the project of this poetry—even though revolutionary aspirations for a *demos* were the aspirations of the previous generation that it sublimated. What is crucial to keep in mind is that the novel scarce became definitive to the nation-building project. If we consider Sadegh Hedayat's novella *The Blind Owl*, or Dolatabadi's *Kelidar*, or the exquisite works of Ebrahim Golestan, Houshang Golshiri, and so on, none of these had any nation-building propensity. The same is true about film and drama. Poetry was the sole carrier of the seeds of imagining the nation anew—in two consecutive moves: the Constitutional period and the Nimaic revolution.

Thus conceived and imagined, the nation is not just indeterminate, which is both a given and a cliché. Any attempt to give that contingency a solid political form has been catastrophic and prone to fascism, from the Pahlavis to the Islamists. Thus poetically imagined, the nation is always contingent, indeterminate, and therefore always suggestive rather than solid, a promise rather than a delivery. Pressures of ethnic nationalism from the four corners of the land have always pulled the homeland asunder, abusing and twisting the term "Persian" from a linguistic and literary marker to an ethnic denomination; thus, paradoxically, today the only thing that holds the fragmented nation together is either the militant fascism of a tyrannical centrist at the center or else a poetic imagination that can only unite the nation by letting it flourish freely. Here is a key poetic idea of Sepehri, usually considered the least political of the six poets whom I study in this book, in which one can see how the sublimated politics is definitive to a sublated poetic moment:

Ary, ma ghonche-ye yek khabim . . .

Yes, we are the budding blossom of a dream:
Budding blossom of a dream?
Do we blossom?
One day, without a leaf moving!
Here?
No, in the valley of death.
Darkness, solitude?
No. A beautiful seclusion.
Who'd come to see us?
Who'd come to smell us?
. . .
And will we with the blowing of wind wither?
And once again will we fall?
. . .[54]

This is poetically narrating the quintessence of the nation by positing a knowing subject to it, where the epistemic shift of poetic thinking has always already run ahead of its politics—and no "migration" will diminish the power of that poetics. It only makes it stronger.

The Event: Poetic Time and Narrative

As I commence this study of the relationship between time and poetic narrative, placing a succession of poets on a temporal platform as they seek to imagine their homeland, paramount in my mind (other than the collective works of these poets themselves) are the meditations of a number of philosophers with no particular relation to each other, except in the cast of my own critical thinking: Baba Afzal Kashani (died 1214), Mulla Sadra Shirazi (1572–1641), and Mohammad Iqbal (1877–1938) on one hand; Ernst Cassirer (1874–1945), Martin Heidegger (1889–1976), Paul Ricœur (1913–2005), and Alain Badiou (born 1937) on the other. Each one of these philosophers, in different times and different contexts, has been concerned with the issue of temporality in their formal grasp of Being (*wujud, hasti*). Baba Afzal Kashani's ontological division of *wujud* between Being (*budan*) and Finding (*yaftan*); Mulla Sadra's revolutionary ontology of "Transubstantial Motion," or *al-harakah al-jawhariyyah*; Mohammad Iqbal's conception of movement in his philosophical preoccupation with the reconstruction of religious thought; Heidegger's definitive dwelling on Dasein in his *Being and Time*; Alain Badiou's articulation of "the Event"; Paul Ricœur's idea of "time and narrative"; and Ernst Cassirer's thinking on the "human world of space and time"— are all in one way or another crucial in helping us think critically about *temporality* as the space in which, so I argue, these six poets have found themselves being, thinking, meaning. Equally important for me and the way in which I see the world are the collective works of Asian, African, and Latin American philosophers such as Kojin Karatani, Y. V. Mudimbe, or Enrique Dussel and Walter Mignolo, with whose work I have been in dialogue for quite some time. Baba Afzal, Mulla Sadra, and Iqbal (among many others) are in the immediate vicinity of these poets, and their relevance is quite clear; as for any European philosopher, I of course always approach them at arm's length through the critical visions of non-European philosophers to debone their inherent colonial gaze at the rest of the world.

What holds these philosophers together in my mind is the formation of Persian New Poetry as an Event, motioning on a poetic time that has defined the national narrative of a people on their most enduring poetic intuitions. Alain Badiou's articulation of the Event is exceptionally helpful for guiding us to understand the phenomenon of Persian New Poetry as a unique and revolutionary moment in which an entire people were destined to re-imagine themselves in the world. The void of inconstant multiplicities, as Badiou has articulated it, forms the patented background to the rise of this poetry as an Event. This is one among many other ways in which Badiou has put it: "In the ontological situation, a pure multiple is natural (is an ordinal) if it is founded by the void alone, and if everything which belongs to it is equally founded by the void alone (since everything which belongs to an ordinal is an ordinal). It is a *void-foundation of void-foundations*. A situation-being is historical if it contains at least one evental, foundational, on-the-edge-of-the-void site."[55] The order of the situation, the dominant ideological *modus operandi* of knowing, makes the excluded and the disruptive invisible. The Event stages the otherwise invisible—as the Persian New Poetry does with the trauma of postcolonial nationhood. I see the rise and effervescence of Persian New Poetry as an Event, which requires for us to locate the poetic time of its successive narratives along temporal stages, in a way that Mulla Sadra considered "Transubstantial Motion," or *al-harakah al-jawhariyyah*, where the quintessence of the Event moves and transforms. I intend to detail more of this philosophical foregrounding of my thinking poetically with these six poets as I progress from one poet to another in the following chapters.

For now, and upstream from all these philosophers, I have found Ernst Cassirer's thoughts exceptionally insightful into the nature of spatial and temporal memory definitive to our understanding of how poetic narrative works. In his seminal text, *An Essay on Man* (1944), Cassirer has devoted an entire chapter to "The Human World of Space and Time." Here he has pointed out how the provenance of memory is instrumental in defining and casting lived experiences in the world. He has explained by way of examples:

This was the reason why Goethe entitled his autobiography *Poetry and Truth* (*Dichtung und Wahrheit*). He did not mean that he had inserted into the narrative of his life any imaginary or fictitious elements. He wanted to discover and describe the truth about his life; but this truth could only be found by giving to the isolated and dispersed facts of his life a poetical, that is a symbolic, shape . . . Poetry is one of the forms in which a man may give the verdict on himself and his life. It is self-knowledge and self-criticism . . . The process is not restricted to poetry; it is possible in every other medium of artistic expression. If we look at the self-portraits of Rembrandt painted in the different epochs of his life we find in the features the whole story of Rembrandt's life, of his personality, of his development as an artist.[56]

In a vein similar to Goethe and Rembrandt, what we read in these six Persian poets is also a memorial vision poetically retrieved and cast on material history, where the poetic as the mythic begins to make sense of the scattered relics of time and space in a particularly traumatic passage from past to present, from old to new, from the absence to the presence of agency. That self-knowledge, poetically mitigated, is not just about the individual poets making sense of their own lives, but it extends and spreads to their poetic imagination that they share with their readers, and through which they become a people, a nation, a self-conscious collectivity. In her poem "Let Us Believe in the Beginning of the Cold Season," Forough Farrokhzad recited:

> The time passed:
> The time passed and the clock chimed four times—
> It chimed four times.
> Today is the first day of winter—
> I know the secret of seasons,
> And I understand the way seconds speak
> The savior is in the grave
> And the earth, the inviting earth,
> Is an allusion to peace . . .[57]

Here, that temporal self-knowledge of the poet beats and repeats the minutes and seconds of existence for an entire nation, the people who thus become a people as they read her revelatory poem. There is a communion between the poet and her readers when they both share and exchange the memorial moment of this intuition of transcendence. This is the moment of the Event, the narrative of the poetic moment, sustained through its internal Transubstantial Motion. On the wings of these six poets, I wish to invite you to ride and witness the birth of a postcolonial nation from the very depth of its conditions of coloniality.

Chapter 1

NIMA YUSHIJ: THE ARCHETYPAL EVENT

Allow me now to carry a few seminal points from that long Introduction forward into my first chapter. I took my time detailing the context and contour of my study in order to acclimate you, my dear precious reader, evidently interested in Persian poetry of our own time, with my particular idiomaticity, with the way in which my mind works in this book; this book with which I have long since hoped to write—in the form of an operatic overture, as it were, with the major themes, tunes, melodies, and trajectories of my thinking—these six poets into the rest of my story. I have offered a temporal trajectory that begins in the early twentieth century with Nima Yushij on top of the North Iranian mountain ranges and ends in the first quarter of the twenty-first century with Esmail Kho'i in exile on the streets, alleys, and squares of London (where I met him on a few occasions), with Nima Yushij establishing the archetypal figure of the whole poetic Event, Akhavan-e Sales, shaping the retroactive gestation of a past for this elegiac assemblage, Shamlou dreaming of a potent future, Farrokhzad defining its present, Sepehri casting its presence in atemporal terms, and finally Kho'i exiting the whole paradigm and making a bitter, Jeremiah-like epic of defeat far away from his homeland in a vacuous space he sarcastically called "*Bidarkoja*/Nowhereville." This located temporal matrix finally facing a timeless, spaceless cul-de-sac has allowed me to offer an epistemological foregrounding with a temporal cast set in Transubstantial Motion, with philosophers such as Baba Afzal Kashani, Molla Sadra Shirazi, and at times Paul Ricœur, Alain Badiou, and Ernst Cassirer as my main, not so hidden, interlocutors.

My contention in this first chapter is now to put forward the idea that, by inaugurating the archetypal framework of Persian New (*She'r-e No*), Nima Yushij both crafted and complicated the idea of "the nation" and with it the articulation of the self-knowing authorial subject that would people it and set it in motion. I am placing his and his progenies' monumental poetic Event in the context of the nation (*vatan* or *mellat*) where they were born, raised, and came to creative effervescence, in order to give a corporeal body to their poetic soul and preempt the collapse of their legacy into vacuous abstractions. They were not just poets in the abstract sense of the term. They were the architects of the idea of a homeland, its past, present, and future. Nima imagined this nation anew, turned the classical Persian prosody upside down, declared it outdated, bid it a respectful farewell, and set upon himself the monumental task of thinking what the texture and disposition of Persian poetry would be for a vastly altered world. This was no mean task, and the poetic heritage of Ferdowsi, Khayyam, Attar, Sana'i, Sa'di, Rumi, and Hafez (and a whole pantheon of other demi-gods) he was planting on a new axis was not so easy to move and shift around. There was much forceful and mighty resistance to his way of thinking poetry anew. But the force of his convictions and the rise of a new generation of poets who were at his beck and call made that epochal epistemic shift possible, almost inevitable. The idea of the nation embedded in this New Poetry, and this New Poetry embedded in that nation, was thus poetically perceived before it was politically posited. As it happens, six seminal poets of the Constitutional period of the late nineteenth and early twentieth centuries came before the six poets of my considerations in this book: Aref Qazvini, Mirzadeh Eshqi, Abolqasem Lahuti, Iraj Mirza, Malek al-Sho'ra Bahar, and Parvin E'tesami. This idea of "the nation" I posit here is therefore always already antithetical to any form of ruling state, and as such anticolonial, postcolonial, and decolonial all at the same time. It is iconoclastic, subversive, and rebellious. It is imagined but not in the way that Benedict Anderson thought in *Imagined Communities* (1983), i.e. out of nowhere and made of nothing. It is rooted in a poetic imagination that is nourished by millennia of sublime and beautiful thinking, which in this study I wish to retrieve and articulate.

As the nation was thus being poetically conceived, it had no proprietor, no claimant to its throne, as it were, no ruling monarch or turbaned mulla to have any legitimate command over it, no political machinery to lay any rightful prerogative to it, no state to confiscate and call it a "nation-state." The state, any state, was constitutionally alien to the nation thus being poetically conceived. If Nima Yushij's sublime poetic imagination symbolized this nation, Reza Shah's military thuggery represented the state—a militant representation that remains definitive to any other state coming after Reza Shah up to and particularly under the Islamist state that Ayatollah Khomeini built to lay a theocratic claim to the selfsame nation. What could possibly Nima Yushij and Reza Shah have in common, except an irrevocable sense of animus, hostility, and irreconcilable differences—between the nation that one poetically imagined, and the state that the other politically superimposed on it? If the Qajar dynasty (1789–1926) was a total state without a nation, brutalizing its subjects and forcing them into servitude to its ludicrous imperial rules, and if after the Constitutional Revolution of 1906–11 a nation was born with no state to lay any legitimate claim on it, then before long the colonial concoctions of the Russians and the British crafted a state that they superimposed on that nascent nation. Given the poetic precarity of the nation thus conceived, no colonially manufactured state could ever lay a total claim to it. Impossible. Thus emerged a perennial bifurcation and chasm between the nation primarily poetically perceived and the state colonially constituted. This binary, this tension between the nation and the state, has remained endemic to the very idea of "Iran" as a colonially crafted nation-state.[1] From the Pahlavis to the Islamists, all the endemic revolts definitive to their histories are poetically inspired, and all the colorful states trying to repress them are colonial, even (or particularly) when they fake and feign opposition to the European or US empire—for precisely at those moments they are replicating the colonial disposition of the very idea of "the nation-state" that they parrot. The temporal texture of this matrix gave the nation a moral, metaphysical, and meta-narrative authority beyond the ideological reach of any state—monarchical or mullarchical.

In his now legendary poem, "Ay Adam-ha/Ahoy People" (November 1941), Nima's moral desperation at the sight of the wretched of the earth became definitive to his politics of defiance that defined the nation in precisely contrarian terms. The poem was composed about November 1941, just a few months after the Allied occupation of Iran, the abdication of Reza Shah, the shaky installation of his son in power, and soon the formation of the Communist Tudeh Party. There is not a single reference to any of these historic events in this poem, and yet all of them and much more are sublated into the quintessence of the politics of defiance definitive to the formation of the nation at this pivotal point.

Ay Adam-ha . . .

Ahoy people!
Sitting there happily on the shore
Merry-making!
Someone is drowning in the sea!
Someone is struggling desperately
In the dark and dangerous sea you know well—
At the time when you're drunk with the thought
You have conquered your enemy,
When in futility you fathom
You have helped a desperate person,
So you may gain even more power—
When you fasten your belt really tightly—
When exactly shall I say?
Someone is desperately drowning in the sea!

Ahoy people!
Sitting at a pleasant gathering by the sea!
Food to eat, clothes to wear—
Someone is calling you from the sea
Beating desperately on the heavy waves—
His mouth wide open, his eyes popping out with fear:
He sees your shadows from the distance,
Swallowing water in the dark maelstrom:
His desperation increasing by the seconds—
Pushing his head now,
Now his legs
Out of the water!
Ahoy people!

> From a distance he is watching this aging world:
> Screaming, hoping for help!
> Ahoy people watching around by the peaceful shore!
> Waves are rushing to the silent shores:
> Spreading like an unconscious drunk,
> Then retreating, yelling—
> And this cry can still be heard from the distance
> Ahoy people!
> And the howling sound of the wind ever so dreadful,
> And in the sound of the wind his voice ever louder:
> From the distant and close waters
> Ears can still hear:
> "Ahoy people!"[2]

Nima Yushij in Context

Fortunately for my purpose here, the preeminent Iranian literary critic Mohammad Reza Shafi'i-Kadkani has produced a solid study of the context in which the poetry of Nima Yushij took place: *Ba Cheraq va Ayeneh: Dar Josteju-ye Risheh-ha-ye Tahavvol-She'r-e Mo'aser Iran/With a Lantern and a Mirror: In Search of the Roots of the Transformation of Contemporary Iranian Poetry* (2011, again please note no sign of anything about "modernity" or "modernism" in the title). The way in which Shafi'i-Kadkani's mind works in this exquisite volume is central to a solid understanding of New Poetry completely cleansed of the colonial category of "modernism." First comes a long introduction, "Harf-Avval/First Word," in which he sets the mode of his probing and authoritative discourse.[3] From here he moves to his first chapter, which he has called "Chashm-andazi Digar/Another Perspective," discussing social, historical, and economic changes of the late nineteenth and early twentieth centuries.[4] Then he offers samples of poets best representing this period, "Pishgaman-e Tahavvol/Pioneering Figures in Transformation."[5] He then devotes a whole chapter to "Ja-ye-pa-ye Sh'er-e Farangi/The Trace of European Poetry," in which he identifies what he believes to be the influence of European poetry on Persian New Poetry.[6] From here, he turns to "Degarguni-ye Sakht va Surat-ha/The Transformation of Structures and Forms."[7] Finally, he develops a chapter on "Safar-e az Sonnat beh No-Avari/The Journey from Tradition to Innovation."[8] At the end, we have a section on what he has called "She'r e jadvali: Asib-Shenasi Nasl-e Kherad Goriz/Crossword Poetry: A Pathology of the Irrational Generation," presenting the harsh critique of a younger generation of vacuous formalists.[9] There are a few appendices that follow, "Nakhostin Gam-ha dar Rah Tahavvol-e She'r-e Mo'aser/Initial Steps on the Way to the Transformation of Contemporary Poetry," dated 1963.[10] There is another short essay on "Tallaqi Qodama az Vatan/The Ancestors' Understanding of Homeland," dated 1971.[11] The last appendix consists of an essay on "Shamayel Ghazal-e Farsi dar Farang/The

Shape of the Persian Ghazal in Europe."[12] To all of this he has then written a "Harf-e Akhar/Conclusion."[13] The entire formal and substrative structure of this book is an authoritative framework in which we see how a leading Iranian poet and literary critic has understood the rise and unfolding of Persian New Poetry.

The first important issue to consider in this learned book on the context and content of Persian New Poetry is how a leading, perhaps the most widely celebrated, literary critic of his time, Mohammad Reza Shafi'i-Kadkani, himself a deeply loved and admired poet, has written yet another volume on contemporary poetry without any need to make even a single reference to words, concepts, and ideas of "modernity," "modernism," or "modernization." This is in sharp and unmissable contrast to those scholars, Iranians or otherwise, who write in English, French, and so on, and who—like a knee-jerk reaction or a nervous tic—opt for and parrot the words "modern" or "modernist" when discussing the selfsame poetry.[14] Why this chasm between Iranians writing in Persian, and anyone else writing in English or other European languages? To be sure, there are Iranians who also write in Persian and under the influence of these European sources and have uncritically imported the term "modernity" and its cognates into Persian.[15] But those, too, are done without the slightest sense of a critical distance as to why they are doing as they do. The evidence of Shafi'i-Kadkani's seminal textual evidence, as a literary critic who is thoroughly aware and even conversant with European sources, helps us place Nima Yushij and other poets following him in a context more in tune with the original perception of their poetry, before and after the colonial concoction of (decidedly European and Eurocentric) "modernity." That "modernity" has always been the dominant ideology of Eurocentric capitalism, and it has had a deeply distorting effect on its colonial shadows.

Beyond this crucial point is the primacy that Shafi'i-Kadkani has given to social changes in the course of the Constitutional period, such as those initiated by the Qajar prince Abbas Mirza (1789–1833), a potent brand of nationalism, the evident presence of militant Islamism and socialism, all anticipating anticolonial sentiments, as well as the rise of women's rights, and then how all of these are translated into a powerful poetic diction. Shafi'i-Kadkani has cited an article in the heat of the Constitutional Revolution, where poetry has been praised as a form of philosophical thinking.[16] The author of this article has praised the advances that poets and other artists have made in Europe, compared to which Iranian poets of his time have been stagnant, so he believed. Published in the progressive periodical *Sur-e Israfil* (widely popular between 1907 and 1909), this tract has been considered by Shafi'i-Kadkani as a poetic manifesto—and in many ways it is. A more critical stance towards this article, however, would show how, through the colonial encounter with Europe, Iran had by now entered the colonial public sphere from a position of moral and normative subjugation; the authors of this period kept regurgitating the names of "Voltaire, Rousseau, Diderot, Schiller, Bacon, Pushkin, Chateaubriand, Hugo, Rafael, and Michealangelo" without any rhyme or reason, just to season their prose with some strange and frightful European names, as if they had any serious grasp of their works. They were frightened out of their wits by virtue of European military and economic might, and they were translating that military might into specific terms of cultural hegemony. They had no critical grasp of how that might and power were contingent on having plundered the world. For this reason you see references to Russian and European icons at one and the same time—namely, the French, the English, and the Russian colonial forces that paralyzed their critical thinking—and even Shafi'i-Kadkani himself, generations later, still failed to see whence this power of influence.[17]

With his aesthetic senses completely attuned to Persian New Poetry, Shafi'i-Kadkani has identified a number of key figures such as Mirza Fath Ali Akhondzadeh (1812–78) and Mirza Malkam Khan (in office 1872–8), or travelogues such as that of Mirza Saleh Shirazi (1790–1845), and he has devoted a special section to European poetry, when samples of its representative poets began to be translated into Persian.[18] He spends a good amount of time with the Constitutional period and then comes to Nima Yushij to praise him for the unique freshness of his poetry, which remains inimitable, even comparing him to Hafez.[19] He praises Nima's poetry for its "ambiguity" and local color, altogether, a kind of wild and strange beauty manifests itself, for which reason the entrenched enthusiasts of classical poetry cannot enjoy his poetry, for a habituated sense of beauty has no place in his poetry. "Nima seeks strange beauties and strange meanings," Shafi'i-Kadkani has said. "We first need to get acquainted with his language and eventually enter his universe of feelings."[20] Shafi'i-Kadkani faults professors of Persian poetry at Tehran University, his own colleagues, for failing to understand Nima's poetry. He eventually moves on to other poets, all of them the subject of my examination in this book: Shamlou, Akhavan, Forough, Sepehri—all except for Kho'i, to whom he makes a few cursory references.

Historical frames of reference of the sort that Shafi'i-Kadkani has accurately and convincingly offered can only help us to better grasp the enormity of the poetic revolution that Nima had initiated in the course of his enormous output spanning almost four decades. This is so because nothing in that history can completely account for the actual texture and power of his poetry. Like all other real revolutions, it could not have been anticipated or its terms foretold. Consider this moment when Nima staged his mastery of pictural memories, turning them into metaphors of a self-consciously meditative life. Nothing in classical Persian poetry can compete with this diction and disposition—and this is quite a serious claim to make in the context of a colossal poetic legacy. This is not to underestimate the poetic power of the classical masters, but simply to mark the freshness and bold and beautiful poetic idiomaticity that Nima discovered, crafted, and performed. Here is a sample of his meditative mind in "Ojaq-e Sard/Cold Campfire" (1944):

Left abandoned from distant nights,
Upon the pathway through the woods,
A stone grate from a small campfire—
In it some cold ashes.

Just like my hazy thoughts
Sorrowful:

Sketches of a picture
Full of everything:
A whole story, painful its ending.

My sweet day that was so in peace with me
Has alas become incongruous:
Turning cold, stonelike,
In the autumn of my life:
Allusions to spring now turning yellowish.

Just like abandoned from those distant nights,
Upon the pathway through the woods,
A stone grate from a small campfire—
In it some cold ashes.[21]

The Life and Legacy of a Poet

Nima Yushij (1897–1960) is the pen name of Mohammad Ali Nuri Esfandiari, who was born to landed gentry and raised in the Yush region of the province of Mazandaran in northern Iran.[22] He was a teenager when his family moved to Tehran, where he attended Persian primary school and received a French education at the St. Louis French Catholic Mission school. His early childhood and youth coincided with the tumultuous years of the Constitutional Revolution of 1906–11 and the Socialist Jungle Movement of Gilan (1915–21)—for which he seems to have had some sympathy. After graduating high school, Nima was employed as clerk in a state ministry. His poetic career was publicly announced with the publication of his first autobiographical poem, "Qesseh-ye Rang-e Parideh Khun-e Sard/The Story of Pale Complexion and Cold Blood" (1921). This was followed by his ground-breaking poem "Afsaneh/Myth" (1922), which announced the confident birth of a fresh new poetic voice. The astonishing aspect of these poems is that in them, there barely exists any trace of the tumultuous political events of the time. He was busy crafting the formative forces of a poetry that would dwarf all these political events in comparison. By 1926, Nima had married his maternal cousin, Alieh Khanom Jahangir, and moved back to Mazandaran. Their one and only son, Sheragim, whom I met in Texas in the 1980s, was born in 1943. Nima's seminal essay, "Arzesh-e Ehsasat dar Zendgani Honarpishegan/The Significance of Feelings in the Life of Artists" (1940), has remained a defining cornerstone of his own poetic disposition. The year 1941 was a pivotal turning point when Reza Shah abdicated under pressure from the Allied Forces, when the Communist Tudeh Party was established, and when, through such sympathetic figures as Jalal Al-e Ahmad, Nima was regularly published in Tudeh-affiliated periodicals. In the aftermath of the CIA-MI6 military coup of 1953, however, Nima was briefly imprisoned, after which he had very little to do with the Tudeh

Party or leftist politics. By the time of his death on January 4, 1960, he had left behind a monumental body of poetry, which would radically redefine the entire legacy of Persian poetry.[23]

The archive of Nima's poetry was entrusted to a small group of his friends and competent scholars who saw through the publication of his work in a professional and competent way.[24] The eminent literary scholar Mohammad Mo'in (1914–71) supervised the publication of his archive. In his brief comments on this archive, Mo'in has pointed out how his poetic output transitioned from classical prosody to New Poetry, but included a period when he kept the classical prosody while introducing new themes.[25] Nima's close confidant and neighbor, as well as the leading public intellectual of his time, Jalal Al-e Ahmad, was one of his literary executors, and he reported how Nima's wife Aliyeh Jahangir was instrumental in protecting her husband's legacy, while Sirus Tahbaz assumed much of the responsibility, along with the supervision of Nima's son Sheragim.[26] There were basically two volumes in Persian and in Tabari, an Iranian language spoken by people in Nima's native Mazandaran. The collection of Nima's poetry that was published during his lifetime extended from *Makh Oula* (the name of a river near Nima's residence, 1965) to *Ab dar Khabgah Murchegan/Water in the Ants' Colony* (1972). Sirus Tahbaz published a first collection in 1987, but it was full of typos (an endemic calamity in the Iranian publishing industry). In 1991, a complete edition was published, including more potent political poems, such as the one praising one of the leading socialist thinkers, Taqi Arani (1903–40), which could not have been published during the Pahlavi period.[27] More recently, two additional volumes of Nima's poetry have been edited and published after his son Sheragim literally sold sacks (*guni*) full of his father's poems to the Academy of Persian Language and Literature (*Farhangestan-e Zaban va Adab Farsi*). *Sad Sal-e Digar/One Hundred More Years* (2017) and *Nava-ye Karevan/The Caravan's Melody* (2019) have added voluminously to the edited archive of Nima's work, although they have not much altered our prior understanding of his poetry.[28]

In its iconoclastic, unexpected, and transcendent totality, Nima's poetry posited the archetypal moment when the classical Persian poetic episteme was broken and supplemented—the venerated prosody that had held Persian poetic intuition for millennia had been fully conjugated and had exhausted itself, now reaching a degenerative point of diminishing returns.[29] There were therefore two seismic events occasioning the Nimaic revolution that happened at one and the same time: first, the full epistemic paradigm of classical Persian poetic prosody was finally exhausted and was not going anywhere, and, second, massive social changes were happening around the Constitutional era (1906–11), so that politically the monarchical episteme had also depleted itself and had nowhere else to go. The two epistemic depletions occurred almost simultaneously. The Constitutional Revolution dismantled the monarchy to prepare the nation to face new realities, as Nima Yushij also broke the classical prosody to liberate the new Iranian persona from its formal bondage to the *ancien régime* and to rise to the occasion of a massive revolutionary momentum. The six poets of the Constitutional period (Aref, Iraj, Eshqi, Lahuti, Bahar, and E'tesami) were preparatory, we might now say, for the rise of Nima and his progenies. This poetic Event was therefore not "modernization" or (*horribile dictu*) "Westernization" at all, and it therefore had nothing to do with the European project of colonial modernity. Quite to the contrary: the Event marked the birth of a decidedly anticolonial persona—at once poetic and political. To the degree that any of these poets paid any attention to European poets, they were equally attentive to Arab, Turkish, South Asian, Latin American, African-American, and African poets. It is, alas, only a colonized mind that disregards these evident facts, picks and chooses a few European references, conflates Christianity and "the West," and jumps on the bandwagon of "modernism" in Persian poetry. Persian New Poetry is not modern, to the degree that modernity is a subterfuge for European colonialism in a gaudy disguise. Fortunately, a new generation of young Iranian scholars has now emerged, deeply steeped in postcolonial thinking, and some of them have turned their critical attention to Nima's poetry. There is a bold and brilliant new comparative study of Nima and William Butler Yeats in Persian, for example, in which their respective use of "nativism" has been articulated and read as a sign and signature of their anticolonial struggles.[30]

This Event in Persian New Poetry occurred under colonial duress and, in fact, in defiance of it, as two epistemic shifts, one political and the other poetic, were breaking loose of their exhausted and overused paradigms. This way of thinking about the New Poetry is not just a superior way of reading Nima Yushij and his poetic legacy after the Constitutional Revolution, but it is also more directly rooted in what historically happened before the false, flawed, and distorting proposition of "modernism" was force-fed into this poetic Event. Consider the following opening stanza of one of the most famous poems of Nima, "Dar Javar-e Sakhtsar/ By Sakhtsar" (1930):

Man keh duram az diar-e khod cho morghi az maqar . . .

Far away from my homeland, like a bird away from the nest,
Just like a lifetime gone by forgotten and elapsed,
My head full of thoughts and yet my lips sealed,
The night whispers of its secrets to me, and I of mine to the night,
Have nothing to say to anyone, nor anyone has anything to say to me,
Here by Sakhtsar: What is the sea telling me?
Why are its waves rushing towards me so heavily? . . .[31]

The poetic power of the moment is at once solitary and social. Nima here demarcated the borderline between solitude and society, where the sense of the poetic self is forming in provocatively dialogical terms.[32] This is universal self-consciousness irreducible to any colonial subjugation, to be marked either as modernity or tradition—two deeply flawed binaries that for generations have distorted the truth of Persian New Poetry and much more. The world misses much about the power and audacity of that poetic self thus formed, if the whole Event is shoved into the platitude of (perforce European) "modernism." The life and legacy of Nima Yushij, now more than sixty years after his passing, is beginning to be assessed and assayed primarily in Persian by Iranian scholars, and by a very small number of works in English or other European languages. Definitive to this yet-to-be-fully-mapped legacy, as evident in this and many other samples of Nima's poems, is the formative coagulation of solitude and society, lyricism and politics, as realities, *sui generis*.

"The Old Man Was Our Eyes"

To this day, Jalal Al-e Ahmad's "Pir-e Mard Chashm-e ma bud/The Old Man Was Our Eyes" (1961) remains one of the most precious documents we have about Nima's life and poetry, published soon after his passing in January 1960.[33] A leading public intellectual of his time, Al-e Ahmad was a close friend, neighbor, publisher, and confidant of Nima Yushij, as well as among his earliest supporters and believers.[34] "The Old Man Was Our Eyes" is a short essay, something of an obituary, which Al-e Ahmad wrote soon after Nima's passing and published in the leading literary journal of the time, *Arash*. The short essay is a homage, a love letter to the future readers of Nima, a deeply felt and beautifully composed prose written in a typically quick and telegraphic style, and yet it manages to touch on every crucial aspect of Nima's life and legacy. In this essay, Al-e Ahmad tells us about his first encounter with Nima, calling him "Pir-e Mard/The Old Man" (a deeply endearing term) at a writers' congress in the summer of 1946, where there was no electricity; as a result, he recited his own poem, "Ay Adam-ha/Ahoy People," in a dark room, with a candle and his big bald head the center of attention. Later, when Al-e Ahmad was in charge of the organ of the Iranian Communist (Tudeh) Party, *Mardom/The Masses*, he would publish Nima's famous poem, "Padeshah-e Fath/The King of Conquest," but would cut out parts of it to make it shorter, of course, much to Nima's chagrin. Here the *crème de la crème* of the Tudeh Party could not make head or tail of Nima's poems and concluded that his lines had to be properly punctuated, for he had broken down the classical Persian prosody. In another incident, Al-e Ahmad told us that in 1947 he and Ahmad Shamlou, at the time a young rising poet, went to see Nima; he described his home on Paris Avenue in Tehran, smoking opium and reciting his poems, while Shamlou, too, was reading his poetry to Nima. Al-e Ahmad finally moved to the Shemiran suburb in Northern Tehran, near Nima's home, where he started building a house for himself and his famous novelist wife, Simin Daneshvar (1921–2012).

Al-e Ahmad promoted Nima Yushij, while a leading Iranian artist, Bahman Mohassess (1931–2020) painted his portrait. They arranged for a celebration of his poetry. Al-e Ahmad was among his earliest supporters, but at the same time he underlined his political naiveté. Eventually, they became family friends and neighbors. Nima received a small salary from the Ministry of Culture where he worked and wasted most of it on his opium addiction, while his capable wife, Aliyeh Khanom, worked for a bank and provided for the family. Nima was a picky eater, cantankerous, and suspicious of everyone. He became the center of attention for young poets, but he was also paranoid that they would steal his poems. He was extremely disorganized, and he did not publish his poems methodically, but only single poems here and there. He was afraid that Parviz Natel Khanlari (1914–90), a relation of his and a leading literary figure, would arrest and incarcerate him for daring to dismantle classical Persian prosody. After the coup of 1953, Nima's paranoia intensified, and he entrusted a sack (*guni*) full of his poems to Al-e Ahmad, who kept it in his attic and later returned it to him. Eventually, Nima was jailed for some time, and Al-e Ahmad brought him a mattress and blanket to his prison cell, hiding inside them Nima's pipe and opium, with a note in French saying where to find them. The leading Iranian novelist and filmmaker Ebrahim Golestan (1922–2023) wanted to make a short documentary about him, but Nima refused, for he believed that Golestan worked for the British who wanted to document his life. He came across as a paradox of both confidence and deep anxiety. This is Al-e Ahmad's final assessment of who Nima was:

> This is how the old man lived among us, with his rustic simplicity wondering about all we did, the more they bothered him the more determined he became, until finally he became familiar with our shortcomings, just like a pearl in the heart of a rough and crooked oyster shell, in the dark corner of a faraway dungeon for years he remained concealed, never wanted to go abroad, nor did he desire the beautiful bosom of a woman, nor [did he have] the wish for another clime or another market. He never wished for the pomposity of fake respect, or tried to disguise this ugly wench as beautiful, and in his eyes, which were the eyes with which we saw our world, there was a serenity that you may have thought was out of submission, and perhaps so, but it was in fact the majesty you see in the eyes of a statue of the pharaonic epoch.[35]

At the end, Al-e Ahmad described the scene of his death with astounding brevity, poise, and dignified respect, as he prepared him for his burial, before sitting down to open the Qur'an and recite a few verses for him: "Wa al-Saffat Saffan . . . By those who set the ranks in order . . ." (37:1). Did this verse of the Qur'an really appear when Al-e Ahmad opened the Holy Book to recite a verse for him, or was it his choice when writing this precious obituary of a monumental man he knew closely? Every time I read this astounding document, I compare it with the graceless prose of academic scholarship on Nima and Al-e Ahmad alike, and I realize that the world that relies on US-made "Area Studies" to learn about "areas" has forever lost a grace now beyond reach. An entire generation of young and brilliant scholars has been wasted on this crooked legacy of the Cold War.

By the time of his passing, Nima was already an iconic figure to a generation of poets, literati, political leaders, and public intellectuals alike. Leading artists, intellectuals, and poets of his time knew that they were in the presence of greatness, even though they were yet to grasp the full parameters of that significance. As I will read them, this constellation of six poets begins with Nima Yushij and in only one generation ends with his immediate followers, centering around a towering visionary poet who radically recast the entire form and prosody of the Persian poetic imagination, at a pivotal moment in their national history. Nima was the single-most significant poet of this bold and brilliant generation for having projected the very prospect of thinking- and knowing- and being-in-the-world (including the very vision of a homeland) in a radically new poetic diction. He was fully aware of his own significance, and in his signature poem, "Morgh-e Amin/ The Amen Bird" (1951), he imagined himself as an omen of this delivery.

A key sign of how highly his contemporaries considered him as the poetic evidence of their time appeared when a leading Iranian dramatist wanted to translate Shakespeare into Persian. Nima once "met" Shakespeare—and yet in that brief encounter, he left us evidence for how he saw the world. When Abdul Hossein Noushin (1907–71), a leading dramatist of the time, wanted to translate Shakespeare's *Othello*, he approached Nima to ask him to translate the poetic part of the play, and so he did. It is astonishing today to read "The Willow Song" in Act 4, Scene 3, of *Othello* in Nima's signature poetic diction. Desdemona only has time to sing two verses before she breaks off to talk to her maid Emilia. Nima took the original stanza and turned it into a refrain—so that Desdemona sings:

DESDEMONA (singing)
The poor soul sat sighing by a sycamore tree,
Sing all a green willow.
Her hand on her bosom, her head on her knee,
Sing willow, willow, willow.

Nima translated:

Bar pa-ye bid-e sabz neshasteh tamam-e ruz

All day she sat at the foot of the sycamore tree
Head down just like the branches of the tree
She was in pain from her torturous love
Everyone could hear her cry
Though the wretched lover sings under the sycamore tree.[36]

My translation of Nima's original could not possibly be entirely accurate, because of the gendered disposition of the English language and the fact that in Persian we do not have gender-specific pronouns. Hence, where I translate "she sat" or "she was," in fact, no such gendered specificity is in Nima's original Persian. The singer of the song could be a man, a woman, or anything else in between. By both the power of his own poetic voice and the miracle of the Persian language, Nima turned a simple passage in Shakespeare into a site-specific lesson of what the Persian New Poetry that he inaugurated was doing with the entire poetic conception of the world. Thus, when Al-e Ahmad said about Nima "in his eyes, which were the eyes with which we saw our world (chashm-e zamaneh ma bud)," both he and the poet whom he so lovingly celebrated had seen a world we can now best hope to remember.

The Fourfold Forces of Nima's Poetry: From Totality to Infinity

I am sitting with a physical copy of the complete works of Nima Yushij, *Majmu'eh-ye Kamel-e Ash'ar-e Nima Yushij*, both his works in Persian and those occasional poems he composed in his native Tabari.[37] Edited by Sirus Tahbaz (1939–99), a literary scholar, children's books' author, critic, and editor who devoted his life to preserving Nima's legacy, this compendium was first published in Tehran in 1991, and it has recently been augmented by two additional volumes from the unpublished works of Nima Yushij. The poems which Tahbaz edited under the supervision of the literary estate that Nima himself had appointed before his death are ordered chronologically: the first one is "Mennat-e Dunan/Beseeching the Lowly" (1921) and the last one "Shab, Hameh Shab/Night, All Night" (1958), about two years before his passing. The two more recent volumes, *Sad Sal-e Digar/One Hundred More Years* (2017) and *Nava-ye Karevan/The Caravan's Melody* (2019), do have archival significance, but nothing in them adds to or subtracts from anything that Tahbaz had not already edited and published following Nima's own will and under the supervision of his most trusted confidants. My earliest copies of Nima's poems all date back to their original publications as single volumes, which I purchased when they were still available in Tehran's bookstores in the early to mid-1970s. The combination of all these versions of Nima's poetry, in their original single volumes and now in their collected editions, sums up the history of their publication and reception for Iranians of my generation. The key question when we read through Nima's poems is how to comprehend this collection of poetry. To understand Nima's poetics, the way in which his poetic thinking composes and unfolds, we need to see how his voluminous work gels and forms an assemblage of multiple and complementary components. Not all his poems are alike—some are palpably *atmospheric*, others *autochthonous* to his authorial voice, yet others boldly *political*, and then there are poems oozing with palpable *lyricism*. These fourfold themes I propose here are the formative forces that should guide us in our reading of Nima's work.[38]

The eminent literary scholar Mohammad Mo'in—a reputable classicist with little to no interest in New Poetry, to whom Nima had entrusted the orderly publication of his compendium—has thought that his poetry went from classical prosody and classical themes to classical prosody with contemporary themes, and from there finally to a radical alteration of both poetic form and themes. This is perhaps fairly accurate, but quite limited in helping us understand how his poetry worked. After Mo'in, other senior Iranian literary scholars such as Mohammad Reza Shafi'i-Kadkani and literary historians such as Yahya Aryanpour became preoccupied with the periodization of Nima's work and the thematic social and symbolic roots at the basis of his poetic revolution. This, too, was exceptionally important and insightful for helping us read Nima's oeuvre in its proper contexts.[39] But, at the same time, those scholars farthest removed from Nima's work, writing mostly in English, French, and other European languages, joined the goose chase of branding Nima's poetry "modern" or "modernist." What both of these groups of scholars have missed, however, are the internal forces and dynamics of Nima's poetics, implicating their social consequences, and yet deeply embedded in his own poetry, in terms definitive to the idiomaticity of his poetic intuitions, which I believe was composed of four forceful factors: (1) the *atmospheric* environment of his poetic imagination; (2) the *autochthonous* voice domestic to his poetic domain, which defined his poetic persona; (3) the *political* presence and power of his poetry; and (4) the *lyricism* that consistently overrides his politics and connects to the atmospheric and autochthonous thematic of his poems. The political force of his poetry, as well as the way in which his legacy constitutes an Event in the long history of Persian poetics, therefore, becomes miasmatic to the general tone of his aesthetic sensibilities. Let me now take time to explain these fourfold dynamics at work in his poetics, offering some key examples.

The first and foremost force of Nima's poetics consists of the atmospheric environment of his poetic imagination—the climactic ambience of his poems, the dramatic gathering of the weather, the rain, the sky, the sea, the river, the mountain, the valley, and the air in which the mood of his poems are all wrapped, pulsating. A solid example of his atmospheric poems is "Hengam keh Geryeh Midahad Saz/ When Weeping Melodiously" (1948):

Hengam keh geryeh midahad saz . . .

When this smoky substance with clouds on its back
Starts weeping melodiously,
When the dark blue-eyed sea
Angrily beats its own face:

From that traveler who's gone from me for long—
So coquettishly, lovingly—
I hold a picture in my chest
Made of familiar excuses.

But alas what's the use of crying, or of this tempest:
It is a silent and dark night: Everything solitary—
A man is playing the flute on the faraway road
His melody we can barely hear—
The other solitary soul is me from my eyes
A storm of tears flows.

When this smoky substance with clouds on its back
Starts weeping melodiously,
When the dark blue-eyed sea
Angrily beats its own face.[40]

When you read the poem and it starts sinking into you, feeling it scene after scene—and I am now thinking of the original in my mind—the first and foremost sensation is that of cloudy, rainy, thundering, stormy weather, fearsome and fearful. The climate has become climactic. The deeply cloudy sky is foggy, smoky, raining thunderously, as if sobbing, weeping, while the sea is stormy, angry, self-flagellating. The moody ambience brings a traveling person to mind; then come the distant melodies of a flute player, solitary, lonesome, aloof. Nothing is happening, just a scene, graphic, cosmic, and fearsome. Such an atmospheric sense of time and space is pervasive throughout Nima's poetry. The first and final epistemic violence *we do not* perpetrate on this gem of a scene is to read it politically: cry means this, sky means that, and cloud the other thing. The scene is not political. It is poetic, formal, atmospheric—it is formidable. We sit quietly and politely and read, and listen, and wonder. We need to keep it that way. The mystery of the poem is on its surface. We are set in this clime, reading him in this amorphous atmosphere. In my youth, I traveled to Mazandaran, Nima's homeland, and I can very well see and sense this weather. But here poetically, formally, atmospherically, the whole operatic scene and sense are foreboding, creating the right scene where the poetic Event is happening. What, if anything, ultimately happens in the poem is entirely tangential to this atmospheric, cosmic moment.

Immediately related to this atmospheric sense of Nima's poetry is his autochthonous voice, domestic and native to his emotive universe, which in turn defines his poetic persona. Here is one of the best examples in Nima's "Mahtab/Moonlight" (1948):

The moon is shining
The firefly is glowing—
Not a moment of sleep
Is broken in the eyes of anyone
And yet:
The troubles of this sleepy bunch
Break the sleep in my teary eyes.

Worrisome: The dawn is standing by me—
The morning wishes me
To awaken this forsaken lot,
And give them the good tiding—
But alas a thorn in my side
Prevents me from this intention.

The gentle tenderness of a flower stem
I planted with all my soul,
And with all my soul I watered:
Alas
Breaks in my bosom—

I wring my hands:
Perchance to open a door,

> Uselessly I persist,
> Hoping for someone to open the door—
> Their ruinous habitat
> Crumbles on my head.
>
> The moon is shining
> The firefly is glowing—
> Feet full of blisters from the long road,
> At the entrance of the village a solitary man,
> His backpack on his back,
> His hand upon the gate,
> Whispers to himself:
> The sorrow of this sleepy bunch
> Breaks the sleep in my teary eyes.[41]

This is Nima's self-image of himself, his poetry, his life, his mission, his persona, his message, and his musings. He is that lonesome solitary man having traveled a long path to bring a message to the sleepy inhabitants of a village, doubtful if he has anyone to listen to his message. This assemblage of atmospheric scenes and autochthonic voices places the poetics in its own cosmogonic sphere, irreducible to geographical and autobiographical specificities. The poetic constellation crafts its own spatial and authorial *loci*. This is where the poet becomes prophetic, his message revelatory, and in the absence of any metaphysics, the poetic Event crafts its own intuition of transcendence—where attending to the political will henceforth be entirely outside the domain of the party poetics or ideological gestations of one sort or another.

We also have a fusion of the atmospheric and autochthonous such as in "Khaneh-am Abri ast/My Home Is a Cloud" (1952), where the authorial persona and the poetic sphere concur and conflate with each other:

> *Khaneh-am abri ast . . .*
>
> My home is a cloud:[42]
> Cloudy is the whole earth with it—
>
> From round the mountain slope—
> Broken, ruinous, and drunk—
> The wind is blowing:
> And all the world is ruined by it,
> And so are my own senses!
>
> Oh you the flutist!
> The melody of your flute
> Has carried you far away:
> Where are you?

My home is a cloud:
The cloud is about to rain—
Thinking of my brighter days
Now all gone
I face the sun:
Overlooking the shores of the sea.

And the whole world is broken and ruinous
From the wind—
And upon the road, the flutist:
Constantly playing the flute:
In this cloud-covered world,
Pacing his own way ahead.[43]

The third potent component of Nima's aesthetic imagination is the political power of his poetry.[44] The best example of this aspect of his work is his by now legendary poem "Morgh-e Amin/The Amen Bird" (1951). The poem reads like an epic encounter between the Amen Bird (an image of Nima himself) and the people pleading with it to be a messenger of salvation and deliver them from their misery. Nima borrowed the allegory of "The Amen Bird" from a folkloric origin, where a bird or angel is believed to fly over the earth and, if people wished for something as it flew by, the wish would come true. Nima's poem begins with a self-description of the poet himself, the narrator, as the Amen Bird:

The Amen Bird full of pain and homeless—
Had flown to the farthest reaches of this tyrannized land
Returned forlorn—
With no appetite for water or seeds—
Wondering about the solution
On the day of delivery![45]

The poet *cum* Amen Bird continues to self-describe—as to who and what it is. It knows the world, is familiar with the wretched of the earth (*jor-dideh mardoman*), and, by saying "Amen," the bird keeps uniting the people, encourages them not to lose hope, and strings together their hidden desires.

The Bird has held in its throat the story of its people.
Pulling strings and strings,
Irrespective of the faults others find with it,
In its beak it holds the tip of threads otherwise lost.
It is a sign of the day of victory,
It holds its hand deep into the hidden labyrinth of life . . .

The Bird begins to listen to people's cry for freedom, and suddenly a protest breaks out, and we can hear revolutionary slogans:

> May the unjust pain of people come to an end
> (while the unjust pain of people intensifies).

The Bird keeps saying "Amen," assuring the masses of the victory soon to come:

> Salvation shall come,
> And the dark night shall turn to bright day.

The people, however, keep complaining:

> But that monster—
> Enemy of the people for the longest time
> Is devouring the world.

The bird prays for them:

> May he never see his wishes come true.

The epic poem continues apace along this dialogical course, as people describe their pains and the Bird gives them hope, until finally:

> The Amen Bird flies away from the roofs:
> On the calm horizon the rooster is singing
> The morning layers crack
> Under the calm cold sky
> Shapes and colors come to light—
> The night runs away
> The morning rises![46]

The "Amen Bird" is Nima's most revolutionary poem, albeit not in the common understanding of the political. He is not advocating any ideological force for any political path or revolutionary mobilization against tyranny. The poem is set between him and his people. His people are in deep trouble and come to him and complain, and he gives them the good tidings that soon the situation will be different and that justice and righteousness will prevail. It is imperative not to reduce Nima's poetics of political liberation to his haphazard affiliation with the (Communist) Tudeh or any other political party. This is poetic politics of an entirely different register. This is the prophetic voice of the poet in communion with his people—the people he poetically imagines and invents.

Lastly, the fourth and final aspect of his poetic disposition is the overriding lyricism that supersedes his politics and connects the atmospheric and autochthonous forces. The political therefore becomes miasmatic to the general tone of his poetics. Here is a good example, "To-ra Man Chasm dar Raham/I Long for You!" (1968):

> *To-ra man chashm dar raham . . .*

I long for you
At night—
When upon the branches of the *talajan*,⁴⁷
Shadows darken
And those who dearly love you
Are saddened:
I long for you!

At night, when the valleys
Like sleeping snakes are fast asleep—
When the hands of Blue Lotus
Weave a trap
Around the feet of the mountain cypress tree:
Whether you think of me or not,
I will never forget you:
I long for you!⁴⁸

This constellation that I propose here—or assemblage, to be more precise—begins and crescendos with seemingly forming a *totality* where politics matters but does not determine or overwhelm the discourse and is therefore released into a poetic *infinity*, if we were to use Emmanuel Levinas's famous terms. The fourfold poetic forces of *atmospheric* environment, *autochthonous* voice, *political* presence, and *lyrical overtones* now form a totality open to its own poetic infinity. In *Totality and Infinity: An Essay on Exteriority* (1961), Levinas has made a crucial distinction between the closed-circuited systems of philosophical totality and the open-ended prospect of infinity when exposed to eschatological theologies.⁴⁹ "The visage of being that shows itself in war is fixed in the concept of totality," Levinas has written, "which dominates Western philosophy. Individuals are reduced to being bearers of forces that command them unbeknown to themselves. The meaning of individuals (invisible outside of this totality) is derived from the totality."⁵⁰ This is Levinas boldly introducing his theological Judaism into his philosophical Europeanism. It works fine for him. From this premise, Levinas has pivoted towards his conception of "infinity"—of which we need to have a full perspective:

> However, the extraordinary phenomenon of prophetic eschatology certainly does not intend to win its civic rights within the domain of thought by being assimilated to a philosophical evidence. In religions and even in theologies eschatology, like an oracle, does indeed seem to "complete" philosophical evidences; its beliefs-conjectures mean to be more certain than the evidences—as though eschatology added information about the future by revealing the finality of being. But, when reduced to the evidences, eschatology would then already accept the ontology of totality issued from war. Its real import lies elsewhere. It does not introduce a teleological system into the totality; it does not consist in teaching the orientation of history. Eschatology institutes a relation with being beyond the totality or beyond history, and not with being beyond the

past and the present. Not with the void that would surround the totality and where one could, arbitrarily, think what one likes, and thus promote the claims of a subjectivity free as the wind. It is a relationship with a surplus always exterior to the totality, as though the objective totality did not fill out the true measure of being, as though another concept, the concept of infinity, were needed to express this transcendence with regard to totality, non-encompassable within a totality and as primordial as totality.[51]

That "prophetic eschatology" or "theologies of eschatology" for Levinas is, of course, inviting the Mosaic into the Platonic, which is fine for him. This is the signature definition of his philosophy. But he does not wish for the Judaic eschatology to be assimilated into Platonic philosophy, or what he calls "Being." He is right in thinking so. He has rightly insisted: "Eschatology institutes a relation with being beyond the totality or beyond history." This is his boldest and most significant Jewish contribution to an otherwise happily Greek ontology. The trouble with Levinas, however, is his militant Euro- and Judeo-centrism. He was pathologically ignorant of the Islamic philosophical antecedent that was ahead of him by centuries; his Jewish ancestors who found their pinnacle in Maimonides (*circa* 1134–1204) were fully aware, yet as a racist European philosopher he was entirely oblivious. But we need not throw the baby out with the bathwater. Levinas's insight is crucial to make a distinction between *totality* (Greek) and *infinity* (Hebraic). We only need to adjust his crucial insight and fine-tune it away from eschatology and towards Nima's poetic intuition of transcendence, for which project we cannot hold myopic European philosophers to account. They, and Levinas in particular, were just too near-sighted and provincial. Given his militant Eurocentrism,[52] Levinas's conception of "eschatology" is limited to the so-called "Judeo-Christian" terms. But there is much still useful in his philosophical prose that could be put to good use elsewhere. Bracketing Levinas's Biblical myopia, what he has said remains valid: "Eschatology institutes a relation with being beyond the totality or beyond history, and not with being beyond the past and the present." An equally important detachment from Levinas must also happen when we shift from his metaphysical phenomenology to the sorts of aesthetic intuition of transcendence evident in Persian poetry in general and in its masters, from Hafez to Nima in particular. We postcolonial thinkers are nomads, pilgrims: we pick and choose what we find useful for our own thinking. These poets have their own openings into an *infinity* beyond the reach of the *totality* that they face. Troubling Levinas, their face is familiar to us. This is what I mean by the *totality* of the fourfold forces at work in Nima's poetry coming together to release itself into opening horizons of an *infinity* beyond their constituent forces.

Nima's Epistolary Poetics

I am holding in my hands the very first edition of Nima Yushij's *Harf-ha-ye Hamsayeh/The Neighbor's Words* (1972). I purchased this book from a bookstore in front of Tehran University upon its publication, when I was an undergraduate student in Tehran. On the first page of this copy, which I keep as a precious icon of an almost forgotten age, I signed my name, as I habitually did those days, and dated it September 1979, when I had just come to Philadelphia and started my doctoral studies at the University of Pennsylvania. I had brought two suitcases full of books when I left my homeland, right before the February 1979 revolution turned everything upside down. I have read this copy cover to cover, underlined in red pen phrases that I liked, and written marginalia on some pages. There is no editorial introduction to this volume, just a note or a letter to a fictitious "neighbor," as Nima wrote. "I plead with you, please collect these letters," we read on the very first page of the book over Nima's signature, "although there are many superfluous and redundant things in them that need to be edited out. But they are certain notes. If I do not live long enough to write that detailed introduction to my poetry, then at least these letters will remain."[53] And remained those letters have—priceless documents of a poet at work detailing what he did to Persian poetry to make it anew.

Nima proceeded to write that he had much to say about poetry, and he specified that the title of these letters should be "Beh Hamsayeh/To the Neighbor" or "Harf ha-ye-Hamsayeh/The Neighbor's Words." He dated it Khordad 1324/June 1945, about five years to the month before I was born in the more southern climes of our shared homeland. You turn to the next page, and the letters start: "My dear, can you find that necessary purity and cleanliness that is required for your own solitude? My dear, ask yourself this question! No one knows what you are doing and [they] cannot see you."[54] The letter continues, and then we come to the next letter: "My dear, you should be able to sit down just like a rock, and feel in your body the circulation of time that the earth's storms have done to you."[55] I still remember and feel the power of the initial sensation when reading these letters for the first time, and that feeling is still with me. It is not clear if these letters were ever meant for someone in particular or, like the Muslim mystic Ayn al-Qozat al-Hamadani's (1098–1131) letters generations earlier, are just an epistolary form that Nima chose to share his ideas with his readers—or no reader in particular—just with posterity, or with himself listening to the echoes of his prophetic words.[56] What is important about these letters above all is their poetic, prophetic, and revelatory prose and disposition. They come out of nowhere; they are oracular, divinatory, uttered with such a mystic certainty, moral clarity, and authoritative power that we inadvertently sit down and listen carefully. Nima knew what he was saying; he wrote from the depth of his poetic convictions, and right from there he wished to share with us what his revolutionary utterances were all about.

It is impossible to exaggerate the simplicity, the power, and the theoretical potency of these "letters." He was speaking to the soul of a poet—any poet, a future poet, real or fictive. Just like the *Letters to a Young Poet* (1929) that Rainer Maria Rilke (1875–1926) wrote to Franz Xaver Kappus (1883–1966), a nineteen-year-old officer cadet, these letters by Nima, too, have an epistolary power to them—although they become far more technical and detailed about form than Rilke's letters. "Why don't you come to see me?" Nima wrote in a letter to this anonymous person. "You have hidden behind a veil and just write letters to me. I have collected your letters and kept them in a safe place. Some of them deserve to be considered in these responses. It is quite clear that, once a clear path has shown itself, a curious mind can locate the hidden treasure of one's consciousness."[57] These letters could be real, written to real people, or they could be just a formal option for the way in which Nima wished to share his ideas. Either way, most of these letters are instructions to a young poet to trust and cultivate their intuitions. Nima offered detailed and specific instructions in that direction—on both the formal body and the defiant soul of the New Poetry that he had just inaugurated.

The letters go into detail explaining Nima's contentious positions *vis-à-vis* classical poetry and Persian prosody. "I told you," so he writes in another letter, "that our old poetry is subjective, which is to say it is internal and deals with interior situations. In that poetry, external manifestations represent the internal dynamics that take place all interior to the person and do not opt to pay attention to external things. For which reason it is entirely useless for theatrical performances or even declamation."[58] This poetic materialism, detailed attention to the objective world outside the poet's mind, becomes definitive to Nima's conception of poetry. In that vein, he offered detailed observations regarding rhyme and rhythm in poems:

> You have asked me about rhyme. I'll explain it to you one day. In the eyes of your friend, rhyme is a music quite separate from rhythm in the content of the poem—a poem without rhyme is like a house that does not have a door and a roof. Your neighbor will not entertain in his thinking anything else other than this idea and what it means. I think both those who follow the classical prosody and those who compose poems without rhyme are wrong. Neither of the two groups, however, have any reason on their side, except that they wish to fly with the majestic falcon who is your friend, trying to do something new, years after he has flown all over this vast sky.[59]

From such specific speculations about formal aspects of poetry, Nima moved to a definition of what poetry is: "You wish to hear from me what is poetry at its best . . . At its best, poetry is a kind of observation (*moshahedeh*) that a handful of people have made for another handful of people. Therefore, my friend, do not expect something like this to be understood by the multitude. Everybody to a varied degree has the capacity to distinguish good from bad poetry, just one step further away from that they may know but not comprehend."[60] Politics was never too far from Nima's mind in these letters: "You have become too political, and I won't say why," he wrote in one letter. Then he specified what he meant by that:

> There has never been a literature that has been irrelevant to poetics, that would be a lie . . . I recall some of the works of Maxim Gorky. He says literature can inspire in a clear and more persuasive way what science and philosophy express. I agree with this position . . . Our nation (*mellat*) more than anything else needs this kind of literature, whether prose or poetry, meaning the kind of literature

that illustrates life ... A poet therefore is not someone who gives rhyme and rhythm to words ... A poet must, in fact, explain ordinary things that science and philosophy have not expressed clearly, and at times do so even better.[61]

In another major collection, *Setareh'i dar Zamin/A Star on Earth* (1975), of mostly letters he wrote in the 1920s and 1930s, we read one of his key self-descriptions in a letter dated 1923: "Don't you think you can see me. I, the real I, am a different truth than the one dwelling in my writings, and still people have not heard my voice, let alone a melody that would explain my heart to them. People avoid me as I avoid them."[62] These are not letters intended to communicate a message to someone. These are meditative moments in which Nima explained himself as much to himself as he did to others, to posterity. He wrote to leading literary scholars, renowned artists, famous personalities, and anonymous friends and family, including his own brother, in all of them mixing together a prose that is quite personal yet equally public—but all the time poetic. The result is a diction that remains always aloof from the mundane and implicates a far more serious set of issues at stake. There are letters, to be sure, to his mother about family matters, but there are also letters that explain how he thinks about the world of art, as well as the world in which poetry is located. In a letter dated 1944, he wrote to his young friend that there were three things that change: poetry, painting, and music—"painting by following nature, music by abandoning monotony and finding a synchrony between motions and more effective qualities and a more perfect style of gestures; and poetry as I have initiated it with a more perfect and simpler style."[63] In another letter dated 1929, he suddenly blurted out: "I am a great magician."[64] There is a self-assurance about him that what he has accomplished would soon be a part of the history of Persian poetry.

What is important about these letters is not just giving us a fuller grasp of their author's cast of mind, of aspects of his biography, or perhaps above all of his own take on the poetic revolution that he inaugurated. What is equally important is that he was writing these letters simultaneously as he was composing his poems. These letters and his poems are integral to and coterminous with each other. It is as if he was proving himself, reassuring himself, with an explanation as to what he was doing in his poems. There was not much of an audience for his poems, and even those at the Tudeh Party, such as Al-e Ahmad, who were sympathetic to his poetry, were not entirely sure what he was up to; they would, as Al-e Ahmad admitted, occasionally censor and butcher his poems before publishing them. These letters are therefore a poetic hermeneutic unto themselves, there to convince more than anyone else Nima himself as to what he was doing. From the range of these letters, it is quite clear that he was a man of profound solitude, for it must have taken him the better part of his days to both compose his poems and write these letters— perhaps even composing a poem, then writing a letter, or *vice versa*. We have therefore a prose account of his own poetic disposition. There is no one-to-one correspondence between the letters and the poems, as he never explained his poems to anyone—and his poetry features an entirely different, almost revelatory, voice. They are on two different but parallel tracks. Basically, for the four decades between the early 1920s and the later 1950s, he composed his poems and wrote his letters almost simultaneously and perhaps, one might even say, obsessively—like a person who has seen an urgent dream, a vision, a premonition of his own poetry and now has very little else to do but to deliver what has been revealed to him. Nima wrote non-epistolary prose as well, like his famous essay "Arzesh-e Ehsasat dar Zendgani Honarpishegan/The Significance of Feelings in the Life of Artists" (1946), but his best output explaining the poetics of his poetry are these letters. In these letters, we see him as solitary, and he spoke directly to the world. This epistolary prose generates a dialogical disposition to his thinking, a Bakhtinian twist in his meditations in two complementary senses, both dialogical thinking in his letters and dialogical harmony between his poetry and his prose. We have a much earlier model for such epistolary prose in the writings of Ayn al-Qozat al-Hamadani and his contemporary Ahmad al-Ghazali (1061–1123). The prose gives a conversational tone to the ideas shared, later developed in the genre of the epistolary novel. The direct model of Nima's letters is the collection of letters that has reached us from Ayn al-Qozat, where he too raised this genre to a *bona fide* philosophical prose.

To be sure, we have highly competent and quite technical accounts of Nima's poetics, such as Mehdi Akhavan-e Sales' two seminal essays, *Ata Va Laqa-ye Nima/ The Pros and Cons of Nima* (1982)—which was initially published in 1979 during the upheavals of the 1977–9 revolution. In this essay, Akhavan-e Sales has praised Nima as "our great contemporary poet and the father, the master, and the leader of Persian, Dari, and Tajik progressive and path-breaking poetry."[65] He has analyzed the technical aspects of Nima's poetry but has not shied away from over-politicization either—as in his reading of Nima's famous poem, "Hast Shab/It is Night," which he has interpreted as a symbolic poem that begins with the promises of the Constitutional period but ends in despair.[66] Mehdi Akhavan-e Sales composed another long essay on Nima's poetics, *Badaye' va Bed'at-ha-ye Nima/ Nima's Innovations and Novelties* (1979), again attending to the technical aspect of Nima's poetic revolution. Akhavan-e Sales subsequently published these two long essays in the form of a book, in 1989.[67] In these two seminal essays, we have one major follower of Nima, by now a solid poet of his own standing, reflecting on the technical particularities of Nima's poetry and the manners in which he had parted ways with classical prosody. These two essays are in effect ways to explain and justify Nima's poetic revolution. But in his own letters, Nima wrote from the emotive heart and the epistemic roots of his poetics.

In his own letters, Nima managed a fusion between the personal and the poetic. In *Donya Khane-ye Man Ast/The World Is My Home* (1971), another major collection of his letters, he wrote in an undated letter to his mother: "If I do not have a financial mind, I have a scientific mind, fully alert in me. I am familiar with the secrets of human morality of all sorts. Today I am the role model of an entire nation who has initiated new laws. I do not need you to admonish me."[68] In most of his letters, he pointed out that he was sending these letters via friends and family, for there was no reliable postal service yet. In another letter to his sister Nakta, he compared her to a flower he identified by its local name, "*michkajumeh*," which is very delicate and should never be touched: "despite the fact that the drops of their tears have fallen on their faces all their lives, they smile, your tears just like those dewdrops must be dissolved into laughter."[69] To his brother he wrote: "I have not done anything sufficient. Although in my own craft and industry I am superior to others, still I feel ashamed in front of the family, because spiritual progress has prevented your wretched abandoned brother from outward progress. I spend my life like a star behind the clouds."[70] Sometimes, his poetic outbursts are almost independent of whom he was addressing: "But a good poem is like an infant, potentially alive and well. It grows with the nation's thoughts, even though at the time of its birth it is rejected."[71] This letter is dated December 27, 1927, according to the Gregorian calendar. In a 1930 letter to his brother Ladbon, he wrote: "Despite all of these, I am not good but also good. I have good times when I go for a pleasant walk, I enjoy myself, and yet I am in pain; I think, and yet I regret spending so much time contemplating the philosophy of things. Altogether I have the true meaning and the philosophy of life. To whatever is said around me, I listen, and if they are contrary to my own thoughts, I consider them the noises of a fly."[72]

By far the most precious letters of Nima—at once personal, political, and deeply poetic—are those from his correspondence with his wife Aliyeh Jahangir, known as Aliyeh Khanom, a deeply cultivated and educated woman, the principal breadwinner of their household, the niece of the prominent Constitutional-era journalist Mirza Jahangir Khan Sur-e Israfil (circa 1870–1908). It was to his wife that Nima Yushij wrote his most heartfelt love letters in which he also confided his conceptions about being a poet. "Oh, even Satan does not shake hand with the poet," he wrote in a letter to her, "except in the depth of the dark night to intuit in him frightful thoughts and long spans of hopelessness."[73] In these letters, the figure of the "*sha'er*/poet" emerged as a particular category with certain revelatory qualifications. The divine and diabolic forces are identical poles, which he invoked in these letters when explaining what a poet is or does. "Oh, if the divine punishment and the fires of hell were not lies, how would God have dealt with the poet?"[74] But at the same time he had both a romantic and a realistic conception of love and marriage, which he wished to share with his wife. "Whenever I think of the institution of marriage," he wrote, "I imagine a simple and modest nest on top of trees where two kindred birds live there without abusing each other . . . But God has not given humans the necessary piety and natural bliss to live like birds."[75] Whatever the real dynamics of their marriage might have been, and they seemed to have had their share of quarrels, these letters transformed them into the elements of a sublime sense of the poet in love with his companion—a love that also occasioned the most potent reflections on who and what a poet is.

Nima Yushij's correspondence with his wife, whom he obviously tried to impress with his own significance as a ground-breaking poet, gave him ample opportunity to reflect on the nature and function of a poet in this world. "God divided all the fruits of this earth—he gave wealth, selfishness, and cruelty to people and heart solely to the poet, and he gave that heart a mysterious majesty that succumbs only to the grace of women."[76] This was, of course, meant as an expression of love to Aliyeh Khanom, but at the same time it identified the category of "the poet" in very specific terms, at once cosmic and common. God has a divine mission for his poets: "He keeps his poet in solitude on this earth in order to test his new ideas—and keeps him that way incongruent with all the other created beings."[77] His poetic gift, however, is also to show his wife how much he loved her: "The waves of the sea that look so beautiful during the sunrise and moonrise: who has been able to rely on them and lay on them? But look at the solid mountain, although on the surface it looks so rough, all the flowers grow on it—come, come sit on my heart!"[78] He was obviously aware of his own poverty, and anytime he writes of power and wealth one can feel a sense of twisting that fact to his own moral advantage. "Think," he wrote at one point to his wife, "Don't regret not having tall palaces and luxurious gardens—all of these are the results of treacheries and crime!"[79] But at the same time, the disposition of the poet was never far from his mind: "The perishable flower that cannot be touched or plucked is the heart of the poet."[80] He was therefore writing to his wife as much as to himself. At times, he did appear to be defiantly misanthropic:

> I have no idea where and how this idea has taken roots in me. About an hour ago when I was in a crowded street in this city (Laleh-zar)—I wish, I were blind so I would not see the unseemly form and shape of humans, deaf not to hear their voices. A bewildered, defiant, and fugitive being from the people nature has not created worse than me![81]

Above all, however, a poet is here to measure the gentlest changes in the human disposition: "The heart of the poet is like a vast sea. Look at the sea how despite its vastness, the slightest breath will affect its surface. Why should the slightest suspicion not do the same and sadden and affect my face—the way nature has created my heart is more sensitive than other hearts!"[82] He described himself both to his wife and to himself, and in the process he cast the very idea of "the poet" in the living world—in terms political, poetic, and personal at one and the same time.

Between Being and Finding: Nima as a Poetic Event

My primary suggestion in this chapter has been that the historic figure and poetic legacy of Nima Yushij form a unique poetic Event in the inaugural history of Persian New Poetry, which he launched, documented, and theorized all at once. He therefore remains the chief symbolic memory of Persian New Poetry. Ernst Cassirer has spoken of "symbolic memory," of which his example is Augustine's *Confessions*. Here is how Cassirer has put it:

> Yet poetry is not the only, and perhaps not the most characteristic, form of symbolic memory. The first great example of what an autobiography is and means was given in Augustine's *Confessions*. Here we find quite a different type of self-examination. Augustine does not relate the events of his own life, which were to him scarcely worthy of being remembered or recorded. The drama told

by Augustine is the religious drama of mankind ... Every line in Augustine's book has not merely a historical but also a hidden symbolic meaning. Augustine could not understand his own life or speak of it except in the symbolic language of the Christian faith.[83]

The same we might say about Nima Yushij's legacy: in and of itself a symbolic memory that at once crafted and posited itself for an entire generation of thinking and being poetically. He was inaugural, real, and mythic all at one and the same time. In the case of Nima, we are talking of a seminal poet who enabled an entire nation to think in terms both poetic and political—and both in an emancipatory aesthetic. "The hidden symbolic meaning" is what the Nimaic revolution inaugurated, like a new episteme, that would take the next generation of his followers to digest, internalize, conjugate, deliver, and eventually to exhaust. That idea that Persian New Poetry began with Nima and ended with Kho'i is central to my argument in this book. It is in that sense that I also turn to Alain Badiou's idea of "Event" for the Nimaic revolution, which I have also identified as archetypal—meaning that it posited a major epistemic shift in the received classical disposition of Persian poetic prosody. Events in this philosophical sense for Alain Badiou introduce a rupture, political, aesthetic, amorous, or scientific (as he has typified them), dismantling the ruling regime of power or knowledge or both, thus disrupting the situation that prevails and hides the potential of any and all Events. As he has articulated it:

> A situation (which means a structured presentation) is, relative to the same terms, their double multiplicity; inconsistent and consistent. This duality is established in the distribution of the count-as-one; inconsistency before and consistency afterwards. Structure is both what obliges us to consider, via retroaction, that presentation is a multiple (inconsistent) and what authorizes us, via anticipation, to compose the terms of the presentation as units of a multiple (consistent). It is clearly recognizable that this distribution of obligation and authorization makes the one—which is not—into a law. It is the same thing to say of the one that it is not, and to say that the one is a law of the multiple, in the double sense of being what constrains the multiple to manifest itself as such, and what rules its structured composition.[84]

Based on this categorical articulation of consistency and rupture, Badiou's philosophical positions offer clear examples of the Event patently in the political field, albeit rooted in his more universal articulation of the idea. Above all, the Event is formal, structural, compositional. It can be political, but for my purposes here I am thinking of the Nimaic revolution as an epistemic rupture, where through a poetic Event the nature of reality is revisioned, recast, reperceived. Nima dismantled the classical Persian prosody and replaced it with a far more immediate, palpable, real prosody closer to the lived syncopation of reality. For Badiou, the Event occurs in the four fields of love, art, science, and politics, as he has put it. The examples he has offered are the Paris commune, the Russian and Chinese revolutions, the revolt of May 1968, the anti-war Civil Rights movement in the US, and later the Arab Spring. Schoenberg's music, George Cantor's mathematics, and Mallarmé's poetry make up some of his other examples.

In his sequel to *Being and Event*, Badiou's *Logics of Worlds* (2006) has identified four typologies of the subject: political subjects, artistic subjects, amorous subjects, and scientific subjects.[85] "In the case of artistic truths," he has said, "the world exhibits a singular form of tension between the intensity of the sensible and the tranquility of form. The Event is a break in the established regime of this tension." He has further added:

> The production of the present is that of an artistic configuration ... From the interior of a configuration, the reactive subject organizes the denial of that configuration's formal novelty, treating it as a simple de-formation of admitted forms, rather than as a dynamic broadening of in-formation [*mise en forme*] ... The obscure subject aims at the destruction of the works that comprise the body of the faithful artistic subject, which it perceives as a formless abomination and wishes to destroy in the name of its fiction of the sublime Body, the Body of the divine or of purity. We go from the pagan statues hammered by the Christians to the gigantic Buddhas blown up by the Taliban, via the Nazi auto-da-fes (against 'degenerate' art) and, more inconspicuously, the disappearance into storage facilities of what has fallen out of fashion. The obscure subject is essentially iconoclastic.[86]

Consider the very last pronouncement—that "the obscure subject is essentially iconoclastic." The Nimaic Even is the occasion of that obscure subject coming to the surface, from potentiality to actuality. In the Persian philosophical imagination, as perhaps best evident in Baba Afzal Kashani's (died *circa* 1214) conception of *wujud* in Arabic, which in his work is divided into two Persian concepts: *budan*/Being and *yaftan*/Finding. In that context, Kashani has been concerned with the issue of temporality in its formal grasp of Being (*wujud, hasti*)—for there is a strong factor of epistemic motion and temporal differential at work between *budan* and *yaftan*. Baba Afzal Kashani's ontological division of *wujud* between Being (*budan*) and Finding (*yaftan*) helps us think critically about *temporality* as the space in which, so I argue, these six poets have found themselves being, thinking, meaning, poetically—having both potential and actual capacities. Here is how one scholar of Baba Afzal has summarized his ontology:

> Potential being is represented by the tree present in a seed, while actual being is the tree itself. Potential finding is life or the soul at whatever level it may be envisaged, from the mineral up to the human; actual finding is the self-consciousness of the intellect, where knowledge, knower, and known are identical. Existence that is only "being" lacks the perfection of "finding," while finding that is only potential has not yet become everlasting. Each higher level of existence contains the lower levels within itself; everything outside the intelligible world of the soul is an imperfect likeness of what is found within.[87]

This ontology obviously has a larger context: "Like most Muslim cosmologists, Bābā Afżal discerns two movements in the universe, that from the origin to the world, or from 'finding' to 'being,' and that from the world to the point of return from being to finding." This is not a mere philosophical speculation, for, "as the microcosm, man contains within himself all levels of the macrocosm; these he must actualize one by one to bring about the Return to God."[88] This philosophical foregrounding, by both Badiou and Baba Afzal, enables us to think of the texture of the knowing subject as it is poetically dwelling in the known and knowable world. Thinking of Nima as a poetic Event trafficking in his poetry between *budan* and *yaftan* enables us to foresee the unfolding legacy of his poetry in terms specifically articulated in the generation of the poetic possibilities that he enabled.

The Nimaic poetic move from Finding to Being was in a decidedly formal shift in the classical Persian prosody (*'aruz*) which he both theorized and performed. This was the revolutionary Event that he boldly imagined and patiently inaugurated. In one of his signature poems, "Mahtab/Moonlight" (1948), Nima projected his own self-image as the *locus classicus* of the poet as pilgrim delivering this liberating message to an unsuspecting nation:

Negaran ba man estadeh sahar . . .

Worrisome: The dawn is standing by me:
The morning wishes me
To awaken this forsaken lot,
And give them the good tiding—
But alas a thorn in my liver
Prevents me from this intention.[89]

Chapter 2

MEHDI AKHAVAN-E SALES: REMEMBRANCE OF THINGS PAST

I have in my possession and am now looking at a two-volume set of Mehdi Akhavan-e Sales' collected works. These two volumes were published in Tehran in 2018 and were recently sent to me by the poet's son, Mazdak Akhavan-e Sales, via a friend traveling from Tehran to New York. The handsomely bound volumes are respectfully inscribed, signed, and presented to me by the poet's two sons, Mazdak and his brother Zardosht Akhavan-e Sales. The precious prose of the inscriptions is exceedingly kind, generous, and deferential. I am too embarrassed, for it would be a sign of immodesty, to cite them here. I cherish these two precious volumes among my most prized possessions in my private library. I feel as if Akhavan (as we affectionately call our beloved poet) has sent them to me from his heavenly abode—in a manner of speaking. I write these words in mid-September 2024, when an ignoramus American senator, John Kennedy of Louisiana, was quoted in the news desecrating the precious name of my homeland "Iran" in a congressional hearing as synonymous with terrorism. Iran for me and millions of people like me is Mehdi Akhavan-e Sales, and the whole firmament of our poets, philosophers, artists, mystics, architects, down to the very ordinary people leading a noble and hard-working life. For this bird-brained neanderthal senator in the US, the precious name of my homeland has been turned into an icon of barbarity. Thus, I write these words and begin my chapter about the precious legacy of Mehdi Akhavan-e Sales possessed by his treasured memories and at a time of deepest anger and anxiety about the fate of my homeland at the mercy of these senatorial savages, bereft of the most basic facts about any culture on this planet, yet sitting behind the weapons of mass destruction with which they terrorize this earth.

The names of Akhavan's sons, Zardosht and Mazdak, are self-explanatory—two iconic Iranian prophets of yore, Zoroaster (*circa* 1000 BCE) and Mazdak (died *circa* 528)—who defined a vast civilization long before Islam appeared on the world stage. The mighty Persian poet of our time who is the subject of this chapter named his own two children after the two towering figures of Zoroaster and Mazdak, in memory of a past that had become definitive to his poetic imagination. Akhavan and his wife Khadijeh had six children—three daughters and three sons. Two of his daughters, Laleh and Tansegol, died young. He was survived by his three sons—Tus, Zardosht, and Mazdak—and his daughter Luli. These are not usual names, certainly not Arabic names, like their father's own name, Mehdi, or my name, Hamid. Most of our names are Arabic and Islamic names which we carry with pride. But beginning with Akhavan's generation there was a rising tendency for parents to give Iranian children mostly Iranian names, such as those of Akhavan's children, or of my own: Kaveh, Pardis, Chelgis, and Golchin. Taken from the *Shahnameh* or other Persian literary and poetic masterpieces, these names signaled the renewed adaptation of a distant past that had by now become a potent sense of the present. Akhavan was the paramount poet of this moment.

Mehdi Akhavan-e Sales (1929–90), his *nom de plume* M. Omid, was a poet and a musician with a powerful penchant for epic tone and tenor in his voluminous work. He was born in Mashhad in the province of Khorasan in northwestern Iran.[1] His father Ali was an apothecary herbalist from Yazd, one of three brothers (thus their last name, which means "the Three Brothers"), and his mother Mariam was from Khorasan. He received his early education in his hometown and was drawn to music, although his father disapproved. "My father's name was Ali," he once wrote in a short autobiographical note:

> He was one of those herbalist physicians who was originally from the Fahraj region in Yazd and who had migrated to and lived in Khorasan. He had a wife named Mariam, born and raised in Khorasan. In 1927, they brought a Mr. Nobody to this world in Tus of Khurasan, that would be me. This Mr. Nobody kept growing up, until one fine day he suddenly noticed that he was gently whispering to himself some songs—and what songs they were! May no Muslim ever hear, or an infidel see![2]

After his high school graduation, Akhavan moved to Tehran; initially, he taught in public schools and eventually found employment in the Ministry of Culture. In 1950, he married his cousin Khadijeh, with whom he had six children. In 1990, he went on a major European tour to England, Denmark, Sweden, Norway, and France—reciting his poetry mostly to Iranian expats. He died the same year at the age of sixty-one, in Tehran.

During his own lifetime, Akhavan was so widely loved and admired and so definitive to the poetic disposition of his age that, when he would write short or long prefaces or conclusions to his own collections of poetry, he would habitually self-deprecate, indulge his readers in his sublime sense of humor, and joke that he did not care much about his own poetry, that poetry at his age was just a pastime or a hobby, like collecting stamps, flying pigeons, or playing cards.[3] But when overwhelmed by poetic seizure, it was as if another human being had surfaced in him—a voice of the divine, deciphering the signs of his age in terms at once far away and immediately present, as when in his "Qesseh-ye Shahryar-e Shahr-e Sangestan/The Ballad of the Prince of Stoneville" (1960) he eavesdropped on behalf of his entire nation on the conversation between two doves overlooking a defeated prince—speculating on the day of his promised delivery:

The signs I see in him
Look like Bahram—
The same [legendary] Bahram-e Varjavand
Who shall resurrect on the Day of Judgement
And do many honorable deeds
Thousands of wondrous glories—
After him Giv the son of Gudarz—
With him stands Tus the son of Nozar—
And then Garshasp: That brave and thunderous lion—
And then the rest and then the rest . . .[4]

Nima Unfolded: From Archetypal to Archaic

If Nima cast Persian New Poetry in decidedly defiant, subversive, and path-breaking ways definitive to his paradigmatic shift, his follower and admirer Mehdi Akhavan-e Sales offered that archetypal cast a definitive mythic past and an archaic diction. Above all, Akhavan was a master storyteller of stories of bygone ages, a reminder and inventor of distant memories that may or may not have been there, but that he poetically imagined. His poetic language is archaic, his rhythm decidedly epic, his content radically contemporary, his politics delivered in a boldly rebellious semantic. But at the same time, his diction, pronouncedly epic, is boldly formal—and because of that cognitive dissonance the devoted "modernists" have been totally baffled by him, as he has sent them spinning after their own tail.

Throughout his illustrious career as a leading poet after Nima, Mehdi Akhavan-e Sales' poetic preoccupation was with the Iranian past, real and unreal at one and the same time. Zoroastrian, Mazdaian, Manicheans, and Mazdakite icons and allusions abound in his poetry. Akhavan's singular contribution to this assemblage of six iconic poets which I have gathered in this book was to craft a past, a mythic chronicle, and a heroic pedigree (all in an updated archaic language) for the history of his nation. If Nima was archetypal in his poetic diction, Akhavan was archaic in his preferred parlance, perforce reminiscent of Ferdowsi in his *Shahnameh*, with whom he was usually and rightly compared. "Khan-e Hashtom/The Eighth Task" (1968) and its sequel, "Adamak/Little Man" (1968), are the best examples of this allusion to Ferdowsi's *Shahnameh* (1010) that capture this definitive aspect of his poetry. The two poems work into and against each other: first describing the scene of a *naqqali* performance and then lamenting the scene when the *naqqal* has lost his audience to a television set. The poet first describes the scene in a cold winter night, lost in a wilderness until a tavern appears, into the warm and welcoming bosom of which he enters to see a mesmerized crowd that has gathered around a *naqqal* telling them a story. Here Akhavan mimicked the performative power of the *naqqali* tradition with a virtuoso performance. The *naqqal* begins by telling his audience how the story of the Seven Tasks (trials, labors) of Rostam has already been told before by Ferdowsi and other ancient storytellers, and now he wants to tell the story of "the Eighth Task."

> This is a story, yes, a story of pain—
> It is not poetry—
> This is the measure of love and hatred
> Manly and cowardly—
> It is not useless pure poetry good and full of nothing
> Excellent nothing like nothing
> This is an old rug of misery
> Soaked with the blood of Rostam and Siavash
> The cover of Takhti's coffin.[5]

In one stroke, just dropping the name of Gholamreza Takhti (1930–68)—a renewed and widely loved wrestling champion—he instantly brought together myth and reality, past and present iconic heroes, and with them their living memories. The story he wants to tell is the Eighth Task of Rostam: he is trapped inside a ditch full of daggers and swords after his own brother has plotted against him. The pinnacle of the story is when Rostam sees the shadow of his brother Shaghad, whom he could have killed, but did not. It is a painful story about being killed by your own brother. But, more pointedly, it is a task which Rostam does not survive. Hence, this last, until now untold, task is one of betrayal of the enemy within, of the foe at your own bosom.

The poem has a follow-up called "Adamak/Little Man," where we see that the selfsame *naqqal* has no audience, for everyone is drawn to the television:

> That which now tells a story
> Comes from inside the magical box of the West . . .
> Ah I am ashamed, so ashamed—
> In a corner by the window sits the *naqqal* of yore,
> Silent, sad, and forlorn—
> His mast like a column in his hand
> His hand under his brow—
> Angry and hurt:
> Sitting on the coffeehouse bench far from the crowd—
> His back bent, his head inside the sleeves of his own cloak—
> Saddened by all those deceitful and shameless sights:
> In his heart a storm of curses and hatred
> The Western magic box busy with its deceits . . .[6]

Everything wrong with technological modernity, with cultural colonialism, with European imperial projects robbing the nations around the globe of their rooted cultures, is evident in this poem. The *naqqal* here is an iconic figure reading all that was good, pure, definitive to Iranian culture, and the television set is the symbolic representation of an age of colonial machinations transforming an entire world and robbing it of its most elemental virtues. How in the world could a poet so visceral in his critique of colonial modernity be read as a "modern poet?" At the end of the poem, Akhavan turns to a damning denunciation of television and all its tricks and how it is draining an entire nation of its definitive features. To do so, he opts for a powerful sarcastic tone.

> For the truth of things come listen
> To the new *naqqal*!
> Let go of (old) stories—
> The heroes of those stories have died along with those stories—
> It is now for quite some time
> That the fire of myth has died out—
> Listen, children, dearly beloved children:
> Let's cheer for the living heroes!
> Listen to us, the past is dead,
> Lovely is the present and the future!
> Come and listen, long live the heroes of our own time—
> Hey, you who love dead things!
> Now we are the living, we are alive:
> Look at us and know us:
> You learn and you read about us!
> And hey, you who love the bygone heroism!
> We are Sam of Nariman, we are Zal Zar;
> We are Rostam of Dastan; we are the heroic Sohrab;
> We are Faramarz; we are Borzu;
> We are the famous Prince . . .⁷

In the end, the *naqqal*, and with him the poet, leave the scene in utter disgust. The nostalgic and antiquarian forces evident in this poem do not remain stagnant at that level and become emblematic of a whole culture of defiance against colonial "modernity," the very term that some Iranist scholars have oddly opted to affix to how to read Akhavan's poetry! Nima's potent archaic language is deeply rooted in Nima's archetypal poetics of his time. The two of them read together frame the way in which an entire nation was now transforming and re-imagining itself against the alienating forces of the Eurocentric onslaught of colonial modernity.⁸

Force-Feeding Eurocentric Modernity

When I was doing research for this chapter to see what new work of scholarship on Akhavan-e Sales I may have missed, I came across a book with a quite intriguing title: *Memories of an Impossible Future: Mehdi Akhavān Sāles and the Poetics of Time* (2016). I manage to locate the book and, upon reading, soon realized that the issue of force-feeding this unexamined European "modernity" down the throat of contemporary Persian poetry (and much else) has assumed an even more violent character in the case of Mehdi Akhavan-e Sales. Early in this book, the author, Marie Huber, a learned professor of Persian and Comparative Literature at Stanford University, shares with her readers an anecdote about someone asking

Akhavan what languages he knew. In a moment of typical sublimity, which Huber has completely missed, Akhavan responded that he only knew a bit of Persian—thereby dismissing the implied intention of that positively puerile question. The interlocutor failed to see the glory of the response and insisted that Akhavan must have known European languages and was therefore influenced by modern European poets. Neither the translator and his colonized mind, who had asked this banal question, nor indeed Marie Huber, now reiterating that encounter, could grasp the significance of Akhavan's response, but they went on a rampage and actually wrote an entire book waterboarding Akhavan's poetry with entirely irrelevant European modernist speculations, no doubt significant for their own European provenance but entirely irrelevant to Akhavan's poetry. Akhavan lived in a world that included Europe and the legacy of all its colonial savageries around the world. Nothing less and nothing more. But turning that vacuous truism into a cornerstone of his poetry? The sheer chutzpa!

The evident purpose of Huber's book is to examine the technical aspects of Akhavan's poetics, including rhythm and metaphor, and particularly the issues of time and temporality in his poetry. This is a perfectly legitimate project, except, as always in these sorts of endeavors, the word "philosophy" is of course reserved exclusively for European philosophy, which in turn becomes the principal culprit in failing to teach us anything important about the matter at hand.[9] "While we should allow for a measure of exaggeration and authorial coquetry," Marie Huber has interjected, "the anecdote nevertheless illustrates an important point: Akhavān, unlike most of his contemporaries, had little regard for intellectual fashions and did not seek inspiration abroad. At the same time—and here the translator's intuition was astute—Akhavān's poetry is most profoundly rooted in our age."[10] What exactly does that mean? "Our age"? Is that supposed to be the European age writ colonially large, perhaps? Or Akhavan's own age as an Iranian poet rooted in a vast poetic and philosophical legacy? We have here in effect two problems in one thick brushstroke. There is no indication that Akhavan was an exception to the fact that his contemporaries were far more rooted in what they knew well than in what they did not; and second, being rooted "in our age" does not mean in the European (colonial) age. We have multiple temporal and spatial frames of reference. People around the world have their own time, place, spatiality, and temporality—diametrically opposed to the Hegelian teleology of the *geist* that must perforce end in European time. We were not all born on the European colonial clock. So "our age" might very well be Huber's own age. Perfectly fine. But it is most certainly not Akhavan's age—a poet sitting at the pinnacle of a monumental poetic legacy long before and even longer after the thing that calls itself "the West," or "Western modernity," has done its deeds and disappeared into thin air.

What follows in Huber's book is even more an act of violent force-feeding "modernity" down the throat of Akhavan-e Sales' poetry:

> Its scope and depth transcend the national boundaries of Iran. Yet can we hasten to apply Western definitions of modernity? Or should we rather speak of pertinence in the sense of a poetry that enacts the dilemmas of the modern age

in its quests and aporias, feats of linguistic prowess and lapses into silence, heteroglossia and unadorned simplicity, desire and disillusionment, alienation and belief in an improbable humanity buried amid the ruins of history? These are the questions addressed in this book.[11]

Right here is the crux of the issue: the fact and phenomenon and the terrorizing consequences of European colonialism (or colonial modernity) have no hint of a presence in a book published in 2016, before we figure out how European modernity and its "aporias, feats of linguistic prowess and lapses into silence, heteroglossia and . . . alienation and belief in an improbable humanity buried amid the ruins of history" may figure and reconfigure under the shadow of the European colonial savageries as the vehicles of its "modernity." Persian New Poetry of the sort that Akhavan best represented was deeply and indelibly rooted in its immediate continental context of the Persian cosmopolis, emerging from its own imperial past and plunging deeply into the globalized European colonial modernity. Its encounter with European predatory colonialism (code-named "modernity") was one among any number of other factors defining its worldliness. Thus, the answer is a resounding no: "can we hasten to apply Western definitions of modernity" to any country and clime at the receiving end of the epistemic barbarism of colonialism? The answer is no. We should not. The rest of the phrase—"Or should we rather speak of pertinence in the sense of a poetry that enacts the dilemmas of the modern age . . . "—is a tautology, the same chimeric construct of European modernity coming back through the window once kicked out the door. The world has nothing but an actively hostile and contrarian stand *vis-à-vis* European colonial modernity, as we just saw in a sublime example of Akhavan's poetry. This is neither specific to Persian New Poetry, nor a singular sign of "nativism." This is the worldly universalism of a different sort, subjugated, denied, and denigrated by the misplaced hubris of European self-universalization.[12]

There is nothing in Akhavan's or Nima's poetry that indicates anything other than their own historically rooted time and place, and any other extension outside those vast and empowering boundaries into Europe or other than Europe goes into multiple directions—into Asia, Africa, and Latin America—without any prerogative given to European modernism, which is a perfectly legitimate project in and of itself for Europeans. Huber's preoccupation with Paul Ricœur, Hans-Georg Gadamer, Emmanuel Levinas, Maurice Blanchot, Michel de Certeau, and Jacques Derrida are all fine and dandy for herself or any other author, but has very little to do with Akhavan, without waterboarding these figures and their presumed "modernism" down his nose, mouth, and throat. Her preoccupation eventually degenerates into name-checking (or name-dropping) Walter Benjamin, Léopold Szondi, Friedrich Schleiermacher, and so on. Why not think of Enrique Dussel and Walter Mignolo from Argentina, or Mudimbe from Africa, Ashis Nandy from India, Kojin Karatani from Japan, Nasr Hamed Abu Zaid from Egypt—or any number of other Muslim and Iranian philosophers? Why this bizarre privileging of European thinkers as Thinkers, and then so without an iota of critical awareness of their colonial encounters with the rest of the world? Should I again rehearse the horrid racism of Kant, Hegel, Levinas, and the rest of them—that they did not think us proper human beings? I think I have done so on enough occasions.[13]

"My readings of Akhavān's poetry are guided by three essential paradigms," Huber tells her readers, "borrowed from Celan, Blanchot and Szondi: meridian, infinite conversation and stretto are figures of signification unfolding in time and space, without final closure."[14] I can only imagine poor Akhavan turning in his grave! This is a perfectly plausible schema to study Paul Celan, Maurice Blanchot, or any other European poet in Léopold Szondi's frame of reference. All the power to them all! But where does the most deeply rooted Iranian poet of the distant past, made politically potent for his readers, enter this production? "While outright comparisons with Western poetic movements are problematic," Huber has admitted, "and the search for real or imagined influences merely deflects attention from the specific modernity, the specific exorbitance of Nimā's and Akhavān's writing, parallels can be drawn to certain concerns of twentieth-century literature in the West."[15] Such free-floating speculations are far more than "problematic." They are deeply flawed, self-alienating, distorting, and outright abusive. There is no specific modernity except colonial modernity, if we were to get anywhere near "the specific exorbitance of Nimā's and Akhavān's writing." "The West" is the singular cause of calamity around the globe, as the world witnesses right now in what this very "West" headed by its Israeli settler-colony is doing in Palestine and Lebanon and the rest of the region. Rudyard Kipling's imperial musing that "Oh, East is East, and West is West, and never the twain shall meet" is the most potent poetic part of this colonial modernity posing as "modernism"—again perfectly enlightening for its European scene, yet entirely prone to epistemic violence to the rest of the world.

After all this misplaced epistemic song and dance, Marie Huber has ultimately gotten the timing wrong and confused the projection of a mythic past with "an impossible future." The trouble at the very root of this way of thinking is to pluck Akhavan's poetry out of his natural and cosmopolitan habitat and to submit it like a cadaver to a European philosophical autopsy table for dissection. There is no philosopher or critical thinker in the immediate vicinity of Akhavan whom she either knows or thinks worthy of her attention. The poor, lifeless cadaver of Akhavan's poetry is thus submitted to some mighty European philosopher for their kind and generous consideration. The result is a calamitous prose that reads like reports on old archeological relics that the British or French stole from Egypt, Iraq, or Iran and placed in their respective museums to produce Orientalist knowledge about their (former) colonies. It is very much similar to Kiarostami's cinema being subjected to film-philosophy of the European gestation, or else when Ferdowsi's *Shahnameh* was submitted to the provincialism of "the oral formulaic theory" to explain itself.

There is, to be sure, nothing wrong with occasionally or even consistently paying attention to aspects of European philosophical thinking about anything, so far as we are fully aware of the always already cosmopolitan world immediately embracing a poet and artist or a filmmaker anywhere else in the world, so far as we take that world in its wholesome totality and infinity seriously, and—above all—so far as we fully comprehend the fact that European modernity spelled colonialism and catastrophe for the rest of the world. Therefore, we must plant an actively decolonial set of lenses on what and where we read anything smelling of European modernity. As a by-product of multiple literary, poetic, philosophical, and moral worlds, in and outside of Iran, deep into Asia, Africa, Latin America, and also Europe, I am fully aware and actively at work in all these traditions and legacies, but always already with a decolonial set of critical lenses and always already in active solidarity and conversation with critical thinkers and literati inside these contrapuntal domains. For my entire academic lifetime, I have been based at a major Ivy League university (Columbia), and I am the product of two others (the University of Pennsylvania and Harvard). I teach Persian philosophical texts in one seminar on one side of my campus before I rush to another to teach Plato's *Symposium* or Enheduana's *Exaltation of Inana*, or Virgil's *Aeneid*, or Claudia Rankine's *Citizen: An American Lyric*, or Toni Morrison's *Song of Solomon*. As an ambidextrous thinker, I am both the host and the guest of these "moveable feasts" at one and the same time. But I remain solid where I am as an Iranian and conversant with the world around me. Otherwise, this blindfolded privileging of European philosophy as "Philosophy" and literature as "Literature" or poetry as "Poetry" is prone to produce a terribly lopsided perception of the world, where, even in the case of an Iranian poet like Akhavan who in bold and precise terms says that he has nothing to do with Europe, his own words are turned around against him and dismissed! The world outside European modernity has its own varied and compelling philosophical legacies, Iran included. Those philosophers may also have, as I contend that they do, something relevant to add to our reading of the world at large, Akhavan's poetry included. Plucking one poet like a dead body from a graveyard and putting them on the autopsy table (forensic or clinical) to humor European ideas is a seriously unseemly scene. The Eurocentric scholar suddenly looks like the captain of an oil tanker exporting crude oil and other raw materials from the Persian Gulf to Europe or the US for their factories to produce finished products and feel reconfirmed in the superiority of their manufacturing and marketing intelligence. We are too far gone into the game to allow that to happen. We reverse the colonial gaze, we look at what European philosophy may have to offer, debone its nasty racist traits, with our feet firmly rooted where we are in Asia, Africa, or Latin America—with our works of art the focal points of the hermeneutics, aesthetics, and poetics of our being, knowing, and imagining (in) the world.

We ultimately need not make any theoretical argument outside Akhavan's own poetry. In "The Eighth Task," at one point we read about the *naqqal*, which is now Akhavan himself, making very specific gestures and bold expressions about "East and West." It would be good for purveyors of European "modernity" and "modernism" to read him carefully:

He paused for a moment and remained silent—
Moved his wooden stick towards the West with hatred and disgust;
And towards the East with contempt—
He then moved his hair just like a lion his mane—

Then he burst into a hateful fury,
With a trembling voice and a painfully rhetorical diction he said . . .[16]

The Invention of Tradition and Modernity

To correct our lenses and see an immediate remedy not to read Akhavan abusively into the project of European "modernity" (what an astoundingly foul calamity), I cannot right now think of a better device than the magnificent scholarship of Gholamhossein Youssefi (1928–90), a leading literary scholar of his time, with a solid command of both classical and contemporary Persian prose and poetry. I am holding in my hand my copy of Gholamhossein Youssefi's *Cheshmeh-ye Roshan/ The Enlightened Fountain* (1990).[17] It is a quite bulky book, and the spine is coming off, as it usually does due to the clumsy craftsmanship of Iranian publishers. Years ago, when I was a graduate student at the University of Pennsylvania, I learned bookbinding and would regularly mend my own precious books. In the aftermath of Covid-19 and the abundance of PDF files of old books available online, this exquisite skill seems to have become antiquarian. Youssefi was a deeply cultivated literary historian who, contrary to many other scholars of his rank and stature, had an open mind and gracious heart to approach contemporary Persian New Poetry with a critical intention to understand and appreciate it. Throughout this book, he has used the word "*tajaddod*/renovation" to designate this recent phase of Persian poetry, a word that has nothing to do with what Europeans understand as their project of "modernity" and the rest of the world sees as an ideology of colonial domination from its European center. *Tajaddod* means "to renew" as it is generally used in scholarship to mean a learned scholar who has renewed a practice to save it from vacuous familiarity. In a more classical context, for example, Al-Ghazali (1057–1111) has been considered a *mojadded*, a renovator of scholastic learning. This is the way in which Youssefi also understood Nima and his followers: that Nima renovated Persian poetry.

What is crucial about Youssefi's book is the way in which he has seamlessly woven together four successive phases in the history of Persian poetry: (1) from the earliest poetry of Rudaki (*circa* 858–941) to the end of the classical period with Abd al-Rahman Jami (1414–92); (2) the transitional period to *tajaddod* from Mohtasham Kashani (1500–88) to Adib al-Mamalek Farahani (1860–1917), when neo-classicism still ruled; (3) from the poetry of Iraj Mirza (1874–1926) and Mirzadeh Eshqi (1893–1924) to that of Aref Qazvini (1882–1934) and his contemporaries during the Constitutional period up to Abolqasem Lahuti (1887–1957), when signs of thematic renovations become evident; (4) and finally from Nima Yushij and his followers to the end of this period in Youssefi's own time. There is no room for introducing, interjecting, and violating this sustained and systemic scheme with European modernity, for each phase is deeply rooted in the preceding phase and anticipates the next, which means that the Nimaic revolution is epistemically intertwined with all its preceding phases, without any need to speculate about "modernity." Youssefi has composed quite insightful chapters on five of the six poets whom I examine in this book—except for Esmail Kho'i, who at the time when Youssefi was writing his book, had already left Iran under duress and who thought of himself as being in exile.

The sense of continuity that entails successive waves of epistemic changes makes one thing abundantly clear: "traditions" are the most potent inventions of "modernity." There is no such thing as "traditional Persian poetry" for us to have "modern Persian poetry." Traditions were invented for the colonized world, as the colonizing world called itself "modern" and the harbinger of "modernity": for much of the ravaged world, this meant colonialism. The critical response to that fact is not to colonize the entirety of the world with the European sense of modernity and to actively ship on an aircraft carrier a platoon of European poets and philosophers to land in the Persian Gulf and start treating Iranian or Arab or any other poets and thinkers like crude oil and other raw materials for the enhancement and enrichment of European modernity. In their edited volume, *The Invention of Tradition* (1983), Eric Hobsbawm and Terence Ranger have collected a number of key essays and put forward the argument that many so-called "traditions" that may appear ancient are in fact very recent inventions. "Nothing appears more ancient, and linked to an immemorial past," they have argued, "than the pageantry which surrounds British monarchy in its public ceremonial manifestations. Yet, as a chapter in this book establishes, in its modern form it is the product of the late nineteenth and twentieth centuries. 'Traditions' which appear or claim to be old are often quite recent in origin and sometimes invented."[18] It is in his own contribution to this volume that Hobsbawm has pointed out: "It is the contrast between the constant change and innovation of the modern world and the attempt to structure at least some parts of social life within it as unchanging and invariant, that makes 'the invention of tradition' so interesting for historians of the past two centuries."[19]

Absent from Hobsbawm's thinking, however, is still the calamity of inventing non-existent traditions for the colonized world to make them susceptible to the savageries of European colonialism, camouflaged as "modernity." To understand that salient fact we need to go to the seminal work of Walter Mignolo, *The Darker Side of Western Modernity: Global Futures, Decolonial Options* (2011). According to Mignolo, what Europeans have sold the world as their Renaissance and Enlightenment (capitalist) modernity had a nasty colonial underbelly of the very condition of conquest, fore-structuring the cultural domination of European ideas and practices over the rest of humanity, driven above all by Christian eschatology. Here, Mignolo has articulated his strategies of decolonization. Early on in this book, Mignolo has given an outline of his critique of modernity:

> Currently there are three types of critique to modernity. One type is internal to the history of Europe itself and in that sense these premises are a Eurocentered critique of modernity (for example, psychoanalysis, Marxism, poststructuralism, postmodernity), and the other two types emerged from non-European histories entangled with Western modernity. One of them focuses on the idea of Western civilization (for example, dewesternization, Occidentosis), and the other on

coloniality (such as postcoloniality, decoloniality). The three types of critiques are analyzed in relation to their point of origination and their routes of dispersion. Postmodernity originated in Europe but dispersed around the world. Decoloniality originated among Third World countries after the Bandung Conference in 1955, and also dispersed all over the world. Dewesternization originated in East Asia, but the dewesternizing argument can be found in other parts of the world.[20]

We outside Europe, in body, soul, and mind, are mindful of the first category that Mignolo has described, but we are driven by our own concerns. My old essay, "For the Last Time Civilization" (2001), falls into the second category that Mignolo has outlined, and much of my work ever since has been in the third category.[21] The project that Mignolo has called "dewesternization" remains definitive to much of the moral, political, intellectual, and theoretical practices around the globe, and in which I place my reading of these seminal six poets, particularly in this chapter on Mehdi Akhavan-e Sales' poetry, on how much of the work produced outside Iran is being abused as fodder for expanding the colonial domain of European modernity.

Let me now turn to a classic example of Akhavan-e Sales' own poetry as evidence of how utterly abusive it is to frame him within European modernity. In his signature poem, "Akhar-e Shahnameh/The End of the *Shahnameh*" (1957), he has issued something of a manifesto of his poetry:

In shekasteh chang-e bi-qanun . . .

This broken harp out of tune
Docile in the hands
Of the old, pale, harpist:
Sometimes seems to dream—
Seeing itself at the bright court of the Mazdaian Sun:
Beholding the splendid sight of Zarathustra—
Strolling with a joyous fairy
On the pure and bright prairies
In moonlight.
It sees on the solemn brows of the inner sanctum
The false lights of
A whole caravan of dead flames in a swamp—
Recalling the glorious days of pride and innocence
Happily sings:
The sad story of exile!

"This broken harp out of tune" might be read as Akhavan's own poetry, as the "old, pale, harpist" would be himself—the poet. We are to hear a panegyric, a Jeramiah, the stormy revolt of a voice crying against the ravages of colonial modernity. Merely read my translation and try to imagine the fury of the original:

"Ahoy, where is it:
The capital of this insane, wicked century?
Its blighted nights like days;
Its dark and tight days like night:
Deep in the bosom of myth?
With its tall and frightful fortresses,
With the vicious smiling of its gates—
Cold and strange?

"Ahoy, where is it?
The capital of this evil century full of turmoil?
The century of ugly faces
Above the moon orbit
And yet so far away from the solid manner of the Sun—
The bloodthirsty century,
The century of fearsome messages:
When with the feces of the bird of faraway delusions
It can instantly wreak havoc in God's four corners and seven climes:
Whatever exists,
Whatever is lowly,
Whatever is high:
Beating it hard
Robbing it clean.

"Ahoy, where is it?
The capital of this shameless faithless century?
When every fresh blossom is pitilessly
At the mercy of the wind?
As the respect of the old—having given the fruits of their lives—
Is the subject of denial, dismissal, treachery, and injustice?"[22]

No one comes even close to Akhavan when he is furious and curses the entire existence for the horrors of this world, national or global, ravaged by European colonial modernity. This is the only solid way to read his mythologization of the Iranian past. It is impossible to miss or to convey in any translation the rage, the depth of anger, at the heart of this poem, looking for the capital of this century dominated by brutal European savagery around the globe. He wages war against this capital, calls for an army, a flotilla, an armada, fully armed, to defeat and triumph over them. Who are "we"—at the heart of this poem?

We
Are the conquerors of the proud fortresses of history,
Witnesses to the glory of cities of every century!

> We
> Are the memories of the sad innocence of all ages!
>
> We
> Are the storytellers of happy and sweet tales:
> Stories of clean skies,
> Pouring light, water,
> Cold darkness, the earth:
> The stories of sweetest messages
> From the purity of the bright rivers of days . . .
>
> We
> Are a caravan of wine goblets and harps;
> Musicians on our harps;
> Mythmakers of our lives;
> Our lives: poetry and myth
> Told by drunken cupbearers![23]

And then comes a cold warning and a reminder to himself:

> Oh you wretched teller of gibberish,
> Change your tune!
> The son of Dastan will not survive the pit of that un-brother
> He died; he died; he died!
> Tell us the story of the son of Farrokhzad . . .

There are all allusions to the *Shahnameh* stories—and at the end . . .

> We
> Are the conquerors of forgotten cities:
> With a weak voice rising from our chess
> Teller of forgotten tales!
> No one takes us seriously or honors our currencies;
> As if they are minted by forgotten monarchs
> Or by a prince whose dynasty has fallen!
> Occasionally we wish to awake from this magical slumber
> Just like the deep sleep of the People of the Cave
> We rub our eyes and we say:
> There is the golden castle, there the sweet morning,
> and yet Daqyanus is immortal!
> Alas! Alas! Alas![24]

Just look at these lines: this is how "Iran" as a "postcolonial nation" was recovered to dwell in this world and to stand up to the bullies internal or external to its pride of place. We became a people, and we had a claim to peoplehood, nationhood, precisely based on these kinds of lines and the sentiments that they immortalized. European colonial modernity? That is not us?

A Pensive Pilgrim Traveling Back to the Past

Poems such as these by Mehdi Akhavan-e Sales mark the living organicity of an epic like the *Shahnameh*, pushing forward its stories, heroes, and dramatic forces into contemporary and entirely uncharted territories. Ferdowsi (940–1020) in effect lives in Akhavan as his *Shahnameh* does in much of his nostalgic poetry. Effortlessly, Akhavan's poetic diction shares Ferdowsi's majestic verses and regal deportment. Akhavan in effect brings Ferdowsi back to life, as if the distant Persian poet had a belated rendezvous with the unfolding history of his people. The Persian epic becomes a living and breathing text in the poetry of Akhavan, its unresolved dramatic tensions retrieved for contemporary history. There is no "translating" this organicity of the text and its "supplements" into any other language or any conception of world literature as we understand it theorized by prominent professors of English and Comparative Literature meditating on North American university campuses. The task at hand is categorically to abandon the failed but still entertaining project of Eurocentric "World Literature" as it stands today and to try to understand the living worldliness of the texts that we read themselves, beyond any strait-jacket admission into the vacuous pantheon of a Euro-Universalist "World Literature." When we read Akhavan we are, just as he said, in the light of a divine dispensation that the poet crafted and summoned, where he was in direct communion with the very soul of his people, his nation, which he made possible through the very words he crafted, sculpted, conceived, and conveyed.

As perhaps best evident in Akhavan's legendary poem "Chavoshi/Pilgrims Ballad" (1946), his poetic disposition breathes a contemporary urgency in the way in which he recalled the past. The poem begins with a description of the travelers of yore, pilgrims, passengers, sojourners, "as it is described in myths," with the image of having a small backpack on their shoulder and a stick in one hand, walking sometimes quietly, sometimes talking, and we are invited to join the journey:

> Three roads appear:
> On each a stone-sign:
> On each carved a story unique to itself:
> The first the path of happiness, peace, and joy—
> Full of ignominy and yet facing urbanity, civilization, and orchards—
> The second path is half ignominy half good name:
> If you were to raise your head full of commotions,
> And if you were to keep quiet then peaceful—
> The third road is the path of no return, no end.[25]

The poet felt sad and forlorn where he was now, in his homeland now, and invited us to join him on the third path: the road of no return and no end. This road is not towards the heavens, he assured us, where stars used to drink with Hafez and Khayyam and today do the same with Nima Yushij and Louis MacNeice (hence four poets: three Iranians, one a revolutionary Irish). He leaves the heavens, the poet said, to Christ and their godly figures. The journey goes through human soul and body, ultimately reaching revolutionary lands where heroes like Taras Bulba—the romanticized hero of the historical novella by the Russian novelist Nikolai Gogol (1809–52)—have been fighting. We might read this poem as a short version of Dante's *Divine Comedy* (*circa* 1308–21), itself perhaps based, among other sources, on the Zoroastrian antecedent of the *Arda Viraf Nameh*, a Zoroastrian text written in Middle Persian. However, this time, in Akhavan's version, the journey is not through the heavens and hell but through the earthly realities that require a critical reading. Here is the key passage as to where this journey is headed:

> Where?
> Wherever is not here
> For here I am scared of caressing as I am of slapping,
> From he who slaps and he who receives a slap:
> In this vision (I see)
> Omar uses the whip of Xerxes
> Though not hitting the sea
> But lashing my back, my disheartened veins,
> Your living body; my dead corpse.[26]

In this poem, Akhavan quoted his own guide and path-breaking model, Nima Yushij, as Dante would Virgil, as it were, and paraphrased a line from the Irish poet Louis MacNeice (1907–63), and in a note he thanked a friend, Hossein Razi, who had translated this poem for him, before traveling to Europe, and he painfully said here in a footnote that the Arabs and Mongols had attracted the brightest Iranian minds in the past while now "the West" stole the best of us.[27] This is what he thought of "the West" (and its "modernity") and of colonialism: as stealing Iranian natural, moral, and intellectual resources. Chavoshi in its entirety is a purgatorial passage of a pilgrim between heaven and hell, right here on earth, where a cosmic battle between good and evil is at work. The poet abandoned the heavens to the battles of stars and saints, demi-gods and prophets, and opted for a journey to a "*pahndasht-e bi khodavand*/a vast godless prairie." There, the journey goes through the poet's own body and soul, infested with narcotics and alcohol, all under the power of poets who declared the end of human salvation, except through revolutionary uprisings. But still by the end of the poem there is a glimmer of hope:

> And upon the green, velvety vastness of the sea
> We cast our boats like walnut shells,
> And teach the white birds of the sails
> To open their bosoms to the gentle breath
> And sail fast at times and gently at others!

Come my forsaken friend—
Like me sad and in despair:
I am so saddened here and forlorn!
Let us collect our little bundle of sustenance for the road
And step on the path with no end![28]

A Poetic Manifesto against Platonic Philosophy

To understand Akhavan's thinking in his extraordinary poetic and critical input, we might place him in the immediate but prolonged context of at least three philosopher-poets who in their aesthetic disposition were his predecessors: Naser Khosrow Qobadiani (1004–88), Baba Afzal Kashani (died *circa* 1214), and Mohammad Iqbal Lahori (1877–1938). While the first two composed both meditative poetry and elegant philosophical prose, the third combined the two and produced his two philosophical masterpieces, *Asrar-i-Khudi/Secrets of Selfhood* (1915) and *Rumuz-i-Bekhudi/Signs of Selflessness* (1917), in Persian poetry. This sustained poetic-philosophical legacy bears witness in Persian language, and for the Persian poet offers a rich and effervescent reservoir at the disposal of generations thinking and rethinking before and including Akhavan. There are reflections of this poetic-philosophy evident in their poetry, but there are also traces of their poetic thinking in their philosophical prose. As one scholar of Baba Afzal Kashani has put it succinctly:

> Bābā Afżal's most universally recognized contribution to Iranian culture lies in the field of literature. In poetry he has been considered one of the two or three greatest masters of the *robāʿī*, while in philosophical prose only Sohravardī stands on the same level. Though Bābā Afżal wrote none of the visionary treatises of the type for which Sohravardī is famous, his systematic expositions of the teachings of the Peripatetic philosophers surpass Sohravardī's similar works in clarity, smoothness, and liquidity. Like Ebn Sīnā (Avicenna; d. 428/1037) in the *Dāneš-nāma-ye ʿalāʾī*, Bābā Afżal employs a great deal of Persian vocabulary where others would have used Arabic, but unlike Ebn Sīnā he chooses only attractive and mellifluous terms, making his works a delight to read; nor does he neglect to employ the corresponding Arabic terms where clarity demands them.[29]

There is, of course, a span of almost two centuries of the growth and expansion of Persian philosophical prose between Avicenna and Baba Afzal, with the epistemic breakthroughs of Naser Khosrow and Suhrawardi's Persian philosophical treatises in between. The issue, however, is more theoretically potent when we consider Baba Afzal's prose and poetry together as well as the poetic disposition of Baba Afzal's philosophical thinking. In addition to dividing the existent being into Being and Finding, he also divided it into a different category, which he called *nafsani/*soul-based and other than soul-based. In between *budan* and *yaftan*, as Baba Afzal put it, the former is rational and the second soul-based, meaning emotive and speculative. The *yaftan* category itself is of two sorts: *yaftan* with reason, which is universal; and *yaftan* through *hess*/feeling and *khial*/imagination, which is particular. Here is how Baba Afzal put it in his original treatise:

> The universal cannot be comprehended the way the particular is perceived, for the particular is understood with the power of feeling and the power of imagination, such as one group of people as opposed to another, or one color as opposed to another, or one taste as opposed to another. With the light of the universal intellect we comprehend all the particulars in a similar way, as for example in the meaning of color where one sees the colors white or black or green in a similar way, though colors are individually different from one another, in their particularities though identical in being color; the particular must be understood through particular means, and the universal through universal means, and particular beings are diverse and changing, while the universal is immune from change and corruption.[30]

We might in a similar vein consider Akhavan's poetic oeuvre as a particular case of Nimaic poetics, or else each individual poetic occasion in his compositions as the case of *yaftan* (particular) in the context of *budan* (universal). But against the backdrop of these previous poet-philosophers, performing their thoughts in Persian prose and poetry, Akhavan took the entire philosophical legacy of Plato to task, precisely by and through his own poetry. Consider Akhavan's poem "Derakht-e Ma'refat/The Tree of Knowledge" (1985), which he dedicated to Abdolhossein Zarrinkub (1923–99), one of the most prolific literary scholars and historians of his time. The point of this poem is to dismiss systematic rational knowledge as useless and misguided. A key segment of the poem is a forceful denunciation of Plato for having disallowed slaves and poets into his republic. This is how Akhavan started and continued the poem:

> Oh tree of knowledge: other than doubt and wonder, what has been your fruit?
> Or at least I have never seen anything other than those growing on you?
> They planted you in the fertile earth and raised you to the heavens,
> As the shrewd and old gardener watered you in secret—
> Either bring me some of those fruits on your high branches
> Concealed from our eyes,
> Or else get uprooted like me and plunge to the soil of death
> So I won't see you ever so green both in Spring and in Winter! . . .
>
> Other than doubt and wonder, other than doubt and awe
> What else has been your fruits? You old tree? . . .
>
> The city of the stupid Plato I have traveled through all its back alleys
> And found them all boring and banal!

> We are slaves and poets: battle tested:
> Throwing you stones and kicks: You idiot!
> Although you fancy yourself immune to all winds
> But I have seen your sycamore move with every wind.[31]

At the end of the poem, Akhavan opted to turn to the city of poetry, as opposed to Plato's republic, and in a note he dismissed the real historical Plato as a homosexual who had forbidden slaves and poets from entering his utopia and compared him unfavorably to "the Spiritual Plato" as imagined by Muslim philosophers. In Akhavan's mind, the entire Platonic legacy was turned upside down with a bitter sarcasm, in effect posing his own poetry as a defiance of the poet against the legacy of the philosopher who had dismissed poets from his republic for spreading falsehoods and corrupting the youth—precisely when he was establishing the foundations of a philosophical mind. Akhavan effectively celebrated that "corruption" and considered it superior to the sort of healthy but useless or even dangerous knowledge that had brought us to the current state of the world. Compared to all the previous philosopher-poets—such as Baba Afzal and Naser Khosrow, or even Iqbal before him—Akhavan was a counter-philosopher, a response and a rebuttal to Plato, whereas all the previous poet-philosophers who came before him had celebrated and embraced the Greek philosopher. Akhavan's defiant tone here, responding in poetry to Plato's denunciation of poetry, is a contrapuntal argument against the futility of a tree of knowledge that keeps producing nothing but fruits of useless speculations as the soul and body of humanity was being wasted. In effect, in this poem, Akhavan declared a poetic manifesto against philosophy as we have received it from Plato down, while articulating another mode of philosophical thinking from the blind spot of Plato where he dismissed the poets as philosophers of a different sort.

The Poet as the Knowing Subject

In a long essay that Akhavan wrote at the end of his collection of poems *Az In Avesta/From This Avesta* (1965), he offered a detailed account of his take on Persian New Poetry and a host of other related issues.[32] The essay starts with a detailed account of the disposition of the formation of the subject "I" in Persian poetry, after which he proceeded to cover a range of issues, chief among them a discussion of the nature of poetry, followed by a bitter criticism of the fields of European Orientalism and Iranian Studies, as well as the absence of a critical frame of reference about what happened in the Nimaic revolution, followed by a meticulous discussion of his own poetic language. The language of this essay is typical of Akhavan's playful, bitter, meandering, and pensive prose, for which one needs patience, perseverance, and trust in that he has something serious to share.

This long essay might be considered a kind of poetic manifesto by someone deeply rooted in Persian literary and philosophical imagination yet now fully committed to the Nimaic revolution in Persian New Poetry. He began this treatise by praising Ahura Mazda, Bozorg Dadar Afaridegar, as he formally declared, as if doing ablutions for a prayer, "the creator of goodness and the beneficent, of kindness and beauty." This is a defiantly non-Islamic mode of salutation in which Akhavan basked and thrived. He proceeded with invoking Zoroastrian deities, praising the four angelic agencies, from there to the revolutionary prophet Mazdak Bamdadan (died *circa* 528) and from there to other prophetic figures such as Buddha and Mani, including Mahatma Gandhi. No sign of Prophet Muhammad here.[33] Akhavan identified himself as a "Chavoshi Khan/Singer of Pilgrim Ballads." Then follows a genealogy of poets actively present in his mind: Baba Taher Oryan, Omar Khayyam, Manuchehri Damghani, Rumi, Hafez, Naser Khosrow, and Attar, followed by Seif Faraghani and Ferdowsi. These are all towering poets in the pantheon of Persian poetry, which he invoked as almost talismanic icons blessing his own poetic heritage. He then proceeded to deliberately make fun of the word "West/Farang" and wrote how in their languages (English, French, German, and so on) any "gibberish/*qil-o-qal*" might be considered poetry, but not in Persian, for which reason he, Akhavan himself, could not claim to be a poet in the Persian language.[34] From there he proceeded to discuss the key concepts of "*man*/I" and "*manniyyat*/I-ness" in Persian poetry, with an abundance of examples from various classical poets. After reviewing a whole range of poetry on "*manyyat*/I-ness," he concluded that the "I" behind poetic diction was different from the "I" of mundane realities. This entire section reads like a deeply informed literary articulation of the philosophical underpinning of the poetic subject, delivered from the depth of his poetic reading of Iranian history, culture, and sacred and literary imagination combined.

From there, Akhavan went on to philosophers and mystics such as Avicenna and Ayn al-Qozat, to argue that "I" is the very quintessence of our humanity.[35] Reading this essay, it is impossible to exaggerate his deep-rooted cultivation in the entire course of Persian literary humanism, poets, philosophers, and prose stylists alike. We soon learn that this essay was meant as an interview that did not work.[36] He then conducted a mock conversation with himself, beginning with the question "what is poetry," to which he responded: "Poetry is the result of the impatience (*bi-tabi*) of a person at a moment when they are at the receiving end of prophetic consciousness (*sho'ur-e nobovvat*)."[37] Finally he reached the point to ask why Persian New Poetry was so disregarded around the world. First, he bitterly dismissed Soviet Orientalism for having absorbed parts of the Persianate world into itself and for right now having no clue about cultural developments in Iran. He equally regretted that Afghanistan and Tajikistan were so cut off from Iran, so that the Persianate world was completely alien to them: meaning that they had been alienated from their own literary background, so that people in Afghanistan, or Central Asia or India were clueless about Nima—who remained the solid index for being aware of the Iranian cultural scene. The same was true for Europe, which he accused of being clueless. He was equally critical of Tehran-centrism in his own homeland.[38] In short, the Nimaic revolution, he contended, was completely foreign to Orientalists and the Iranian (Area) Studies domain, for these fields were originally conceived basically as the intelligence arm of the Cold War.

Akhavan-e Sales' poetic manifesto here in its prose diction and power is in the longer legacy of other philosopher-poets from whom he derived inspiration: Baba Afzal Kashani, Naser Khosrow, Suhrawardi, Attar, Sana'i, and so on—the list is long, and their collective thinking was at the roots of the way in which Akhavan thought about his own or Nima's poetry. These are the poet-philosophers whom he read and admired in their original, not the haphazard translation of any European poet whom he may have run into in a magazine or journal. Akhavan was harshly critical of Orientalists and had an obscene phrase for the very idea of "comparative literature." Not every turn of phrase that he produced in the heat of the moment is, of course, as important as the trajectory of his thinking about what had happened in Persian New Poetry and Nima's unique place in it. But the sheer power of this prose takes us to the heart of a poetic legacy that was in the heat of imagining a poetic past for the people, the nation which he unabashedly loved. Consider one of his famous (late) poems, "To Ra Ey Kohan Bum-o-Bar Dust Daram/I Love You, oh Ancient Home and Land" (1989), composed about one year after the Iran–Iraq War (1980–8), in which hundreds of thousands of Iranian (and Iraqi) youth had perished, and where his love of his homeland took bold and broad brushes in a famous *qasideh*:

Zeh puch-e jahan hich agar dust daram
To ra ey kohan bum o bar dust daram . . .

If I love anything in this meaningless world
I love you, oh ancient home and land!
You, oh ever youthful ancient and old:
I love you if I ever loved anything—
You, oh precious thing, ancient Iran,
You, oh priceless jewel, I love you!
You ancient homeland of the great heroes
Majestic and gallant, I love you . . .[39]

The poem unfolds apace and finally proceeds to declare his deep love and affection for all things Iranian, particularly the three prophets: Zoroaster, Mazdak and Mani—each for a particular reason, but for Mazdak his love is rooted in the utopian socialism that he historically represented. From there, he went on to a succession of poets from Ferdowsi and Khayyam to Rumi and Sa'di, Hafez and Nezami. From there, he went around the country and various provinces, from there to the surrounding countries and climes that were part of greater Iran, to express his love for his homeland. It is crucial to make a clear distinction between the poetic articulation of a sense of nation and homeland, on one hand, and on the other hand the ideological gestation of political nationalism that at least since the nineteenth century had defined a significant component of the Iranian political project in direct and open contradiction to equally evident forces of third-world socialism and militant Islamism. Never did any one of these totalizing ideologies triumph over the others, except through violent imposition and the elimination of their rival factions, as in the violent formation of the Islamic Republic.

To see what Akhavan was doing in adopting pre-Islamic leitmotifs in his poetry, it would be helpful to compare, for example, his poetry with the prose of the dissident Qajar prince Jalal al-Din Mirza (1827–72), who represents a particularly potent form of racialized nationalist discourse prevalent in the nineteenth century in which pre-Islamic Iranian history was being imaginatively retrieved for a sustained nationalist historiography—as best evident in his multi-volume tome titled *Nameh-ye Khosrowan/Book of Monarchs* (1868–71).[40] In this narrative, dominant for generations among the white-identified monarchists, the Arab and Mongol invasions were being marked as particularly disruptive for Iranian history. In this discourse, we read about an active partaking in European and Eurocentric "Arianism" in which non-white peoples were at once racialized and identified as particularly barbaric. Paramount in this historiography was an active identification with Europe and European white supremacy. Akhavan's poetry, to the contrary, is of an entirely different gestation. He was fully aware and severely critical of European colonialism—and as a result his poetic retrieval of pre-Islamic Iranian motifs stood at the service of a pride of place against colonial domination. As a result, he had no desire for the nonsense of "pure Persian" in his prose and poetry, and Arabic words freely abound and happily sit next to Persian, together forming a coherent and consistent language irreducible to Persian or Arabic etymologies or indulging in myths of "origins."

The Moment in Transubstantial Motion

The epistemic movement from Nima to Akhavan, or from Nima to Shamlou, and so on, is the movement best articulated, or perhaps envisioned, by the towering Iranian Muslim philosopher Mulla Sadra Shirazi (1572–1641) in his theory of "*al-harakah al-jawhariyyah*/transubstantial motion," in which he proposed the provocative idea of the systemic unfolding and reiteration of existent beings—a sense of being in motion.[41] Here is how one scholar of Mulla Sadra has put the dynamics of this movement in his ontology:

> Sadra distinguishes between essence and existence. Essence is static where each instance of an essence is identically the same. No instance of an essence is a unique individual (*fard*) but only a case (*hissa*) . . . Existence on the other hand is dynamic ever unfolding itself in new and higher forms (*wujud munbasit*), and it has unique individuals (*afrad*) not just cases (*hisas*) of existence. It is this dynamism of existence which creates those modes which result in essences in the mind. Real existences have no names such as properties and description, while essences have names and describable properties. Reality then is the proper place for existence, while mind is the proper home of essence, concept and static notions. Sadra then emphasizes that existence is existence of an essence, not of something which is then asserted of an essence. Existence is simply the status of being real, not an attribute of something which is in its own right already something real.[42]

The classical distinction between essence (*mahiyyah*) and existence (*wujud*) might be extended in this way here: the essence here might be considered the nature of the Nimaic poetic Event, while the existence is its paradigmatic unfolding (transubstantiation) in Akhavan and other poets who followed his revolutionary sublimation of Persian poetry. The result is a sense of being in motion:

> Since motion means moving as a verb, that is "a continuous renewal and lapse" (*al-tajaddud wa al-inqida*') of the parts of motion, it is impossible that its immediate cause should be something with a stable or enduring being. For a stable or enduring entity will contain in itself the passing phases of movement as a present fact, and this togetherness of all passing phases would amount to stability, not movement. Movement therefore cannot be established on the basis of a stable entity. Such an entity can have a stable essence, but not a stable being which must consist simply in change and mutation. There is therefore a more fundamental change beneath the change of accident, that is "a change in substance."[43]

We might think through Mulla Sadra's idea of Transubstantial Motion in a number of ways in the making of Persian New Poetry: from Nima to his followers, through and among his followers, and even from one poetic Event to another in all this mode of poetic thinking, being, and knowing—the active formation of an episteme, within which we move from one conjugation of the paradigm to another. But we might also consider that what is paramount in Akhavan's poetry is the encapsulation of this motion in one static poetic moment, for example, in his signature poem "Peyvand-ha va Bagh/Grafting and Garden" (1962), where an entire event is held together in one iconic moment. The poem begins in the form of a dialogue with an anonymous interlocutor. It starts abruptly, as if in the middle of a conversation:

> For a moment she remained silent then
> Threw up in the air
> The red apple she had in her hand:
> The apple turned around in the air a few times and came back—
> She smelled the apple
> Then she said:
> "Enough of grafting and watering
> So
> What's up with you?"
>
> Ah, what could I say?
> Nothing![44]

We now read a detailed account of the lovely dress the interlocutor is wearing, and soon we realize that we are witness to the soul of the neighbor's garden, "drunk and sweet, walking and talking."[45] The voice of the poet telling us this story begins to cry and turns around and looks at his own garden, where the brooks have dried up, the flowers and bushes shriveled and wasted away. What follows is one of the most powerful curses in the entire history of Persian New Poetry, and as such almost impossible to translate. But here is an approximation:

> I swear by your pending demise, oh you ignoble garden!
> Long after you have been forever lost,
> May every cloud of hatred made of tears and disgust be pregnant
> Just like my silently pouring cloud!
> Oh you barren trees with your roots buried in the soil of devious contempt:
> Not a single noble bud will ever grow from any part of you!
> Oh you bunch of dirty leaves, weft and warp,
> Debris of a long dusty drought!
> No rain can ever wash you clean![46]

The entire poem is just one instance, one moment, from beginning to end. But in it we see encapsulated an entire history, of two neighboring gardens: one green, luscious, and fruitful; the other dried, dilapidated, and abandoned. The poet stands on the side of the dilapidated garden, furious with the fate of his lot, now standing for his homeland. The instance is the entire episteme of the Nimaic Transubstantial Motion in one snapshot of history, where time has stood still for us to see the horror of a national trauma.

In his "Qesseh-ye Shahryar-e Shahr-e Sangestan/The Ballad of the Prince of Stoneville" (1960), Akhavan-e Sales captured a lasting instance summarizing that Transubstantial Motion:

> Two doves
> Sitting on a branch of an old cedar tree:
> Having grown far from its peers
> On the slope of a mighty mountain—
> Two kindred souls, kind and gentle to each other:
> Two sad souls—
> Storytellers of the sorrow they share:
> How happy elsewhere
> How happy the bygone time of the two souls together:
> Two pilgrim doves together:
> The caresses of one consoling the other;
> The consoling of one caressing the other!
> If they were to address each other: "Dearest sister!"
> In response: "Yes my sweetest sister!!"
> "Tell your loving sister the story of your pain and sorrow!"[47]

Ending the Episteme

There is another way, equally fruitful, in which we might extend Mulla Sadra's notion of Transubstantial Motion to the entire oeuvre of Akhavan's poetry, from beginning to end, as an episteme that rises, culminates, and concludes. A look at the evolution of Akhavan's poetry reveals how the rise and height of his poetic output in the 1950s and 1960s all culminated at the point of the 1979 Revolution and ultimately declined and ended as the Nimaic episteme came to a closure. The violent Islamization of the Iranian revolution of 1977–9 brought the entire gamut of Iranian cultural effervescence to an end, to an epistemic shift, awaiting future schemata yet to be determined. In Nimaic poetry specifically, the episteme ended at the threshold of the 1977–9 revolution, when the idea of the nation at the heart of this poetic paradigm was formed and, thereafter, its poetry fully conjugated and concluded. Soon, of course, Iranian cinema resumed its historic course in more potent terms, but not so Nimaic poetry.

In this context, Akhavan's poetry can be divided into two major parts: before and after the Iranian revolution of 1977–9—where his best work and the work most relevant to the Nimaic episteme was done only until the revolution, after which he lost his momentous touch, even though he remained quite active and productive. He was the same powerful poet that he had always been, but he had lost his moral and political cause. Here are the main titles of his poetic output: (1) *Arghanun/Organon* (1951); (2) *Zemestan/Winter* (1956); (3) *Akhar-e Shahnameh/ The End of the Shahnameh* (1959); (4) *Az In Avesta/From This Avesta* (1965); (5) *Dar Hayat-e Kuchak-e Pa'iz dar Zendan/In the Small Yard of Fall in Prison* (1975); (6) *Zendegi Miguyad Amma Baz Bayad Zist/Life Though Says We Must Continue to Live* (1978); (7) *Duzakh Amma Sard/Hell but Cold* (1978); (8) *To Ra Ey Kohan Bum-o-Bar Dust Daram/I Love You, oh Ancient Home and Land* (1989). Most evident in these collections are the earliest fusions of lyrical and political poetry, both contingent on an acute social consciousness, evident throughout his first period; by the second period, he was the same exceptionally gifted poet, but one searches in vain for the thunder that had once defined the glory of his poetry.

Form and substance go hand to hand in this division. *Arghanun* is a collection of Akhavan's earliest poems in classical prosodies, although signs of an emerging poetic consciousness in tune with his immediate surroundings are also evident. The Akhavan we know and love in effect begins with *Zemestan*, where the eponymous poem becomes the national anthem of the entire post-1953 coup generation. His poetic diction increasingly yielded to Nima's poetics. *The End of the Shahnameh* is fully blossomed Nimaic poetics in tune with his post-coup anger and anxieties. This continued apace until we reach *Hell but Cold* at the threshold of the 1977–9 revolution, and a decade later, by the time he published *I Love You, oh Ancient Home and Land*, we are witness to the complete depletion of this youthful power and synergy. By now the Islamists had taken over, and Akhavan had very little to say or offer for the post-revolutionary age. The duration of the episteme to which Akhavan was integral lasted from the late Qajar to the early Islamist period, from the Constitutional Revolution of 1906–11 giving rise to Nima, to the Islamist take-over of the 1977–9 revolution putting an end to what Nima had made possible, and what Akhavan and his other followers had delivered. Akhavan was fully aware of this closure as early as in the mid-1980s, when he composed his short but heart-breaking "Akhar-e khat/The End of the Line" (1988):

> Me and my turn have come to the end of the line!
> Stop! Let the young ones get in!⁴⁸

Except: no young ones were getting on that bus. The bus only had six passengers. The journey had ended. At the back of that bus forever-moving sat one singularly powerful poet, who could only look forward by looking backward. As we see the bus speeding away on an open-ended road and journey, the image of Akhavan gets ever smaller and yet his voice ever defiant, ever heroic, ever commanding in our ears, ever stronger:

> "Ahoy where is it:
> The capital of this insane, wicked century?"⁴⁹

Chapter 3

AHMAD SHAMLOU: THE TROUBADOUR OF A HOMELAND TO COME

"Man Bamdadam . . . " I still remember the shiver in my spine moving up to my shoulders when I first heard this phrase in one of Ahmad Shamlou's autobiographical poems, "Dar Jedal ba Khamushi/Battling Silence" (1984): "I am Bamdad!" How did that come about? What confidence, what pride of place, what historical force had come together to have him make that announcement? It sounds like "Call me Ishmael," the opening sentence of Herman Melville's *Moby Dick* (1851). These two opening words in Shamlou's poem form no ordinary phrase from an ordinary mouth. This is an entire history, an entire people, speaking from and through the depth of those words—and yet the ordinariness of it, matter-of-factness, the loving, caring, amorous ring of it:

> I am Bamdad
> A citizen of medium height and average intelligence—
> My ancestors, with just one link,
> Reach the slaves of Kabul—
> My first name is Arabic
> My tribal name Turkish—
> My pen name Persian—
> My tribal name is ashamed of history—
> I don't like my first name—
> Except when you call me:
> Then it is the most beautiful name in the world—
> And your voice the saddest
> Call for help![1]

Predicated on the archetypal formation of the Persian New Poetry that Nima had enabled, empowered, and staged, Ahmad Shamlou (1925–2000) was the poet of the future, of a homeland yet to come, with little to no interest in the Iranian or any other past, except when Biblical allusions to iconic figures such as Abraham or Christ or occasionally *Shahnameh* heroes like Esfandiar would pop up as metaphors in his poetry. If anything, Shamlou held disdain for the Iranian past and was severely critical of some iconic aspects of Persian culture—from his brazen criticism of the *Shahnameh* to his disrespectful dismissal of classical Persian music. Shamlou was the sleek, bold, and beautiful voice and vision of the future of the nation that he imagined—worldly, happy, flamboyant, deeply erotic, and rebelliously joyous. Here is a good example from his poem "Sar Cheshmeh/ Fountainhead" (1956):

> I sought your eyes in the dark,
> In the dark I found your eyes—
> And my night became full of stars
>
> I called you:
> In the darkest nights
> My heart called you—
> And you came to me in the echo of my voice—
> Your hands sang a song for my hands,
> For my eyes with your eyes,
> For my lips with your lips,
> With your body for my body
> You sang a song.[2]

Above all, Shamlou was a lyricist, and yet a deeply political poet, the erotic and the violent intimately coming together in his sublimated poetry. In this he was perhaps closest to Hafez, whose poetry he recited and promoted in precisely those terms— the master lyricist's bitter and defiant political urges. When we read Hafez and Shamlou next to each other, the temporal span shrinks, and we think that the time from the fourteenth to the twentieth century are held in the same poetic embrace. Tapping into that poetic past was definitive to Shamlou's temporal imagination of a future which he staged in his own poetry.

Born on the Planet Tomorrow

Ahmad Shamlou was born on December 12, 1925, in Tehran and died on July 23, 2000, in the village of Fardis near Tehran. During his lifespan of three-quarters of a century, the Qajar dynasty collapsed, the Pahlavi dynasty came to power and collapsed, and the Islamic Republic defeated all its rivals and established a theocracy. Shamlou's father was an officer in Reza Shah's military service and would roam around the country with his family, for which reason Shamlou and his siblings frequently had to change schools. He soon abandoned schooling altogether and became an autodidact throughout his life, suspicious and dismissive of formal education. During the Second World War, he became politically active and was briefly incarcerated. He was again back in jail in the aftermath of the CIA-MI6 military coup of 1953, and throughout his life he had an affinity for political prisoners, for whom he composed many of his legendary poems. From this we should not conclude that he was a political activist. He was not. This is a false conclusion that many of his die-hard supporters wish to imagine, with no basis in facts. The revolutionary disposition of Shamlou's legacy was in decidedly poetic terms.[3]

In his early youth, Shamlou discovered Nima's poetry and soon befriended him. He would be instrumental in publicizing and popularizing Nima's poetry. I remember when I was a graduate student at the University of Pennsylvania in Philadelphia around the time of the Iranian revolution of 1977-9: Shamlou visited the US in 1977-8, and I attended his talk at the International House on the University of Pennsylvania's campus on February 26, 1978. "Nima was a distant star," I remember him telling us on this occasion, "and we were stars closer to our people, but we received our lights from Nima beaming it towards our readers." That metaphor has stayed with me ever since. He would eventually part ways from Nima in some of his poetic predilections that would later be identified as *she'r-e sepid*/free or blank verse, in which neither the classical nor the Nimaic prosody were evident. But as he would repeatedly confess, Nima for him was the inauguration of his own poetic voice.

From his early youth onwards, Shamlou was drawn to the French and German languages, but he never had a serious command of any foreign language, despite the fact that he would fake "translating" books from these languages into Persian. He just revised, edited, and rewrote what had already been translated by other capable and serious translators. By 1946 he had abandoned all formal schooling and began working in a bookstore; at that time, he had started reading Nima and commenced publishing his own poetry. By the early 1950s, he was busy promoting Nima and developing a potent reputation as a journalist. He continued to publish his own poems. At that time, he also developed a serious interest in the eminent Spanish poet Federico García Lorca (1898-1936), even though he had no evident knowledge of Spanish. He also collaborated with filmmakers in writing scripts and dialogues, including documentaries—none of them of any enduring significance. During the heated years of the 1977-9 revolution, Shamlou published the periodical *Iranshahr* from London in 1978-9. It was a key critical engagement with the unfolding social uprising. He had a lifelong interest in the Japanese Haiku and the poetry of Langston Hughes, even though he had no demonstrable knowledge of Japanese or English. He returned to the US in 1990, where I once again met him at a dinner party in Princeton in his honor. In such gatherings he was treated as a demi-god.[4]

Ahmad Shamlou traveled to Europe and the US on a number of occasions, both for medical and professional purposes. While abroad he would generate a sensation among his fans and followers. Shamlou married twice before he finally met his lifetime love, companion, and collaborator Aida Sarkisian (born 1939) in 1962, whom he immortalized in his poetry. Shamlou, like many leading Iranian intellectuals of his time, was a severe alcoholic. When I met him in Princeton in 1990, his sycophantic fans were competing to buy him more expensive brands of vodka. Aida was there, gracefully trying to discourage these fans from fueling Shamlou's addiction. In the aftermath of the Iranian revolution of 1977-9, Shamlou became mostly withdrawn, and his poem "Dar in Bon-bast/In this Dead-End" (1979) was a signal event declaring his having reached a momentous dead-end, along with the Persian New Poetry that he had been instrumental in defining.

Dahanat ra mibuyand...

They smell your breath
Lest you may have said: "I love you!"
They smell your heart
It's a strange time, my love!

They lash love
By the pole of the checkpoint:
We need to hide love behind closed doors...
Don't you dare to think:
It's a strange time, my love!

He who bangs on the door at nighttime
Has come to kill the light—
We need to hide the light behind closed doors...
The victoriously drunk Iblis
Has sat down celebrating the feast of our mourning
We need to hide God behind closed doors...[5]

The best sources about Shamlou's life and legacy are not the outward signs of his mundane and haphazard life, but his unflinching, pure, and powerful poetry. In an autobiographical poem, "Dar Jedal ba Khamushi/Fighting Silence" (1984), Shamlou left behind a deeply moving account of how he saw himself in the autumn of his life, when he was in his late fifties, more than a decade before he passed away. He identified himself as Ahmad Shamlou, pen name Alef Bamdad, and confessed to his readers that he disliked his first name, except when his beloved partner Aida called him by that name. The poem has a mournful air about its tone and diction, feeling the approaching death, both confessional and combative yet resigned. He traced his consciousness to when he was five years old, when he already regretted his birth.

At five
A pitcher in hand
I was chasing after a mirage in a barren desert—
Just ahead of my sister
Who was still a stranger to the magnetic draw of man...

I am Bamdad
Tired of fighting with myself
Tired of the *saqqakhaneh*, *khanqah*, and mirage,
Tired of the desert, the whip, and the imposition,
Tired of the shame of Abel
Been silent for quite a while,
Time to scream from the depth of my being
For at least here Satan is charging at me...

> I am the first and the last Dawn!
> I am Abel:
> Upon the pedestal of humiliation
> I am the honor of the universe
> Whipped by myself!
> The black fire of my sorrow
> Shames the Hellfire of its meagre wherewithal . . .
>
> Naked I lie chained to the surgical table:
> I need to scream:
> I am the dignity of the universe, as it were—
> I am Abel
> And in my skull, looking like a pumpkin bowl
> Is saved a breakfast for the head surgeon,
> With a bitter scream
> I'll make the meal taste like a snake's venom—
> For I am Bamdad
> The rising of the sunshine![6]

All the material evidence of his life, his birth, and his twisting and winding years, spent mostly under an autocratic monarchy and then a theocratic republic, are always summoned and sublated in his poetry—as if he only lived to find the elements of his poetic diction as the material evidence of his aesthetic imagination. He was rooted, evident, knowing, and knowable. The precarity of his nation lived in his fragile life. Less than a decade before his passing, in his "Dar Astaneh/At the Threshold" (1992), Shamlou would revisit his habitual autobiographical voice, albeit this time with a vision of his own death:

> One must pause and bend
> At the threshold of a door that has no knocker handle
> For if you have come at the right moment
> The doorkeeper is waiting for you—
> And if it is not time, it is useless to knock at the door.
> The door is short
> So you better be humble!
> A mirror might be there
> So you can look at yourself to make sure you look proper!
>
> Though the commotion you hear from the other side of the door
> Is more your own imagination—
> Not because there are lots of guests!
> For no one is waiting for you
> For there might be motion there but nothing moves . . .
>
> Farewell, farewell
> Thus says Bamdad the poet

I dance my way through the inevitable threshold
Happy and grateful . . .

The time was short
And the journey difficult
But it was precious and lacked nothing
I oblige wholeheartedly and gratefully
Thus spoke Bamdad, tired![7]

There is a sense of resignation in this poem, the poet reminiscing and mediating at the end of his earthly sojourn, a sign of his believing in nothing but his lived experiences and passing life. His poetic voice and vision, above all, are the forces of any conviction or trust in an afterlife, towards which this threshold opens to either fame or infamy, praise or punishment. The poem operates on the borderline of an eschatology, evident in the image of a door, of an end and a beginning, that is neither Islamic nor anti-Islamic, neither metaphysical nor materialist. It is poetic, rooted in his own flowered tapestry of things visible and invisible, known or knowable. By now, the Persian New Poetry that Shamlou best represented had crafted its own inner convictions, in a world at one and the same time moral and imaginative, particular and universal. In another poem, "Va Hasrati/And a Regret" (1969), he anticipated this eventuality:

Nah in barf ra digar sar-e baz istadan nist . . .

No, this snow is not about to stop!
The snow that sits on our eyebrows and on our hair
So into the mirror you look at yourself
That you would—frightened—
From the height of a gorge, like a scream
At the depth of the valley—

At any rate: you better set the polar fire on!
As the kind thunder of your look
Casts the sun upon the metal of a dagger
That I must valiantly endure
The pain of its nocturnal light
When with its sharp edges
It tests the versatility of my heart!

No there is no doubt!
Except for the certainty of your existence
That makes me doubt my fate:
For you are that sip of water
That slaves have the doves drink
Just before putting a dagger to their throat![8]

How to live on the edge of that un/certainty was the art of Shamlou's potent poetry: the moment that anticipated a future on the basis of a fragile present. He made life on that edge, just as Khayyam would, both precious and tenuous at one and the same time. This is where the formal space of his free verse was best prepared to serve his way of poetic thinking. He had no ready-made answer for that fragility of the necessary language to define that moment, and with it the precarity of the nation that the language defined and that he now both personified and enabled. His poetic thinking was the sole sign of how that nation of sentiments might be able to become the historic unfolding of the persona of a poet. As a result, Shamlou's poetry reads like the autobiographical account of the soul of a nation, made a nation precisely through the labyrinth of his poetry and the poetry of the other five iconic figures gathered in this kaleidoscopic sextet.

The Poet Laureate of a Nation

Shamlou's poetic output began quite early in his life. Usually *Ahan-ha va Ehsas/ Irons and Emotions* (1944–50) is believed to be his first published collection of poems.[9] This timing places the poems published in this collection somewhere between the end of the Allied occupation of Iran during the Second World War and well into the reign of the second Pahlavi monarch, Mohammad Reza Shah Pahlavi (1919–80). At this point, Shamlou's homeland was under occupation, the ruling monarch had been forced into abdication and exile, his son installed in power, and the Iranian Communist (Tudeh) Party had been formed in active collaboration with the Soviet Union. This initial collection of poems was followed by "23" (1951) and *Qat'-nameh/Proclamation* (1950–1); at that time Shamlou was still experimenting with his newfound voice. Nima was still alive, Akhavan had joined the Nimaic revolution, and Shamlou had announced himself among the contenders in the active formation of the Persian New Poetry. By the time Shamlou published *Hava-ye Tazeh/Fresh Air* (1947–56), he was thoroughly established as a major voice in Persian New Poetry. The next two collections, *Bagh-e Ayeneh/Garden of Mirrors* (1957–8) and *Lahzeh-ha va Hamisheh/Moments and Forever* (1960–3), marked the height of his emerging reputation as a bold and resounding poet of his generation. The Shah was now firmly in power; Ayatollah Khomeini had launched his first unsuccessful attempt to overthrow him and was forced into exile. The Pahlavi dynasty was fully in control. The Shah had married his last wife, Farah Diba, who had a genuine interest in the arts and letters of her homeland, which was a mixed blessing for Iranian artists and literati. Shamlou by now constituted a major voice of his people's sentiments and politics.

Soon after Shamlou met Aida, the love of his life, her name began to appear in the titles of his collections of poems: *Aida dar Ayeneh/Aida in the Mirror* (1962–4) and *Aida, Derakht, Khanjar, va Khatereh/Aida, Tree, Dagger, and Memory* (1964–5). By now Shamlou's amorous and political poetry had merged in the following collections: *Qoqnus dar Baran/Phoenix in the Rain* (1965–6), *Marsiyeh-ha-ye Khak/*

Earthly Elegies (1966–9), and *Shekoftan dar Meh/Blossoming in the Fog* (1969–70). But when he published what was arguably his magnum opus, *Ebrahim dar Atash/ Abraham in the Fire* (1969–73), followed by *Deshneh dar Dis/Dagger on the Plate* (1974–7), he marked entirely new heights in his poetic diction. By now his poetic paradigm had completely matured and exhausted itself. What he would publish from this point forward, in the dreadful shadow of an Islamist theology, would be merely nostalgic, archival, memorial. Volumes such as *Taraneh-ha-ye Kuchak-e Ghorbat/Short Songs of Exile* (1977–80) and *Madayeh bi-Saleh/Thankless Panegyrics* (1990) were of this period. The volume he called *Dar Astaneh/At the Threshold* (1985–96) marked the maturest phase of his later poetry. *Hadis-e Bi-Gharari-ye Mahan/The Story of Mahan's Restlessness* (1972–99) was his swan song, published just about a year before his passing.

In a pioneering study of Shamlou's poetry in the late 1970s, Taghi Pournamdarian, a leading literary scholar, has divided his oeuvre into two parts: before and after *Fresh Air* (1956), before turning to such thematic subjects as imagination, musicality, and poetic structure.[10] Pournamdarian has basically categorized Shamlou's poetics into three distinct phases: classical prosody, Nimaic prosody, and *she'r-e sefid*/blank verse.[11] Key aspects of Pournamdarian's study are the social and political dimensions of Shamlou's poetry, where he has identified the following successive phases: the social foregrounding of his poetry, protest against injustice, hope for victory, disappointment and defeat, seeking a haven in love, the tapering off of passion, and finally the passage of time and meditation on death.[12] All of these are plausible and evident—although not in the teleological thrust that Pournamdarian has suggested. What is crucial here, however, is the fact that Shamlou's vision of the future colors all of these passing and transitional sentiments. At the height of his disappointments, in the loving embrace of Aida, he placed his poetry, and in the political fury of his rebellious defiance, there was always a vision of the future he wished to convey.

Paramount in Shamlou, and what underlies his poetic disposition towards a liberating future, is the character of Nima and the empowering volcano of his poetry. Throughout the prodigious outpouring of his poems, Shamlou was emphatic in his debt to Nima. He considered Nima as the oracular voice that had envisioned and imagined his generation. Even after he found his own unique take on Persian New Poetry and abandoned both classical and Nimaic prosody, he still remained under the spell of his shadow. This is how he once described Nima's significance:

> Nima dismantled the idiotic metric balance between the hemistich and considered the harmony and the phonetic impact of words sufficient for poetry ... In his own poetry he brought together the words and the spirit of the poem, the poem with its rhyme, its rhythm, along with the natural music and the art of declamation and made this the foundation of his poetics. I spent much time with him and for me he was the very manifestation of respectful admiration ... The importance of Nima is not to dismantle the length of the hemistich. The critics only see the surface of things. The significance of Nima is laying the very

foundations of the culture of poetry. Something we never had. He introduced this to the poetic perception. We may have become good drivers. But he invented the car.[13]

Shamlou's own sign and signature was no less iconic, emotively charged, and politically potent. Imagine that: an entire nation, a whole civilization, on the verge of a rebirth, one by one, men and women, the most learned and literate of them, falling in love, marrying, and parenting their precious children, all on the premise of a poem by Shamlou that they had read or heard in the prime of their youth! Here is one sublime example, "Bar Sarma-ye Darun/Upon the Cold Inside" (1973):

Hameh larzesh-e dast-o-delam . . .

All the shivering of my hand and my heart
Was for love to become
A haven—
Not a flight
Just a refuge.

Ahoy love,
Ahoy love,
Your blue countenance is nowhere in sight!
And the cooling of an ointment
Upon the fire of a wound;
Not the commotion of a flame
On the cold inside.
Ahoy love
Ahoy love
Your red countenance is nowhere in sight.

A dark dust of consolation
Upon the presence of futility;
And a corner to be free
On the flight of presence—
A blackness
On the blue peace;
And the greenness of a leaf
On the color purple—
Ahoy love
Ahoy love
Your familiar countenance is nowhere in sight.[14]

Examples are countless, impossible and unnecessary to list or enumerate. Soon after Forough Farrokhzad (1934–67) had died in an automobile accident, Shamlou composed an elegy in her memory that became a definitive signature of his lyrical poetry: "Marsiyeh/Elegy" (1970). What is peculiar about this poem is one poet mourning another in terms idiomatic to both of their poems.

Beh jost-o-ju-ye to . . .

Searching for you:
I cry on the threshold of mountains
At the gate of sea and grass!

Searching for you:
I cry at the passageways of winds,
On the crossroad of seasons,
In the broken frame of a window
That puts an old edge on the cloudy sky—

Awaiting you
This empty notebook
Will have to turn so many
So many pages.

To accept the flow of the wind
And of love—
The sister of death:
And the eternity shared its secret with you!
Thus you appeared like a treasure
Splendid and causing envy:
Treasure troves of the kind
That makes belonging
To the land and homelands
So precious!

Your name is a rising sunshine
That crosses the forehead of skies
Blessed be thy name!
As for us:
We still turn around days and nights
And the yet![15]

Love was not an abstraction for Shamlou, nor accidental to his poetry. After he met Aida, it was as if all his love poetry were written for her: real, immediate, palpable. It was a particularly poignant love story, rendered poetic by Shamlou, where Aida stood both as a real person whom Shamlou loved, and as a metaphor for all objects of joy and desire anywhere else in the world. More than anything else, Shamlou's love for Aida made his poetry worldly and particular, universal and translatable.

Mara to bi-sababi nisti
Berasti selat kodam Qasideh'i ay ghazal! ...

You are not out of nothing for me
Truth be told:
The reward for what elegy are you:
Ey Ghazal!
The showering stars
Of which greetings to the sun are you
From a dark little window?
Words take shape when you look at me:
What beautiful flirtations your looks commence!
Behind the back of your pupils
The cry of which prisoner is it—
With swollen fractured lips—
Throwing a red rose
To freedom?
Otherwise: such fire-play of stars,
Oh no way,
Owes nothing to the sun!
My sight feels secure from your voice:
Oh how piously you call my name!
And your heart: Is a dove of peace
Soaked in blood upon the rooftop of pain!
And yet how high, how soaring, you fly![16]

The classical metaphors of *selat*/reward, *qasideh*/panegyric, and *ghazal* easily weave together to form the opening stanza of the poem, before they perform their functions and disappear to reach for fresh and palpable metaphors of his own making. The love and yearning are real, the desire potent, the love manifest. Shamlou's lyricism was definitive to his poetic diction, at the heart of his aesthetic imagination. But at the same time, he never lost his pending existential anxieties, as in his signature poem "Oqubat/Punishment" (1970):

Miveh bar shakheh shodam ...

I became a fruit on a branch and a stone in a child's hand:
The talisman of a miracle might only save me—
The way I have launched an assault upon myself!

You precious tall beloved
Walk just like the velvety cloud
Onto my gaze.

When I return home!
Like a homeless bird

Come to the balcony before I open the door
With a face made of rain and whisper!

Do as worthy of the little time we have
For the one who swings the axe of events
Has no full control of his tired hands!

Who said I am the last wise man on this earth?
I am that beautiful monster
Standing on the equator of the earth—
Drowning in the purity of all the waters of this earth,
And the horizons of his devilish gaze
Is the horizon where a star is rising!

I have a cottage at the end of the earth
Where the solidity of the *terra firma*
Just like the dance of a mirage
Relies on the deceit of thirst.

Upon the edge of Human and God
Yes
Where the earth and the naught meet
I have an unstable cottage!
And the wind that blows over the dark sea
Sweeps my lackluster cold balcony . . .

My house is at the end of the world
Where the earth and nothingness meet.

They had told us:

"We will teach you that sacred word—
But to earn it you must endure a terrible punishment!"

We endured the grueling punishment so hard
That the sacred word suddenly escaped us.[17]

The futility of the point of the poem resides precisely in its full ecstatic power. The poet narrator is at once earthly and divine, humble and proud, and witness to a cosmic event only he can see. The poet speaks from that point, that interface, of care and confidence. Here, Shamlou the poet stands for humanity at large: fearful, futile, yet epic in their desperation. The nation at the epicenter of which he stood to compose this poem was as heroic as it was futile, in either case fraught, fragile, and historical.

Ahmad Shamlou as Troubadour

Shamlou was a restless soul, impatient and jubilant, defiant and combative—full of songs and furies. His poetic soul would not, could not, sit still and be content with anything. He dabbled in translating poems from Federico García Lorca, Langston Hughes, and others, including the Gilgamesh epic, although he did not know much of any foreign language. In some of these translations, his then wife Tusi Hae'ri (1917–93)—who was an accomplished literary scholar, had a solid command of French, and had studied literature in Paris—was actively involved. He wrote stories and scripts, including children's stories, edited journals, published an encyclopedic collection of colloquial expressions in his monumental project *Ketab-e Kucheh/ The Book of Streets*, even though he was not a trained linguist or folklorist, and none of his film scripts amounted to anything in the larger context of Iranian cinema. It is quite obvious that he engaged in such activities mainly for financial reasons, as his primary source of income. All of these amateurish activities gave his political enemies or less gifted rivals much to criticize and therefore dismiss Shamlou altogether, which is, of course, an entirely ludicrous proposition.

All these circumstances aside, and here is the rub, nothing endeared Shamlou to his contemporaries more than his glorious poetry, especially when he recited it himself, and the poetry of other iconic figures of the Persian pantheon which he vastly popularized with his declamations. The best way, therefore, to come to terms with Shamlou's poetic legacy is not just the substance of his own oeuvre, but also the melodious diction of his declamations of his own poetry accompanied by the musical compositions of contemporary musicians such as Fereydoun Shahbazin (born 1942) or Farhad Fakhreddini (born 1938). Shamlou had an astonishingly commanding voice, and an entire generation grew up listening to and understanding the power of his own texts and those of other masters of classical and contemporary Persian poetry. He recited the poetry of Hafez, Rumi, and Khayyam from the past and those of Nima and his own in his time. This vocal fusion of classical and contemporary poetry created an alchemical texture from which he sang his own songs and shared his own vision of things, unlike anything else that had happened during his lifetime. We had love and admiration for him, not because we were deaf and blind to the nonsense that he uttered about classical Persian music or the *Shahnameh*, or because we disregarded the fact that he was not an authority on Persian colloquial expressions and folklore. We just ignored them and stayed tuned in to his poetic diction. If we wanted to read a learned critique of Shamlou's amateurish dabbling in folklore, all we had to do was to turn to the literary scholar leading in this subject, Mahmoud Omidsalar, and read his exquisite essay reviewing the *Ketab-e Kucheh*, in a civilized tone and precise terms, without any of the political gymnastics of people who were and are as amateurish about such technical matters as Shamlou was, yet harbor an entirely irrelevant political animus against him because of his politics.[18] The highlights of my own undergraduate years in Tehran, and for millions of others like me, was when the Institute for the Intellectual Development of Children and Young Adults (*Kanun-e Parvaresh-e Fekri-ye Kudakan va Nojavanan*) released the LP and audio cassettes of his recitation of his own poetry and that of Nima, Hafez, Rumi, and Khayyam. We would buy a copy and get together in a room with other provincial students simply to listen to his recitations. We were mesmerized by what we heard, felt, and experienced.

We might therefore sidestep all the irrelevant noises and read Shamlou as a singer-songwriter, a minstrel-poet, a troubadour like the mythic figure of Barbad at the famed court of the Sasanian king Khosrow II Parviz (reigned 591–628), although this time around entirely outside any court affiliation and right at the center of the crafting of a poetically anchored public sphere. Another key figure closer to Shamlou would be the legendary constitutionalist poet Aref Qazvini (1882–1934), who also was a singer and songwriter personifying the joyous and defiant spirit of his time. Both Shamlou and Aref can therefore be read like an *ashiq*, as understood, for example, in the Azerbaijani or Armenian context, referring to a singer-poet, or a bard, who accompanies his songs with a lute. The iconic figure is prevalent in Anatolia and Central Asia, with traces also in Safavid Iran, where the Safavid monarch Shah Ismail (1487–1524) considered himself an *ashiq*.[19] Even more distant than the figure of the *ashiq* is the institution of the *gosan*, a Parthian concept with Armenian traces that refers to a "poet-musician, minstrel, that was revived in the eleventh-century classical Persian text, Fakhr-al-Din As'ad Gorgani's *Vis-o-Ramin*, among other sources."[20] Today the word *khonyagar* has a similar meaning.

As I write, I am listening to Shamlou reciting one of his own poems to the music of Esfandiar Monfaredzadeh on a classic LP that *Kanun* issued in 1972. I purchased this LP when I was a college student in Tehran, at the time of its initial release. Right now, its digital version is available online. Framed by Monfaredzadeh's exquisite music, Shamlou is reciting one of his signature poems:

Bi ankeh dideh binad . . .

Without the eyes seeing:
One can still sense
Through the zigzag-winding pattern of the wind—
In the garden:
The majestic sadness of a leaf
That unhurriedly falls on the ground

Upon the window glass panes, the dewdrops are in commotion:
There is no way for the sight
For you to gather in solitude and look
At your inner sanctum!

Neither the sun nor the fire any longer
Have warmth or light
So you search the heap of the cold soil in vain
Dreaming a spark of fire!

This is another season:
So cold from within that it
Complicates any clear conception of beauty!
Blessed be the memories of autumn
With the storm of colors it cast upon our eyes!
The brazier of the sun is the same as always:
The oven is not cold just as last year!
Cold is I!
This is the story:
Something is wasted in my chest in my body.[21]

As he admitted on many occasions, Shamlou wished that he could have become a musician, but he did not, and he sublated his musical urges right into his own poetry, the so-called *she'r sepid* or blank verse, which Nima enabled but also curtailed—given his own predilection for a prosody different from the one he had dismantled. Shamlou rooted his own voice in Nima, yet flew freely on to the blank verse to compose his repressed musicality right into the body of his poetry. He wrote his poems as if composing a nocturne by Chopin, for example, for which reason he named many of his most precious poems "Shabaneh/Nocturnal." Precisely for that reason, he became a master performer of his own (and other poets') poetry. After he published his first audio cassettes reciting his own poetry, we could no longer recite his poetry except by mimicking his voice, as if humming a piece of music. He was the troubadour, the *khonyagar*, as he would say, the *gosan* of his time. Everything else about his sometimes-flamboyant character fades into irrelevance—except for the musically and poetically deaf people who seek to make a reputation for themselves by attacking Shamlou at his weakest spot, for they are too blind to look at his shining glory. The fact that Shamlou uttered nonsensical comments about classical music, or about Ferdowsi, or his *Shahnameh*, or about Zahhak, and so on—all mostly spontaneous speculation to which he was encouraged by an adoring and uncritical audience that dare not question his audacity covering for his lack of authority, precision, and erudition. He was no learned scholar. He was a divine poet. He read Hafez in the way in which he wanted Hafez to be read. His so-called critical edition of Hafez was effectively mimicking the way in which he recited Hafez for a vast audience. His edition of Hafez had very little to do with Hafez and much more with Shamlou himself.[22] I recall from the first day when I purchased his version of Hafez in Tehran: I thought that this was not Hafez, this was Shamlou, a new book of poetry by Shamlou. His poetry, and his poetic disposition, as he would say in one of his poems, was his dwelling, his house of being. Here is his famous poem, "Ta Shokoufeh Sorkh-e Yek Pirahan/ Until the Red Blossom of a Dress" (1950):

Sang mikesham bar Dush . . .

I carry stones on my back
The stone of words
The stone of rhymes

And from the turning moments of these sunsets
That awaken the night in its depth
And the color becomes pitch dark
In the blindness of the coffin,
And music becomes breathless
Fearing the explosion of silence:
I work
Work
Work—
And from the stones of words
Make a solid wall
So I can build the roof of my poem on it
Sit under it
Be imprisoned in it.

This is how I am:
Maybe I am stupid
Who can tell
That I must carry the stones of my own prison
On my own back
Just as the son of Mary did his Cross!

And certainly not like you:
Carving the bone of your brother
Into the handle of your executioner's whip—
And weave the whip of your executioner
From your sister's hair—
And from the broken teeth of your father
Putting a bezzle on the handle of the tyrant's whip.[23]

As a troubadour, a *gosan*, a *khonyagar*, Shamlou invoked and provoked in his audience the distant and close memories of the poet as the prophetic voice of a power beyond his immediate time and space. In a recent book, *The Persian Prince* (2023), on the archetypal formation and deconstruction of the Persian prince, I have argued how under colonial duress the archetype broke down into its constituent forces: a prophet, a poet, a rebel, and a pilgrim.[24] Here in Shamlou, as indeed in all the others among these six poets, we see the poet as precisely that rebel, as that prophetic voice, and above all as a homeless pilgrim. The fusion of these four sub-archetypal forces gathers in Shamlou's poetry precisely as a troubadour. He sings in a prophetic voice, he declares in that rebellious disposition, and he mobilizes an entire emotive universe in building a nation before and beyond its colonial predicaments.

The Troubadour as a Revolutionary Witness

The poet as rebel exudes with a prophetic voice as a pilgrim—with the entirety of the nation, the fact and the idea of it, as both its point of origin and final destination. Shamlou was perhaps the most boldly political poet of all the six figures in this constellation, with the exception of Esmail Kho'i, who became particularly political in an exilic sense after he had left Iran and lived in England until the end of his life, where he cut an iconic persona as a permanent pilgrim who emerged from this sextet and never returned to his point of origin. Shamlou could never last outside Iran. He had to return to his point of origin, and he did. In one iconic poem after another, Shamlou would push the boundaries of political poetry to new heights and new depths at one and the same time, as in this legendary poem titled "Ebrahim dar Atash/Abraham in the Fire" (1973):

Dar avar-e khunin-e gorg-o-mish . . .

In the bloody ruins
Of dawn
When you can't tell a wolf from a sheep:
Ecce Homo!
Who wished the earth green
And only love
Worthy of the most beautiful women!
For this to him
Was no ordinary gift
To deserve dust and stone!

What a man!
What a man!
Who used to say:
The heart better soak
In seven swords of love!
And the throat better utter
The most beautiful names!

And the lion-iron-mountain
Of a man
Like this paced the bloody battlefield of fate
With an Achilles' Heel.
An Immortal

The secret of whose death
Was the sorrow of love,
And the sadness of solitude.

Oh Sad Esfandiar:
You are better off with your eyes closed![25]

Most of these poems were composed on the occasion of the death of a particular political activist, and yet they would instantly assume transhistorical and iconic significance. Shamlou had by now become the chronicler and sojourner of the truth of the most valiant heroes of the revolutionary uprisings: his poetry became the pantheon of those who had given their lives for a cause. This pantheon was not limited to Iranian revolutionaries. In "Khatabeh Tadfin/The Funeral Elegy" (1973), published in his collection *Kashefan Forutan-e Shukaran/The Humble Discoverers of the Hemlock*, he began the poem by dedicating it to Che Guevara:

The oblivious
Are all identical—
Only storm
Gives birth to uneven children.

Harmonious
Are the shadowlike
Careful:
On the borderlines of the Sun!
Looking alive
Though dead!

As for these:
They have headed towards the sea—
Keeping the flame high!
Their lives
Shoulder to shoulder with death,
Ahead of death
Always alive
After being with death
And always with the same name
With which they lived—
For degeneration
Ashamed and admonished
Pass by the tall entrance of their memories!

The discoverers
Of fountains;
The humble discoverers of the hemlock;

Seekers of happiness
In the mouth of volcanos;
Conjurers of a smile
Hidden in the magicians' top hat of pain—
With a footprint deeper than happiness
On the passageways of birds:
They stand facing the thunder,
Light the house
And die![26]

This was an elegy for the whole pantheon of the revolutionary heroes whom he loved, admired, and eulogized. Shamlou would invariably turn to folkloric diction in his political poetry, as for example in one of his signature poems, "Pariya/Fairies" (1953)—where we can see his command of the colloquial and folkloric diction of the Persian language staged at his full disposal.

Once upon a time
Under the cobalt dome:
Head to toe naked
three fairies were sitting by the sunset—
The fairies were crying
Inconsolably
Pouring tears as clouds do in spring!
Their hair long as a bow,
Longer than a bow!
Dark liked coal
Darker than coal!
In front of them
On the horizon the city of chained slaves;
Behind them cold and dark
The castle of old myths.
From the horizons
Ring-o-ring-o-ring
One could hear the sounds of chains:
From behind them
From the tower
One could hear moaning
All through the nights!

"Fairies are you hungry
Fairies are you thirsty
Fairies are you tired?
Why do you look like captured birds?
Why do you cry so hard?
Such moaning, bemoaning, cries?"

> Fairies did not say a word
> Fairies kept crying
> Unconsolably
> Just like spring thunder
> Fairies were crying...

The commotion of the Fairies continues apace, until finally...

> The city is now ours:
> It is the feast of the people!
> The demon is unhappy!
> The world is ours!
> The demon is unhappy!
> Light is victorious!
> The demon is unhappy!
> Darkness is ashamed
> The demons are unhappy!...[27]

A similar folkloric spirt informs Shamlou's other equally loved poem, "Dokhtara-ye Naneh Darya/The Daughters of Mother Sea" (1960), where he extended his command of Persian folkloric diction into the making of a lyrical allegory of his own:

> Once upon a time
> When except for God
> There was none:
> Under this cobalt dome
> Neither a star
> Nor a song—
>
> Uncle Desert
> Fat and floppy
> With two rosy cheeks,
> Small hands and feet,
> His beard and his soul like a twain:
> His pipe was cold and empty,
> His little heart a sea of troubles—
> He had closed the door to his garden
> Sitting by the door!
>
> "Uncle Desert! Where are your sons?"
>
> "By the sea are my sons—
> They are madly in love with the daughters of the sea...
> My precious children night to dawn
> They cry:

Refuse to sleep
Pour their salty tears into the sea singing—
Oh how sadly they sing:

"Daughters of Mother Sea!
Our cottages are cold and dark
We hope for the best
First from God and then from you! . . .

The poem is replete with nostalgic memories, and meanwhile . . .

The daughters of Mother Sea
At the bottom of the sea
Are sitting drunk and in pain—

"Oh sons of Uncle Desert
Your lips like rock candies
Hundred years of yearning
For you just a little cost for seeing you!
The sea is full of your salty tears and lost—
Our fortunes lost and gone!
Don't spill the secret of love into the desert!
Your tears are salty, don't shed them in the sea."[28]

The two sides yearn for each other—and a burning desire defines the entire allegory. As evident in these poems, Shamlou was a political poet not in the sense of having been jailed once or twice or having been in active solidarity with some political activists. He was political in the very cast of his poetic thinking, being, and knowing. To understand this, we need to go back to the single-most significant treatise on classical Persian prosody, Shams al-Din Muhammad ibn Qais al-Razi's (flourished 1230) *Al-Mo'jam fi Ma'a'ir Ash'ar al-'Ajam/Compendium on the Principles of Persian Poetry*. Al-Razi divided his book into two main chapters: the first on *'aruz* or prosody,[29] and second on rhyming and poetics.[30] These two main parts are then followed by a brief and concise conclusion that brings these two sections together and that he has called "Haghighat-e Elm/The Truth of Science."[31] Here, al-Razi has identified the two main components of a good poem: *alfaz*/words and *ma'ani*/concepts that have to be perfect and perfectly harmonious with each other in every respect—good thoughts poured into good words and cast in appropriate prosody, that is the very definition of good poetry.[32] The second issue that Shams al-Razi has raised consists of proportionate rewards paid to the poet by the person they have praised, for no good poetry in praise of a prince should go unrewarded.[33] The third factor is warning poets against plagiarism (*saraqat*).[34] Finally, the fourth and last factor recommended is that poets should know a little bit of every form of knowledge, so that when they refer to it, people will not ridicule their ignorance.[35]

The important aspect of Persian New Poetry that Shamlou here best represents, almost a millennium after al-Razi's systematic theorization, is how every item of these four final recommendations has been broken and overcome. As we read him today, we see how he first specified "meaning" and then expressed that meaning in suitable poetic phrases. In the Nimaic revolution, poetry became a mode of thinking in and of itself, not expressing the thinking that had already taken place elsewhere outside the poem. For classical Persian poetry we may argue that Hafez was the only poet who thought poetically, while other masters—such as Ferdowsi, Khayyam, Sa'di, and Rumi—had already done their thinking before the poem commenced and now had a compelling way of expressing it. This is not the case with Hafez. He had not done the thinking before and now expressed it. He thought with his poetry. He thought poetically. Ferdowsi thought heroically in epic and performed it magnificently in his *Shahnameh*, in which he in fact worked from a prose *Shahnameh* to which he had access. Omar Khayyam already had his view of life and now performed it to perfection in his quatrains. The same is the case with Naser Khosrow, a philosopher with volumes of philosophical prose to his credit, who now opted for a poetic diction more or less sharing the same philosophical ideas. Rumi thought mystically and performed it gloriously in his *ghazal*s and his *Masnavi*. He was a storyteller, working, again, from stories that had already been told, but putting a moral, philosophical, or allegorical twist on them. Sa'di was a wise and worldly thinker with a sublime command of Persian prose and poetry. None of these are applicable to Hafez, who did not think before commencing his poetry. He thought poetically. We may include the sublime South Asian poet Muhammad Iqbal Lahori (1877–1938) in the same category, who especially in his two masterpieces, *Asrar-i-Khodi* and *Rumuz-i-Bekhodi*, also thought poetically. The same was true for Nima and his followers, who came to sublime fruition in all their poetic diction, now specifically with Shamlou. These six poets define the specificity of a poetic revolution where the poets are thinking through and as they dwell in the world poetically.

Shamlou's politics was poetically thought through. His politics, therefore, were not socialist or nationalist, Islamist or anti-Islamist. He commanded his own unique poetic politics. He thought poetically through the politics of his homeland and beyond, and to do so he began with the most vulnerable moments of the revolutionaries arrested, jailed, or executed. Here is an excellent example, "Keyfar/Punishment" (1957), from his collection *Bagh-e Ayeneh/The Garden of Mirrors*:

Dar inja char zendan ast . . .

There are four jails here:
In each cell twice as many tunnels,
In each tunnel a few hollows,
In each hollow a few men in chains.

Among those in chains:
One has murdered his wife with a dagger in the heat of suspicion.

Among these men:
One has, on a hot summer day,
Bloodied the bread of his children
With the blood of the stubborn stingy baker . . .

But I have not killed anyone in a dark and stormy night,
Nor have I sat one night in the dark waiting for a money lender,
Nor have I in the middle of the night jumped from one roof to another!

In the heart of these mountains of my own dreams
I do not listen to anything
But the echoes of these cold melodies
Of these wild grasses that grow, decay, dry, and fall!
If it were not for these chains
Perhaps early one morning
Just like a breeze
Just like a distant memory
I would have crossed over the limits of the lowly cold earth . . .

That is the guilt!
That is the guilt![36]

Imagine a nation: a constellation of six consecutive poets in search of their homeland, in time and space, sense and sentiments, politics and poetics. By now Nima had posited his archetypal and timeless vision of that poetics. Akhavan had dreamed of an empowering past and Shamlou was envisioning a liberated future for it. Shamlou was a visionary poet, in the specific sense of the term: he had a liberated vision of his homeland for the posterity yet to come. To prove it, he was living it. In his poetry he personified, exemplified, the future of a liberation he desired, imagined, and poetically performed. All his flamboyant criticism of everything classical about Iranian culture, from Persian music to Iranian mythology, was at the service of this vision of a liberated future. Things that he liked about the Iranian past—Hafez, Khayyam, Rumi, and so on—he sublimated in his own defiant renditions. To his critics, these appeared as flippant, amateurish, and disrespectful. But more than anything else his frivolity and iconoclastic disposition was always already performed at the service of a liberated future where he had already imagined himself. The overriding Aristotelian conception of mimesis (imitation, representation) is at the heart of his liberating poetics. Equally definitive are the temporal divisions between past, present, and future, as for example the French philosopher Paul Ricœur has noted in his *Time and Narrative*.[37] That temporal demarcation was all fictional, all contingent on the vanishing now. Such assumptions are all contingent on the poetic narrative of the moment that Shamlou at this point best represented, enabling the nation to tell its stories anew. Shamlou therefore posited a future contingent on the past that Akhavan had articulated—the two were coterminous with each other.

As evident in his poems, the poetic voice of this generation is emblematic of the postcolonial disposition of a political culture in which the figure of the monarch and the performance of the molla have lost all premises of legitimacy. The lifespan of Shamlou, as indeed of the rest of this sextet, began in the twilight of the Qajars and around the rise of the Pahlavis, when Iran was in the grip of Russian and British colonialism, eventually yielding to Soviet and American imperialism and their Cold War. The archetypal figure of the Persian Prince had by now completely collapsed and dissolved under colonial duress and reverted to its fourfold formative forces: the poet, the prophet, the pilgrim, and the rebel. Shamlou's agential self-proclamation is in the spirit of the prophet rebel, now a pilgrim in the dispersion of a world history.

Consider Shamlou's "Marg-e Naseri/The Death of the Nazarene" (1965), composed in celebration of the moment of the crucifixion of Jesus Christ:

Ba Avazi yek-dast . . .

With a monotonous song
Monotonous,
The tail end of the wooden load
Drew a heavy and shivering line behind him—
Upon the earth.

"Put a crown of thorns on his head!"
As the long song
Of the load behind him—
In the hallucinations of his pain—
Wove a fiery thread.

"Hurry up, Nazarene, hurry up!"
He felt light
From the forgiveness he found in his own soul
And like a proud swan
He gazed on his own purity.

"Whip him!" . . .
"Hurry up, Nazarene, hurry up! . . .
The overcast heavens
Heavily
Lowered upon the silencing song of forgiveness—
The mourners
Climbed the mount:
And the sun and the moon embraced.[38]

By now the nation of sentiments that Shamlou and his ensemble of poets had gathered around Nima had transcended all its sectarian and denominational divisions. They were crafting a new nation, rooted in the poetic legacy of the Constitutional Revolution, from the pangs of colonialism imagining a homeland liberated, not just from aging tyrannies, but equally from the outdated phrasing of their worldly whereabouts.

The Poet as Agent Provocateur

Above all, Shamlou was a poet—first and foremost—and in his poetic disposition a rebel, a prophet, and a pilgrim. Whatever else he did ultimately amounted to a wasteful avocation that in the end became fodder for the force and power of his poetic voice. If he turned to *Farhang-e Kucheh/The Culture of the Street* to catalogue them, it was not because he was a trained philologist, linguist, or folklorist. He was none of those. He was a poet and wanted to dwell on the poetic power of folkloric diction. If he prepared his own version of Hafez, it was not because he had the patience and perseverance of painstakingly preparing a critical edition of the *Divan* of Hafez, but because he wanted to dwell in and cohabit with Hafez a moment of poetic intimacy. He wanted to show that he was as good as Hafez. Vastly more erudite and patient scholars such as Mohammad Ghazvini, Qasem Ghani, and Parviz Natel Khanlari had prepared critical editions of the *Divan* of Hafez, and there was no logical reason for him to pretend that he was their match. He was not. Apples and oranges—as it were. If he uttered nonsensical gibberish about Ferdowsi and his monumental *Shahnameh*, it was not because he was a literary historian and had carefully weighed what he wanted to say, but because he wanted to declare that he was a better poet than Ferdowsi. If he revised and recast other people's translations and passed them as his own, it was not because he had a serious command of any foreign language. He did not. It was because he wanted to lay a claim to global prose and poetry to feel at home in the world. If he spoke disrespectfully of Persian classical music, it was not because he understood how a rich and glorious musical tradition worked. He did not. It was because he wanted to ask people to see how his own poetic melodies were superior to anything else they might have heard.

Look at me, read me, listen to me: a Persian Narcissus very much in love with his own image at work—and through him and in his mirror his readers could read, watch, and bask in that beauty. For he was them—the best of them manifest. He loved, and rightly so, what he saw in the public image of himself—and they in him. "Ayeneh-'i dar barabar Ayeneh," as he once put it in a poem, "a mirror in front of a mirror." Above all else, Shamlou basked and thrived in reciting his own words and other master poets' melodious poems. He became Hafez. He became Rumi. He became Khayyam. All the icons of Persian poetic scholarship who prepared critical editions of these texts stood to one side, and on the other an entire generation of the Persian-speaking world growing up listening to him, reciting Hafez, Rumi, and Khayyam. Not the scholars preparing the critical editions of these poets, but the echoes of Shamlou's voice reciting their poetry was what meant most. He was more influential in having a vast majority of literate Iranians and other

Persian-speaking people listen to him reciting Hafez than even the most beloved vocalist of his time, Mohammad Reza Shajarian (1940–2020), singing his *ghazals*. He was Hafez incarnate, Rumi, Khayyam, and all other masters of Persian poetry coming back to whisper in his ears, as he sang their songs for an entire nation.

"The future" that Ahmad Shamlou envisioned and lived poetically was deeply embedded in the troubled truth that he and his nation experienced. He never lived to see that future come true. No one could ever actually see and live that future for real. It was a dream, an apparition, a hope, born of despair. Like Akhavan's past, Shamlou's future was atemporal, amorphous, metamorphic, a poetic trope. He was busy casting his people on the scaffolding of an imagined nation that was more real than the real nation, and as such he would endure any and all of its endemic adversaries. In his lifetime, he connected and lived through two monarchical dynasties and one Islamist theocracy. He waved them all away and survived through their vile and militant adversities. Like Nima and Akhavan, Shamlou was busy building a poetic edifice: real, towering, rock-solid, taller than the walls that any state could build around itself to lay a false claim on an unruly nation that he had helped imagine. He always remained expectant, awaiting the gathering of love and politics, of rebellion and Eros, as here in his "Taraneh-ye Tarik/Dark Song" in "Abraham in the Fire":

> Against the silvery background of the morning
> A horseman
> Stands still—
> And the tall mane of his horse
> Waves in the wind.
>
> Oh God, oh God!
> Horsemen should not stand still
> When the event is warning!
>
> By the burned hedges
> A silent girl stands by
> And her thin skirt waves in the wind!
> Oh God! Oh God!
> Girls should not just stand still
> When men—
> Disappointed and tired—
> Get old.[39]

Chapter 4

FOROUGH FARROKHZAD: THE POETICS OF THE PRESENT

The crowning achievement of them all, a generation delivering its promises, Forough Farrokhzad (1934–67) was a poet of the present: no interest in the past or preoccupation with the phantom promises of a future, neither Akhavan and his preoccupation with a past, nor Shamlou and his fixation on a future delivery, and in between them both, the supreme poet of the present. "Parishadokht-e She'r-e Emruz," Akhavan once called her, the Queen Fairy of the Poetry of Today, and this honorific praise resonates in more than one sense. Dwelling on the momentous Now and Here was definitive to Farrokhzad's poetry. She was a poet of the present and of the evident, a counter-metaphysician of the material force of body and soul, detailing a poetics of interiority definitive to her present and her palpable sense of the world, bringing the joyous and fragile materiality of a decidedly female voice to the idea of homeland, which she at once satirized and yet paradoxically confirmed. Here is a good example of her sense of the present from her "Vahm-e Sabz/Green Apprehension" (1963):

> What summit exactly?
> What soaring height?
> Protect me:
> You worrisome lights,
> You lit suspicious homes—
> Where cleanly washed clothes—
> Embraced by aromatic smoke—
> Are waving on your sunny roofs!
>
> Protect me:
> You complete, simple women—
> Who from behind the skin of your thin fingers
> Are tracing the contours
> Of the ecstatic trembling of a fetus—
> And in the low cut of your collar
> The air is always filled
> With the aroma of fresh milk.[1]

This summons a sublimated reading of reality—evident, real, present, and true—sustained through and embedded in evident facts turned into metaphors: "cleanly washed clothes," "the aroma of fresh milk," "the low cut of the collar," "the ecstatic trembling of a fetus," and so on—all evident faces of the real, of the visible, of the evident, of the now. In her poetry, Farrokhzad perfected and staged this particular mutation of the factual into the metaphoric, of the poetic of the present into the metaphysics of the ordinary. She was a metaphysician of the evident, escaping and overcoming the received legacies of the theo-ontological, of the there and then, brought down to earth to the Here and Now. She did not seek to dismantle that aging theo-ontology front and center and face to face. She put the simulacrum of the sacred to work, to a renewed significance, and of that metamorphic power she made a poetic legacy, her singular signature carved into the very timber of her time.[2] Rarely would any other poet, let alone the gathered crowd of the US-based imperial (bourgeois) feminism of the expatriate Area Studies cabal that has amassed at the doorsteps of her glorious poetry, come even close to grasping that metaphysics. In an essay I published on Farrokhzad's poetry more than thirty-five years ago, I began dwelling on this potent part of her poetry—the materiality of her metaphysics.[3] In this chapter, I plan to expand on that theme in more extended and rooted directions.

A Short Life, a Long Shadow

Forough Farrokhzad lived a short but exceptionally rich and fruitful life.[4] She was born in Tehran on December 18, 1934 and before she died in a tragic automobile accident on February 14, 1967 at the age of thirty-two, she had already published four collections of her poetry and made one iconic documentary film, *Khaneh Siah Ast/The House Is Black* (1962), which became definitive to the rise of the Iranian New Wave. Her final collection of poetry, *Iman Biavarim beh Aghaz-e Fasl-e Sard/Let Us Believe in the Commencement of the Cold Season*, was published posthumously in 1973.[5] She was still a teenager when she famously fell in love with her cousin Parviz Shapour (1924–2000), a renowned satirist, married him (perfectly normal at the time in Iran and many other Muslim countries), and moved to my hometown of Ahvaz. The fruit of that marriage was Farrokhzad's only biological son, Kamyar, whose custody she lost in a bitter and nasty divorce. She returned to Tehran, had a nervous breakdown, recovered, and soon met Ebrahim Golestan (1922–2023), with whom she carried on a lifelong extramarital affair. He was a major novelist, a minor filmmaker, and a flamboyant and pathologically egotistical public intellectual, who for the longest time would suck the air out of Farrokhzad's otherwise overwhelming and towering significance. Farrokhzad published three collections of her poetry in rapid succession: *Asir/Captive*, *Divar/Wall*, and *Esyan/Rebellion* in 1952, 1956, and 1957, respectively. Before she published her final masterpiece, *Tavalodi Digar/Another Birth*, in 1963, she also made her legendary documentary film, *Khaneh Siah Ast/The House Is Black*, in the fall of 1962.[6] After her death, her posthumous collection of poetry,

Iman Biavarim beh Aghaz-e Fasl-e Sard/Let Us Believe in the Commencement of the Cold Season (1973), consolidated her significance as the soaring poet of her time.[7]

Nothing about Farrokhzad's short life could have anticipated, might explain, or else offer any clue as to her emerging poetic brilliance. She was a very ordinary woman, born and raised in a relatively well-to-do family, married very young, had a child whom she had to abandon after her divorce, conducted a lifelong affair with a famous married man, soon began to compose and publish her poems, briefly traveled abroad, came back to make a documentary film masterpiece and to publish the maturest collection of her poetry, and then died in an automobile accident. That is about it. The only thing particular about her life was the fact that she took her thoughts and emotions very seriously, and that she had a gift for articulating them boldly and plainly. Here in this poem, "Tanha Sedast keh Mimanad/Only the Voice Will Remain" (1973), we have all we need to know to understand the exquisite spirit of her life as a poet:

> I am a descendant of trees:
> Breathing the captured air sickens me!
> The dead bird taught me
> To remember the flight!
> The end of all forces is to unite:
> To unite with the bright principle of the Sun,
> And to pour into the consciousness of the light!
> It is of course natural
> That wooden windmills rot—
> Why should I stop?
> I hold the young wheat spikes
> Under my breast and breastfeed them.
>
> In the land of the midgets
> Measures always rotate on the axis of zero:
> Why should I stop?
> I follow the Four Elements—
> And the drafting of the constitution of my heart
> Does not follow the working of
> The blind local rulers!
>
> What do I have to do with
> The long moaning cry of barbarism
> In the sexual organ of the beast?
>
> What do I have to do with the
> Pathetic movement of the
> Worm in the meaty vacuum?
> The bloody genealogy of flowers
> Has committed me to life—

> The bloody genealogy of flowers
> You know?[8]

Being "a descendant of trees" completely shifts the aura of a poetic voice—as does the bold and defiant: "Why should I stop?" Before we even reach the glorious metaphor of "I hold the young wheat spikes/Under my breast and breastfeed them," by the time we get to "The bloody genealogy of flowers/Has committed me to life—/The bloody genealogy of flowers/You know," Farrokhzad has turned the poetic of every politics upside down. Turning her own body, boldly feminine, into a metaphor of sublime confidence, she was both rooted in the mundane and dreary ordinariness of a woman's life in Iran of her time yet soaring above them all. Where would a phrase like "the bloody genealogy of flowers/Has committed me to life" come from? From the depth of that volcanic eruption against the mundane, the evident, the everydayness. And yet that very mundane evidence was the molten lava of her poetic eruptions. Today it is impossible to imagine Forough Farrokhzad to have lived a full and fulfilling life beyond her brief and volcanic eruption: as if she willed that automobile accident to terminate her life in the prime of her creativity. It is as if she was destined, fated, to have thundered into and brightened the sky above her homeland in a rainbow of her emotions and commotions and then to suddenly disappear into the thin air, immortalized there and then to recast the entire fate of her inherited universe.[9]

Enheduana, Sappho, Sor Juana Inés de la Cruz, Rabe'eh, Farrokhzad: Poets as Metaphors

No other poet among the six whom I study in this book captured and defined the temporal spontaneity of her time as much as Farrokhzad did in her poetic diction; among all her other works her masterpiece, "Tavallod-i Digar/Another Birth" (1963), is the quintessence of this temporal poise, confidence, and presence.[10] The first stanza of the poem hits the reader like a dark and foreboding proclamation and it takes the entirety of the poem to unpack and to locate our presence in its spellbinding force. From the very first line we realize that we are in the presence of a prophetic (revelatory) voice at once archaic and yet immediate and contemporary. Our time and narrative became spontaneously sacred in the instance of this poetic coil. The echoes of the Qur'anic verses and Hafez's *ghazals* resound in this poem:

Hameh-ye hasti-ye man . . .

> All my existence
> Is a dark verse
> Repeating you in itself
> Taking you to the early dawn
> Of eternal blossoming and growing.
> I sighed

You in this verse!
I sighed you!
In this verse
I rooted you in Tree, Water, and Fire.[11]

Hameh-ye hast-ye man! All my existence! It is impossible to exaggerate the majestic character of that opening phrase. The verb that holds this whole inaugural stanza together is *"tariki ast"* from the compound verb *"tarik-budan,"* used here in the present tense, *"tariki ast."*[12] "My entire existence is a dark verse." What is a "dark verse," exactly? A strange combination, but still so astoundingly evocative. The whole diction is declaratory, evocative, decidedly oracular. How and when did she ascend that mountaintop where these verses were revealed to her? Three distant poets, farthest removed from Farrokhzad's mind and world, come to the learned mind of her readers: the Sumerian priestess Enheduana, the Greek singer and songwriter Sappho, and the Mexican poet Sor Juana Inés de la Cruz. Enheduana was the high priestess of the moon god in the Sumerian city-state of Ur during the reign of her father, Sargon of Akkad (reigned *circa* 2334–2279 BCE), while Sappho (*circa* 630–570 BCE) was an Archaic Greek lyricist from the island of Lesbos, whose evocatively homoerotic poetry was to be sung accompanied by instrumental music.[13] We can proceed to think of the sublime Mexican poet nun, Sor Juana Inés de la Cruz (1651–95), and her exquisite love poems. As we read Farrokhzad today, echoes of Enheduana, Sappho, and Sor Juana Inés de la Cruz resonate in her poetry, especially here in "Another Birth," where the prophetic and the lyrical are powerfully infused together. We may therefore consider Enheduana, Sappho, and Sor Juana Inés de la Cruz not just as three distant sister-poets of Farrokhzad from classical antiquity to the Americas, but also as three complementary metaphors of prophetic and erotic binaries that come together in Farrokhzad's poetic legacy. We might equally think of the distant and legendary descendant of Enheduana, the Iraqi Muslim mystic poet Rabe'eh al-Adawiyeh (713–801), as she was recollected generations later by Farid al-Din Attar. All of these poets and many more, from Enheduana and Sappho to Rabe'eh al-Adawiyeh, assume metaphoric power when we read Farrokhzad in their extended shadows. From that metaphoric fusion we can now read the rest of Farrokhzad's poem more palpably—especially when she moves to tell us what life is:

Life is perhaps
A long street where a woman,
Carrying a basket,
Walks every day!
Life is perhaps
A rope with which a man hangs himself
From the branch of a tree,
Life is perhaps
A child returning from school,
Life is perhaps

> Lighting a cigarette
> In the lethargic span between two embracing,
> Or the bewildered look of a passer-by
> Who lifts his hat
> And with a meaningless smile turns to another passer-by and says:
> "Good Morning!"
> Life is perhaps
> That closed circuited moment
> When my gaze
> Ruins itself in the pupil of your eyes—
> And there is a feeling in this
> That I will mix with an understanding
> Of the moon and a grasp of darkness.[14]

Is this poetry or philosophy, mysticism or dissent, meditative or revelatory, or both, or neither? A whole different tertiary space is crafted, where life is made meaningful in precisely its moments of meaningless ordinariness. Early in his "Madarej al-Kamal/Stages of Perfection," the philosopher-poet Baba Afzal Kashani (died *circa* 1214) specified what kind of people his interlocutors were: neither the incomplete (immature) people nor the complete (mature) but those who are in the middle, "our interlocuters are the intermediary people, and by that we mean people who are traveling, neither the static nor the hesitant . . . those who are restless, never satisfied with that which they have achieved, and as they mature they become even more eager and in a rush, prompted by the joy that comes with motion towards perfection, and saddened by that which halts them."[15] We need to place Farrokhzad comfortably in the company of such philosopher-poets as Baba Afzal, who seek to capture their interlocutors somewhere in the midst of their journey— when they have already started moving but have not yet reached any certain destination. Consider Farrokhzad's poetic focusing on what life is: "Perhaps/A long street where a woman,/Carrying a basket/Walks every day!/ . . . A rope with which a man hangs himself/From the branch of a tree,/A child retuning from school,/ . . . / Lighting a cigarette/In the lethargic span between two embracing,/ Or the bewildered look of a passer-by/Who lifts his hat/And with a meaningless smile turns to another passer-by and says:/"Good Morning!"/ . . . That closed circuited moment/When my gaze/Ruins itself in the pupil of your eyes." What holds these successive images and metaphors together? It is their ordinariness, of course, and yet their present mobilities from the mundane to the ecstatic. From here forward we are invited ever deeper into the poet's inner sanctum, with Enheduana, Sappho, and Rabe'eh, as three metaphors (prophetic and erotic and mystic) on Farrokhzad's poetic mind:

> In a room the size of solitude
> My heart
> That is the size of a love
> Looks at the simple excuses of its happiness:

At the beautiful withering of the flowers in the vase,
At the seedling you have planted in our garden,
And at the warbling of the canaries
Singing within the framing of a window.[16]

This is sublime simplicity of not just love but of being: Farrokhzad as the metaphysician of the sublime and the beautiful. This is the sustained sublimation of Persian lyricism of millennial heritage into something new, real, palpable, contemporary. This is reality shorn to truth—any claim to truth, except for the self-evident in the poetic act itself. This is not partaking but inventing solitude and selfhood, akin to the sort of selfhood someone like the Danish existentialist philosopher Søren Kierkegaard (1813–55) would invent in his decidedly Christian context. Just think of the image: "the beautiful withering of the flowers in the vase." Here we sense the precious passing beauty in the moment of death and mourning, resignation, and sublimation at one and the same time. It is as if we, along with Farrokhzad's persona, have died and come back to life, and this is our second life, a resurrection, a renewal, a resumed consciousness, where we see and sense differently.

Oh
This is my share,
This is my share—
My share
Is a sky that hanging a curtain takes away from me,
My share is to descend a dilapidated stairway,
Reaching down for something in emptiness and exile,
My share is a sad stroll in the garden of memories,
And to die for a voice that tells me:
"I love your hands!"[17]

Is this a moment of love or an instance of despair, desolation, or hope? Both and beyond. In her deeply entrenched poetic persona, Farrokhzad recast and redefined the whole conception of love, standing against the entire history of a rich and overwhelming Persian metaphoric tradition. She became Hafez manifest: thinking, feeling, being, and knowing poetically. The imageries that she invoked, the metaphors she coined, only a fleeting phrase such as "I love your hands"—all gather to become the simulacrum of a truth beyond evident facts. In these moments, she becomes like Rumi, with a poetic move beyond anthropocentricism, where plants, animals, and humans connect from the inanimate objects to the angelic ascent. Here is the moment:

I plant my hands in the little garden:
I shall grow
I know
I know

I know
And the sparrows shall lay their eggs in between my inky fingers![18]

This above all is a prophetic voice pure and simple, a fusion of Enheduana, Sappho, and Rabe'eh coming together—and yet its metaphors and images are so immediately accessible, physical, real, ordinary, and above all unmistakably Persian. Being planted as a human and resurrected as a plant conflates and crafts a whole new perception of post-humanism, stipulated in poetic speculations. The imagery continues apace along the same lines:

I hang a pair of earrings on my ears
From a pair of identical cherries:
And I stick petals of dahlia
To my fingernails.
There is a street
Where the young boys who were in love with me—
With that disheveled hair, long necks, and thin legs
Recall the innocent smiles of a young girl
Who was carried away by the wind one night!
There is a street
My heart has snatched away from my childhood neighborhood.[19]

Images are familiar, innocent, resonant—yet the mood is prophetic, deeply reminiscent of Enheduana in her exultation of Inana, albeit in a decidedly immediate sense. The invocation of Enheduana is particularly apt here because Farrokhzad, too, speaks in this poem in a distinctly prophetic diction. If so, then the prophetic, the poetic, and the disposition of a pilgrim, as I began to introduce them from the chapter on Shamlou onwards, has by now assumed a decidedly feminine tenor, from which emerges a mystic force:

A voluminous journey upon the line of time
And with a volume impregnate the barren line of time
A volume of a conscious picture that has just returned from a festive
gathering with a mirror
And that is how it is that someone dies and someone lives
No fisherman will ever find a pearl in a pathetic brook pouring into a marsh
I know a sad little fairy
Who lives in an ocean
And who plays her heart on a wooden flute
Ever so gently
A sad little fairy who dies by a kiss at night and resurrects
With another kiss in the morning.[20]

This is a metaphoric voice becoming also metamorphic: "Safar-e hajmi dar khat-e zaman/A voluminous journey upon the line of time"—followed by "Va beh hajmai khat-e khoshk-e zaman ra abestan kardan/And with a volume impregnate the barren line of time." The image is clear: a shapely volume is traveling through a barren line, "impregnating" it. By now the poetic metaphor has metamorphosed into a philosophical (semiotic) proposition, with the act of poetry itself, Farrokhzad's own poetic event, as a metapoetic act, generating meaning, as a volume would impregnate an otherwise barren line. With Enheduana, Sappho, and Rabe'eh walking by her side—more as persona than as persons, metaphoric rather than real—Farrokhzad has by now carried the power of Persian poetic diction into a revelatory moment, with echoes of the metaphoric powers of generations of poets from Enheduana over Sappho to Rabe'eh resonating in her revelatory voice. The poet has become prophetic, the prophetic rebellious, the rebellious always a pilgrim.

Ghaybat *and* Zuhur: *Eschatology and Parousia*

All appearances and false impressions aside, Forough Farrokhzad was a Muslim woman and a Shi'a. False categories such as "secular" or "modern" return from her door embarrassed. She, to be sure, cut a radically different figure of being a Muslim woman in the world—diametrically at odds with the supposition of a Muslim woman dominant in the Islamophobic stratosphere East and West, North and South, where the white-washed, Eurocentric, Iranian bourgeois feminism deeply partakes in the most entrenched European and American Islamophobia. The incurable Islamophobia of Iranian "secular" feminism cannot fathom imagining Farrokhzad as Muslim poet or person, for that does not gel well with the deeply colonized image of themselves. Like millions of other Iranian women, and indeed millions of other Muslim women around the world, Forough Farrokhzad did not wear a hijab or cover her hair with a scarf, as some other Muslim women choose to do. Today, that scarf, especially in the US and Europe (where the heart of Iranian bourgeois feminism dwells), has falsely become fetishized as the singular and universal icon of being a Muslim woman. That assumption is false and misleading. What Muslim women wear, how they choose to show aspects of their piety in public, may radically differ. In addition, Farrokhzad was a single woman, a divorcée, who created a scandal with her extramarital relationship with a married man. Her poetry palpitates with erotic themes and metaphors. What kind of a Muslim woman is this? Certainly not the kind of Muslim woman whom the ruling Islamist regime in Iran would embrace, or whom the racist and Islamophobic ruling regimes in the US and Europe could fathom, or *a fortiori* the equally if not more Islamophobic Iranian bourgeois feminism rampant among the "Area Studies" crowd would or could stomach. For she was a normal, honest, truthful, and bold kind of a Muslim woman—with both her eroticism and her piety, at one and the same time. As a sign of her Muslim faith, we must abandon all the false appearances that the world has singularly decided to be the sign of a Muslim woman and enter the inner sanctum of her poetry, where we find her in the sublimest mode of prayer: her poetic impulses. Her poetry was her piety, her prayers, her meditations, her mysticism, and her dissent, in communion with her prophetic soul.

Farrokhzad's poetic persona was one of the most powerful voices of a Muslim poet, a poet aware of her Muslim faith, conversant with its iconic themes, and her poem "Kasi keh Mesl-e Hichkas Nist/Someone Who Is Like No One Else" (1973) is the most powerful evidence of that fact. In many of her other iconic poems, such as "Another Birth" (1963) or "Earthly Verses" (1963), signs and metaphors of an Islamic piety are equally present and put to powerful poetic uses. But it is in this singularly visionary poem that she posits a powerful liberation theology cast in potent poetic poise. In Shi'a Islam, the two simultaneous ideas of *ghaybat*/occultation and *zuhur*/ Parousia are tantamount to the concepts of Christian Eschatology. Eschatology and Parousia are two Greek words at the root of the Christian messianic doctrines. Eschatology points to the end of time, anticipating the second coming of the Messiah. Parousia, meanwhile, means the "presence" or "arrival" of an anticipated royalty, meaning the momentous circumstances of his re-appearance as the promised Messiah. In Shi'ism, this messianic idea gathers around the figure of the promised Mahdi and is identified as *ghaybat*/occultation and *zuhur*/Parousia or re-appearance. "Someone Who Is Like No One Else" reads on the borderline of that dialectic of occultation and Parousia, of *ghaybat* and *zuhur*, and as such can be read as a powerful political declaration staging an eschatological manifesto, of the coming Messiah/Mahdi. It is impossible to exaggerate the power of this poem, precisely because it is composed in colloquial terms and from the perspective of a little girl, an elementary school girl, more innocent and more powerful than the most sophisticated theological treatises on the Day of Judgment (*ruz-e qiyamat*). In the Shi'a doctrines of *ghaybat* and *zuhur*, Muslims are to look for the *ala'im-e zuhur*, or signs of Parousia—namely, certain indications that the Mahdi is coming. This is the eschatological doctrine at the heart of this poem, which Farrokhzad cast in the form of reporting a dream that the narrator has had:

> I have had a dream—
> Someone is coming:
> I have dreamed of a red star–
> And my eyelashes keep batting,
> And my shoes keep pairing,
> And cross my heart, hope to die, if I lie! . . .[21]

The dream here reads like a revelation, for the narrator speaks from the unseen and the unheard, but intuited in a vision that Farrokhzad now unfolds. The narrator is a prepubescent girl, as a sign of her innocence and truthfulness, of her immaculate infallibility—whereby she becomes a truth-teller, like a prophetic voice. Shoes that keep pairing and eyelashes that keep batting are signs, in folkloric terminologies, that this is a truthful dream, and the prophet and the messenger, both as the seer and as the interpreter, are telling the truth, a truthful dream that would, or should, come true.

> Someone is coming,
> Someone is coming,
> Someone is coming:

> Someone better
> Someone who is like no one:
> Not like the father, not like Ansi, not like Yahya, not like mother
> They are like the one they should be like.
> They are taller than the trees of the Architect's House
> And their face
> Is brighter than the face of the hidden Imam—
> And he is not scared of Seyyed Javad's brother
> Who has become a police officer
> And he is not even scared of Seyyed Javad himself
> Who owns the rooms in our house![22]

The stanza recites like a chant with repetitions as emphasis through incantation. The body of that somebody to come is not corporeal, for he (or she) is not like the father or any other familiar figure—fearful or mortal. I have opted for the pronoun "they" in my translation, for in Persian we do not have gender-specific pronouns, and I do not wish to prejudice the translation towards a male savior in a poem composed by a Muslim woman. That exquisite gender ambiguity adds to the power of the poem, despite the fact that the figure of the Mahdi as the Twelfth Imam in Shi'ism is a male descendant of Ali and his wife Fatima, the Prophet's beloved daughter. Thus, the person of the Mahdi in Shi'ism is a decidedly male figure, but not so in Farrokhzad's poem. Kasi is just someone, a person. Paramount here is the political atmosphere that Farrokhzad created: Seyyed Javad's brother is a police officer who bullies the people of the neighborhood, and Seyyed Javad himself is a landlord in the same neighborhood. The political force of the stanza is already declared. This is a form of liberation theology platformed through its poetic intuition of salvation. The constitution of fascism, the fusion of militarism and wealth, is marked with the gentlest and most effective references. But who exactly is the savior to deliver us from this horror?

> Their name as the mother says when she is praying
> Is: Oh the Judge of all Judges,
> Oh the Hope of all Hopes!
> And they can recite all the difficult words
> Of the third-grade textbook
> With their eyes closed—
> And they can even deduct
> The number one thousand from the number twenty million,
> Without missing anything!
> And they can buy all they need
> From Seyyed Javad's grocery store!
> And they can do something
> So that the lightbulb that reads "Allah"—
> And that was green just like the early morning green—
> Comes back to light the sky over the Meftahian Mosque . . .[23]

The reference to "deduct the number one thousand from the number twenty million/Without missing anything!" we always read and understood as an allusion to the 1,000 ruling families (*hezar famil*) over and above the then 20 million people of Iran, and the declaration that, if they were to be eliminated, nothing would be amiss. The rest of the stanza is replete with the insignia of Islamic messianism, beginning with the lightbulb that reads "Allah" and casts its light upon the entirety of the city and the poem where it is composed. Rarely can the particular power of a liberation theology within a specifically Islamic context be seen so seamlessly written into the folkloric idiomaticity of a culture. What follows is a prayer, an incantation, a messianic chant—all replete with political poignancy:

> Someone is coming,
> Someone is coming,
> Someone who in their heart is with us:
> In their breath is with us,
> In their voice is with us—
> Someone whose coming cannot be arrested
> Handcuffed
> Or jailed . . .[24]

By now the images of the handcuffed and the jailed have pushed the political force of the poem forward into familiar territory. The heart and soul of the prophetic voice as a prepubescent girl is in communion with the Mahdi as Messiah to come—it is impossible to exaggerate the moral imagination and radical spontaneity of the poetic moment that by now has assumed revelatory power. What follows is a socialist dreamworld, rooted in the liberation theology that Farrokhzad has provoked and staged:

> Someone is coming from the sky
> Over Topkhana Square
> On the night of fireworks—
> And who will spread the dining cloth,
> And divide the bread,
> And divide Pepsi Cola,
> Divide the national park,
> Divide the cough syrup,
> Divide the day of school registration,
> Divide the hospital admission tickets,
> Divide the rainboots,
> Divide the cinema of Fardin—
> And divide everything that has been hoarded!
> And they will give us our share too!
> I have had a dream![25]

Here all the insignia of poor people's iconography are staged: bread, Pepsi Cola, access to a public park, cough syrup, rainboots, and tickets to see a film in which Mohammad Ali Fardin (1931–2000)—a famous and widely popular actor—plays are the lead tropes. These are all from the perspective of a young girl, a middle schooler, whom Farrokhzad makes the mouthpiece of her eschatology. This eschatology is neither doctrinal nor "secular," a concept that has no place in this potent Parousia. These are the hopes and aspirations of ordinary folk that the coming Mahdi will deliver, and the young girl at the epicenter of the dream as revelation has seen and is now making believable the unseen. The dream as revelation comes shortly after the Khomeini uprising of 1963 and long before the Iranian revolution of 1977–9 in which Khomeini played a central role. Therefore, neither can the Islamists claim this poem for themselves, nor can the militant Marxists dismiss it as irrelevant to their cause. The poem stands somewhere in between both and all divergent ideological claims to leading a revolution. The poem is a revolution in and of itself, an eschatological resurrection to make the aging grandfathers of the Shi'i eschatology stand aside and behold how the new revelation has announced itself.

Consider, for example, the Shi'i poet, philosopher, and theologian Abd al-Razzaq Lahiji's (died 1662) seminal text *Gohar Morad/The Desired Jewel*, where he discussed the public (*nass-e jalliyeh*) and private (*nass-e khafiyyeh*) declaration of Imam Ali as the Prophet Muhammad's successor (Imam).[26] For the Shi'is, the Twelfth (Hidden) Imam is a direct descendant of Ali as the last messianic figure of the Mahdi. If Lahiji were alive and were to read Farrokhzad's poem, as both a poet himself and a theologian, he would have been overjoyed with it. In Farrokhzad's poem, the evident and the symbolic are pointedly contemporary, and as such they replace the doctrinal public and the private indications in Lahiji's theology. The point in Farrokhzad's poem is that the narrator has experienced a truthful vision. Farrokhzad's poem is rooted in Shi'i eschatological doctrines, but at the same time it transcends them in diction and disposition—pushing the poetic boundaries of the expectation of the Hidden Imam into radically contemporary, decidedly socialist, dimensions of a renewed liberation theology.

The Captive, against the Wall, and the Final Rebellion

Forough Farrokhzad's road to *Another Birth*, and after that to *Let Us Believe in the Commencement of the Cold Season*, was short but eventful.[27] Her first three volumes of poetry were finger exercises on the keyboard of her soul, intertwined with her poetic excitement: self-centered and daring, yet lacking in any serious vision of her own persona or her time and being, but still probing and heartfelt, as she paced her way towards a purposeful life to season and mature. The three rapid and consecutive volumes of *Asir/Captive* (1955), *Divar/Wall* (1956), and *Esyan/Rebellion* (1958) established Farrokhzad's reputation in the small group of emerging poets of her time. This was the era of the post-1953 CIA-MI6 military coup in Iran, where she found ample time to think and feel and excavate her mind and body. She was reading vociferously, as she once put it, and her agitated soul began to pour out. She was a solid follower of Nima, while in full command of Persian classical prosody, and she could easily traffic between Nimaic and classical forms. She had asked Shoja al-Din Shafa (1918–2010), a classicist literato, to write an introduction to her first volume, which consisted of her first attempts at poetry. In the second volume, we notice a rebellious soul at work, with the famous poem "Gonah/Sin" declaring to the world at large that she meant business. With *Esyan/Rebellion*, her courageous and defiant voice became pronounced and self-evident. Based on these experiences and the interlude of her documentary film, *The House Is Black*, she published her masterpiece *Another Birth* (1963). Her final collection of poems, *Let Us Believe in the Commencement of the Cold Season*, was ready for publication by 1963, but was not published until after her untimely death in 1967.[28]

Captive consists of forty-four poems, composed between 1953 and 1955. *Wall* includes twenty-five poems, composed between 1954 and 1956, chief among them "Gonah/Sin." *Rebellion* consists of seventeen poems, mostly composed between 1956 and 1958. The majority of these poems are in the classical prosody of the quatrain, although exuding in more intimate and personal thematics, signs of an emerging poetic self-consciousness. In these collections, Farrokhzad staged her command of the classical forms while delving deep into her own troubled soul, with which an entire generation of young Iranian women, at least high-school- or even college-educated, now actively identified. After *Rebellion* she altogether abandoned classical prosody and joined the Nimaic camp in earnest. As I have argued elsewhere, the link between the first and the second phase of her poetry is the making of her documentary *The House Is Black*, which renders the transition far smoother than otherwise imagined.[29] Students of her poetry have usually disregarded her film, and conversely those who know and admire her extraordinarily significant documentary and other minor or major roles in documentary filmmaking exhibit a prosaic awareness of her poetry.[30] Each of these three (not two) phases has its own formal force. The first three volumes have their internal formal dynamics, punctuated by *The House Is Black*, and they resumed in a third phase with *Another Birth*, with the final posthumous volume, *Let Us Believe in the Commencement of the Cold Season*, staging her swan song exit.

In his encyclopedia entry on Farrokhzad, Michael Hillmann, a leading scholar of Farrokhzad's life and poetry, has drawn necessary attention to the forms of her early poetry and argued against dismissing them as "juvenile." This is a very important argument, until he begins to racialize critical perspectives on poetic forms and to posit the presumably "Iranian critics" against the evidently "American formalist critics" who take form more seriously, as if before these "American formalist critics," who seem to be racially predisposed to be "formalist," Iranian, or African, or Latin American poets were entirely clueless about form! In addition to being the rather nasty left-over of an old-fashioned Orientalist trope that Iranians and other Persian-speaking people do not understand their own poetry well, it is a patently wrong assumption that non-American poets or critics were bereft of any serious understanding of form, in both classical and contemporary readings of poetry. The entire gamut of Persian literary theory from Shams Qais Razi in the thirteenth century to Shafi'i-Kadkani in the twenty-first, and scores of others in between, is of course completely devoted to form, and scarcely anything but form.[31] This is, of course, to disregard entirely Iranian literary critics such as Abd al-Qahir al-Jorjani (1009–78), who were busy extending their theorization of form to Arabic poetics. American, Iranian, American-Iranian, Arab, Indian, and the like are all sordid racialized categories, not schools of thought of literary theorization. The slightest facility with any aspect of Persian or Arabic or Sanskrit literary criticism clearly shows that people of varied literary cultures have been deeply aware and informed by form, long before "American formalist critics" were anywhere to be found.

Form is, of course, crucial in Farrokhzad's poetry, in all her poems, from her very first to her very last and into her posthumously published volume. But the form she seamlessly infused with the subversive forces of her poems is what made them both—form and substance now inseparable—so potent and publicly subversive. Consider her seminal poem from her collection *Wall*, "Gonah/Sin," which works through her earliest preoccupation with narrative, "Do-beyti/Quatrains" or "Char-pareh/Four hemistich." The bold, daring, and defiant disposition of the poem is precisely in putting a classical form (also known as *fahlaviat*) that goes all the way back to Baba Taher Oryan and Omar Khayyam and puts it to use in a subversive encounter, which she makes public through the Trojan Horse of a beloved classical form. The original form of "Do-Beyti" is a staccato, Haiku-like event, whisperish and subversive. But here in Farrokhzad's "Sin" it becomes the unit of telling a story, narrating an event, an illicit sexual encounter:

> I sinned, a sin full of pleasure—
> In an embrace that was hot and burning,
> I sinned in between two arms
> That were sizzling, vengeful, and fierce.
>
> In that dark and quiet hide-out,
> I gazed at his eyes full of mysteries,
> My heart trembling impatiently in my chest
> From the desires of his eyes full of needs.
>
> In that dark and silent hideout
> I sat by his side bewildered,
> His lips poured lust onto my lips,
> Saving me from the sorrows of my heart.
>
> I sang into his ears the story of love:
> "I want you my sweetheart,
> I desire your life-affirming embrace
> I desire you my insane lover!"
>
> Lust was aflame in his eyes,
> Dancing like red wine in a goblet—

My body on the soft bed
Danced shimmeringly on his chest.

I sinned, a sin full of pleasure,
By the side of a body shivering and unconscious—
Oh God, I have no idea what I did,
In that dark and silent hide-out.[32]

This short and defiant poem suddenly gendered the nation in which it was composed, recited, published, whispered, and now read out loud with disbelief and incredulity. For a young woman, a divorcée, having an extramarital affair with a married man to come out and publicly share a poetic moment of sexual intimacy (fictional or real) was the most subversive and yet real force of this poem. Poetry is always a form of ventriloquism: the poet composes but someone else, someone inconspicuous, is reciting. The result is at once subversive and liberating, absented yet formidably present: the entire nation, we might say, entered its liberated postcolonial moment with this poem, when the very condition of postcoloniality was decolonized in its gendered forms, as all its inherited taboos were daringly dismantled: a woman, a poetic voice, declared her desires and ecstasies publicly.

Love and Eros: Forough as Diotima

Today I was working on this chapter just before rushing to class to teach Plato's *Symposium* (*circa* 385–370 BCE), and while discussing the position of Diotima as voiced by Socrates, it occurred to me that Forough Farrokhzad did not have a situation too different from the prophetic voice of a woman among seven rambunctious and eloquent men competing to tell each other what love/Eros is. As you may recall, in Plato's *Symposium* a party of seven men discuss the meaning of love. When it is time for Socrates, he introduces the figure of Diotima, a prophetess, and states his position through the absented voice of hers. Why did Plato opt for Socrates to become the mouthpiece of an absentee prophetess and speak of love, not of the beloved, articulating the transmutation of earthly to divine love? When discussing this passage in Socrates' speech, my mind wandered off to Forough Farrokhzad's poetry:

> Then who are these lovers of wisdom, Diotima, I said, if they are neither the wise nor the ignorant? Why, at this point it's clear even to a child, she said, that they are those intermediate between both of these, and that Eros is among them. For wisdom is surely among the most beautiful of things, but Eros is love of the beautiful, so Eros is necessarily a philosopher, a lover of wisdom, and, being a philosopher, intermediate between wisdom and ignorance. His birth is the cause of this too: for he is of a wise and resourceful father, but of an unwise and resourceless mother.[33]

I have always thought that Persian poets have been our true philosophers, for even the most potent philosophers who performed their philosophies in Persian or even in Arabic were also poets: from Naser Khosrow (1008–88) in the eleventh, over Baba Afzal Kashani (died *circa* 1214) in the thirteenth, to Muhammad Iqbal (1877–1938) in the twentieth century. But in the case of Forough Farrokhzad, this proclivity assumes a particularly erotic disposition, as best here described by Diotima in effect providing the most compelling account of Eros in the *Symposium*. By far, Farrokhzad's most pronouncedly erotic poem, "Asheqaneh," is almost entirely untranslatable, beginning with her title, for which there is no straightforward English equivalent, but something like "lovingly" or "loveliness." Yet, as soon as I say so, these suggestions fail to come close to the expression "*asheqaneh*"—which means something akin to amorous, being in love, where the word for love/*eshq*/ Eros and Lover/*asheq* assume the suffix "*aneh*," which makes it something like "in the mood of love." Therefore, "lovingly" is the closest I can bring myself to suggest. I am now going to venture to translate it in its entirety as best as I can, not to convey its sublime passion but only to share (hopefully) its compositional disposition and power:

Oh you who have colored the night with my dreaming of you
Made my bosom heavy with the aroma of you!

Oh you who have spread yourself over my eyes,
Given me more joy than sorrow—
Just like rain washing the body of the soil,
You have cleansed my being from pollution!

Oh you the palpitations of my burning body:
A fire in the shadow of my eyelashes—
Oh you more bounteous than the wheat fields,
More fruitful than golden branches!

Oh you the opened gates to suns:
Against the darkness of all doubts—
With you I am no longer afraid of any pains,
If anything, I have the pain of happiness!

My tightened heart and so much light!
The commotion of life in the depth of the grave!
Oh your two eyes my green pastures:
The seal of your eyes burned into my eyes!

If I had you in me before,
How would I confuse others with you?
It's a dark pain, the pain of desire:
To go on and self-deprecate in vain!

Resting your head on darkened chests,
Polluting your chest with the dirt of hatred—
Finding in caresses the fangs of snakes,
Detecting venom in the smiles of lovers!

Putting gold into the hands of thieves,
Getting lost in the vastness of the bazaars—
Oh you intertwined with my soul:
Resurrecting me from my own grave!

Like a star with two golden wings:
Descending from the farthest skies!
Because of you my solitude vanished —
My body smelled of love-making!

You the water in the dried brooks of my chest!
You the flood in the flows of my veins!
In a world so cold and dark:
My steps locked with your steps!

Oh you hiding under my skin,
Like blood boiling through my skin!
Burning my hair with your caresses—
Setting my cheeks on fire with desire!

Oh you stranger to my dress:
Familiar with the pastures of my body!
Oh you the bright sunrise with no sunset:
The sun of the southern climes!

Oh you more joyous than the dawn!
Fresher and more bountiful than spring!
This is no longer love, this is madness—
Like a chandelier in silence and darkness!

When love awakened in my chest,
Top to toe I am selfless:
This is no longer I, no longer I:
Wasted is the life I lived with myself!

My lips the place of your kisses!
My eyes fixed with expectations of your kisses!
Oh you the shivering of ecstasy in my body:
The contours of your body my only dress!

Oh I want to burst open:
So my joy is mixed with sadness for a moment!
Oh I want to stand up straight
Crying like a cloud ceaselessly!

This tight heart of mine and such rising smoke of incense!
Loud music of harp and sitar from a basement?
Such a tight space and these soaring flights?
This dark night and such songs?

Oh your looks like a magical lullaby!
Like a cradle for a restless child!
Oh your breathing like a gentle breeze when half asleep:
Washing away the trembling of my anxieties!
Oh you asleep in the smiles of all my tomorrows—
Deeply penetrated all my worlds!

Oh you having stirred in me the temper of my poetry—
Having set so much fire to my poetry!
When you raised the fever of my poetry so high,
You set my poetry all on fire![34]

As I was translating this poem, one line after another, I had a sense of Farrokhzad looking over my shoulder, as it were, motherly, sisterly, lovingly, and for every line that I translated she would look at me disapprovingly and whisper: "Oh really? That's the best you can do? Try again!" And I would try again! What I have offered is mostly a verbatim translation of the poem, with the full understanding that the passion and power of the original, which I feel as I write, is impossible to translate into any language, as it would be ludicrous to translate a Chopin nocturne, or a music piece by Hossein Alizadeh. This untranslatability itself is integral to Farrokhzad's poetic mystic and metaphysics. It is only a signature definition to be a reader of her poetry in her and my mother tongue. It is the sign of a privilege, a rite of passage, with which one is born into a language, not in a certain geographical territory but in fact in her poetry.

The Metaphysics of the Here and Now: From Temporal Hal *to Mystical* Ahval

Paramount in the poetry of Farrokhzad is a sense of the Here and Now, a material metaphysics of the Here and Now, as we might call it, of the present tense and evident space, where the past has ended and the future has not yet started. She was the contemporary, the mother and single parent of our being-in-the-world. The Persian and Arabic word "*hal*/now" or "*aknun*/this instance" has a constellation of significance, among them the condition of being, as in "how are you" or "*hal-e shoma chetoreh*," implying how you feel at this moment, or how your moment feels.³⁵ A related concept is *zaman*/time, but it also means death in the sense that the time has lapsed and that it is time to die. Hence, there is an existential anxiety built into the moment of the now/*hal*.³⁶ The plural of *hal* is *ahval*, which assumes even more mystical significance in Persian literary and poetic legacy. *Hal* here is a passing thought, feeling, sensation, while the plural of it is a succession of such feelings. They are transient and passing, and may only last for a moment, as opposed to *maqam*/station, which has been earned through prolonged periods of meditation and exercises. Forough Farrokhzad was a master diagnostician of *hal*, of how and where we were in the world. In her poetry she literally invented the condition of being in the moment. This needs more explanation—specifically, in the Persian Sufi sense.

In his *al-Tasfiyyeh fi Ahval al-Mutesavvefeh: Sufi Nameh/Purification in the Conditions of the Mystics: Sufi Nameh*, the prominent Sufi theorist Qotb al-Din Ardeshir al-Ebadi (1098–1152) identified seven stages in the external and seven in the internal *ahval* of a mystic. The external ones include *showq*/ecstasy, *muraqabah*/spiritual exercises, *haya*/shame, *vafa*/loyalty, *sama'*/ritual dance, *vajd*/ecstasy caused by *sama'*, and *sohbat*/socialization.³⁷ These external conditions are coupled with the following internal stages: *tafakkor*/thinking, *basirat*/perception, *ma'refat*/gnosis, *mohabbat*/love, *jam'iyyat*/presence of the mind, *moshahdat*/perception, and finally *tamkin*/resignation.³⁸ Look at these *ahval*, conditions of ecstatic being, one more time: all of them, internal and external, are gathered in Farrokhzad's poetic moment, oscillating, as they often do, between temporal *hal* and mystical *ahval*. She seduced her leaders into the bosom of her poems, and we all feel at home there and then. This is an atemporal time, perhaps best evident in one of her most glorious poems, "Ghorubi Abadi/An Eternal Sunset" (1963):

Ruz ya Shab? . . .

Is it day or night?
No, my friend: It is an eternal sunset!
As two doves fly into the wind
Like two white coffins—
And some sounds
Of commotion from a distance—
From that strange prairie—
Unstable and wandering
Just like the motions of the wind—

Something ought to be said!
Something ought to be said!
My heart wishes to pair with darkness!
Something ought to be said!

What a heavy obliviousness:
An apple falls from the branch,

The yellow seeds of linen
Break under the beaks of my loving canaries!
The flowers of fava beans
Submit their cobalt senses
To the ecstatic winds,
To the liberation from the vague fears of change!
And here in me,
In my mind,
Oh . . . there is nothing on my mind:
Except for the whirling thick red particles,
And my gaze—
Just like a lie—
Is ashamed and broken!

I think of a moon—
Of a word in a poem!
I think of a fountain—
I think of a delusion buried into the earth—
Of the rich aroma of a wheat field,
Of the myth of bread,
Of the innocence of playful games,
And of that long narrow alley
That was full of the aromas of acacias!
I think of the bitter awakening after a game,
And of a bewilderment after an alley,
And of a long emptiness after the aroma of acacias!

Heroisms?
Ah . . .
Horses are so old!
Love?
It's lonesome and from a low window
It stares at the deserts bereft of legendary lovers!
At a passageway with a confused memory
Of the crawling of an ankle through an anklet!
Wishes?
They lose themselves
In the cruel synchrony of closed doors—
Eyes permanently closed!
You'd get tired!

I think of a home
With the languorous breathing of its ivies,
With its lights
Brightened just like pupils of eyes,

With its lights
Meditative, lazy, worriless—
Of a child with bounteous smile,
Just like concentric circles on water
And a bloodied body just like a bunch of grapes!

I think of ruins,
And of the plunder of dark blowing,
And of a suspicious light
That penetrates through the window at night,
And of a tiny little grave,
As tiny as the body of a child!

Work . . . Work?
Yes, but inside that big desk
A hidden enemy lives
That chews on you slowly—
As it does on wood and notebook,
And on thousands of other useless things,
And ultimately you would plunge into a cup of tea,
Just like a boat into a whirlpool
And into the depth of horizons where
You'd see nothing but the thick smoke of a cigarette
And some incomprehensible sketches!

A star?
Yes, hundreds upon hundreds but
All beyond the incarcerated nights—
A bird?
Yes, hundreds upon hundreds but
All in distant memories
With their useless pride in flapping their wings!

I am thinking of a scream in the streets,
I think of a harmless mouse
Who occasionally passes through the wall!

Something ought to be said,
Something ought to be said:
Early in the morning
In moments of trembling,
When the air—like the sensation of pubescence—
Suddenly mixes with something ambiguous:
I wish to submit
To a rebellion—

I wish to pour
From that massive cloud!
I wish to say:
No, No, No!

Let us go!
Something ought to be said:
A drink, or a bed, or solitude, or else sleep?
Let us go!³⁹

Just read these lines again—the English works better in this particular translation. We are all in a revelatory moment, a *hal*, a condition, that has seized Farrokhzad and with it she has grabbed hold of us. "The Eternal Sunset" is neither here nor there, it is the moment of the birth, life, and death of the whole of humanity, all gathered in one. The repeated pleading: "Something ought to be said!/ Something ought to be said!" rings like the TICK-tock, TICK-tock of a cosmic clock. All of this reads through a sudden, spontaneous, and sustained material metaphysics of the Here and Now! There is no other way of reading this astounding poem, except as a moment of revelation, irreducible to anything that we have ever heard or read before. This is thinking, being, feeling, and knowing poetically. This is Rumi, Hafez, and Khayyam all coming back to life and living a radically real contemporary life! I was much happier with this translation than I would ever be with "Asheqaneh." This works better, I think, because the original poem is meditative, not ecstatic. There is very little left to be said after this poem, a moment of naked truth unveiling itself. There is no rhyme or reason moving from one stanza to the next, nothing except the inner force of a *hal*, of a sensation, that accepts and celebrates and lets loose its extemporaneous encounter with truth.

Invention of the Present

In *Inventions of a Present: The Novel in Its Crisis of Globalization* (2024), the late Fredric Jameson has gathered a number of his as usual brilliant essays to underline our literary location in the present world and the history that has made it happen. The insights are plausible, and the novels he has marshalled to discuss in this volume help make the point. To justify his preoccupation with the contemporary novelistic voices, Jameson has written:

> What is new and distinctive about the novel today, what is historically unique about the emergent situation of the works discussed here, is that they try to write the collective or at least register the crisis of the individual attempting to do so. Not even the nation-state functions any longer to frame our innumerable destinies, although it is still there to mark its failure to do so: still national-historical in their singularities, other forms of collectivity, residual or emergent, offer to heal a breach its subjects may not have been aware of until registered in

the works examined here . . . "There is no present," cried Mallarmé, "no—a present does not exist . . . absent the voice of the Multitude, absent-everything. Poorly advised, those who would declare themselves their own contemporaries." In these novels we can begin to hear, however faintly, the voices of contemporaries.[40]

"To write the collective": novelists, poets, filmmakers, and artists of all colors and ranks share the same point of departure. Entirely against the grain of Mallarmé's declarative, I hear in Farrokhzad's resounding voice of writing the collective that Jameson has heard in the novels that he has examined, the radical contemporaneity of a voice that was the singing melody of her time and the people she shared it with in fact and with ferocity. And yes, the nation, not the nation-state, remains the paramount and most potent form of feeling, knowing, being, and claiming the collective. Not the post-national, not the "DissemiNation," as Homi Bhabha is wont of saying: but the nation as the collective that the poet sings. In one poem by Forough Farrokhzad there is more alacrity and awareness of that sense of the present, both rooted and liberated, than in volumes of politically imbalanced declaratives. Nima Yushij's archetypal inauguration of the voice of that present soon rooted and branched and flowered in Mehdi Akhavan-e Sales' sense of the past and Ahmad Shamlou's vision of a liberated future, before it reached Forough Farrokhzad's present, "*hal*," and from there to anticipate Sohrab Sepehri's "presence" or "*hozur*," and then rest its case with Esmail Kho'i's Nowhereville, "*Bidarkoja*," in his permanent exilic condition in England, of all places. Here, in one of her signature masterpieces, "Mordab/Swamp" (1963), Farrokhzad captured that momentous evidence of the present, of her mind, soul, and above all body "writing the collective":

Shab siahi kard o bimari gereft . . .

The night darkened and became sick:
Eyes are rebelling in awareness!
The eyes can't stop seeing, alas!
The eyes can't cover themselves, alas!
They went deep and found me an old death swamp,
Found my entire existence an aging expectation,
They saw my desert and my loneliness,
My paper moon and my paper sun:
Like an old embryo fighting with the uterus,
Tearing the wall of the uterus with its fangs.
Alive but desperate to be born,
Dead but the desire of dying in it . . .

Wow, if I had a way towards a sea!
Why would I fear ever plunging . . .

Oh deer, deer of prairies!
If some time on the crossings of wildflowers

You found a river singing,
Flowing to the blue color of the seas,
Laying on the back of its rebellion,
Flowing from the silky flow of itself,
The mane of the horse of wind in its fist,
The red soul of the moon on its back,
Shot through the green thighs of shafts,
Stealing the virgin perfume of bushes . . .
Remember the sleep of that sleepless swamp
Recall the death in a swamp . . .[41]

The contrasting imageries of the fresh hope of prairies and the dreadful fact of swamps holds the running river, and with it the poem, together. The insomniac narrator dreams while wide awake, as the observing eyes are both conscious and troubled. The self-description is quite overwhelming, a living organism wishing to be born, a dead corpse hoping to die. Paradoxes here come in parallels. From the swamp the dream is to reach the sea, to travel through the prairies, although the dream is futile and the narrator succumbs to the overwhelming (inevitable) fate. But still, the collective is singing, dreaming, dreading, and it is fully aware of the nightmares and the wrong sentiments that trouble the fated destination. Keep in mind that the poems in *Another Birth* were written between 1959 and 1963, and published in 1963, in effect pouring out the troubled soul of the nation in the aftermath of the US-UK military coup of 1953, when the nation was interrupted by the diabolic forces of domestic tyranny and imperial thuggery.

A Solitary Soul

During my graduate studies years at the University of Pennsylvania in Philadelphia, for about five years (1979–84) I was the chief doctoral student of Phillip Rieff (1922–2006), eventually writing my doctoral dissertation under his guidance. The most renowned Freudian sociologist of his generation, Rieff used to teach a seminar for which he did not accept more than ten to twelve students, and each of his seminar sessions was devoted to the study of only one single text, and only a few pages of that text. Max Weber's "Politics as a Vacation," for example, or Nietzsche's *Beyond God and Evil*, Paul's Letter to the Corinthians, and Kafka's "In the Penal Colony" were among these texts that we read during these precious years of my apprenticeship with him. One semester, Rieff devoted the entire seminar to a close reading of Kierkegaard's *The Present Age*. I became deeply invested in Kierkegaard after that seminar and began an independent reading and tutorial with Rieff on the rest of Kierkegaard's work. Something quite strange began to happen in the back of my mind: as I read Kierkegaard closely and widely, the poetry of Farrokhzad assumed a renewed significance. This was not entirely unusual, for my undergraduate years in Iran had been formative to my intellectual disposition for the rest of my academic career. It was at that point that I began to realize there was a solitary world at the heart of Farrokhzad's poetic persona that no scandalous love affair could have filled or fulfilled or compromised. That sense of solitude is decisive to come to terms with her poetic persona. She came from the depth of our history, with pain and pleasure alike. A generation of US-based cliché feminism remains tone-deaf to her material metaphysics, as her admirers of this brand have turned her into fodder for their own limited courage and compromised imagination. She has not been saved from her most ardent supporters and their jaundiced feminism. In my mind, Rieff, Kierkegaard, and Farrokhzad have a perhaps unsuspecting, perhaps perfectly logical, conversation.

Teased out of that banal "feminism" of the suburban Virginia vintage, Farrokhzad shines in her bold poetry, the sustained textual evidence of her material metaphysics of the Here and Now. How else would we find in her poetry the evidence of our own existential angst if our moral contingency is not educated by her sensitivities. Years after my earliest exposure to Farrokhzad, I would remember her when reading Kierkegaard with Philip Rieff, particularly *The Sickness unto Death* (1849), through which I would rediscover Farrokhzad's poetry. It would take me years to distance myself from all the variations on the theme of the Area Studies soft-Orientalism "field" and the abuse to which Farrokhzad's poetry (among many other gems of a national heritage) was subjected by the generation closest to her, laying a false claim on her. As I cleansed my mind from those banal and abusive readings, I eventually found my way back to her own precious poetry totally distanced from such credal clichés—except as professional duty to know the details of "the work" done on Farrokhzad to make her read North American feminism. It was now that I realized what abusive terror these nomenklatura and the apparatchik of the "Area Studies" cabal had perpetrated on Farrokhzad, as they did with everything else they touched. The field was flawed, weak, ill-educated, and above all blasé.[42]

The remarkable fact that Farrokhzad has had an enduring influence on how I have read Kierkegaard points to something even more serious: this constellation of the six poets I explore in this book has shaped and colored and formed how my generation has read just about anything else since our adolescence, when, as a provincial student in Tehran, I effectively grew up with these poets—perhaps Forough Farrokhzad in particular, because I was still in high school when my cousin Sharifeh Parvizi, who was a few years older than me, and my other cousins, began reading and interpreting her work to me. Years later, Kierkegaard in turn helped me understand Farrokhzad better, as Farrokhzad helped me decipher the particular moments of existential despair which she enabled us to decode. Kierkegaard's *The Sickness unto Death* (1849), which he published under the pseudonym Anti-Climacus, is usually read in the context of Christian existentialism, where the Danish philosopher has concentrated on the concept of despair, which, as in all his other works, he Christianizes. But it is this passage of Kierkegaard on solitude that now most appealed to me as I was rereading Farrokhzad:

> Generally the need of solitude is a sign that there is spirit in a man after all, and it is a measure for what spirit there is. The purely twaddling inhuman and too-human men are to such a degree without feeling for the need of solitude that,

like a certain species of social birds (the so-called love birds), they promptly die if for an instant they have to be alone ... In the constant sociability of our age people shudder at solitude to such a degree that they know no other use to put it to but (oh, admirable epigram!) as a punishment for criminals. But after all it is a fact that in our age it is a crime to have spirit, so it is natural that such people, the lovers of solitude, are included in the same class with criminals.[43]

She taught us not to shudder at solitude—hers or ours, or the world's—but to embrace and own it. She elevated the condition of solitude into a moment of feeling, knowing, being with her. That solitude in the case of Farrokhzad is closer to the Sufi idea of *khalvat*/solitude and *hal*/condition, both tantamount to a present in the light of a self-conscious soul, for which sensation we might turn to the seminal poem of Farrokhzad in her posthumous volume "Iman Biavarim beh Aghaz-e Fasl-e Sard/Let Us Believe in the Commencement of the Cold Season"—a revelatory, prophetic moment, where we learned how to live, breathe, and anticipate death, or else how to think of life at the end of the cold season:

Va in manam
Zani Tanha ...

And this is I:
A lonesome woman—
At the commencement of the cold season,
At the beginning of grasping the polluted essence of the earth,
And the simple and sad sorrow of the sky,
And the incapacities of these cement-like hands!

Time passed,
Time passed and the clock struck four times,
Struck four times:
Today is the first day of Winter!
I know the secret of seasons,
And understand the words instances speak!
The savior is buried in the grave
And the earth, the welcoming earth,
Is an allusion to peace ...

At the threshold of a cold season:
In the memorial ceremony of mirrors,
And the sorrowful gathering of pale experiences,
And this sunset:
Pregnant with the knowledge of silence:
How can you command someone
Who walks so patiently,
Heavily,

Bewilderedly,
To stop!
How can you tell the man he is not alive,
That he has never been alive? . . .

Oh my beloved!
My one and only beloved!
What dark clouds await the feast of the sun! . . .

In the street the wind is blowing:
This is the beginning of the ruins!
The day your hands were ruined
The wind was blowing, too!
The precious stars,
The precious paper stars,
When in the heavens the lies begin to blow
How can we seek solace in the verses of the prophets
With broken heads?
We reach each other like people dead for thousands of years,
And then the sun will judge our rotten corpses!

I am cold:
I am cold and I can never be warm again!
Oh beloved,
My most precious beloved:
How old was that wine?
Look how heavy time is in this place,
And how the fish are gnawing on my flesh!
Why do you always keep me at the bottom of the sea?

I am cold and I detest shell earrings!
I am cold and I know
That from all the red delusions of a wild anemone
Nothing will remain except for a few drops of blood . . .

I told my mother "it's all over":
I told her it always happens before you expect it,
We need to send a condolence message to the newspapers . . .

Perhaps truth was those two young arms,
Those two young arms
That were being buried under the relentless pouring of snow!
And next year when spring makes love with the sky
Behind the window,
And in her body gushes forth the green light branches of blossoms,

Oh my Beloved, my most precious beloved:
Let us believe in the commencement of the cold season . . .⁴⁴

Forough Farrokhzad, Audre Lorde, and Claudia Rankine

Cut: some thirty years later I was teaching Claudia Rankine, the Jamaican-American poet's *Citizen: An American Lyric* (2014), and noticed that I was reading her as if I was reading Farrokhzad, or perhaps more accurately I was reading her in light of my active memories of Farrokhzad. This prompted me to do a bit more research on how Farrokhzad is being received here in the US, and I found out that she is invariably compared with Sylvia Plath (1932–63)—which on the surface seems perfectly logical. This, in turn, reminded me of how I have always thought of Audre Lorde (1934–92) as being much closer to Farrokhzad's sensibilities.⁴⁵ All of these comparisons with Sylvia Plath, however, I thought were a bit overblown. But it then began to dawn on me why it is that, when I read Farrokhzad, I hear American poets such as Claudia Rankine, Audre Lorde, and Maya Angelou, or even jazz singers like Nina Simone. Closer to her neighborhood, I have also always taught her in my classes next to the Egyptian painter Inji Aflatoun (1924–89) and the Algerian novelist Assia Djebar (1936–2015). Then I began to wonder why it is that none of these "Area Studies" folks go anywhere near an African-American, Latin American, Caribbean, or Arab poet or artist when reading Farrokhzad comparatively. There are two issues at work here, I thought: a deeply colonized, white-identified mind and an astounding ignorance of the full tapestry of American life beyond its white culture. Consider here Farrokhzad's "Beh Aftab Salami Do-bareh Khaham Dad/I Shall Greet the Sun Again" (1963), where her global character requiring such comparisons comes through. The globality of that character is deeply compromised if we do not read her in a wider frame of reference:

> I shall greet the sun again!
> The brook that was flowing in me,
> The clouds that were my extended thoughts,
> The painful growing of the poplar tree
> That were keeping me company crossing
> Through the dry seasons,
> The flocks of crows
> That were bringing me the aroma
> Of nocturnal farms,
> My mother who lived in the mirror
> And who looked like my old self,
> The earth
> That the lust of repeating me
> Filled its agitated interiors
> With green seeds:
> I shall greet them all again!

I am coming!
I am coming!
I am coming!

With my hair locks
The extension of the aromas of the subterranean earth,
With my eyes
The thick experiences of darkness,
With bushes
That I have picked from the woods
On the other side of the wall!

I am coming!
I am coming!
I am coming!

And in the threshold
That is filling with love:
I shall greet one more time
Those who love!
And I shall greet the girl
Who is still standing there
In the vestibule
Filled with love![46]

The more we place her in that globality of comparative reference, the more rooted she becomes in her poetic particularities. Consider how in her poem "Delam Bara-ye Baghcheh Misuzad/I Feel Sorry for the Flowerbed" (1963) she gives a family portrait of herself and her parents and siblings, all gathered around a flowerbed:

Kasi beh fekr-e golha nist . . .

No one thinks of the flowers,
No one thinks of the fish,
No one wants to believe
That the flowerbed is dying—
That the heart of the flowerbed
Has swollen under the sun!
That the mind of the flowerbed
Is being vacated of all green memories,
And the feeling of the flowerbed
Seems to be something abstract:
Rotten in the solitude of the flowerbed.

Then comes a family portrait: the father could not care less about the flowerbed and is mostly in his room reading history books; the mother meanwhile is constantly praying on her prayer rug, fearful of hell; the brother considers the flowerbed a graveyard, laughing at the chaos and confusion of the grass; the sister meanwhile is friendly to the flowers, whispering her sorrows to them. At the end of this portrait comes a depiction of the courtyard:

> Our courtyard is lonesome,
> Our courtyard is lonesome:
> All day long
> We can hear from the outside
> The sounds of things
> Blowing up into pieces—
> And of explosions!
> Our neighbors are all planting
> Grenades and machine guns
> In their flowerbeds—
> Instead of flowers!
> Our neighbors have all covered their ceramic pools
> And the ceramic pools have unwillingly,
> All become hidden ammunition depots,
> As the children of the neighborhood
> Have all filled their school backpacks with little bombs
> Our courtyard is confused!
>
> I am scared of the time
> That has lost its heart,
> I am scared
> Imagining the futility of so many hands!
> Of imagining the alienation of so many faces!
> Just like a student who is madly in love with trigonometry
> I feel lonely!
>
> I believe we can take the flowerbed to the hospital—
>
> I think . . .
> I think . . .
> I think . . .
>
> And the heart of the flowerbed is swollen under the sun—
> And the mind of the flowerbed is—
> Slowly ever so slowly—
> Forgetting its green memories![47]

As I finished this translation, I realized that this has been the most precious chapter for me to write. Repeatedly I have had to stop to catch my breath—for these poems literally take your breath away. I am now confident that these poems were lost on all of us in and through our youth, especially to professional feminists on North American campuses (bless their captured imagination) making pitiful careers out of these precious poems, misreading, abusing, and appropriating them without the slightest pause to ponder the power of their underlying aesthetic imagination.

Va pensiero: Oh, mia patria sì bella e perduta

Farrokhzad thought through and on the borderline of two vastly different conceptions of her homeland: one deeply dark and foreboding, and the other rambunctiously satirical and hilarious. "Ayeh-ha-ye Zamini/Earthly Verses" (1963) is one and "Ay Marz-e Por Gohar/Oh Most Precious Homeland" (1963) the other. When we read these two poems back-to-back today—a revolution, a war, and a succession of social uprisings against Islamist tyranny after they were originally composed—they still define the contours of a conception of homeland at once scarily dark and yet equally and defiantly self-deprecating. In between the two overwhelming sentiments, Farrokhzad located and defined the existential parameters of her homeland. The paradoxical feelings were the past indices of the post-CIA-MI6 military coup era that had brought the runaway Pahlavi monarch back to power. These two poems are the results of that paradoxical moment; having been published in the volume *Another Birth*, they mark Farrokhzad at the maturest phase of her short life-time career as a poet. Let us first consider "Earthly Verses"—and here is an almost verbatim translation of some of its key stanzas:

> Then the sun grew cold:
> And all blessings abandoned the earth,
> And the grass dried all over the prairies,
> And the fish dried in the seas,
> And the earth refused to accept any more corpses!
>
> Through all the pale windows
> The night—
> Just like a suspicious vision—
> Was in constant commotion!
> And the roads
> Abandoned their ends
> In darkness—
>
> No one thought of love anymore,
> No one thought of victory anymore,
> And no one thought of anything anymore:

In caves of solitude
Alienation came to life—
Blood smelled of opium and hashish:
Pregnant women gave birth to headless children—
And mortified cradles
Sought refuge in graves!

What dark and bitter times!
Bread had conquered
The glorious power of prophecy!
Hungry and pathetic prophets
Run away from the divine rendezvous!
As Christ's lost lambs
Could not hear the voice of any shepherd
In the bewilderment of any desert! . . .

The sun was dead:
The sun was dead and tomorrow
In the minds of children
Had a vague and lost meaning—
And they drew the meaning of this old idea
In their homework
With a big black dot!

The People:
The forsaken people—
Sullen, sad, and bewildered—
Under the bad-omen weight of their bodies
Run away from one exile to another,
As the painful urge of murder
Was swollen in their hands.

Sometime just a spark,
A little spark,
Blew up this lifeless silent society
From the inside!
They would charge into each other,
Men cut each other's throat
And in a bed of blood
They raped prepubescent girls!

They were lost in their own fears,
And the frightful sense of sinfulness
Had crippled their blinded and perturbed souls.

During the execution ceremonies
When the rope
Exploded the frightened eyes of a condemned
From their sockets,
They would sulk into themselves—
And their old and tired nerves
Would moan from a frightful lust!

And yet on the margins of the squares:
You would still see these little criminals
Standing and staring
At the ceaseless falling waters
From fountains!

Perhaps still
Behind their deserted eyes—
In the depth of frozenness—
Something half alive and confused
Had remained
Wishing
In this anemic struggle
To believe in the purity of songs of water!
Perhaps!
But what an endless emptiness!
The sun has died
And no one knew that the name of that sad bird
That had run away from the hearts
Was Faith!

Oh the voice of the prisoner:
Could from any side of this hateful night
The splendor of your hopelessness
Carve a tunnel towards light?
Oh the voice of the prisoner:
Oh the last of all voices . . .[48]

Complete darkness and a desperate search for light: she saw a terrorizing fact behind the phenomenon of humanity that she faced. She sometimes sensed a sign of salvation, but only ephemeral and passing. The terror of the time has become internalized in character traits. Society is at a loss, politics futile, hope fruitless. This dark and menacing image is in sharp contrast with her most satirical poem of the same period, lampooning her homeland and the range of its hypocrisies. Both poems appeared in the single volume *Another Birth*, one after the other, offering a deeply conflicted and contradictory vision of the homeland. "Oh Most Precious Homeland!" (1963) is also self-referential and mocks autobiography, when the poet goes and secures a birth certificate for herself!

I succeeded:
I registered myself!
I adorned myself with a name on a birth certificate,
And my existence was identified by a number!
Therefore Long Live Number 678!
Issued from District Number 5 resident of Tehran!

I can now rest assured in every respect:
The beloved bosom of my motherland,
The pacifier of all the glorious historical heritage,
The lullaby of Culture and Civilization!
And all the gobbledygook of Law!
Oh yes:
From every respect I can now rest assured!

I was so happy that
I rushed straight to my window
And for 678 times I inhaled and exhaled
The air full of the stench of manure, garbage, and piss—
And under 678 promissory notes
And under 678 job applications, I signed:
Forough Farrokhzad . . .

With my first official glance
From behind the curtain
I can see 678 poets
Who—oh bastards!—
Disguised as alien beggars
Are looking for rhyme and rhythm
In dumpsters![49]

The poem continues apace in the same vein, making a mockery of all the official icons of pompous nationalism, but at the same time positing the nation as the unit of thinking, feeling, and imagining the collective. Put together, these two pieces place Farrokhzad at the crossroads of two major currents of her time, one politically daunting and the other frivolously emancipatory. In poems such as "Earthly Verses" and "Oh Most Precious Homeland!" Forough Farrokhzad detailed her existential angst about belonging to a nation—and in doing so she invented the present on which the entirety of a history rests. When we place her next to poets such as Audre Lorde and Claudia Rankine, her political prowess becomes more potent, in our reading them altogether speaking of a defiant recasting of the real. There is, to be sure, a solitary soul at the very pulse of Farrokhzad's poetry, but from that solitude she also defined the society of sentiments that defines a nation. As such, she wrote the collective in her invention of the present in both poetic and political terms, with a defiantly postcolonial nation as the premise of her poetic consciousness. There and then she would articulate a metaphysics of the Here and Now: from temporal *hal* to mystical *ahval*—wedding, as it were, the metaphysics of her homeland to the poetics of its present. Love and Eros would mark Forough as Diotima, speaking in tongues but still overwhelmingly present and powerful. In her poetry, she went through the purgatory of three successive volumes—*The Captive, The Wall,* and *Rebellion*—to get there. At the moral core of her poetry, all the while she remained a defiant Muslim woman who recast the doctrinal ideas of *ghaybat* and *zuhur*: Eschatology and Parousia to speak the materiality of her lived experiences to a theology of discontent beyond the clerical reach of the doctors of law. This would place her next to Enheduana, Sappho, and Rabe'eh, where poets themselves have become metaphors. And as such she lived a very short life to cast a very long shadow. We still live under that shadow.

Chapter 5

SOHRAB SEPEHRI: A METAPOETIC OF PRESENCE

Whenever I read a poem by Sohrab Sepehri, almost inadvertently I read it out loud, and if I am in public, I may then lower my voice and whisper it to myself. This is true even when I am reading his prose. It is as if he wrote those poems and those letters and reflections for me, just for me, or for anyone else like me, millions of Persian-speaking people around the world, who have learned how to listen to his voice. His poetic voice is amorphous; it morphs into the inner voice of whoever comes near him and hears him whisper:

> If for one day I did not watch the sunrise, the sunset felt I had committed a sin. The dusk and dawn made me a contemplative person. They taught me how to meditate and behold the unknown. I used to pray for years. The elders used to pray, and so did I. At school they used to take us to the mosque to pray. One day the door to the mosque was closed. The greengrocer on the street corner said: "Go pray on the rooftop of the mosque. You'd be closer to God by a few meters."[1]

His playful soul a kindred spirit of Forough Farrokhzad, Sohrab Sepehri (1928–80) exhibited an almost mystical (numinous, to be more precise) dwelling on the metapoetics of the Here and Now—although not on the temporal present of the time (*hal*), as she did, but on the atemporal presence (*hozur*) of the moment. Yes, allusions to Biblical and Qur'anic figures, or even the *Rig Veda*, would occasionally pop up in Sepehri's poetry. But this was all in metaphoric passing—as they all joined the preponderance of his attention to the luminous allure of the presence—of being-in-the-world, of where and when and whence and how of where we were, of where we are. Sepehri's poetry thrived on the numinous grasp of a metapoetic of presence (*hozur-e ashia'*, as he called it), giving the souls of the nation which he had mesmerized with his poetry a place to be, to find in and of themselves. Farrokhzad's sense of the present (*hal*) was external, while Sepehri's sense of presence (*hozur*) was internal. That sense of presence, of in-dwelling in the world, was the single most important feature of Sepehri's poetry, the force with which he cast a metapoetic predilection onto the entire epistemic force that Nima Yushij had inaugurated. Without Sepehri, the Nimaic temporal episteme, as well as Akhavan, Shamlou, and Farrokhzad's articulation of it, would have been vacuous and purposeless. Sepehri anchored that temporal grid with evident interiority. If the whole assemblage came together to gather and imagine a nation at the epicenter of its poetry, Sepehri's role was to give that nation a metapoetic of presence, the ease of self-evidence. Here is an example from Sepehri's poem "Hamrah/Fellow Traveler" (1961) of how that *hozur* worked:

> Between us
> The wandering deserts,
> The lightless nights,
> The dusty beds of exiles,
> The forgotten fires—
> Between us
> The "One Thousand and One Night" of searching.[2]

This is a metapoetic of presence—a presence that is fully aware of itself, a poetry that addresses itself to itself, a sense of the self that does not privilege but posits a conscious awareness of presence as *hozur* that suspends the metaphysics of meaning and purpose and replaces it with a full consciousness of the interiority of the knowing, feeling subject. It poetically suspends the assumption of a metaphysics of presence that projects a one-to-one correspondence between concepts and contexts, or meaning and perceptions. Words in Sepehri's work become poetic and therefore allegorical: words allude to the presence of the world, but they do not speculate delusional claims in assuming that knowledge infers truth. Here, poetic signature does not signify, it merely implicates. There is therefore a poetic suspension of meaning at work here, where concepts become allegories not categorical. We are therefore placed where we no longer seek a metaphysical truth but dwell in a poetic of presence. As a poet-painter, Sepehri wrote with broad and precise brushes at one and the same time. His poetry is exceptionally ocularcentric, much like, in fact, his canvases are visual poetry in action.

The Quiet Revolutionary

Painting, poetry, and traveling: Sepehri's precious and short life was triangulated in what he loved most and did best. A quiet revolutionary in matters of mind, soul, and indomitable spirit, and therefore in politics in the most subterranean sense, Sohrab Sepehri (1928–80) was born to a learned, cultivated, and prominent family that eventually settled in Kashan in central Iran, a city that left a lasting impression on his poetry and painting. Both his parents were poets and painters, and from his earliest childhood onwards he began sketching on the white walls of his house.[3] His early education in the 1930s was memorable but uneventful, growing up in a small town in the care of a loving family. By the 1940s, shortly before he turned twenty, he was introduced to Nima Yushij and Vincent van Gogh at one and the same time—under the spell of these two earliest impressions, to his last days Sepehri remained a poet-painter, with painting and poetry mixing and matching in his creative soul. He finally left his hometown of Kashan and went to Tehran to enroll in the Faculty of Fine Arts. By the 1950s he was solidly in Nima's poetic camp, while he was preoccupied with his painting. For the entire decade of the 1950s he basked in his friendship with a whole rainbow of painters and poets, chief among them his kindred soul Forough Farrokhzad, with whom he had a lasting friendship, and whose untimely and tragic death deeply affected him. This was not a romantic involvement. Sepehri never married, nor was he ever reported to have had any close and intimate relationship with anyone, male or female. More than anything else he seems to have been extremely private, solitary, and perhaps even asexual. Physical intimacy does have a pale presence in his poetry, to be sure, but compared to Forough Farrokhzad, he appears like a tame and bashful brother who left such matters to his bold, brilliant, defiant, and iconoclastic younger sister. Farrokhzad was six years younger than him—and boldly sexual in her poetry.

Sepehri's first volumes of poetry and his exhibited artwork were coming out apace. Today we remember the title of Sepehri's volumes of poetry only in an archival and retroactive way. It was not until he collected them all in 1977 and published them in one volume, which he called *Hasht Ketab/Eight Books*, that the collection of these eight books staged his monumental significance in Persian New Poetry. His earliest volumes began to appear in the early 1950s: *Marg-e Rang/The Death of Color* (1951) and *Zendegi Khwab-ha/The Life of Dreams* (1953), all the way through the tumultuous years after the CIA-MI6 coup of 1953, of which there is barely any trace in his poetry of this period. He resumed the publication of his subsequent volumes at a fast pace, with *Avar-e Aftab/The Ruins of the Sunshine* (1961) and *Sharq-e Anduh/The East of Sorrow* (1961), until we reach his iconic masterpieces, *Seda-ye Pa-ye Ab/The Sound of the Water's Footstep* (1965), *Mosafer/Traveler* (1966), *Hajm-e Sabz/The Green Volume* (1967), concluding with *Ma Hich, ma Negah/We Nothing, We the Look* (1977). He ultimately published all of these eight volumes in a single volume, *Hasht Ketab/Eight Books* (1977). The title of this collection of his books, of course, immediately brings to mind the title of Amir Khosrow Dehlavi's masterpiece *Hasht Behesht/Eight Paradises* (1302). Sepehri was a deeply learned and erudite poet, and most of his knowledge came primarily through Persian, but also through French and English, of which he seems to have had a working command.

By the mid-1950s, he had commenced his lifelong fascinations with traveling abroad, East and West, with extended stays in Paris, New York, and Japan to study painting and exhibit his artwork. He even exhibited in the Venice Biennale. By the early 1960s, he had traveled to Japan and then to India—travels that left an enduring impact on him. He composed his most famous poems and exhibited his artwork to increasing critical and commercial acclaim. He continued with his travels far and wide in Europe, India, Pakistan, Afghanistan, and deep into the Arab and Muslim world—all the way to the US, where he lived in New York for a few months.[4] His travels in Europe, the US, Japan, India, Egypt, Pakistan, and Afghanistan became definitive to his thinking. The collection of his notes by his sister, *Hanuz dar Safaram/I Am Still Traveling*, sums up this preoccupation with traveling.

Sepehri had a nomadic soul rooted in the Here and Now, much like Farrokhzad. But where she was real, he was ethereal. She dwelled. He traveled—physically, emotively, imaginatively. She rooted herself in what she saw. He sublimated whatever she saw. Born and raised in the capital city of Tehran, Farrokhzad had a proprietary claim on the entirety of her homeland, where she dwelled authoritatively. Born and raised in the provincial expanse of Kashan, Sepehri was never centripetal in his nomadic imagination. He wanted to leave. She wanted to remain. Sepehri was atemporal, ephemeral, amorphic. By placing his poetic voice at the ground zero of all other times—his own neither past, nor future, nor present, not even archetypal, but entirely atemporal—Sepehri gave meaning to all others who had this temporal disposition about their poetry. Without Sepehri, the constellation, the episteme that these six poets established, would have been too timebound to last. He made all their temporalities atemporal. He was the poet of the presence of things, of the *hozur* of things, of a mystic dwelling in the thingness of things. His poetic metaphysics was metapoetic, and as such it was physical, material, evident. There is not an iota of symbolism in or about Sepehri's poetry. He saw everything for what it was: real for real, on its surface, and then he sublimated it to his own precise poetic penchant for the sublime and the beautiful, for allusions and indirections.

There is no reading Sepehri's life without, or outside, his precious autobiographical poem, "Seda-ye Pa-ye Ab/The Sound of the Water's Footstep" (1964)—the poem that defined his moral, aesthetic, and metapoetic whereabouts.[5]

Ahl-e Kashanam . . .

I am from Kashan,
I get by fine!

I have a bit of food to eat,
A tad of intelligence,
A smidgeon of taste—
I have a mother,
More precious than a tree leaf—
A few friends,
Dearer than running water.
And then a God who is nearby:
In the midst of these Evening Primroses,
By that Pine Tree
On the surface of the self-consciousness of water,
On the law of plants!

He knew himself and he declared himself a Muslim, although in a language entirely his own, rooted in its formal allusions to who and what a Muslim is, and yet he recast the entire metaphysics of scholastic certainties into a metapoetic of his self-consciousness:

I am a Muslim:
My Qibla is a red rose,
My prayer rug the fountain,
The clay on which I pray light
The prairie is my prayer spread!

The poem unfolds apace. The poet repeats that he is from Kashan, that he is a painter, that once in a while he paints a cage of his solitude to sell to his customers, that his "ancestry" (tongue in cheek) may go back to a prostitute from the city of Bukhara—then we get to learn more about his parents and siblings, all uplifted from the ground to an ethereal identity:

My father died beyond all time spans—
When my father died, the sky was blue:
My mother suddenly woke from sleep,
My sister became beautiful,
When my father died, all police officers were poets,
The greengrocer asked me:
How many kilos of melon would you like?
I asked him:
How much will a happy heart cost per gram?
My father used to paint,
He used to make *tar* too,
He played *tar* too,
He also had beautiful calligraphy handwriting!

Then we learn more about the garden in which the poet grew up, where he used to drink water without philosophy, as he says, and would pick mulberries off trees without knowledge. He happily grew up in that Garden of Eden before knowledge, before philosophy, theory—until finally he grew up enough to move out into the world. Here I shiver as I translate:

Man beh mehmani donya raftam . . .

I went to the festive gathering of the world—
To the prairies of sadness,
To the garden of mysticism,
I went to the twinkle-lighted balcony of knowledge,
Then I ascended the ladder of religion,
Until I reached the end of the street of doubt,
And came to the cool air of full satisfaction—
I went to the wet night of kindness,
I went to visit someone on the other side of love,
I went forward, I went until I reached woman—
Until I came to the light of pleasure,

The silence of desire—
Until the full sound of solitude!

The poet then starts describing to us what he has seen in the world, a child who was smelling the moon, a doorless cage where light was fluttering ... he sees a poet who, when addressing a flower, would use formal prose ... he sees poets, jurists, trains:

I saw a train carrying light,
I saw a train carrying Islamic Jurisprudence—
And it went so heavily,
I saw a train carrying politics—
And it went so lightly ...

The poet travels, sees things in motion, sees things grow, sees wars and battles, like the battle of a parrot with eloquence; he sees invasions, like the invasion of a word against the chin of a poet. He sees conquests, like the conquest of an entire century by a poem; he sees murder, like the murder of a story on the street corner of a map; he sees people, cities, prairies, plants, and then he reveals to us where he is actually from:

I am from Kashan
But Kashan is not my city,
My city is lost—
With hard work I have feverishly
Built a house on the other side of the night,
In this house I am close to the wet anonymity of grass,
I can hear the sound of the little garden breathing
I can hear darkness when it pours from a leaf ...

The poet keeps telling us what hidden sounds he can hear: "I am close to the beginning of the Earth!" He speaks of his soul, of the generosity of things he sees, how he is happy with just one apple—and then his sublime recognition of how precious life is:

Life is such a pleasant custom:
Life has feathers and wings as wide as death,
A jump the size of love ...
Life is to wash a plate
Life is finding a penny in a little brook on the street ...
It makes no difference where I am—
Wherever I am, I am,
The sky belongs to me:
The window, thought, air, love, the earth are all mine.
So what if once in a while the mushrooms of solitude grow ...
We need to wash our eyes,

We need to see things differently,
We need to wash the words,
The word must be the wind itself,
The word must be the rain itself,
We need to close the umbrellas,
We need to go under the rain,
Thoughts, memories,
We need them all under the rain,
The whole people of the city
We must take under the rain . . .
We need to make love with woman under the rain—
Under the rain we must play games . . .
Life is to take a bath in the pond of Now.

The ecstasy unfolds, words must become truth, the world must exude itself, we must realize that, if there were no worms, life would have lacked something, and if there were no death, our hands would have searched for something . . . and we should not be scared of death, for death is not the end of a dove, for death comes anytime we bite into a grape—and finally he reveals with the disarming power of the simplest words:

Sadeh bashim . . .

Let us be simple,
Simple,
Whether at a bank-teller or under a tree!
Our task is not to decipher the secret of a red rose—
Our task is perhaps
To swim in the mystery of a red rose!
Let us camp on the other side of knowing . . .
Our task is perhaps
Between the waterlily and the century!
To run after the song of truth!

He signs the poem: Kashan, Chenar Village, Summer 1964—and he is done. Quietly he has turned our world upside down, held our heads gently in his hands, turned towards the sun and said: Look!

The Painter, the Poet, the Ascetic

Sohrab Sepehri was perhaps closest to Forough Farrokhzad in their shared poetic dispositions, characters, and demeanors. As scholars of Sohrab Sepehri's legacy have correctly pointed out, "[t]he death of Forug̱ Farrokzād in a car accident on 13 February 1967 had a profound impact on Iranian literati in general, and Sepehri in particular. As reflected in his famous elegy for her called 'Doust' . . . with her death Sepehri lost not only a close friend, but a fellow poet who shared much of his world vision and sensibilities, both emotional and poetic."[6] To understand the significance of this closeness, we need to take a closer look at the poem Sepehri wrote when Farrokhzad died in the automobile accident. Here is the poem:

Bozorg bud . . .

She was majestic
And she was native to our time—
And she was related to all opening horizons—
And how well she understood
The dialect of water and earth.

Her voice
Had the shape of the discordant sadness of reality—
And her eyelashes
Pointed out to us!
And her hands
Thumbed through the soft air of generosity:
Sending kindness towards us!

She had the shape of her own solitude:
And she interpreted the most loving twists of her time
For the mirror!

And just like rain,
She was full of the freshness of repetitions!
And just like trees
She used to cast herself in between the salvation of lights!

She always called on the childhood of winds—
And she always tied up the direction of her speeches
To the binding of water.

For us one night
She interpreted the green prostration of love
So boldly
That we could all caress the kindness of the surface of earth—
And just like a bucket full of water
We were all refreshed.

And so many times we saw
How with so many baskets
She went to harvest for just one bunch of good news!

And yet she could not sit
Face-to-face with the evident luminosity of pigeons—
And moved to the edge of nothingness,
And she laid down
behind the patience of lights.

And she did not think
For a moment
How lonesome we would all be—
In the midst of the confusion
Of the pronunciations of all these closed doors—
For eating an apple.[7]

The poem begins by citing in English the line "I should be glad of another death" by the American poet T. S. Eliot (1888–1965), which appears in Eliot's poem "The Journey of the Magi."[8] Above all, as evident in this eulogy, Sepehri was an ascetic mystic of radical contemporaneity. Everything that came his way, death or life, or that he touched in body and soul, became instantly iconic, sublimated to something ethereal. It suffices to look at the way in which he remembered Farrokhzad after her death. Nothing tangible, palpable, or intimate. Everything about their friendship is ethereal. It is by now a clichéd assumption that "in his vision of the world and of mankind's place within it, Sepehri believed above all in the importance of people's direct relationship with nature, one unencumbered by the anesthetizing effect of daily habits and preoccupations with preconceived ideas."[9] This is a deeply flawed and misleading assumption. He was not preoccupied by nature. He was the chief architect of a poetic aesthesis with which he saw the world: the whole world, nature or culture, physical and moral, political and historical. Yes, there is an abundance of references to nature in his poetry. But this is not the physical nature that he and everyone else witnessed. This is his formal rendition of the nature into the *modus operandi* of his aesthetic imagination.[10] Consider what he once wrote about his paintings very specifically: "We had a lot of trees in our garden. But my tree had no match. There was nothing in the garden like it. My sun, too; it was unlike other people's sun. It was similar to the chalkboard-carved sun on the fireplace. The mountain of my paintings was an imaginary mountain. It had nothing to do with the Three Pointed Mountain."[11] By the same token, there are traces of Taoism in his perception of the world, but so are traces of Zen Buddhism, Hinduism, and of course Sufism, and even European Romanticism, but all such traces he sublated into something else in his own poetry, which was not the sum total of his archival knowledge of facts but the sublimated truth of how he saw the world.

More accurate is to suggest this:

Unwavering in his belief in a delicate yet essential unity between mankind, nature, and a greater cosmic order, Sepehri spent the length of his artistic life in search of the most effective expression of this central belief. To this end, he freely crossed over to a variety of myths and philosophies ranging from Zen Buddhism and Taoism to Sufism and European Romanticism, retaining from each those tenets most organically suitable to his vision.[12]

The last point is critical, but not sufficient. It would be a misguided trajectory simply to catalogue various "influences" on him to reach for his poetry or painting. He read, he lived, he breathed, he painted, and he wrote his poems, all in an organic whole. There is an alchemical disposition in his poetry which is uniquely his and his alone, but of course all such elements were evident in them. We will lose something serious about his poetry if we are simply satisfied with archiving such influences on him. It is equally plausible to think of him as an ecumenical humanist who embraced "the whole of mankind." But not so in a politically dictated, or jaundiced "humanist" way. He was after revealing a luminous cohesion in Being-in-the-world. And in his painting and poetry, he was that luminosity. Above all, the painter-poet on him was an ascetic, perhaps not celibate, but not exactly lusting after anything immediate or palpable. Everything palpable was there to be sublimated, arisen to overcome itself and become what was hidden in it, but evident to him. After him we all began to look at water, air, life, our own bodies, and the whole world we bodily inhabited in the Here and Now differently, as if for the first time.

The Blue Room

A collection of three autobiographical essays that Sepehri had drafted and left behind, and that his sister Parvaneh Sepehri edited and published, came out in one volume as *Otaq-e Abi/The Blue Room*. This volume gives us a fuller picture of Sepehri's state of mind as he traveled widely through East and West to locate himself poetically, aesthetically, and above all emotively and existentially in the world around him. In the first essay, "The Blue Room," Sepehri was preoccupied with a room painted blue in a garden, where as a child he and his family had lived and where he had encountered snakes that had stuck in his mind. In his adulthood, he remembered these snakes together with active Hindu and Buddhist metaphors: "The blue room was a mandala. I had easily entered the mandala."[13] As an adult, now deeply steeped in Indian religious metaphors, Sepehri turned the blue room into a Hindu domain with which he rehearsed his knowledge of Hinduism, Buddhism, and other mystical traditions, from the Indian over the Egyptian to the Native American domains. The prose is somewhat forced and archival, picking up any sign, color, or shape and casting it in Hindu or Buddhist terms. It is a youthful piece, unedited, unprepared, incomplete, perhaps not ready for publication. The same is true about the second essay, "Our Painting Teacher," where Sepehri recollected his early schooling. Here he recalled the sadistic corporeal punishment that he and his classmates endured at school. He bitterly recalled his teacher admonishing him for his artwork.[14] Altogether he was a restless student: "My grade in etiquette at school was A Plus at home F-." He added: "At school I was scared. At home I scared [others]."[15] This piece, too, is rash and rushed, some important biographical sketches, but nothing more.

In the third and final essay, "Conversation with the Master," Sepehri recalled a conversation he had had with a French teacher of his and eventually plunged into a discussion of the difference between Eastern and Western artwork that commenced with the issue of "*qarineh-sazi*/parallelism" in Persian gardens and Persian carpets, for the legends have it that the Sassanid kings wanted to have a vision of the garden in winter, for which reason they commissioned Persian carpets mimicking their gardens. He sought to theorize the significance of parallelisms in Eastern art when he said that "time is meta-time and space meta-space."[16] In following this course of recollections, which had remained incomplete at his death, Sepehri walked through a historical progression, where in his estimation "the West" dominated by Reason and "the East" with spirit and soul. The third essay, the most theoretically informed and insightful, is incomplete, but it is by far the most cogent and coherent attempt to theorize his understanding of Western and Eastern art, not in generic clichés but in detailed attention to examples and samples. The saddest thing about *The Blue Room* is that it is incomplete—not just because we do not get to read his full and polished account of his life as a painter, but because he was onto something meditative and exploratory and never managed to bring it to a refined closure. What we read in these interrelated essays is a restless but confident soul, informed and cultivated, in search of aesthetic confidence. Yet, by the end of the fragmented pieces we are certain that he seems to have found it, at least in his own mind, which in turn flourished with full and bourgeoning confidence in a poem such as "Dar Golestaneh/In Golestaneh," where he abandoned all anxieties of meditative articulation and simply sang:

Prairies so expansive,
Mountains so high!
What an amazing fragrance
Of grass comes from Golestaneh!

In this village I was looking for something:
For a dream perhaps,
For a light, a pebble, a smile.

Behind the poplar trees
There was pure oblivion—
Calling me!

I stopped by a canebrake:
The wind was blowing!
I listened:
Who was talking to me?
A lizard slid—
I started walking:
A hay field was nearby,
Beyond it a cucumber field,

And after that bushes of colorful flowers,
And then the forgetfulness of the soil!

By a little pond
I took my slippers off
And sat down:
Put my feet into the water—
Oh how green I am today!
And how alert my body is!
Oh I so hope
No worries come my way
From behind the mountains!
Who is it behind the trees?
Nothing, it's just a cow grazing in the field!
It is noontime in summer:
The shades know what kind of a summer this is—
Spotless shades—
A corner: Light and pure!
The children of feelings:
Here is the place to play!
Life is not empty:
There is kindness, there is apple, there is faith!
Yes:
As long as there are anemones
We must live!

There is something in my heart:
Just like a forest made of light,
Just like the early morning slumber—
And I am so restless
That I wish to run to the end of this prairie,
To the top of that mountain,
I can hear a sound from the distance,
Calling me.[17]

Hozur-e khasteh-ye ashia': *The Tired Presence of Things*

When we read Sepehri closely, the evident signs of his exposure to Indian, Chinese, Japanese, Egyptian, and Native American cultures are quite evident and frequently appear in his poetry. He was perhaps the most learned of all these six poets in his knowledge of Eastern religions and philosophies. But his poetic imagination picked and chose the particularly soothing and luminous aspects of all these traditions—with Nirvana as the ideal state of peace, freedom, and soteriological delivery and happiness at its ontic epicenter. All of these poetic allusions, however, remain at a citational level and are subsumed and sublimated into an aspect of his poetry which we can call and consider as *Indwelling*—meaning that they enabled him to sink deeper into his poetic consciousness. We would move in the wrong direction if we simply were to tally and archive his varied influences. We need to begin with the organicity of his poetic voice and acknowledge certain formative forces syntactically, not analytically. This will enable us to see his sense of "nature" as artful, not factual. In his poem, "Neda-ye Aghaz/The Sound of the Beginning," he says:

> Like a cloud
> My heart becomes so heavy
> When from the window I see Houri,
> Our neighbor's daughter,
> Sit by the rarest Elm tree on earth
> And read a book on Islamic Jurisprudence![18]

That Elm tree (*narvan*) is not "nature." It is a poetic rendition of nature, and therefore the comparison is between reading Islamic jurisprudence and reading Persian poetry. Hence, this allusion is not just to the tree but to the tree as an unmitigated reality, whereas *fiqh* (Islamic jurisprudence) is entirely scholastically mitigating not just the tree but the whole world around it. Seeking a direct connection to that tree and the world around it, Sepehri poetically went into the world (tree and all), not out—seeking cosmic union and organicity, or interiority, in effect in-bounding into the world instead of out-bounding. The subject that is thus formed is internal to the world, not external to it. In between *totality* and *infinity* (Levinas's language), Sepehri opted for the organicity of both. He did not appear either *total* or *infinite* but *organic*. His gift to his people was to discover their own interiority, subjectivity, and agency. This is the reason, when we recite his poetry out loud to ourselves, why we sense that these poems were composed almost exclusively for our voices. The same is true about anyone else who recites Sepehri's poems—contrary to the poetry of, say, Shamlou, or Akhavan, or even Farrokhzad, and so on—poets who were quite adept at reciting their own poetry for the public to listen. Others have recited Sepehri's poetry, which I found intolerable to hear (especially the late Iranian actor Khosrow Shakiba'i's recitation, which I find utterly unbearable), for I believe that these poems are all meant to be recited out loud to ourselves in solitude—by every one of us. There is a reason why I believe this: we are all meant to read them to ourselves, so that we can hear the sound of our own presence/*hozur*. Sepehri invested his own *hozur* in them, his own solitude, his own presence. All we need to do is to look and carefully read the opening stanza of his legendary poem "Mosafer/Traveler":

> *Dam-e ghorub,*
> *Mian-e hozur-e khasteh ashia':*
> *Negah-e montazeri*
> *Hajm-e vaqt ra midid . . .*

Consider these phrases carefully: "dam-e Ghorub" is the time when dusk is just about to begin, and so it is a liminal moment when the event takes place. But the temporal dimension, the sunset, also has a spatial dimension to it: in the midst of the tired presence of things. This is absolute luminosity, where and when things declare their own presence. Then comes the subject, the gaze of an expectant person, someone waiting for something to happen, and what the person sees, the traveler senses, is the palpable parsing, phrasing of time. This, in short, is the moment of *moraqebeh*, which I have translated as "meditative beholding" in order to bring both its etymological and idiomatic meanings together. Once we do that, Sepehri has been brought closer to the famous gnostic idea of *wahdat al-wujud/* unity of being, usually attributed to the Andalusian mystic Muhy al-Din Ibn Arabi (1165–1240), but equally applicable to Rumi (1207–73), where everything is nothing but God. Let us look at the word Sepehri uses, "*moraqebeh*," a bit more closely.

Moraqebeh affords the constellation and the episteme that Sepehri helped form a certain sense of interiority—matching with and corresponding to Farrokhzad's sense of presentist exteriority. The two contemporary poets are the closest together in the very soul of their poetry—with another kindred soul, Ahmad Reza Ahmadi (1940–2023), having kept both of them close company; much like Akhavan and Shamlou were closest in their temporal disposition, with a past and a future, Farrokhzad and Sepehri were closest in terms of their presentist exteriority and presence of an interiority—or, to put it in different terms, Farrokhzad was *temporally* present (*hal*), while Sepehri was in a condition of atemporal presence (*hozur*), in this constellation. However, Nima had inaugurated the whole epistemic event, and Esmail Kho'i, as we will see in the next and final chapter, closed it by leaving and exiting it altogether. None of these six poets entirely on their own would be complete or would make complete sense from this long-shot perspective, where they have all become iconic in terms beyond their own immediate and specific poetry. Without Sepehri giving the postcolonial persona of the renewed Persian cosmopolis this sense of interiority, the whole epistemic paradigm that he helped form would have been bereft of its sense of moral agency and intuition transcendence. The "tired presence of things" is what Sepehri saw and received from the world around us, and in his poetry, he rejuvenated our perception of those things anew.

The Poet, the Prophet, the Pilgrim

Let me now look at the opening stanza of the poem "Mosafer/Traveler" and take it to the rest of the epic which it inaugurates and unfolds. Now I intend to translate the entirety of the poem into English, as I reread and whisper it gently and repeatedly in the original to myself. This is the only way I know how to convey to my readers the sense of awe and wonder, of peace and confidence, that we have in the presence of Sepehri's gentle and oracular voice when reading his canonical masterpiece: just to feel the power of his prophetic voice, not in soundbites but in its full and complete totality, infinity, and above all organicity, from beginning to end. The long poem is divided into thirty-five long and short stanzas—each anticipating the other, folding into the other, although the whole poem is composed as a stream of consciousness, as in a travel diary of feelings, emotions, observations, and wondrous meandering. The stanzas are not numbered in the original.[19] Yet, I have numbered them in my translation for you to be able to sense their thematic progression. Soon after we start reading the poem, we realize that it is actually a conversation between the Traveler and a friend and interlocutor—and we, too, are now made privy to that conversation, or perhaps we are that friend to whom the Traveler is speaking, recalling and recording his wondrous journey into and out of this world.[20] Words fail to describe the mesmerizing power of the poem in its original Persian: the simplicity and oracular potency of the phrasings. It is Delphic, as it were, simple and sound, yet gently overwhelming. As I translated this poem, I repeatedly had to stop and catch my breath, collect my bearings: smile, cry, burst into audible diction, swallow my voice, and read more quietly to myself. The poem starts gently, imperceptibly, matter-of-fact-ly—just like a musical composition by Mozart—where the thick description of a sunset first sets the scene:

(1)
Dam-e ghorub ...

By the sunset:
In the midst of the tired presence of things
An expectant gaze
Could see the volume of time—
And upon the table:
The commotion of a few fresh seasonal fruits
Was pulling towards a vague grasp of death—
As the wind blew the aroma of the little garden
On the resting carpet—
Presenting it to the gentle edges of life,
And just like a handheld fan
The mind
Held the sunny surface of the flower
In hand
Fanning itself.

We know that we are about to be told a story, sharing an experience, witnessing the moments of a revelation, all in the midst of this perfect *mise-en-scène*. The key phrases here are "hozur-e khasteh-ye ashia'/the tired presence of things" and "negah-e montazeri/hajm-e vaqt ra midid/An expectant gaze/Could see the volume of time." The volume of time (*hajm-e vaqt*) stands still, and in it things have a tired presence. It is like watching a painting, a still life, of Sepehri's own, or else of Cézanne's, or Caravaggio's, or Van Gogh's. We just watch: except the words are moving, and the still life is coming to life.

(2)
The Traveler
Got off the bus:
"What a clean sky!"
And the extension of the lonesome street
Carried him away.

The scene is almost cinematic, like one of those in the Roads photography series of Abbas Kiarostami. The Traveler gets off the bus and disappears on the long road. Imagine Sohrab Sepehri coming back from a journey—and he undertook many distant journeys, East and West of his homeland. But those physical journeys are now all being transmuted into a poetic sojourn, his as much as ours. The entire epic poem reads like watching a road movie: John Ford's *Grapes of Wrath* (1940), Fellini's *La Strada* (1954), Bergman's *Wild Strawberries* (1957), Kiarostami's *And Life Goes on* (1992)—all of them combined, and yet none of them comes even close to the mythic power of Sepehri's "Traveler."

(3)
It was a sunset!
One could hear the sound of the intelligence of vegetations.
The traveler had come
And sat on a comfortable chair
By the lawn.
"I feel sad!
I feel so sad,
All through the way
I was thinking of only one thing:
And the color of the hillsides
Was making me unconscious!
The contours of the road were lost
Into the sorrow of prairies—
What strange valleys!
And the horse, do you remember the horse?
It was white:
And just like a pure phrase
It was grazing on the green silence of the greenery!
And then: the colorful loneliness of the villages on our way,
And then: the tunnels!
I am so sad—
I am so inconsolably sad—
And Nothing—
Not even these aromatic minutes
Going silent on the branches of the orange blossoms,
Not even the honesty of the words exchanged in silence
In between the two leaves of the evening primrose—

No, Nothing
Can rescue me
From the onslaught of the emptiness about me:
And I think this sad melodious song
Will be heard forever.

The references are full of allusions; they are citational, and they refer to something that we do not know quite yet. The Traveler is a master storyteller. He has just come back from a pilgrimage around and through the world, his reports are becoming mythic, and he knows that he has an audience. As we read the poem apace, a few critical concepts come to mind, and we need to consider them both textually and contextually. One is the concept of *ziarat* and *za'er* and its plural *zovvar*, all referring to Shi'i pilgrims' visits to the sites and mausolea of their saints and Imams—say, to Karbala or Mashhad, or else to Mecca to perform the *hajj*. However, this one is entirely worldly. The other is the equally compelling idea of "visiting horizons and souls" (*seyr-e afagh va anfos*)—a particularly poignant mystical concept of the necessity of traveling to purify one's soul. These doctrinal articulations of the facts and metaphors of a journey have given rise to a precious body of literature that begins with the pre-Islamic *Arda Viraf Nameh*, continues with the Prophet Muhammad's journey to the heavens, or Mi'raj, in the Quran, and countless mystical and philosophical renditions of this journey, culminating in texts such as Hakim Sana'i's (*circa* 1080–1141) *Seyr al-Ibad/Journey of the God's Servant* and Farid al-Din Attar's (*circa* 1145–1221) *Mosibat-Nameh/The Book of Tragedy*, among countless others.[21] In all of these journeys, the soul visits the afterlife, through life. These are all augmented by the legendary Isma'ili philosopher-poet Naser Khosrow Qobadiani's (*circa* 1004–88) philosophical treatise *Zad Al-Mosaferin/Sustenance for Travelers*. We continue to think along these lines, and Dante's *Divine Comedy* (1308–21) comes to mind, as well as John Bunyan's *Pilgrim's Progress* (1678). We are now in a whole panorama of spiritual domains, both physical and spiritual pilgrimages. What Sepehri did with this metaphor, however, was to materialize its meaning to turn it into a literal journey around the world and thus metaphorize that world anew. The journeys he took were real—to India, Egypt, Japan, the US, Europe, and so on—and then in his poetic fiction those journeys became the evidence of a renewed allegorical force driving his *alter ego* Traveler forward. We are in the midst of the metapoetic account of a spiritual journey through but beyond this world. Sepehri was reporting what he had seen and done, and he sublated these all to what they metaphorically meant to him, and now to us.

(4)
The gaze of the traveling man
Was cast upon the table:
"What beautiful apples!
Life is the ecstasy of solitude."
The host asked:

What does "beautiful" mean?
"Beautiful means to interpret forms lovingly—
And love, only love
Can get you used to the warmth of an apple,
And love only love
Took me to the vast sorrow of lives
Took me to the possibilities of becoming a bird—
As for the panacea of sadness?
The pure voice of the elixir can give you this potion.

(5)
And now the night had arrived
The lights were on, and they were having tea.

(6)
Why are you so sad?
It seems you are lonely!
How lonely indeed!
I believe
I am afflicted with that hidden vein of the colors of existence—
Afflicted?
Afflicted means in love—
And think how lonely it would be
If the little fish was afflicted with the blueness of the endless sea!
What a thin sad thought!
And sorrow is the covered smile of the look of a plant
And sorrow an imperceptive allusion to the denial of the unity of things,
How lucky are the plants who are in love with light,
And the expansive hand of the light is upon their shoulder
No reaching is impossible,
There will always be a distance,
Although the curve of the water is an excellent pillow
For the pleasant and fragile sleep of the water lilies
There is always a distance,
One must be afflicted
Otherwise, the bewildering whispers in between two words
Would be wasted,
And love
Is a journey to the mobile light of the solitude of things
And love
Is the sound of the distances
The sounds of the distances
That are drowned in uncertainties—
No,
The sound of the distances that are cleansed like silver

And with the slightest hearing of a "nothing" they get smudgy,
The lover is always alone,
And the hand of the person who is in love
Is in the fragile hands of the seconds,
As love and those seconds move towards the other end of the day
And love and the seconds sleep on the seconds,
And love and the seconds dedicate the best book of the world to water,
And they know only too well
That no fish ever
Untied the one thousand and one knots
Of the river—
And yet halfway through the nights
With the old boat of Illumination
They sail upon the rivers of Guidance
All the way to the Immanence of Wonder.
Oh the air of your words carries the listener
Through the garden paths of stories,
And through the veins of such fictions
What a sad, fresh blood!

Where exactly are we as we read? Consider the signposts: reflections on a basket of fruits, on solitude, things that are in the midst of words, distance is paramount, and above all there is a sense of wonder. Things are there, all worldly, but they all point to something else. We see familiar words and things in unfamiliar settings. Things are allegorical, allusive, substitutional. A sad, fresh blood is flowing. The time of the narrative is oscillating between the time of the stories being told and the time of the Traveler with his interlocutor: common between them is the miasmic presence of the stories and observations being shared. By now we have been transformed into the epicenter of that *hozur*, that presence, where things are stripped of their inherited meanings. We might therefore consider this poem, "Mosafer/Traveler," a contemporary rendition of Shihab al-Din Yahya Suhrawardi's (1154–91) "Qesseh Qorbat Gharbiyeh/The Ballad of the Occidental Exile," which begins with this, not the other, world, in effect turning this to the other world. In Suhrawardi's rendition, we encounter a narrator who begins with iconic citations of the Qur'an before plunging into a story that purports to pick up from where Avicenna had left off in his own allegorical stories of Hay ibn Yaqzan and Salaman and Absal.[22] In Suhrawardi's version, the narrator and his brother travel from Transoxiana to the Maghreb and from there to the city of Qairawan, where they are captured and incarcerated in a dungeon at night, and during the day they can see a castle and look around to discover their whereabouts. Finally, a hoopoe bird brings them a letter from their father Hadi, who asks them to come back home to the East, which they do by way of an arduous journey punctuated by Qur'anic allusions. As we read Sepehri's poem, we might see how this story of Suhrawardi is kept in form and overcome in substance from archetypal Qur'anic allusions to real life and this world, as its archaic geography has metamorphosed into a worldly geography.[23] I am not suggesting that Sepehri consciously followed Suhrawardi's model. I am placing both Sepehri's poem and Suhrawardi's ballad in the same archetypal domain. Consider, for example, how the image of the hoopoe appears in the following stanzas of Sepehri's "Traveler":

(7)
The courtyard was lit
And the wind was blowing
As the blood of the night was flowing
In the silence between the two men.

(8)
"It is a clean solitary room—
What simple proportions it has
For thinking!
I am so terribly sad—
Couldn't possibly go to sleep" —
He went and sat by the window
On a soft cloth chair:
"I'm still traveling
Thinking to myself
As if there's a boat floating
On all the rivers of this world and I—
Sailing on this boat—
Have for thousands of years
Been singing the living song
Of ancient mariners
Into the hollowed ears of seasons
As I sail forward—
Where will this journey take me?
Where will my footprint cease and
The gentle fingers of rest untie
My shoelaces?
Where's the place
Where I will have arrived—
Where I can spread
A little carpet and sit on it
In peace
Listening to the sound of a dish
Being washed at a nearby faucet?

(9)
And in what Spring
You would pause
And the surface of the soul
Would be covered with green leaves?

(10)
We must drink wine
And we must walk
In the youthful shade—
That's all!

(11)
Which way towards life?
How do I get to a hoopoe?
And listen to how this very word
All through the journey
Kept disturbing
The window of sleep!
What was it singing in your ears
All through the journey?
Think carefully:
Where is the hidden kernel
Of this mysterious melody?
What is putting pressure
On your eyelids?
What a warm delightful weight!
The journey was not too long,
The flight of sparrows reduced the volumes of time—
And in the conversation between the wind and the gable roofs
All the allusions would turn to the commencement of intelligence,
In that very minute when from the height of summer
You were looking at the thundering Jajrud River!
What happened
When the starlings interrupted your green sleep!
And the season was the season of crops,
And with just one starling sitting on the branch of a cypress
The book of seasons turned a page, and the very first line was:
"Life is the colorful negligence of just one minute of Eve!"

We need to consider such allusions cautiously and purposefully—for they may not be conscious, but they still remain iconic. Throughout the poem, Sepehri crafted his own unique and irreducible allusions to visions and vistas that help guide us towards a particular grasp of the journey—which leads to the point: "Life is the colorful negligence of just one minute of Eve!" Suhrawardi alluded to Avicenna but was not reducible to Avicenna. In the same way, Sepehri reminds us of Suhrawardi but is not reducible to Suhrawardi. What is common to them all—Avicenna, Suhrawardi, and Sepehri—is an allegorical domain to which in this particular genre we might add Ibn Tufail, Sana'i, and Attar on one side, and the Book of *Arda Viraf*, the Mi'raj literature, Dante, and Bunyan on the other.

Now we are reading Sepehri within a larger frame of reference so that the materiality of his poem dwells in the imaginative power of an entire genre of poetic imagination.

(12)
You were looking:
In between a cow and the grass, the mind of the wind was blowing.

(13)
You were looking at
The commemoration of the blackberry marking the skin of the season
The presence of an Indian Roller in the midst of the clover field
Was repairing the scar on the face of feelings!

(14)
Look:
there is always a scar on the face of feelings,
there is always,
as in the alertness of being awake,
approaches like gentle steps of death
from behind, and puts its hands on our shoulders,
And by the side of the incident
We drink
the warmth of their lit fingers
just like a delicious poison.
Do you remember Venice
On the gentle canals?
In that ringing quarrel between water and earth
Where we could see the time from behind a prism,
The jolt of the boat jolted my mind
The dust of habit always blocks the vision,
We must always walk with a fresh breath
And we must blow
So that the golden face of death is spic and span.

(15)
Where is the Ronus Stone?
I am returning from a close encounter with a tree
On its trunk
The simple hands of solitude had left a mark
"I write this line in memory of my deadness!"

(16)
Pass me the wine—
We need to rush:

I am returning from a journey
Through an epic—
And I know
The story of Sohrab and the Elixir
By heart —

(17)
The journey took me to a garden
I knew in my early youth—
And I stood there for a while
For my heartbeat to calm down—
I heard a palpitating sound
And when the gate opened
I suddenly fell on the ground
When Truth rushed out—

As I was translating these stanzas, I had to rush to my class in Hamilton Hall on Columbia University's campus to read Virgil's *Aeneid* with my students, and as I sat there in 309 Hamilton dutifully discussing the Roman epic, recasting Homer's *Iliad* and *Odyssey* for a decidedly imperial project, all I was thinking to myself was this moral edifice which we can read in Sepehri's "Traveler." Oh, I so wished I could have interrupted Virgil and told my students what Sepehri was doing in this infinitely superior epic of the journey of a soul, from which Dante and Virgil could both learn, as would Ferdowsi and Sana'i alike, and all other epic prose and poetry of all other kinds. The problem with Franco Moretti's excellent study *Modern Epic: The World System from Goethe to García Márquez* (1996) is how he has taken Immanuel Wallerstein's idea of a "world system" completely for granted and thus has been blindsided in terms of how nations resist that unjust world order by epics of an entirely different sort—the sort that places Goethe's *Faust* in front of Sepehri's "Traveler" and thus epistemically denies him access to a vastly different conception of the "Modern Epic." Let me proceed with my translation:

(18)
And one more time under the sky of the Psalms
During that journey when by the River Babel
I came to consciousness
The sound of the lute was silent
And when I listened carefully, I could hear someone cry
And a few restless lutes
Were hanging by the fresh branches of the willow tree.

(19)
On my roads of travel
Devout Christian monks
Were pointing towards the silent portrait

Of Prophet Jeremiah—
While I was reciting out loud
From the Book of Ecclesiastes—
As a few Lebanese farmers
Were sitting under an old cedar tree
Counting the oranges on their branches
In their minds!

(20)
By the roadside as I was traveling
I could see blind Iraqi children
Looking at the script
Of the Code of Hammurabi!

(21)
All through my journey
I was catching up
With the latest newspapers
From around the world.

(22)
The journey was full of flowing commotions,
And from the uproar of industries
The entire surface of the journey
Was black and tight
Smelling of kerosine!
On the dust of the journey
Empty bottles of liquors
Groves of instinct, shadows of chances,
Were all standing by each other—
Halfway through the journey
I could hear the sound of coughing
From a sanatorium!
Whores were looking at the jets' grooves
On blue skies!
And children were chasing
After pinwheels!
The street cleaners were singing
As the great poets
Were prostrating to migrant leaves,
And the long path of this journey
Passing through humans and irons
Was passing through the hidden quintessence of life,
Joining the wet strangeness of a small brook,
The silent sparkle of the scale of a fish
The familiarity of an accent, the vastness of a color.

(23)
The journey took me
To Equatorial climes where
In the shade of that green,
That mighty Banyan tree:
How well do I remember
The phrase that descended
Upon the summer site
Of my mind:
Be vast, be solitary,
Be humble, be unbending.

This is the moment of revelation: "Be vast, be solitary,/Be humble, be unbending." The Banyan tree here stands for and is tantamount to the Tuba Tree in Paradise with the same power and awe, divine majesty and poetic presence. The miasmatic stanzas by now have become like verses of an earthly divination, and from the depth of the ordinary rises an extraordinary sense of the sacred, an awareness of our self-transcendence. The Traveler visits cities and crosses prairies, farms, and borderlands, as he sums up the earth in a final formal gathering. New York and Palestine, Iraq and India, Europe and the United States, East and West of the Globe, its North and South, have all come together, a view of the earth both from its Edenic origin and through all the terror it has seen. This is the panoramic vision of the earth from above, from below, from within: both God's and the human's points of view colliding.

(24)
I am returning from the conversation
With the sun—
Where is the shade?

(25)
But still the steps are dizzy with the twisting of Spring
And one might smell the aroma of picking from the hands of the wind!
And the sense of touch
Has passed out
Behind the dust of the shape of an orange!
In this colorful commotion
Who knows
Where is the stone of my solitude on which point of the season?
Still
The woods do not know the full proportions of its countless proportions,
Still
The leaf
Is riding the first word of the wind!

Still
The human is telling something to the water
And in the mind of the grass
Is turning the brook of a little argument
And upon the orbit of a tree
The echoes of the wings of a dove
Is the inconspicuous presence of human behavior.

(26)
A commotion can be heard:
I am the solitary interlocutor
Of the winds blowing all over the world
And all the rivers of the world
Are teaching me the pure secret
Of disappearance—
Just to me!
I am the interpreter of the sparrows of the Ganges Valley—
And right by the road leading to Sarnath—
I have interpreted
The Tibetan earrings—
Studded with mysticism—
For the ears of the girls of Benares—
Lacking in any adornment.
How lucky are the plants
In love as they are with light!
See how the expansive hand of light
Is cast upon their shoulders:
No, it is impossible to reach—
For there will always remain a distance . . .
One must be afflicted—
Otherwise, the whisper of wonder
In between two spoken words would be wasted.
Set upon my shoulders
Oh the early morning hymns of the Vedas
The whole weight of freshness—
For I'm afflicted
With the warmth of Speech—
Oh, all you olive trees of Palestine:
Address all the abundance of your shades
To me:
To this lonesome traveler
Having just returned
From the vicinity of Mount Sinai
Feverish with
The heat of the Divine Word—

(27)
But conversations will all
One day disappear—
And the highways of the air
Will all become white
By the majesty of the butterflies
of the dissipation of senses.

(28)
How many poems
Have been composed
For this melodious sorrow!

(29)
But still someone
Is standing by the tree,
But still a rider
Is waiting beyond the gate of the city citadel
Upon the shoulder of whose wet eyelids
Lays the pleasant slumber of the Battle of Qadisiya,
Still the neighs of restless Mongol horses
Are rising from the emptiness of the hay fields,
Still merchants of Yazd
By the Spice Road
Lose their senses when smelling Indian goods,
And upon the banks of Hamoun Lake
You could hear:
"Evil has covered all earth."
A thousand years passed by,
No one could hear the sound of someone swimming
And the picture of no old maiden reflected on any water.

These are all historical references to wars and conquests in gentle and melodious terms. By now, this and the other world, the one the Traveler has visited and the one he is visiting upon us, have come together. We are in and out of history. The world is being remapped for us—physically and emotively. In a previous study, I have cited parts of this poem as my opening passages for a study of a constellation of travelogues from the late eighteenth to the early twentieth century.[24] Those travelogues, written by travelers from Iran and India going around the globe, were the preparatory stage to create this intuition of transcendence in Sohrab Sepehri in this act of poetic pilgrimage. All those travelers were roaming the world in anticipation of Sepehri's "travelogue," as it were, anticipating his poetic rendition of what they were seeing and yet could not quite read. This poem is the summation of them all, of us all, we as we have declared ourselves as a people, a nation, a part of humanity on this fragile earth. Just look and whisper any of these lines to yourself: "A thousand years passed by,/No one could hear the sound of someone swimming/And the picture of no old maiden reflected on any water," as Sepehri brings all mythic and Vedic wisdoms to one poetic summit. This is how an Iranian became a person, a worldly character, with moral agency and visionary awareness of themselves. This is the poetic recasting of the Persian cosmopolis in terms at once real, immediate, and self-transcendent.

(30)
Halfway through my journey
I was sitting on the banks of the Yamuna River
Watching the reflection of the Taj Mahal in water:
The marble perpetuation of an elixir moment
And the intrusion of the volume of life into death.
Look: two big wings
Are traveling towards the edges of the spirit of water.
There are strange sparks
In the vicinities of two hands
Come and adorn the darkness of apprehension with lights
For just a signal is enough
Life is a gentle stroke on the rock of Magar!

(31)
And on my journey's path
The birds of Nishat Bagh
Washed the dust of experience from my eyesight,
They showed me the health of the cypress tree
And in prayer of emotions and
In gratitude to the feeling of the moment
I sat by the Lake of Suraj Tal
Whispering warmly to myself!

(32)
We ought to move on—
Walking by the distant horizons,
Sometime dwelling in the tent of the vein of just one word
We ought to move on—
And sometime eat mulberries from the branches of a tree.

(33)
I was walking by lyrical poetry
It was a bountiful season,
Under my feet, numbers of sand grains were being crushed
A woman heard

Came by the window, took a look at the season,
She was at the beginning of herself,
Her primitive hands
Were picking gently
The dewdrops of minutes
From the body of feelings of death.
I stopped
The sunshine of lyrics rose
I was mindful of the vaporization of dreams
And I counted the palpitations of a strange plant
On the body of my mind
We thought
We had no boundaries
We thought
We were afloat
In the mythical body of the ecstasy of rhubarb
And a few minutes of forgetfulness
Is the presence of our existence.

(34)
We were at the momentous beginning
Of plants,
When the woman saw me:
I could hear your footsteps,
I thought the wind was passing
By the old curtains.
I had heard your footsteps
On the edge of things—
Where is the celebration of lines?
Look at the waves,
Look at the expansion of my body,
Which way do I reach the grand surface?
And fill my extension to the top of the wet glass
With thirst!
Where would life become precise to the point where a dish breaks?
And the secret of the growth of the mallow flower
The heat of the mind of a horse
Would melt?
And in the beautiful, crowded gathering of hands
One day
We could hear the sound of picking a bunch from the tree,
It was upon what earth
Where we sat on nothing,
And washed our hands and our faces
In the heat of an apple?

The sparks of impossibilities were ascending the existence,
Where the fear of watching would become gentle
And more imperceptive
Than the path of a bird towards death?
And in the conversation of bodies—
And how lightened was
The path of white poplar trees—
Which garden was taking me to the garden of distances?

(35)
We must cross and wander—
We can hear
The wind blowing—
We must cross and wander—
I'm a traveler—
All you perennial winds!
Carry me to the vastness of where
The leaves are formed!
Take me to the childhood of salty waters!
And fill my shoes
With the mobile beauty of
Humility:
Until I reach
The full maturity of the body of grapes!
Soar all my minutes high
To the white skies of instincts
Where flocks of pigeons are flying!
And transform the accident of my being
To a pure lost connection
By a tree!
And in the breathing of my solitude
Flap the windowpanes of my intelligence!
On that day
Send me running after a kite!
Take me to the solitude
Of the hidden proportions of life
And show me the gentle presence of Nothingness!

"The gentle presence of Nothingness?" Where did that come from? "Khalvat-e ab'ad-e zendegi," meaning the "solitude/of the hidden proportions of life" where the Traveler is to be shown "the gentle presence of "Nothingness."[25] This is where the Traveler rests their case. I pause here and catch my breath: it is mesmerizing when reading these lines in the Persian original, hypnotic in its poetic power, as every line magnetically affixes itself to our soul, indissoluble, indescribable, as we read, we move, we listen to our own voice giving voice to what Sepehri was thinking, whispering, to himself when he originally composed this epic journey of his and now our soul. This journey reads happily next to Sana'i and Dante's respective journeys, modeled on the *Mi'raj Nameh* attributed to Avicenna, based on the Isra' in the Quran.[26] It is easy to recognize those masterpieces generations after their canonization. More urgent is to recognize someone who has lived in our own midst and who had the courage, the imagination, and the moral capacity to write an epic journey of his and our souls around the globe, and all in a language to immediately realize and embrace. Sepehri himself traveled around the world, to India, Japan, Egypt, Europe, and the US. But it is only the Arab and Muslim world, right next to India and its continental vastness, that appear so effortlessly in his poem. He felt at home in "the East." He had no animosity or rancor against that which calls itself "the West." He went there, too, exhibited his art, lived there for long or short intervals, but only and always as a pilgrim.

The poet, the prophet, and the pilgrim: these archetypal figures all come together in this seminal poem, in Sepehri's poetry in general, as the metapoetic of the presence evident in his oeuvre, sitting solidly in the midst of a poetic legacy that in six successive moves rose to the occasion, rested its case, and forever disappeared—except in the active memories of a generation that was blessed to have known and heard them and is now in the autumn and winter of their lives, sitting quietly in a corner and whispering these poems to themselves.

Chapter 6

ESMAIL KHO'I: THE VOICE FROM NOWHEREVILLE

To cut to the chase immediately from Sohrab Sepehri to Esmail Kho'i, let me remain with Suhrawardi's "Ballad of the Occidental Exile," which I introduced in the last chapter; here, I will suggest how in Kho'i the allegory completely reverses direction, for while Sepehri roamed the globe and ultimately pivoted back to the Eastern climes of his homely imagination, Kho'i was born and raised in that Eastern clime yet ended up suffering the indignity and anger of exile in "the West" for the final phases of his life. We might therefore see the fate of Kho'i in precisely the reverse order of Suhrawardi's allegorical tale that Sepehri best personified in his persona and his poetry. Kho'i left the peaceful gathering of his East and went to the chaos of the West, carrying within his poetry the painful memories of the wholeness of which he had once been an integral part. He stayed in that exilic chaos, never to return home. Was that not strange that Sepehri and Kho'i were to live their respective poetic fates in two diametrically opposed directions of Suhrawardi's allegorical tale? One going around the world to come home to rest his case, and the other to leave his Oriental abode to get lost in the chaos and confusion of his Occidental exile. Yet, one in one direction and the other in the opposite direction, Sepehri and Kho'i both remained true to their allocated fate to complete and perfect a schema of their homeland and then entrust it to their posterity. Was it fate or accident? It makes no difference, for each in their own poetic ways came to complete the episteme of imagining a nation that was and remains the signature definition of Persian New Poetry.

Although Kho'i began his life and illustrious career as a major poet in his own homeland, with notable achievements and multiple collections of his poetry published, it was not until he was forced to leave Iran, fearing for his life, and until he finally resided in London that his poetry assumed its potent exilic tone and his life became significant precisely in his character as an exilic poet. It is as if, but only as if, he was destined to leave his homeland and see the full fruition of his poetry surface in exile. There certainly was a bitter, angry twist to Kho'i's poetry in exile. But, at the same time, he thrived in that anger and bitterness. One can scarce imagine him to have remained in Iran despite the political circumstances and to become a poet with his unique signature, which flourished in exile. The Persian New Poetry, in effect, "ended"—meaning that its episteme had been fully conjugated—when Akhavan and Shamlou had died and when Kho'i was actively thriving outside Iran. In exile, he became a free spirit, mostly reminiscing about other master poets of his generation whom he personally knew and loudly loved and praised. Here is one example, "Akhavan Jaan/My Sweetest Akhavan" (1990), in which he shared his devotion to and admiration for Mehdi Akhavan-e Sales:

Hich kas ba man dar ghorbat-e man nist mo'aser,
Chon adam gu'i birun zeh zamanam, Akhavan Jaan! ...

No one in my exile is my contemporary,
Just like non-existence:
I am outside time, my dearest Akhavan!
I have no friend, no colleague, neither from the West nor from the East,
Just like God:
I am outside this world, my sweetest Akhavan!
I know the solution is to become just like anyone else, I know this!
But what can I do?
I can't do that, my sweetest Akhavan!
I neither wish to boss people around just like the reactionaries,
Nor am I a dime-a-dozen fake lefty,
My sweetest Akhavan!
I recognize neither an East nor a West,
For I am neither from one nor from the other,
For neither of them means anything to me,
Except two places, my sweetest Akhavan!
And from every creed and every religion and every nation whoever it is,
I know no one but just a human being,
My dearest Akhavan![1]

The poem is in the form of a complaint, sharing a painful experience with a poet whom Kho'i most loved and admired, hailing from his own Khorasan region, like a spiritual father, now visiting him in his exile. A similar sentiment is evident in yet another poem that Kho'i wrote to praise Ahmad Shamlou, "Dar Setayesh-e Ahmad e Shamlu/Praising Ahmad Shamlou" (1991):

Dar kar-e khod beh zat-e khoda mimanad ...

In doing what he does
He resembles God,
For he knows all he needs to know,
And he can do whatever he wants—

Like a cloud he raises his tent
On summits—
Like a tiger

On cliffs
He stands arrogant!

He wishes to clasp the moon's hair,
He is standing, as if on the shoulders of winds . . .

Outside poetry, however, the soul of his world has thorns, too,
Snakes, too . . .
The Rostam of words kills Sohrab, too,
But no, let me not complain,
He is sea-hearted,
His heart is like the sea—
And the sea has storms, too,
As the beautiful monster speaks truth—
And he is indeed a beautiful monster,
And even a beautiful monster has horns and a tail,
And the monster hits with his horns, too . . .
And like the form of his poetry, he is beautiful . . .
Yes, he is beautiful
Like a monster
He is beautiful,
We, too, can boast of our timely presence in the world—
For he is our contemporary.[2]

It is impossible to imagine a fairer and more balanced love and admiration for Shamlou's character flaws, which Kho'i here both acknowledged and beautified. Both Akhavan and Shamlou here in the poetry of Kho'i received their most heartfelt praise by one of their own, by their kindred soul in exile. In exile, Kho'i saw in these master poets of his time his own soul, had it just been left to live in his own homeland; now, from the emotive distance of an irrevocable exile, he saw himself in their familiar and reassuring mirrors. Echoing and mirroring their voices and visions, Kho'i's voice emerged from the depth of his exilic space, from *Bidarkoja*, as he termed it—from Nowhereville.

To the Poetic Manner Born

Turning from Sepehri to Kho'i is like sitting gently by a calm, soothing pond and suddenly noticing that a thunderous flood is headed towards you! The two could not possibly be more different poets—and yet in the assemblage I propose here they complement each other in working towards the formation of a formidable force definitive to the formation of their homeland as a poetically potent polity. Sepehri was gentle, calm, quiet, and ethereally confident. Kho'i was thunderous, defiant, inconsolably angry, and above all a committed revolutionary. There is, however, a limit to the sharpness of this contrast. Neither was Sepehri entirely apolitical, nor was Kho'i devoid of supreme moments of gentility, calm, expansive love, and confidence about his own poetic persona. But still, having met Kho'i in both his poetry and person and Sepehri only in his poetry, prose, and painting, I see traces of each in the other, complicating the radical demarcation between these two seminal poets.

The trajectory of Kho'i's life leading to his exile in England is not very dissimilar from many others in his or, slightly later, my generation—except that he actively and correctly considered himself in exile, while I do not—for the very simple reason that he literally ran for his life, while Iranians like me only left their country to continue their higher education abroad. These are two vastly different circumstances. I left Iran before the 1977–9 revolution to come to the US to pursue my doctorate. Kho'i was a revolutionary activist who had to flee after the revolution, for which they had earnestly fought the Shah's regime, which was usurped by the militant Islamists. This does not mean that I have any sanguine illusion about the violent Islamist regime ruling our homeland, or that I have felt perfectly at home in the US. But still I have happily made English—the colonial language I have made my own, as have many others around the world—our moral and intellectual home. Most of our thinking and writing—postcolonial and decolonial in its diction—are done in English, in the company of other immigrant scholars and thinkers, with Aimé Césaire, Frantz Fanon, Edward Said, and Gayatri Spivak as my generation's exemplary models. Most of Kho'i's poetry and prose was in Persian, our shared mother tongue, as it should have been, yet performed and mourned at one and the same time in the inhospitable capital of British nostalgia for their lost empire. Kho'i was like that proverbial fish out of water, flourishing in Persian in a country and clime with a nostalgic residue of its colonial world domination with its imperial English.

Esmail Kho'i (1938–2021) was born and raised in Mashhad in northwestern Iran, in a loving, caring, and erudite family. His mother was the second wife of his father, who had been disappointed about his first wife not bearing a child. Soon after Kho'i's birth, his stepmother had more children. He has loving memories of both his parents, his stepmother and his siblings.[3] He started composing and even publishing his poems while still in high school in Mashhad. Although he completely assumed the official Tehrani accent in his Persian, he could, if he wanted, when recalling his childhood memories, speak in that accent—as many of us provincials do. Some of his poems also have the mark of the Khorasani accent. His earliest published poems brought him to the attention of his grandfather, whom he remembers fondly and reverentially for having taught him how to read and understand Mawlana Jalal al-Din Rumi. To his dying days he gratefully remembered that privilege. Also, he recalled a high school classmate giving him a copy of the Persian translation of the Hungarian Jewish philosopher György Politzer's (1903–42) widely popular book *Osul-e Moqaddamati-ye Falsafeh/The Elementary Principles of Philosophy*. That book was a staple of our Marxist education well into my generation. I still have my own copy in my possession. The friend continued to give him Marxist literature until he moved to Tehran to attend college. His earliest education in Mashhad, his attempts at poetry, his grandfather's love for Rumi, and his earliest Marxist education all happened in the 1940s and 1950s, during the tense years of the Allied occupation of Iran and the subsequent CIA-MI6 military coup against Mosaddegh to keep the Shah subserviently in power.

Kho'i's first collection of poetry, *Bitab/Restless* (1956), came out when he was still a teenager, a book that he deeply regretted publishing and that remained a source of embarrassment for him throughout his life, as was a long essay which he evidently wrote against Nima's poetic revolution. Literary classicists of his beloved hometown warned him against Persian New Poetry and considered Nima a British conspiracy to destroy Persian poetry![4] But the publication of Akhavan's *Zemestan/Winter* (1956) turned him upside down, and he became deeply drawn to Akhavan and, by extension, Nimaic poetry. While in college in Tehran, Kho'i was equally drawn to another major influence: Professor Mahmoud Houman (1908–80), who taught European philosophy. Houman was the author of a hefty four-volume textbook on European philosophy that was instrumental in our education in European philosophy. Kho'i considered Mehdi Akhavan-e Sales and Mahmoud Houman as the two major influences on him. Houman was also a major scholar of Hafez, and he published his own edition of the seminal Persian poet's works. Houman and Kho'i were of divergent political views, but still very close in their scholarly and intellectual pursuits.

After graduating from college in Tehran, with a degree in European philosophy, Kho'i received a major state scholarship to go to London and continue his education at a graduate level. He returned to Iran in 1965 and began teaching at the Teachers' College, at which time he became captivated by the poetry in Mehdi Akhavan-e Sales' recently published collection *Zemestan/Winter* (1956). By now, Kho'i had been deeply influenced both by his philosophical education and by his irresistible attraction to what he repeatedly called "*she'r-e Akhavani*/Akhavani poetry," rooted in but still distinct from the Nimaic. Although Nima was still alive, Akhavan had put a powerful new twist on his poetics, informed by Nimaic vision yet deeply rooted in his immense knowledge of Persian classical prosody. Kho'i clearly indicated his debt to Nima, Akhavan, and Shamlou. For more than a decade he was active in Iran, publishing his poetry at a regular and steady pace until the militant take-over of the Iranian revolution, when his friend Said Soltanpour was arrested and executed by the Islamist regime on July 26, 1981—soon thereafter Kho'i went into hiding and eventually surfaced in London in 1984.

Kho'i volunteered to his admirers that his poetry became ever angrier after the revolution and his move to England, so that his oeuvre must be divided between the poems of "Esmail Kho'i" and "the Angry Esmail Kho'i." He had his doubts about his angry poetry and said that he would not mind if his angry poems did not remain after the collapse of the Islamic Republic, for half a sea is still a sea. His assessment is, of course, correct: his poetry can be divided into two major parts, before and after the Iranian Revolution of 1977–9. Among his pre-revolutionary collections are *Bitab/Restless* (1956), *Bar Kheng-e Rahvar-e Zamin/Upon the Fast Steed of the Earth* (1967), *Bar Bam-e Gerdbad/On the Roof of the Whirlwind* (1970), *Az Seda-ye Sokhan-e Eshq/From the Sound of the Word of Love* (1970), and *Faratar az Shab-e Aknunian/Beyond the Night of the Contemporaries* (1971).

Reading the poems in these collections reveals a highly competent wordsmith, full of a loving command of his poetic diction, but still no defining signature to distinguish him from a whole slew of other similar or even better poets. Houshang Ebtehaj, Mohmmad Reza Shafi'i-Kadkani, and Fereydoun Moshiri, among scores of others, could very well be considered poets far superior to Kho'i at this early stage, when he left his hometown Mashhad, came to college in Tehran, went to London for his graduate studies, and returned home to make a name for himself as a poet with a penchant for European philosophy. He did not become a poet with a bold, defiant, and definitive signature to his name until the revolution happened and he was forced to leave his homeland. He was born, to put it boldly and fatally, to be an exilic poet. Without the pain and trauma of exile, Kho'i would not have become Kho'i, and Kho'i would not have become the final, missing closure of the Nimaic poetic revolution.

After the revolution and the commencement of his exile in England, Kho'i's volumes were published in rapid succession, among them *Kabus-e Khun Sereshteh Bidaran/The Bloody Nightmare of the Awake* (1984), *Dar Na-behengam/Suddenly* (1984), *Dar Khwabi az Hamareh Hich/In a Dream of the Perpetual Nothing* (1988), *Gozareh Hezareh/The Millennial Testimony* (1991), *Jahan-e Digari Mi-afarinam/I Will Create Another World* (2000), *Sha'er-e Khalqam, Dahan-e Mihanam/I Am the Poet of the People, the Mouth of the Nation* (2000), then a few others, and finally the last volume released in his lifetime, *Dir Nemishavad Delam/My Heart Will Not Be Late* (2020). If we consider the cities where Kho'i's collections of poems were published, initially Mashhad and Tehran figured before the revolution, and then suddenly London, Los Angeles, Frankfurt, Toronto, Stockholm, and Atlanta after the revolution—a clear indication of where his second and definitive stage was located. Here in exile Kho'i became Kho'i, the poet we now know, love, and admire, for he became the voice of the Nowhereville that was destined to be the final destination and resting place of the Nimaic poetic episteme. After Kho'i, the Nimaic poetic episteme came to a closure and ended. There are countless other poets both before Nima and surely after Kho'i who have and will have experimented to varied degrees of success with his and other ways of thinking Persian poetry anew. But Nima and five of his most potent and towering followers—Akhavan, Shamlou, Farrokhzad, Sepehri, and Kho'i—completed his vision and rested their case. The singular signature of this period came when in poetry, his poetry, Kho'i found a home where he could sing a song that only he could now sing. The best evidence of it is "Az She'r Goftan/On Composing Poetry" (1987)—a poem so powerful, so majestic, that I barely dare to come near and translate a few stanza of it, much like when a pilgrim to a sacred site reverentially takes off his shoes, performs an ablution, and approaches a sepulcher:

Bara-ye to ey she'r . . .

For your sake: Oh Poetry!
It is for you
If I have anything to do with anything else,

Or I endure abuse from anyone else!
It is for your sake
If I fly beyond the reach of eagles,
Or if I sit on this spread of the cadavers of vultures!
It is you,
It is you that in the desert of where you are not
Every love and every death,
Wherever they might be,
Are as cheap as any mundane event!
It is you, and for your sake,
That the swamp of whatever else there is
Turns to a dying wave
That by your playful throwing of a pebble—
Smiling—
Blossoms and prides in its countenance!

You turn the rainbow into a word,
You turn the word into a rainbow:
Speech, because of you,
Has the shape of the world,
Because of you
The world is in the shape of a mouth:
Silent and yet singing,
And your shape is the fountain
Of a suddenness
Passing and yet permanent!

Without you the world is like a mountain of cold stone
From the coldness of stone! . . .

Without you the world is like a wall:
Yes,
I have this piercing gaze from you—
Piercing and searching!
You are the cry of the cry,
The silence of the silence,
The memory of memory,
You are the vision of the vision,
The sorrow of all sorrows,
Joy of all joys,
You are the sound, you are the meaning,
You are the sound of the meaning,
You are the meaning of the sound,
You are the meaning of the meaning,
You are the sound of the sound! . . .[5]

I am overwhelmed. I am listening to Kho'i's recorded voice reciting this astounding poem as I write. I translate and feel ashamed of my own or any other translation. How do you translate a Beethoven sonata, a Goya painting, a Parviz Meshkatian composition? We are blessed, this is all I can say, as we are damned at the same time, to have lived our lives with these poets. I stopped translating, stopped writing, and I think that I will close my laptop and simply sit down and listen to Kho'i for a while, reciting this poem in the silence and privacy of my office. The glory of this poem in praise of poetry is matchless. Nothing like it is to be found anywhere else in this pantheon. I am convinced that Kho'i could not have possibly composed this sublime poem in praise of poetry had he not left his homeland, that no other poet, from Nima to Kho'i himself, could have written that poem except in exile, where poetry itself had become his homeland. All major Persian poets—from Ferdowsi over Attar to Naser Khosrow, Sa'di, Rumi, and Hafez—have on occasion reflected on the nature of (their own) poetry. But this is something else. This is a poetic philosophy of poetry, performed in poetry. I am not the only one thinking this way or in awe of this poem. After hearing Kho'i recite this poem, Mehdi Akhavan-e Sales, the solid master of the domain throughout his poetic life, stood up, walked towards Kho'i, and gave Kho'i his jacket to wear—a contemporary version of *"kherqeh pushandan,"* giving someone a cloak, a distant mystic ritual that means officially considering Kho'i a master and now his successor.[6]

Exile as Poetic Ontology

In an essay that Esmail Kho'i published in June 1978, while he was still in Iran, on the globally celebrated Iranian graphic artist Ardeshir Mohassess (1938–2008), Kho'i stated that just a few months before the revolution broke out and Ayatollah Khomeini returned to Iran, he made a few cogent observations about being a *local* as opposed to a *global* artist. His argument was that the only way in which an artist—visual or literary—can become universal is, in fact, to be deeply local. He then compared Mohassess to his own model for poetic excellence, Mehdi Akhavan-e Sales, who also was a poet of the Here and Now, as Kho'i put it, and it was only from the Here and Now that he had become global. This is how Kho'i articulated it:

> As I said, art in its essence is a local phenomenon. Does this then mean that no artist can become universal? Is there a paradox between the local and the global? One might say to become universal is the noblest aspiration of any artist. But only in one way, and solely in one way, can an artist become universal: by being local ... Ardeshir [Mohassess] is the best evidence of this claim. He has now become global, and he will be eternal.[7]

Let us turn this wisdom around and apply it to Esmail Kho'i himself. Was he local or global, and if he was local, as he would say, did he become global when he moved to England and continued mostly, almost exclusively, to write in Persian, with occasional quick roundtrips into (a hesitant and tentative) English? From Iran to England, Kho'i did not go from being local to being global. He went from the dignity of a homeland to the precarity of exile. He did not become global by joining the ranks of Mohassess or Akhavan, but by first being local. He went from being local to being global in the company of an entirely different constellation of exilic poets, literati, and intellectuals. That would be the geology of his exilic poetry.

From Ovid and Dante to Bertolt Brecht, Pablo Neruda, and Mahmoud Darwish—there are countless poets who have at least spent parts of their life in exile.[8] Esmail Kho'i being in exile outside his homeland and living mostly in London (where he had lived as a graduate student in his twenties) is therefore nothing entirely unusual. The Iranian revolution of 1977–9 was a deeply divisive event that caused massive emigration, and hundreds of thousands, perhaps millions, of Iranians moved away from their homeland and lived as new immigrants abroad. There was, of course, something specific to Iranian poets, literati, and intellectuals who had invested deeply in a revolutionary aspiration that did not include, for it could not even fathom such a thing, a violent Islamist component to it. The violent Khomeini ascendency to power, and then the Islamist forces that had enabled it, seized power by brute force, pushed the other revolutionaries (or counter-revolutionaries) out of their country and established a viciously repressive theocratic regime. The diversionary tactic of the American Hostage Crisis (1979–81), the eight years of the brutal Iran–Iraq War (1980–8), as well as the subsequent successive waves of university purges, mass executions, and cultural revolutions helped Khomeini and his followers to consolidate their power and, in turn, create a deeply disappointed, bitter, and angry diaspora. A number of leading Iranian poets, novelists, filmmakers, and other artists left Iran for good and sought to create a working environment for themselves, while the overwhelming majority of them stayed put in Iran, seeking to carve out a space for their arts and remaining conversant with the next generation of Iranian artists abroad.

Esmail Kho'i was not the only member of this exilic community who left Iran for good, never to return, but he was a major figure in it. While in London, where I visited him on multiple occasions, Kho'i was, for example, a frequent visitor to Ebrahim Golestan, an ostensibly wealthy man who lived at Wykehurst Place, a Gothic Revival mansion in Bolney, West Sussex, which is a cross between a French châteaux and an English manor house—surrounded by a significant collection of priceless artworks decorating his endless walls. Other Iranian poets, satirists, and scholars also lived in London at this time, and they still do. In the 1980s, I would see Ebrahim Golestan, Esmail Kho'i, Hadi Khorsandi, Fereydoun Adamiyat, Homayoun Katouzian, Farhad Daftary, and Mashallah Ajoudani for breakfast, lunch, or dinner. Golestan was an exceptionally welcoming and hospitable focal point for such gatherings, at which I would regularly see Kho'i—a gentle, affable, soft-spoken alcoholic with a pleasant and caring demeanor. I have in my private library a number of first editions of his books that he kindly inscribed for me.

When I had just joined Columbia University, I also invited him to our campus in New York to recite his poetry to scores of his admirers.

London in the 1980s and 1990s was a crowded and rambunctious place for all sorts of expats. The Edgeware Road area of London near the Marble Arch and Hyde Park was and remains crowded by a significant number of new immigrants from the Arab and Muslim world, as well as from Asia and Africa. Restaurants, cafés, newsstands, fresh fruit and vegetable stands, spotted by red telephone booths plastered with advertisements for prostitutes, gave the neighborhood a particularly warm, cozy, and welcoming character. Idle men were sitting on plastic chairs on the pavement, smoking their nargilehs, reading Arabic, Persian, or Urdu newspapers, debating politics, as their wealthier womenfolk were roaming and shopping at the Harrods and Marks & Spencer department stores. "Little Kuwait" was one particular square near Edgeware Road, nicknamed so soon after the Iraqi invasion of Kuwait in 1990 and the arrival of wealthy Kuwaiti families. I loved that neighborhood. Fresh fruit and vegetable stands featured familiar produce, while Lebanese and Persian restaurants were competing for customers. A Lebanese, Syrian, Kuwaiti, Iraqi, or Iranian expat could spend an entire evening in such a neighborhood feeling somewhat at home. Esmail Kho'i was a spot in this landscape.

I have turned to Kho'i in this last chapter, for in his condition of exile he represents and personifies the closure of the poetic episteme (which began in temporal terms and concluded in spatial terms) of the Persian New Poetry I have detected and outlined in this book. With Kho'i in exile, the Nimaic poetics came to a sad and somber end and finally rested their case. Other younger poets in and outside of Iran might and indeed do continue to practice their homely or nomadic poetry, sometime with exquisite results.[9] But the souls of the Persian New Poetry that Nima first breathed into classical Persian poetics and that came to flower in five other poets (Akhavan, Shamlou, Farrokhzad, and Sepehri) culminated and concluded with Kho'i in exile. It is this exiled condition that best represents both Kho'i and the final demise of Nimaic poetics. The soul of Persian New Poetry left Iran and abandoned the spirit of the age with the dawn of the Islamist theocracy— while inside Iran delivering its most glorious moments to the emerging Iranian New Wave cinema. Exile as a poetic ontology came to full fruition in Kho'i's personal and poetic legacy. Like Kho'i, so too did Ardeshir Mohassess, about whom he wrote so eloquently early in both of their careers, opt to live in exile in New York. They both began their visual and poetic arts in their own homeland and lived the maturest moments of their lives in exile. They were both local and native to their birth and upbringings and became global precisely in their exilic conditions. In one of the last poems that Kho'i wrote shortly before the thunderous rise of the Iranian revolution, he lovingly anticipated the coming uprising, not yet knowing that this very seismic event would wash him from the shores of his beloved homeland and land him in what he had always in despair called "*Bidarkoja-ye Landan*/The Nowhereville of London." This is that poem, "Soroud-e Azadi/Song of Freedom" (1978), published in the collection of his poems in the spirit of the Siahkal uprising:

Midahand bas yaran jan beh rah-e azadi . . .

So many comrades give their lives for freedom
So that many would live one day
In the shade of freedom!
What is freedom, what is it?
Death of all tyranny,
For the homeland: Prosperity,
For the people: Happiness!

March towards the village:
Upon the fruitful earth!
Watch the shadow of the tyrant,
Or else look at the cities,
Look at work and capital,
See the asymmetrical warfare!

Though now, in the battle
Of those who have arisen,
The time of the evil-doers
Has no doubt turned around!

Look now, look
How it would rise:
And what a torrent it will cause
Against the warmongers,
Against those with power and wealth!
The workers in front,
The peasants by their side!

March towards the village:
Or else look at the cities!

Now from every direction,
Throughout Iran
Blood runs like a river
To wash this ruinous abode
So that it can wash Iran
Of all ruins!
So that it can build an Iran
For the happiness of Iranians!

Yes, freedom, yes!
Yes, freedom, yes!
This paradise of the awakened,
The inferno of the wicked.

Yes, freedom, yes!
This dawning of humanity!
The true dawning of the soul,
The cradle of faith!

Yes, freedom, yes!
Death of all tyranny,
For the homeland: Prosperity!
For the people: Happiness.

And now in this abode:
So many comrades give their lives for freedom!
So that many might one day
Live in the shade of freedom![10]

"A Suitcase Full of Culture"

Exile, shall we say, is a paradox: a condition of both freedom and entrapment, where and when the idea of homeland becomes at once painfully overwhelming yet increasingly distanced, fading, and above all irretrievably fetishized. Esmail Kho'i's poem "Bazgasht beh Borgio Verezzi/Return to Borgio Verezzi" (1983) is rightly celebrated as perhaps his most significant initial poem in exile. Like many of my contemporaries, I have heard Kho'i recite this poem twice—once in New York at Columbia University, when I invited him to come and read his poems, and another time in Sussex, England, at Ebrahim Golestan's mansion, where we both were among his frequent guests. To this day, the poem carries the tone and diction of Kho'i's earliest pains of exile. It describes a visit to an Italian village that the poet had visited before—hence the word "return" in the title. The figures of three women dominate this poem: one is an unnamed female lover accompanying the poet on this trip, another an old Italian woman who reminds the poet of his own grandmother, and the third Forough Farrokhzad as she is cited in the poem. The poem begins abruptly, with the poet and his lover sitting on the train as it is about to enter a tunnel:

Haman dahaneh-ye tariki-ye tunel . . .

The same dark opening of the tunnel—
And then a nameless feeling,
And a split second—
When the train becomes like a coffin—
And then the commotion.
Of all the colors
Cast upon the bluish green embrace
Of silence,

And the suddenness
Of the tree-covered hills,
And then
The cold absence of tourists
On the idle shores,
And that coral reef
On a pale backdrop of sadness
And those two lover-rocks
Staring at each other
In a perpetual pause
Amidst the magic of their granite bewilderment—

And then the fact of my absolute awakening
From a doubtful slumber in my imagination—
Punctuating its fluent texture
Line by line
The flying scream
Of the seagulls![11]

The poet is traveling and sits on this train with a lover; he declares himself in love, even though he is getting old, and that thought reminds him of a line by Hafez. He sees a kind old lady who reminds him of his own grandmother, and in his mind, he begins to edit the old woman's face in a way that would resemble his grandmother even more. He tries to explain to the old lady that he is from Iran, but she has no clue where Iran is. He remembers a line of Forough Farrokhzad about the idea of homeland and edits that poem, too, for the word "Iran" to rhyme with "*viran*/in ruins." He starts talking Persian to the old lady and tells her how in his homeland, cannibals have been resurrected from history. The woman is bewildered and asks him in Italian what language he is speaking. She does not speak Persian. The poet does not speak Italian. But in Persian he assures the old lady that he has brought along a suitcase full of culture from his homeland. It is futile, a mismatch, a non-conversation. The poet goes to the sea and considers how he is now twenty years older than the last time he was there. Standing amidst youngsters who all appear to have zero years to their names and faces, he recalls the twenty years in the span of which the poet has lost a homeland. He then recalls the last time he was there: he was an Iranian poet and a student of philosophy, visiting an Italian village; now he is an exile in the same spot, where the village has lost its name, where its inhabitants are all zero years old, and where the thick description of the landscapes is the only way to describe it.

The lover, the grandmother, and the poet: the three images that define the poem are the most potent insignia defining the poet in exile.[12] The young woman whom he now loves, the grandmother he has forever lost, and Forough Farrokhzad as the poet's "sister," as he calls her, or more precisely, "*khwahar-e talkham*/my bitter sister," frame the poet in terms at once domestic and yet now foreign to his arrival as an exile. The figures of the grandmother and sister are here poetically and personally to welcome the poet and his lady friend to this village. The poet lives with the ghosts of his grandmother and sisters, both long since gone, now here, as part of that suitcase full of ghosts to welcome their son and brother and his European girlfriend. In that sense, the poet is not taking his girlfriend to see a village that he knew in his youth, but actually to visit the ghosts of his grandmother and sister, whom he is carrying in his suitcase.

The Perils and Poetics of a Noble Anger

Much has been said about Kho'i's anger and boldly political poetry after he left Iran and about whether these poems would endure. Kho'i's critics in this regard seem to have a puritanical conception of poetry, with which his defiant revolutionary voice does not quite gel. Some have even falsely compared him with Sepehri, as if Sepehri's poetry was not political. This is a false binary. These are two very different poets who nevertheless come together to form and complete a formidable episteme or paradigm—like the conjugated verb "TO BE" that looks like "AM" in one case and "ARE" in another. But they still are from the same paradigm. Kho'i's poem, all of his poems, will endure—both as historical evidence of an era and as deeply rooted political poetry of a fearless master poet who was in tune with the deepest aspirations and anxieties of his people—whether in exile or at home. A seismic historic event happened in Kho'i's homeland, which divided a nation between those who violently supported an Islamist ideology and those who boldly opposed and resisted it. In the prime of his moral and political imagination, Kho'i invested much in the revolutionary aspirations of his people, aspirations that were, in fact, rooted in the poetic legacy that Nima had inaugurated, that all his followers had expanded in one direction or another, and that Kho'i now best represented and completed. By being true to his political convictions and exilic condition, Kho'i made of exile an existential truth definitive to the homeliness of his homeland. Every single word he uttered, in prose or poetry, was replete with his inconsolable homesickness. He made of his defiant poetry the simulacrum of a home—Iranian in its character and Persian in its poetic disposition—where he would remain true to his vocation as an exilic poet. His poetry would be infinitely more definitive to the principled opposition to the Islamist theocracy than any mundane and/or corrupt monarchist regime-changer on the payroll of US neo-con chicaneries.

To be sure, there were times during his prolonged sojourn in exile when Kho'i's hatred of the ruling Islamist regime in Iran would degenerate into visceral Islamophobia, and his penchant for precise Persian words would trespass into a deliberate avoidance of Arabic words that had found a comfortable place in Persian diction. He would also come to be boldly in support of Salman Rushdie, which in and of itself was fine, but he would totally disregard his major role in fomenting Islamophobia in Europe and the US. Kho'i and a few other Iranians in exile wrote a public letter in which they rightly and correctly condemned Khomeini's edict against Salman Rushdie. But nowhere did any single one of them ever utter a word about the rampant Islamophobia in the US and Europe, which Rushdie himself had actively endorsed and encouraged. The signatories to this letter declared:

> The signers of this declaration who have shown in many different ways their support for Salman Rushdie now and in the past, believe that freedom of speech is one of the greatest achievements of mankind, and point out, as Voltaire once did, that this freedom would be meaningless unless human beings had the liberty to blaspheme. No one and no group has the right to hamper or hinder this freedom in the name of this or that sanctity.[13]

This was, of course, all good and dandy to endorse for a coterie of expat intellectuals who had remained entirely oblivious to the rise of the nasty white supremacist fascism in Europe and the US that much benefited from and trumpeted the Salman Rushdie Affair. By putting their names to this statement, Kho'i and his friends were now in the company of Ayaan Hirsi Ali, Azar Nafisi, Bill Maher, Richard Dawkins, Christopher Hitchens, and scores of other notorious promoters of Muslim hatred in the US and Europe, with calamitous consequences for the militant warmongering of these countries in places such as Afghanistan, Iraq, Palestine, and Syria. Kho'i and his friends freely staged their perfectly correct celebration of freedom of expression, yet they were completely blindsided by the terror of Muslim hatred that successive waves of Muslim immigrants would have to endure in these countries, as well as *a fortiori* in a vicious militarism that now (as I write these words) has staged itself in the genocidal Zionist slaughtering of tens of thousands of Palestinians, Lebanese, and Syrians. With complete impunity. It is odd, strange, and disconcerting that the legitimate criticism of the Islamist regime in Iran would result in a blind hatred that would place Kho'i next to the most notorious neo-con fanaticism to plague the world for generations.

Most of the signatories to this letter—and Kho'i, in particular—lived a decidedly exilic and insular life in the US or Europe and were almost entirely alien to the lived experiences of poor Muslims and millions of other immigrants in these countries; they were deeply white-identified in their politics. They were, willy-nilly, dancing to the tune of a white supremacist xenophobia that has resulted in the rise of neo-fascist parties in Europe and the presidency of Donald Trump in the US. In these flawed sentiments, Kho'i partook in the rooted fear and loathing rampant among his expat contemporaries. In the heat of a moment, Kho'i endorsed, praised, and even published a poem in praise of Shahin Najafi, a notorious expat Iranian rapper and vulgar *agent provocateur* who ended up in the camp of expat monarchists actively supporting the puppet son of the late Shah, the demented Reza Pahlavi! So, was Kho'i a monarchist, too—after a lifetime of commitment to Marxist revolutionary aspirations? Of course not. Kho'i's life in exile was replete with dangerous pitfalls against his own name and reputation as a critical thinker and revolutionary poet, and he would occasionally fall into those cracks. We therefore need to focus on the quintessence of his poetry, which had every reason and rhyme to be replete with anger. He dwelled and thrived in that anger, even though that very anger would occasionally and paradoxically blind him to his own revolutionary heritage. To redeem his precious name against his own bad judgment, let me now read and translate one of his most glorious poems, "Sha'er-e Khalqam, Dahan-e Mihanam/I Am the Poet of the People, the Mouth of the Nation," in which we have a principled measure of who he was and how far from the heart of his politics he would occasionally move in moments of terrible judgment:

Bum niam man zeh cheh zari konam . . .

I am not an Owl, why should I moan?
Be saddened by this dark night,
Be like a distraught night
And push happiness away from myself . . .
The face of the world is all made of this year
Why should I keep thinking of the year passing,
Just like a cloud I will rinse myself of myself
Make my dusty soul shine anew . . .
Don't mock me that these are all illusions and nothing more:
I am a poet, and I can do miracles!
That which is in the depth of your heart
I will reflect in the mirror of my heart!
It is a "We" to you this "I" that I
Make the poet of this poem a slogan!
I am the poet of the people, the mouth of the nation,
It behooves me if I am boastful! . . .[14]

In the same vein we might read his other now legendary poem: "Nuruzaneh/A New Year Song" (1996)—which reads as an uncanny combination of love for Norouz and hatred for the ruling regime in Iran. The point in this poem is the pitch-perfect balance that he found between his celebration of beauty, love, and joy, and the simultaneous denunciation of the horrors of the Islamist regime. Most of the time, the poem walks a perilous line between the denunciation of militant Islamism and of Islam itself. But the balance of the poem is still fairly solid in staying on the side of a critical stance against a theocracy rather than a visceral contempt for the religion in whose name this theocracy rules.

Kam-e hamegan bad rava, kam-e shoma nah!

May everyone's wishes come true, but not yours!
May the life of everyone be happy, but not yours!
You're so spiteful, it is as if the wine of Norouz
Pours into everyone's goblet, but not yours . . .
Oh you who cherish death, I did my research and I found
Every religion finds its way to God but not your Islam . . .
You're so far away from love and beauty
As if the mother of everyone is a woman but not your mother . . . !

This earthquake of science has shaken the foundation of all superstition,
Has bewildered the slumber of everyone, though not yours! . . .
I examined, and I found there are signs of progress
In Nero's Decrees but not in your mandates,
Omar had more magnanimity for the precious culture of Iran
Than you do! . . .[15]

Much of the anger of this poem is targeted against the ruling theocratic regime in the Islamic Republic of Iran, not against Islam itself, and even the phrase "your Islam/*Islam-e shoma*" is quite specific. But still, one can sense the shaky and porous borderline between the principled critique of a militant ideology ruling the poet's homeland and the dangerous domain of hatred of Islam in its entirety—the faith of billions of human beings on this earth. Much of the Iranian left, alas, would remain on that porous borderline, to this day. We must also balance all such angry lashing-out against the overwhelming moments when Kho'i questioned the varied warring "I"s battling inside him, as he did in his crucial poem, "Qazal-qasideh-ye Man-ha-ye Man/The Panegyric-lyric of All My 'I's." For example, he said:

Dar khwish ham bengar . . .

Look inside yourself, too:
That ugly evil
Is perhaps rising from inside you!
You see, perhaps
You might be it!
Perhaps the enemy is inside you,
Might be you, yourself,
The devil who in every task manifests
Itself differently,
And in each station
Has different shapes!
Perhaps outside of you this shadow
Is just this shadow
That you give it existence—
And it walks with you
Wherever you go!
Hmm? What do you think of that?[16]

In that state, in yet another long poem, "Gozareh Hezareh/The Millennial Testimony," the poet might even consider himself a Muslim—of a particular kind:

For myself
I became a Muslim of a different sort
A Muslim made of blasphemy,
Of the Zoroastrian and the Christian,

And I believed in doubt
The doubt of fear and questioning . . .
I dragged the Arab God
To Mother Iran, entrusted it to Zoroastrian Mazda
And the dream of Mazdak . . .[17]

From there he moved to Mani, Socrates, Plato, Buddha, where he created another God, another Islam, to be another Muslim. In short, it is difficult to pinpoint the poet in one particular moment at the expense of the varied gestations of his poetic persona.

The Exilic Community as a Hermeneutic Circle

I am sitting in my office in Knox Hall on Columbia University's campus in New York City, having collected from my bookshelves all my books by or about Esmail Kho'i and placed them next to me on my desk. I look at the stack of books with a sketch of Esmail Kho'i's face on the cover of one of them: *Yek Tekkeh-am Aseman Abi Beferest/Send Me a Patch of Blue Sky!* I am one among the happy few who have seen and known Kho'i and shared his life outside our homeland. The books that I own, some of them signed and kindly and generously inscribed for me by Kho'i himself, are all published in the US, Canada, or Europe. They are palpably inexpensive editions, making them available to Kho'i's admirers who do not have much disposable income to buy books. Editions are clumsy, fonts awkward, the bindings pitiful, print qualities uneven. This pile of books in front of me is the very definition of exilic life for the poet himself and his loving admirers alike. As I look and thumb through my books by and on Kho'i, I also listen to his own voice reciting his poetry, widely available online. He has a powerful and compelling voice, accompanied by music sometimes matching, sometime contradicting the sentiments of the poems: "Kam-e hamegan bad rava, kam-e shoma nah!/May Everyone's Wishes Come True, But Not Yours!" I have spent hours and hours searching and reading about him on the Internet, mostly shorter or longer pieces in Persian by his friends and admirers. I have also watched and listened to short and longer videos: the useful BBC conversation with Jamshid Barzegar, a sad and undignified funeral ceremony, countless videos and audio tracks where he recited his own poetry. Put together, this is the indexical summation of the exilic community in person and online forming a hermeneutic circle around the towering presence of Kho'i among his contemporaries abroad.

During his own lifetime, Kho'i witnessed the publication in Iran of a major book on his life and poetry: Mahmoud Mo'taqedi's *Beh Rasm-e Haghighat va Ziba'i: Zendegi va She'r-e Esmail Kho'i/In the Tradition of Truth and Beauty: The Life and Poetry of Esmail Kho'i* (2014).[18] This is a perfectly legitimate, widely informed, reliable, and even competent book, yet entirely counterintuitive and out of place, for by the time of his death on June 25, 2021, Kho'i was an entirely exilic phenomenon and a widely read, loved, and admired poet precisely by the expat community of Iranians around the world, and as such he lived, died, and belonged to that Nowhereville that he both mourned and marked as the abode of his fateful existence. His friends and admirers have even created the Esmail Kho'i Foundation (*Bonyad-e Esmail Kho'i*) in his honor in Atlanta, Georgia, where, in fact, he attended my lecture at Emory University and brought me some of his most recent books. It is therefore somewhat odd and bizarre to read a book published on Kho'i in his homeland, where he as a poet was not welcomed and would have instantly landed in jail or worse, had he ever gone back to Iran. "Qesseh-ye Ghorbat Gharbiyeh/The Ballad of the Occidental Exile," the title of Suhrawardi's poetic allegory, was the very summation of Kho'i's life and poetry. Kho'i's physical presence and celebrated poetry helped to consolidate this community of both exiled and immigrant Iranians and to enable the rise of a new generation of expat poets and critics— such as Majid Nafisi, Sa'id Youssef, and Ziba Karbassi, whose poetry Kho'i deeply admired and endorsed. Much of the output of this generation was of course and necessarily in Persian, but a significant part was also in translation. Rarely did this body of work exit the limited domain of expat parochialism. Be that as it may, this exilic condition expands the rooted Persian cosmopolis well into the European and North American environs. While in its natural habitat in a vast part of Asia, the Persian cosmopolis overshadowed the colonial languages that came its way— from Arabic to English. In the exilic parochialism of these translators and Area Studies specialists, Persian has been overshadowed and has never been able to express itself against the dominant culture, either performed in Persian or else in the calamitous conditions of securitization of an entire language and its cultures.

In Samsam Kashfi's edited volume with the title *Jan-e Del-e She'r: Negahi beh Chand Sh'er-e Esmail Kho'i/The Heart and Soul of Poetry: A Glance at a Few Poems of Esmail Kho'i* (2002), we read a collection of learned essays, all in Persian, in which Kho'i's poetry is examined from a variety of perspectives.[19] This is a learned volume, and all the luminaries of Iranian expat intellectuals are gathered in it. Mashallah Ajoudani, for example, a prominent historian of modern Iran who also lives in London, has written the essay "Sha'eri va Vasvaseh-ye Sokhanvari/Being a Poet and the Temptation of Speechmaking," in which he has reviewed a collection of Kho'i's poems, distinguishing between his poetic core and his occasional penchant for speechmaking, by which he has meant a kind of formalism that he has deemed without substance.[20] Ajoudani has considered the temptation of *sokhanvari* or verbose speechmaking, a flaw and fault that Kho'i occasionally exhibited. When we look at the list of the other contributors to this volume, all except one are writing in Persian, and they are all expat Iranians, with the exception of Michael Beard, a learned American scholar of Persian literature. The editor tells us in his introduction that he decided against the Persian translation of the English essay included in the edited volume when he realized that it was based on the English translations of Kho'i's work and not on the originals.[21] This volume is representative of the tight hermeneutic circle that has gathered around Kho'i's poetry, comprised almost exclusively of Iranian expats writing in Persian.[22] This phenomenon is a double-edged sword: on one hand, it offered Kho'i a precious extension of the Persian cosmopolis deep into Europe and North America; on the other hand, the linguistic politics of these very regions almost instantly ghettoized and nativized his poetry, preventing it from reaching a more global critical reception in the humanities and a wider readership. The quality of translations afforded Kho'i has always been mixed—some excellent (Hakkak and Beard), others limited and misleading. The quality of analytic and theoretical insight has been equally wanting, limited, and prosaic. Some US- or Canada-based scholars would write a whole treatise based on such wanting translations, rather than care for the originals. The result has been quite chaotic but still insightful.[23] Nothing, we regrettably must admit, has come even close to Kofi Anyidoho's edited volume, *The Word Behind Bars and the Paradox of Exile* (1997), produced around Kho'i and other Iranian poets, artists, and filmmakers in exile.[24]

Kho'i himself, in a famous poem, in fact raised certain existential questions about the whereabouts of a homeland:

Vatan kojast?
Delam bara ye cheh tang ast? . . .

Where is the homeland?
What do I miss—
I occasionally ask myself.
Who is the friend?
Whom do I miss?

Your message still rings in my ears:
"You are not safe here anymore!"
And I recall your advice:
"For God's sake, leave! Don't stay here!"

Then why is it now
That whatever gift comes my way from your side
Is nothing but admonition, and the bitter poison of reprimand?

What have I done?
Except wholeheartedly follow your advice—
And as a result, I am now condemned
To this accursed land of silence and forgetfulness!

Why are you so bold in condemning me?
God forbid, are you demented tyrants?
Or else appeasing the pure and pious Muslims?
Or else you are just being hypocritical and duplicitous? . . .

Alas!
Once I collected my belongings and left a homeland
That would have been the executioner of either my life or my conscience

Were I to stay!
Wish you could come to the custom from which I run away
And searched me to see
There was nothing in my suitcase except my life
And nothing except my life is my suitcase:
Priceless of course
For it is made in Iran
Full of the silk of poetry—
Tapestry made of heart and soul
Protected by its divine gift of grace
From any search . . .

I left so that in a pond somewhere
To be the extension of your sea, . . .
Your lantern you graciously say
Burns there!
Well, may your shining light and soul
Be always bright!
But what does that mean exactly, pray say,
For God's sake, what does that even mean?
What are you saying, and whom are you addressing?
Where and for what else is my petty light burning? . . .[25]

Kho'i, Exile, and the Assemblage

With Esmail Kho'i, the inherited repertoire of the poetic tropes of this assemblage radically changed from the temporal disposition of the homeland to the spatial location of exile, for soon after the Islamist take-over of the Iranian revolution of 1977–9, Kho'i moved into permanent exile in Europe and lived in the UK until the end of his life. In his poetry he de- and subsequently reterritorialized the *locus classicus* of this epistemic assemblage, which, as such, leads us towards a critical conception of ontological diversity in the making of postcolonial agency. The postcolonial subject is here poetically formed and framed, from within the matrix of this aesthetic assemblage—a system at once fluid and amorphous. Therefore, only in historical retrospective can we heuristically break it down, as I have done in this book, to its formative forces (Nima, Akhavan, and so on), to see and perceive their varied but ultimately interpolated forces. Kho'i's was the sad fate of completing, concluding, and exiting this assemblage and seeing his homeland from afar, as well as the ideals and aspirations of other poets, which he shared and saw betrayed and maligned by the theocratic take-over of his homeland—a theocracy that violently shifted the anchor of Iranian culture from cosmopolitan humanism to Islamist scholasticism. Kho'i's poetry had become increasingly bitter and angry, vindictive and hateful, justly defiant against the fate of a poetic legacy that had begun with Nima and ended with him in exile. Paradoxically, or perhaps not, the angrier his voice became, the more poetically elegant and precise his diction turned. Here is an example from "Ja'i keh Vatan Shavad/Where We Might Call Homeland" (2016):

Ja'i keh Vatan Shavad . . .

Here we have everything
But they don't mean anything.
This is not where I can be part of any "we"—
Your entire world
Is my little patch of exile—
This is not where it could ever be
My homeland.[26]

In some remarkable ways, Esmail Kho'i is the historical repetition of Naser Khosrow (1004–88)—a poet-philosopher like him, who also was forced into exile and who also was a revolutionary adherent of Isma'ilism, a radical ideology of his time, akin to Kho'i's commitment to militant Marxism. Kho'i, we might say, was the contemporary version of Naser Khosrow. Kho'i's penchant for poetic philosophy, some of it best captured in his quatrains, was equally reminiscent of Omar Khayyam (1048–1131). Here are some samples of Kho'i's quatrains:

You ask me why do I drink:
And then where, with whom, and when do I drink—
Until I am I and life is what it is,
I drink with everyone, everywhere, and ceaselessly.[27]

He said Freedom, I said it is my Prince,
He asked, what about Happiness?
I said, that is my elixir!
He said, future, I said there is my son!
What about Hope, I said he is my Spiritual Master![28]

When I am no longer the enemy of any Shah or sheikh,
Nor do I follow any particular path,
I wish for a grave in my homeland, so that one day
In a corner of that land, I'd grow as a plant![29]

Let us listen to a song of birds on this green pasture,
Let us breathe happily early in the morning,
Then let you and me embrace,
Perchance to forget our sorrows![30]

What is solitude? Undoubtedly the mother of poetry!
The silent partner of my heart: the spouse of poetry!

Your bewitching beauty: the daughter of poetry,
My sorrow? Alas, the other daughter of poetry.³¹

Comparisons with Naser Khosrow in terms of his exilic condition, and with Omar Khayyam in terms of his taste for quatrains, place Kho'i next to two philosopher-poets, comparisons that would make more sense of his own fusion of the two traits of thinking poetically and philosophically at one and the same time.

Case Closed

Esmail Kho'i was the conclusion, the closure, and the final exhaustion of the poetic episteme that had started with Nima Yushij and unfolded apace for the entirety of the Persian New Poetry that lasted for about a century and that was destined to exit Iran in its last figure altogether to rest its case in exile. It was a cruel paradox that the final chapter of the six poets who imagined their homeland anew was forced into exile and died farthest removed, not only from his physical homeland, but also from the closure and conclusion of the idea of the homeland that they had collectively imagined. But, at the same time, that was perhaps also a closure befitting a cosmopolitan conception of the homeland that, from the very inception, existed beyond all physical borders. Paradoxically, like a fish out of water, no other poet among these six poets lived and died an Iranian poet as did Kho'i. He closed the episteme, rested his case, and in the bitter anger of his death outside his homeland he extended that homeland, as well as the glory of his poetic power, deep into the exilic indignity of not just Iranian but all exiles.

As he lay dying in exile, Iranian cinema had already picked up from where that poetics had enabled and enacted the sublime.

Kho'i in exile—the last Persian poet of the Nimaic revolution far away from his home in a nutshell: to the poetic manner born, he was forced into exile when his closest friend and comrade Said Soltanpour was summarily executed. In exile, he became the evidence of a poetic ontology that he best summarized and collected in the image and allegory of "a suitcase full of culture" and signed always as "from *Bidarkoja*/Nowhereville." Here we must make a definitive distinction between exile and migration. Kho'i did not emigrate to Europe: he was forced into exile, and he fled for fear of his life, and rightly so. A number of Iranian artists made a name and reputation for themselves claiming lucratively to be in "exile" when they were no such thing. They had merely immigrated to Europe or the US, where they exoticized and Orientalized themselves for their white-identified customers. Poets such as Kho'i, and artists such as Ardeshir Mohassess or Nicky Nodjoumi, and filmmakers such as Amir Naderi, were in real exile—and their homeland was ever so poorer when they left it. They had a potent political twist to their arts and a defiant politics against the Islamist theocracy that would have landed them in prison or worse, if they were to return home. Kho'i had to smuggle that proverbial suitcase from his homeland to arrive at a destination that he could never completely call home. The poetics of a noble anger thus became definitive to his life and legacy, central to an exilic community that formed a tight hermeneutic circle around him and his poetry and thus made them meaningful, significant, and historical precisely in an exilic context. With his exile, Kho'i paradoxically padlocked and fastened the assemblage, both completed and closed it at one and the same time—before the whole episteme finally made and rested its case. The irony of all ironies, or not, is that he lost his son Houman while in exile. His son died while the father was still alive. The man ended, the poet came to a closure, before his time. His poetic progeny could now only remember their parents, from Nima through Farrokhzad to Kho'i, in their repressed dreams of themselves. There is one poem, among many others, that perhaps sums up his self-doubting, soul-searching, poetic persona and that might be considered his political and philosophical manifesto. It is called "Khod-sanji/Self-Appraisal":

Man an rahju-ye rah-puyam . . .

I am that seeker of the path,
Walking on the path
Towards the truth, that did
Wrong as long as I did,
I did wrong, I did wrong, I did wrong,
Truth is the human and any absolute
Is a manifestation of falsehood
How many untruthful things
I did with truth, the dogmatist that I was
I became an atheist
For I had seen harm from religion,
And yet I turned atheism into a God
Without knowing it,
I thought religion was the first of all ills, for example,
And yet:
I cured that ill with yet another ill,
Meaning with one wrong I negated another
Wrong, meaning with one ill I cured another ill . . .
I brought the God from the sky of religion
Down to the earth of hatred
The name I gave it here first was the proletariat
Then I placed an organization instead of the people,
then I placed a tyrant
Where the Divinity was placed . . .
I have made a mistake
But you might forgive me
If I did wrong, I did them all for you![32]

Conclusion

SIX PERSIAN POETS IN SEARCH OF A HOMELAND

Time to wrap things up: in 1975, only a year before I left Iran for good, Mohammad Hoghughi, a prominent literary critic of his time, published a seminal assessment of Persian New Poetry, *She'r-e No: Az Aghaz ta Emruz, 1301–1350/New Poetry: From the Beginning to Today, 1922–1971* (1975).[1] Nothing of "modern," "modernity," "modernization," or similar is in the title. Like the rest of us, Hoghughi had no need or urge to use it. Just "New Poetry/*She'r-e No*" would do. Except for a few colonized minds here and there, the misapplication of the term "modernity" or its variants to non-European sites is the product of mostly North American and Western European university campuses and nefarious think-tanks. Hoghughi's learned volume was a seminal event at a crucial moment in the rich and effervescent history of Persian New Poetry, for what Hoghughi did was, in effect, canonizing the unfolding history of this seminal event in Iranian literary and intellectual history. Who were the poets who were collected, anthologized, and thus canonized in this volume? The book is divided into five decades. In the first decade (the 1920s), we obviously have Nima Yushij. In the second decade (the 1930s), we still have Nima Yushij and no one else. In the third decade (the 1940s), we continue to see Nima Yushij, as well as a number of other poets, among them Fereydoun Tavalloli, Siavash Kasra'i, and Houshang Ebtehaj, all of them distinctly popular and important poets of their time, but none of them with a vision of their age based on Nima's model. In the fourth decade (the 1950s), Nima Yushij continues to reign supreme, to which now the names and works of Ahmad Shamlou, Mehdi Akhavan-e Sales, and Forough Farrokhzad are added, among half a dozen other important poets. They are all widely popular and capable poets, but only Shamlou, Akhavan, and Farrokhzad exude a distinctly visionary perspective on their Time and Place, expanding on the archetype that Nima had initiated. In the fifth and final decade (the 1960s), Nima now disappears for he was no longer alive, but Shamlou, Farrokhzad, and Akhavan are joined by Sohrab Sepehri and Esmail Kho'i, as well as a handful of other important poets. By now we see all the six seminal poets I have gathered in my book—for a specific theoretical purpose—solidly evident and canonized by a literary scholar immediately related to and contemporary with these poets, squarely located in the historical context of their defining times and poetic sentiments.

Almost half a decade later, in 1979, at the threshold of the Iranian revolution of 1977-9, another prominent literary historian, Hamid Zarrinkub, published a similar book, *Cheshm-andaz-e She'r-e No-e Farsi/A Perspective on Persian New Poetry* (1979).² In this book, we see that all of the six poets in Hoghughi's volume—Nima, Akhavan, Shamlou, Farrokhzad, Sepehri, and Kho'i—are present, in the midst of more than a dozen or so other equally important, but less visionary, poets. What distinguishes my way of thinking in this book from the work of these seminal literary historians is that they are mainly archiving, anthologizing, and thus canonizing a crucial period in Persian New Poetry, while I have selected six seminal poets whom they also thought significant yet placed them inside an episteme that I believe to be at work, which makes them complementary to each other in forming a singular vision of their time and place. All the other poets anthologized here are and remain crucial in what they did, but not in the same way in which these six poets defined their age and formed a constellation and the subterranean forces of an assemblage, where they located their aesthetic imagination in the framework of forming and framing the collective subconscious of a nation, a people, a *mihan*, a *vatan*, and so on, while casting the character of their homeland in their poetic midst. Published at the threshold of an Islamist take-over of Iranian cosmopolitan culture, Zarrinkub's volume gives a sense of setting the historical record straight before things are lost to collective memories.

In 1989, a solid decade after the revolution, Morteza Kakhi, a learned member of the literati, edited *Roshan-tar az Khamushi: Bargozideh She'r-e Emruz Iran, 1300–1357/Brighter than Silence: An Anthology of the Poetry of Today, 1921–1978* (1989), which begins with the eminent Constitutional-period poet Ali Akbar Dehkhoda (1879–1956) and ends with a contemporary poet, Ali Mousavi Garmaroudi (born 1941).³ In this volume we see gathered all the canonical figures of Nima, Shamlou, Akhavan, Farrokhzad, and Sepehri, as well as a detailed chapter on Esmail Kho'i, with all his poems from the 1960s and early 1970s included—and nothing from his exilic period, for obvious censorial reasons. A couple of years later, in 1991, now more than a decade after the revolution, another literary historian, Shams Langerudi, published a much more detailed three-volume compendium, *Tarikh-e Tahlili-ye She'r e No/The Analytical History of New Poetry* (1991), in which he offered a far more extensive account of this historic momentum in Persian New Poetry, and again we see the prominent place of Nima, Akhavan, Shamlu, Farrokhzad, and Sepehri, as well as a however minor reference, in only one section, to one of Kho'i's poems.⁴ Langerudi has identified Kho'i's poetry simply because of the influence of Akhavan and "philosophical" themes in his poetry. By now the principal six figures in the pantheon of Persian New Poetry have been solidly erected, defined, formed, and framed.

Post-Orientalism, Area Studies, and the Fate of Persian New Poetry

The poets I have introduced and discussed in this book are not entirely unknown to English-speaking people around the world. There are some perfectly competent

Arabic, English, Turkish, French, Urdu, Italian, and German translations of some of these poets available. Some of these translations are quite reliable and readable and actually read as poetry. Other than these translations, there exist also some fairly insightful studies of these poets, and I have had occasion to refer to and cite them in this book. Still, the collectivity of this poetic phenomenon that we call "She'r-e No/New Poetry" and its historic significance remain fairly unknown outside Iran, by and large a *terra incognita*. My purpose in this book has been not just to introduce these poets to the larger world outside Iran, particularly Asia, Africa, and Latin America, places with which we share our appropriation of English or any other European language as a confiscated post/colonial vernacular. Standing in between my study introducing these poets within a specific theoretical frame of reference and my reading public, specialist or otherwise, stands a deeply flawed, outdated, ghettoized, and even outright reactionary field called "Area Studies," and I have had occasion in this and my other work to alert my readers to this sad state of affairs. I have done so not because I particularly enjoy airing a vituperative prose, but because of the extraordinary significance of what I wish to share and thereby hope to encourage my readers to read more, and also to explore this exceptionally beautiful and powerful pantheon of poetry, and to not assimilate it backward into what they may or may not know about classical Persian poetry. This poetry is contemporary with our current world, with our fears and anxieties, hopes and aspirations, and it has to be read that way. The constellation of poets that I have discussed in this book has introduced and exercised a seismic change in the long and illustrious history of Persian poetry, in both form and substance, in form as substance, and in substance as form.

As evident in these and many other similar studies that I introduced at the beginning of this Conclusion, the state of scholarship on the six poets whom I have studied in this book is solid, insightful, detailed, and trustworthy in Persian and in Iran, but quite abysmal (with some notable exceptions) if one is limited to English or any other European language. Still the best studies on these poets are written in Persian and published in Iran, understandably so. The formation of this poetic episteme was definitive to a national consciousness, and reading it requires a critical intimacy with the texts and contexts of that epistemic formation. Given the logic of this episteme, there are countless other poets who are rightly considered masters of their crafts, such as Houshang Ebtehaj, aka H. A. Sayeh (1928–2022), or Nader Naderpour (1929–2000), whom I have not included in this study. This is not a matter of taste. There are countless poems by Ebtehaj, in particular, that I dearly love. It is a matter of collectivity, of an epistemic cohesion, an assemblage, that I have sought to delineate and articulate in this book. That sense of collectivity, of a well-conjugated paradigm, is otherwise lost to both neo-Orientalist foreigners and the new generation of an Iranian expat professoriate beholden to the mantra of "modernism," "modernity," and the like, in their limited, colonially mitigated, Eurocentric, and reactionary imagination.

In the course of writing this book, and as I navigated the field for any serious new work on these six poets in European languages (which by virtue of colonialism have become global languages) over the past few decades, there were moments when I was elated at the crucial work that has been done by serious, principled, and deeply learned scholars, and there were times when I was aghast at the rampant illiteracy, bare-faced careerism, and above all vicious backbiting that has afflicted an entire generation of the emerging "Area Studies" professoriate. The tyranny of the coveted tenure-track positions on North American and Western European campuses has produced a generation of bitter and odious Area Studies specialists who, in an increasingly dwindling job market, have been forced into the rabbit hole of pitiful rivalries, taking full advantage of the anonymity of the review process to backbite each other's work. The sight is quite unseemly. The damage is not only to individual careerists caught in the myopic labyrinth of hateful rivalries, but far more importantly to the subject of their purported scholarship: myopic, parochial, insular, blinkard, and above all pitiful. And to think that the fate of some of the most precious poets of the last century is entrusted to this coterie of blindfolded careerists!

More to the core of the issue: the field of Iranian Studies, as I see it from the vantage point of a lifetime in this domain, is still very much squarely trapped within the debilitating epistemic limitation of neo-Orientalist Area Studies, which is busy parroting English department "modernism" or the Political Science departments' broken hobbyhorse of "modernization *cum* Westernization" mantras.[5] With little to no grasp of the exigencies of colonial, post-, and decolonial projects at work around the globe, they keep regurgitating tired old clichés raised and dismissed decades ago in Eurocentric disciplines, and thus they think that, if they drop a "form" here and a "poetics" there, they have raised the status of Persian literary critical thinking to be admitted into their self-Orientalizing hall of fame (shame). This is a truly miserable and demeaning spectacle to behold. They are still at a point where, if a white American or Italian writes an essay on or translates a poem from Farrokhzad or Sepehri, then they presume these poets have achieved "global" recognition![6] They remain willfully ignorant of an extraordinary body of scholarship published in these fields in Persian and in Iran or Afghanistan or Tajikistan. The politics of citation is pathologically limited to English or French sources, with texts of poets treated like cadavers snatched away from their natural habitat. No Iranian, Afghan, or Tajik scholar writing in Persian is cited, as if Nima, Farrokhzad, or any other of these poets simply composed their poems to be read by a born-again second-generation expat in conversation with their professors with a limited and clumsy command of Persian, Arabic, Urdu, or any other neighboring language. This is a new form of Orientalism, this time around performed by the born-again Orientals themselves!

The reasons for the superior nature of scholarship written in Persian in Iran on this particular subject are very obvious: (1) very few non-Iranians or non-Persian-speaking people actually understand (the significance) of this body of poetry under the rubric of Persian New Poetry (*She'r-e No*); and (2) the abysmal state of post-Orientalist Area Studies, which has now extended into the new generation of a professoriate self-ethnicizing as "Iranian-American," or "Muslim-American," and so on, from the heart of French or English departments, with an astonishing ignorance of the fields in which they aspire to produce readable scholarship. There are, to be sure, spectacular exceptions in the works of serious scholars such as Nesrin Rahimieh (University of California at Irvine), Peyman Vahabzadeh (University of Victoria), or Rebecca Ruth Gould (School of Oriental and African Studies), just to name a few that I have read and much admired while writing this book. The succession of work that, for example, Rebecca Ruth Gould (more recently in collaboration with Kayvon Tahmasebian Dehkordi) has been doing has advanced the field of Persian New Poetry by leaps and bounds.[7] I do, of course, remain critical of all uncritical assumptions about "modernism" and "modernity." But they need not agree with my critical theoretical stance for me to acknowledge their remarkable competence and scholarship.

Exactly the opposite, with the typical and most cliché abuses hurled against the whole phenomenon of New Persian Poetry, is evident in works such as Amr Ahmad's La "Révolution littéraire": Étude de l'influence de la poésie française sur la modernisation des formes poétiques persanes au début du XXe siècle, which is entirely rooted in and beholden to the false assumption of attributing the phenomenon of contemporary Persian literature and poetry to the following claim: "Poetic modernity in Iran is at the heart of a wave of Westernization which affected literature as a whole, and more generally all aspects of the political, economic, social and cultural life of the country."[8] Such archaic and reactionary Eurocentric assumptions are categorically flawed and are by now a worn-out cliché, inaccurate, and about half a century late for a study published in 2012.

Against the grain of this background, and cognizant of the stellar scholarship of serious scholars of the field—of my own generation (Nasrin Rahimieh and Peyman Vahabzadeh) or younger (Rebecca Ruth Gould and Atefeh Akbari Shahmirzadi)—I have offered a theoretical framework that I suggest to be at work among these six poets, at once poetic and political: poetic because political and political because poetic, exploring the intersection of a national imagination in a crucial period of Iranian history. In these six poets, I have detected a historic pattern and a poetic episteme, thereby arguing that what has been branded as "modernist poetry" is not modernist at all. Quite to the contrary: it is, in fact, an allegorical poetics rooted in the Persian literary imagination and reaching for a new public sphere beyond the false binary between the tired old cliché of "tradition versus modernity." These poets were imagining a nation, fathoming a collectivity, unearthing a moral subconscious, in entirely allegorical terms. The critical interface between formal and political, or poetics and politics, foreshadowed the unfolding revolutions of the period, in both transformative and political terms. All these poets were actively rethinking Persian prosody ('aruz) in decidedly defiant terms, which I have detailed in the preceding chapters. My articulation of an epistemic shift in the midst of these six poets shapes precisely the contours of that formal breakthrough in both poetic and political terms. Breaking down and overcoming the Persian classical prosody, as Nima and his followers did, let loose not only words, meters, rhymes, and their regimented prosodies, but with them also the entire normative imagination and disciplined tyranny at the cornerstone of any political subconscious of the nation that enabled, empowered, and celebrated them. Here I have invited you to read these six poets through a critical lens that connects them to the metapoetic of a homeland both specific to these Iranian poets and shared among prominent twentieth-century poets around the entire world. My constellation here works through an assemblage of differences that at once differ and defer (as Derrida's conception of *différance* would have it). From Nima to Akhavan, Shamlou, Farrokhzad, Sepehri, and finally Kho'i, the episteme gathers momentum and works through their specific differences in mostly temporal but finally spatial terms, and yet those differences are evident in the way in which they defer to one another.

Form as Substance, Poetics as Politics

My contention in this book has been to show how the poetic episteme gathered in and by these six poets has now completely formed and finally exhausted itself, that an era has ended. Despite the fact that pioneering poets such as Shams Kasma'i (*circa* 1883–1961) had begun experimenting with free verse before Nima, and despite the fact that some very gifted poets have emerged in the aftermath of the militant triumphalism of the Islamic Republic, none of them could be part of this episteme. What form, if any, the post-revolutionary poets are to gather and call theirs is yet to be seen. This poetic paradigm could only be seen in a rearview mirror, as I have done in this book, where we might suggest that these six poets form a poetic paradigm, an epistemic whole, each of them constituting a particular conjugation of a verb in a unique and distinctive way. I have opted to detect and present this poetic paradigm in specifically temporal terms—archetypal (Nima), nostalgic past (Akhavan), defiant future (Shamlou), rooted present (Forough), luminous presence (Sepehri), and finally vituperative exilic terms (Kho'i). The paradigm began and ended in the twentieth century, from the first poem of Nima to the first poem of Kho'i—with the two Iranian revolutions of 1906–11 and 1977–9 as the polar zeniths of when the poetic paradigm first announced and finally exhausted itself.

Of course, the creative effervescence at the heart of that poetic episteme did not disappear into thin air. We might see and suggest that, in the aftermath of the Iranian revolution of 1977–9, Iranian cinema picked up where Persian New Poetry had left off. With the selfsame traumatic event, both Persian New Poetry ended and the Iranian New Wave began, even though the aesthetic energies of the Iranian New Wave actually go back to the 1960s, with Forough Farrokhzad's seminal film *The House Is Black* (1962) linking the two events together. In the same way in which these six poets had picked up from the previous six poets of the Constitutional period, about a dozen or so filmmakers picked up from these six poets to sustain the soul of defiant creativity and bring it to global attention and admiration—thereby giving us a full panoramic view of the subconscious landscape of the nation.[9] In this context, Farrokhzad made her own film, and Abbas Kiarostami (so we might argue) picked up from Sepehri, while Bahram Beiza'i's fascination with the archaic past was akin to Akhavan's—as they all came together crafting a national cinema that eventually became the subject of global admiration.

Nima lived a full life and passed the torch; Akhavan died at the height of his success, but unfulfilled; Farrokhzad lost her life in a tragic automobile accident at the prime of her creativity; Sepehri died at the cusp of the Islamist revolution; Shamlou lived a long and fulfilling life in the company of the woman he loved; and Kho'i fled his homeland to deliver the legacy of this whole poetic paradigm to the exilic anonymity of the colonial capital. In her one spectacular short film, Farrokhzad planted the seeds of her poetic legacy and entrusted it to the whole pantheon of filmmakers to carry forward. It would not be an exaggeration to suggest that the entire spectrum of the Iranian New Wave emerged from the seeds of that one film that Farrokhzad made and entrusted to her posterity. As I have detailed in my book *Masters and Masterpieces of Iranian Cinema* (2007), Farrokhzad and all the subsequent filmmakers whom she enabled became the parabolic twelve who imagineered, sublimated, and concluded the aesthetic heights of Iranian cinema. The Iranian New Wave reclaimed Persian New Poetry, visualized, aestheticized, and brought it to global attention. When Sohrab Sepehri said in a poem "Man beh mehmani donya raftam/I went to the festive gathering of the world," he probably had no clue how absolutely prophetic he was, that in his painting and poetry he had, in fact, anticipated the absolute prince of the Iranian New Wave, Abbas Kiarostami.

My contention in this book has been that what we today understand of Iran as a postcolonial nation is the byproduct of a succession of literary, poetic, visual, and performing arts—and, in this particular case, six seminal poets who carried the dexterity of its moral imagination from the Constitutional to the Islamic revolution. Since my book *Iran: A People Interrupted* (2007), I have consistently argued that Iran as a nation was more poetically imagined than politically stated. As a result, the state is entirely superfluous and sticks out as an appendix to the centrality of Iran as a nation, as a reality *sui generis*. This sustained course of poetic legacy is neither ideological nor discursive. It is metapoetic in the sense that it is a poetry aware of its poeticality. Based on much earlier forms of such self-conscious poeticality in the works of the masters of classical Persian poetry, Nima and his followers were all self-conscious and composed poetry about their poetry. Here is the perhaps most famous such metapoetic moment in a poem, Ahmad Shamlou's "For Blood and Lipstick" (1950):

Hey, you, Poet, Hey!
Red is red—right?
Lips and wounds:
Though before your wretched eyes
See the teeth of your lover through her smile
Like "strings of wet pearls on blossoms of pomegranate,"
To my eyes it appears like a gushing wound
Through which I can see pieces of bone—
For long before Hitler—
The butcher of Auschwitz—
Killed my friends in his death chambers,

His fellow traveler
Had bottled syrups of African blood in Harlem and Bronx
And stored them to make lipsticks for your lover![10]

This momentous event, when Shamlou recollects global events from the Jewish Holocaust to African-American slavery, is the defining result of an anticolonial consciousness in Persian New Poetry, which dates back to such pioneering poets as Mirzadeh Eshghi (1894–1924), Prince Iraj Mirza (1874–1926), Aref Qazvini (1882–1934), Parvin E'tesami (1907–41), Mohammad-Taqi Bahar (1886–1951), and Abolqasem Lahuti (1887–1947), before we reach the generation of Nima, Akhavan, Shamlou, Forough, Sepehri, and Kho'i. These latter six poets, the subject of my examination in this book as they imagined their nation, and the other six that came just before them, ushered Iran as a postcolonial nation into its worldly presence and gave it an intuition of transcendence. They linked the Constitutional period to the Pahlavi era, and from there to the threshold of the Islamist take-over, from the late nineteenth to the late twentieth century, between the two revolutions of 1906–11 (the Constitutional) and 1977–9 (the Islamist)—with the CIA military coup of 1953 in between the two cosmic events. For roughly a whole century just before that, from the late eighteenth to the late nineteenth century—namely the entirety of the Qajar dynasty (1789–1926)—literary historians considered the era as *Bazgasht-e Adabi*/The Literary Return, when poets began to return to the classical period, abandoning the post-Safavid stylistic proclivities known as *Sabk-e Hendi*/Indian Style (represented by Saba Kashani, Neshat Isfahani, and Azar Bigdeli), when classical poetry began to assume more colloquial and popular forms; Mohammad-Taqi Bahar and others have suspected that this was a reaction to the so-called Indian Style. This was a neo-classical style, but the poetic style that it staged pales in comparison to prose, as best represented in progressive journalism and travelogues of this period.[11] The sextet I have outlined here consists of those who benefited from and then became the crowning achievement of these earlier and successive developments—deeply cultivating a poetic intuition of self-transcendence never before experienced in the history of Iranian encounter with colonial modernity, which is the chief reason why it is such a sordid distortion of truth to call it "modern" or "modernist."

We might therefore see and suggest these three successive phases in the genealogy of Persian New Poetry: (1) the Qajar period and the rise of the Khorasani Style or Return to Neo-Classicism in reaction to the so-called "Indian Style" that had become too obtuse; (2) the Constitutional period and the rise of a potent anticolonial nationalism in Persian poetry; and (3) the Pahlavi era and the rise of Persian New Poetry. During the Qajar period (1789–1926), we witness the rise of the Isfahani Style, which, with some success, sought to reclaim the classical period after the Indian-Style interlude, but this was coterminous with the emancipation of Persian prose in progressive journalism and expansive travelogues. The Constitutional period (1906–11) saw the seeds of the liberating poetry being planted by six poets—Eshqi, Iraj, Aref, Lahuti, E'tesami, and Bahar. In the Pahlavi period (1926–79), the six poets whom I have closely examined in this book pushed the diction and disposition of the liberated Persian New Poetry from merely qualitative to quantitative changes. In this last stage, thinking in poetic terms was made possible, which in turn posited a radical epistemic shift in the very constitution of the Persian poetic imagination—in both form and substance. It is here during the last two phases that the archetypal figure of the Persian Prince was deconstructed into its formative forces of the poet, the prophet, the pilgrim, and the rebel. The figure of the poet now embraces all the other forces of the prophet, the pilgrim, and the rebel, and as such it completely dismantles the figure of the Persian Prince as either monarchic or mullarchic archetype. In this final stage, form becomes substance, and poetics and politics coalesce.

Metapoetics as the Liberating Politics of the Sublime

A close reading of these six poets during the pivotal twentieth century reveals how the Persian cosmopolis was radically recast in decidedly anticolonial terms.[12] The idea of the "Persian Cosmopolis" has been argued in detail in the excellent work of Richard Eaton, in his major essay "The Persian Cosmopolis" (2021).[13] But he has falsely limited it to its origins and sustained developments from the ninth to the nineteenth century, while I consider the project unfolding apace with Iran as its epicenter. Richard Eaton's assumption that Iranian state-sponsored nationalist ideology appropriated the vast Persian cosmopolis for itself is deeply flawed, for he has disregarded the far more potent and culturally productive anticolonial and postcolonial nationalism that preserved and advanced Persian language and literature for precisely the opposite reasons and purposes of the Reza Shah period, which he paradoxically seems to share. The metapoetics at work with these six poets whom I have closely examined here was rooted in that Persian cosmopolis that they were now transforming and recasting in decidedly postcolonial directions. An ignorance of this fact has, in turn, led to the categorically flawed concept of "Persianate modernity" that leaves the colonial concept of "modernity" intact and takes the truism of the Indian and Iranian world, mitigated through Urdu language and literature, into deeply flawed and actively depoliticized and reactionary directions.[14] The argument that Urdu language and literature influenced Persian literary historiography is a perfectly plausible consideration, but entirely misplaced when located in the Eurocentric notion of "modernity" and abusively applied to countries, climes, regions, or continents historically at the mercy of this idea. What Europeans call their "modernity" spells calamitous colonial savagery and a subterfuge for plunder around the world. Even worse is the idea of "modernization as in Westernization," as if the vastly rich and powerful cultures of China, India, Iran, or Egypt were sitting idly by to be civilized, modernized, or "Westernized." "Westernization" as "modernization" was and remains the cruelest force of European savagery around the world, depriving nations of their heritage and self-respect. Modernization as Westernization is another European term for the old colonial adage of *mission civilisatrice*, which French and other European colonial savages used when plundering Asia, Africa, and Latin America. The critique of

Iranian nationalist historiography is all good and well, and even necessary, and has been done competently by Iranians and in Persian for generations, but in this gestation of "the Persianate," it has fallen squarely within a bizarre form of Iranophobia, performed now mostly by a new generation of expat Iranians and their American colleagues thinking themselves liberated by a jaundiced liberal criticism! The flawed category of "Persianate Modernity" constitutionally sidesteps the decolonial and postcolonial power of the Persian New Poetry rooted in the Constitutional period and after.

The road towards this decolonial phase was built in nineteenth-century travelogues. However, in their rush to stage not their criticism (which is perfectly legitimate) but evident hatred of Iranian national (anticolonial) consciousness, this new generation of "Persianate" enthusiasts has staged an astonishing domain of Iranophobia that feels completely at home in the Bush to Trump America that privileges its own fascistic white supremacy while denouncing the anticolonial nationalism of colored people at its military mercy. You will search in vain in such now emergent prose of "the Persianate" variety for the slightest awareness of the big elephant in the room of colonialism. Categorically erasing the geographical and moral map of Iran as a multi-ethnic plurality and dissolving it into the vacuous domain of its "Persianate World," this project is now completely at the service of US imperial designs for the pacification and eradication of any and all national resistance to its hegemonic militarism. The entire field of what henceforth calls itself "Persianate" has now emerged with a decidedly colonial character that partakes in a potent Iranophobia, where the entire history of literary historiography has been metamorphosed into a depoliticized "transregional" imagination.[15] This poorly educated, ill-informed, and anxiously liberal generation of Iranophobic scholars has made a career mostly on North American campuses, where the hatred of Iran and Iranians is a quite lucrative business, especially if it is shifted to the Hindu nationalism of the BJP in India. The term "Persianate" as a result has degenerated from its innocent origin into something akin to "Farsi," when yet another generation of expat Iranians was running away from the word "Iran" as a nation and Persian as a language because of its associations with the Iran of the Islamist regime. People were running around in Los Angeles, calling themselves "Persians" (not Iranians) speaking Farsi (not Persian)! This is particularly informed by a deep-rooted illiteracy in the Persian New Poetry of the sort I have examined in detail in this book—which is entirely produced by Iranians and in Iran—until one of them, Esmail Kho'i, was forced into desperate exile. The issue is, of course, not with the term "Persianate," which was rather innocuous when the American historian Marshall Hodgson (1922–68) coined it back in the 1960s; among others, I have had occasion and reason to adopt and adapt it in my own work.[16] But the way in which it has now been abused and degenerated into a reactionary mantra is not just Iranophobic, but equally Islamophobic and predicated on a bizarre and thinly disguised anti-Arab racism and anti-Iranian bigotry, given the fact that it categorically disregards the Arabic cosmopolis always adjacent to the Persian cosmopolis, as well as the fact that the Persian cosmopolis has been deeply rooted and coterminous with the Arabic and Sanskrit cosmopolis. The entire region has always been historically multi-lingual and multi-cultural, and Arabic, Persian, Turkish, Urdu, and Sanskrit elements and forces have been coterminous with each other. We can therefore only separate the Persian cosmopolis as a heuristic technique fully aware of its Sanskrit and Arabic resonances. There is hence a bizarre Hindutva BJP kind of phobia of Islam and Iran informing this purportedly anti-nationalist project of "Persianate" studies. The perfectly legitimate and accurate term "Persian Cosmopolis," as scholars such as Eaton have articulated it, thus makes it entirely superfluous to use the term "Persianate world," except when agitated by a nasty case of Iranophobia.[17]

Despite its innocuous roots as a geographical and cultural designation, however, the term "Persianate"—or even worse, "Persianate modernity" or "Persianate world"—is now the form that the reactionary post-national professoriate has assumed on North American college campuses after the rise of an anticolonial nationalism that they now either fail to understand or else deliberately seek to sabotage. In its original gestation, it was the connected framework left over from the bygone Persian cosmopolis that enabled literary historians from Iran and India to learn from each other in their comparative projects, as well as to rework the literary texts of the earlier tradition into national heritage. It is an astounding sign of illiteracy to think that any one of these six poets I have examined in detail in this book, or the entire intellectual tradition that they represent, were "nationalist" in the way in which Reza Shah was a nationalist. Forough Farrokhzad and Ahmad Shamlou were decidedly anti-nationalist—their sense of nation (*mihan, vatan, keshar*) is a collective consciousness, not a political ideology. In the case of Akhavan and Kho'i, their sense of nationalism is the overriding platform for their anticolonial and anti-imperial frames of reference. The "Persianate" coterie notices when Reza Shah organizes a Ferdowsi celebration, but they are clueless when poets from Mehdi Akhavan-e Sales over Siavash Kasra'i and Fereydoun Rahnema to Bahram Beiza'i and countless other artists, filmmakers, and poets turn the *Shahnameh* radically upside down and put it to the most progressive, anticolonial, anti-monarchical uses.

These emerging Persianate enthusiasts are turning this otherwise innocent term into an ideology of rootless regionalism, flattening the earth, as it were, robbing it of its national frames of resistance to tyranny and colonization and thus making it ready for any sort of imperial (particularly American) conquest. Whether they know it or not, this is in the service of an amorphous imperial project that now the US leads and its Israeli settler-colony systematically implements, from Palestine over Lebanon to Syria, Iraq, Yemen, and so on, all the way to the borders of Iran: the active fragmentation of all multi-cultural and multi-ethnic national sites of resistance to imperialism and colonialism. Like "the Persianate world," the term "Persianate modernity" is an equally bogus concept: it overrides the nasty colonial origins of European and Eurocentric modernity and actively partakes in Iranophobia and Islamophobia. I do not wish to attack any particular person *ad hominem*. But those who now actively advocate this term and aggressively weaponize it against Iran and its national history are hostile to and ignorant of postcolonial politics and poetics, in which both Iranian and Islamic leitmotifs resonate in literary, poetic, visual, and performing arts. If political at all, all artistic and cultural forms are not modern, or modernist, or anything but waged against domestic tyranny and colonial modernity, both anticolonial and decolonial. The trouble is not with the innocent term "Persianate," but with the post-national generation of the born-again American expat professoriate failing to understand the anticolonial nationalism of their parental generation, partaking in a nasty neo-conservative regionalism, because they think through a deeply colonized mind. Their hostility to national thinking is because of their acutely reactionary investment in the colonial and neo-colonial projects of the sort that Israel is violently pursuing as I write these words late in December 2024, under the full protection and participation of the United States. Anticolonial nationalism has always assumed and imagined the idea of *the nation* and therefore nationality and nationalism in decidedly anticolonial terms. India is India, Iran is Iran, Egypt is Egypt, Turkey is Turkey, as the idea of the transnational was beyond these boundaries but formed within these boundaries. In the guise of opposing ethnic nationalism, this new generation of "Persianate" specialists has falsely perceived an ethno-nationalism at the heart of Iranian nationalism, and by doing so they do not just disregard but, in fact, depoliticize the powerful anticolonial nationalism of the era, which never understood the term "Persian" as a marker of ethnicity or nationalism but as a designation of the linguistic domain. By overriding anticolonial nationalism, this most reactionary gestation of the American "Persianate Studies" clique invests in a racist Iranophobic thrust that feeds into the rise of fascism now riding high in the MAGA fascism of Trump's America.

By failing to make a distinction between colonial and anticolonial nationalism—two vastly different and, in fact, diametrically opposed projects—these born-again Persianate enthusiasts conflate and confuse the fascistic nationalism of Reza Shah and Ataturk with the anticolonial nationalism of Gandhi, Nehru, Mosaddegh, Nasser, and the like. They instead opt for a rootless, shapeless, and amorphous regionalism, leaving nations to be conquered, fragmented, and erased by the amorphous empire, in the metropolitan delusions of which they live and earn their salaries, and by settler-colonies like Israel, which now let loose on defenseless nations such as those of the Palestinians, Syrians, Lebanese, Iraqis, and, of course, Iranians. The six poets of the Constitutional period and the six poets of the post-Constitutional period whom I have identified and studied came one after the other, to form the central core of Persian New Poetry, as the poetic foregrounding of an idea of the nation in decidedly anti-, post-, and decolonial terms. The six poets I have examined here brought the poetic imagination at the heart of the nation to full thematic and poetic fruition, as their poetics transcended their politics and gave the citizens of that nation a sense of selfhood and agency. All of the six poets were working towards imagining a nation, which stands against the actively depoliticized, selfless "selves" mechanically descripted based on the biographical dictionaries of poets, but not what those poets were actually writing, or else on a fraught notion of the "Persianate world" or "Persianate modernity." From the first to the last, these poets felt, thought, and imagined and thus wrote their nation beyond all ethnicities, ethnic nationalisms, or political tyrannies;

therefore, their constellation saw through the way in which the otherwise innocuous idea of "Persianate" is now twisted and propagated by a coterie of US-based scholars awash with a nasty streak of Iranophobia. As such, the idea of "Persianate" now forcefully manufactured by these US-based ideologues actively seeks to neutralize the anticolonial forces of nations on the false pretense of opposing ideological nationalism. What, in fact, this business of "Persianate" studies does is actively neutralize the political potency of the nation as a site of defiant resistance to colonial and imperial designs, at a time when US imperialism and Israeli Zionism work hand-in-hand to eradicate violently any site of national resistance to their genocidal savageries in the region. The nasty politics of this mode of knowledge production on North American college campuses is not accidental. They are actively denationalizing sites of national resistance to imperial domination and colonial conquest.

In a magnificent new study, *Chinese Cosmopolitanism: The History and Philosophy of an Idea* (2024), Shuchen Xiang has demonstrated how the formation of identity and difference in the Chinese context was not predicated on the varied forms of Western savagery that ranged from imperial conquest to settler-colonialism, from plunder of natural resources over slavery to genocide, in order to demarcate who and what the conquerors were.[18] In comparison, it is important to consider that the *modus operandi* of the Persian cosmopolis (still a far more potent idea after these abuses of the term "Persianate") was not based on any military conquest on the model of Islamic empires but entirely predicated on literary humanism. The Persian cosmopolis was the creation of Persian literary humanism or *adab*.[19] But this fully documented Western savagery at the heart of their capitalist modernity is a global and not merely a cultural proposition. The Chinese treatment of the Uyghurs and the Myanmar treatment of the Rohingya show that these peoples are capable of barbarism as much as the West, which they seem to oppose. In the same way, Hindu fundamentalism and Buddhist fanaticism compete with the Islamist savageries of the Taliban, ISIS, and the like. The condition of the Persian cosmopolis therefore must be extended to the anti- and postcoloniality option against Western barbarism to see it generate its own agonistic cosmopolitan culture.

Resting my Case

To sum up and rest my case: this study of six seminal Persian poets of the Pahlavi era is predicated on the idea of "nation" as principally the site of anticolonial, postcolonial, and *a fortiori* decolonial projects—the site, to be more precise, of the rise of a new human being. This is the political premise of my study, upon which I then make my case with how six seminal poets in the course of the twentieth century paradigmatically coalesced to give a poetic potency to that idea of the nation beyond its ideological and political limitations—before and after the idea of "the nation" degenerated from a site of resistance and rebellion against tyranny into an ideology of self-negating nationalism. These six poets, so I have proposed, came on the heels of a previous generation of another six poets, who during the Constitutional period (1906–11) had paved the way for the formation of the very idea of their homeland, articulated against domestic tyranny and foreign conquest alike. But whereas those Constitutional-period poets were actively political and while poetry was accidental to them, these six poets of the Pahlavi period reversed the order and were deeply and primarily concerned with their poetic voice cast in a defiant and new prosody, and yet the undercurrent of the political was contingent on their collective episteme. I have cast the formal disposition of these six poets whom I have examined closely in *temporal* terms, before I turn to the *spatial* by examining the one final figure (Kho'i) who both factually and figuratively exited the national paradigm when forced into exile. On the interface of this temporal and spatial grid, I propose a fusion of politics and poetics, of aesthetic form as metapoetic metaphor. The revolutionary poetics that Nima instigated and implemented in the received classical prosody—*'aruz*—was therefore poetic and political at one and the same time: it was political because of its radical poetics, and it was poetic precisely in the political cast of its episteme.

There is a global context to this particular articulation of the poetics of a postcolonial subject that both connects with and parts ways from the European site of colonization. But how, precisely? In a bold and persuasive study, *Subject without Nation: Robert Musil and the History of Modern Identity* (2000), Stefan Jonsson has offered a critical reading of Robert Musil's unfinished classic novel *The Man Without Qualities* (1930–43). Jonsson has persuasively demonstrated how the central character of the novel, Ulrich, is "a man without qualities," the product of a first post-imperial Austria caught in the purgatorial passage between the collapse of the Austro-Hungarian Empire (1867–1918) and the imminent rise of the avalanche of European racist nationalism and ultimately Nazism. In that singular figure of Ulrich, we therefore witness the formation of a sapless subject bereft of a European imperialist and/or nationalist frame of identity formation. Reading Jonsson's insightful study, we see how what emerged as a bloody tapestry of racist nationalism in the European context was the extension or direct result of their imperial conquest of the world.

Jonsson, however, has presented an insightful detour to come to that conclusion. He has begun his book by citing the Saint Lucian poet and playwright Derek Walcott (1930–2017), who in his Nobel Prize Lecture of 1992 envisioned a city which "would be so racially various that the cultures of the world—the Asiatic, the Mediterranean, the European, the African—would be represented in it, its human variety more exciting than Joyce's Dublin." Jonsson has continued to compare Walcott's assessment with what he sees in the Austro-Hungarian Empire, when "a notion of human subjectivity ... has emerged in late-twentieth-century art, literature, music, architecture, cinema, and cultural theory." Then he has made a crucial stipulation: "Musil's Austria was the first post imperial culture in modern Europe. Although the Austro-Hungarian Empire had no overseas colonies, it ruled over a vast array of nationalities, and in terms of cultural diversity and conflict it is therefore comparable to the major colonial powers." That insight then brings him to make a startling observation:

The rapid modernization of the empire and its eventual collapse in 1918 triggered an intense intellectual activity commonly discussed under rubrics such as "fin-de-siècle Vienna" or *modernité viennoise*. Behind these labels, I would like to suggest, we find a historical experience that is structurally akin to a phenomenon that was to affect other European states only later, the experience of postcoloniality. Indeed, Austria's postimperial culture was characterized not only by explosive conflicts between a residual feudal system and an emerging capitalist society, but also by the struggle between a crumbling imperial regime and various movements of what we today would call identity politics: Zionism and anti-Semitism; women's movements and antifeminism; nationalism, racism, and fascism. These conflicts compelled Musil and other intellectuals of his time, such as Sigmund Freud, Georg Lukács, Hermann Broch, Elias Canetti, Karl Kraus, Otto Bauer, Franz Kafka, and Joseph Roth, to examine the force of collective identities of ethnicity, nationhood, or masculine authority. Today's intellectuals address similar issues, mapping a world of postcolonial migration, globalization, and intercultural conflicts. Robert Musil's works projected a "new human being," one who would resist assimilation into imperialist, nationalist, or fascist communities. I would like this study to honor that intention and to convey a sense of its theoretical and political urgency.[20]

This crucial passage offers us a key link between the European dynamics of internal colonization and the European colonial conquest of the world at large—and thereby solidly dispenses with the blindfolded extension of the European event of modernity to the larger world that could only hear the fact of coloniality echoed in that European word. As I have argued in my book *Iran without Borders: Towards a Critique of the Postcolonial Nation* (2016), the formation of the postcolonial nation is always already transnational, meaning that it was framed and placed from outside its fictive borders. In the case of Iran, in particular, it was imagined by Iranian expat intellectuals and literati and poets in India, on the Ottoman territories, in Istanbul, Cairo, all the way up to Central Asia, and so on. It was also actively imagined and articulated, as I have shown in my book *Reversing the Colonial Gaze: Persian Travelers Abroad* (2019), by global travel narratives, including the encounter with Europe and from there deep into Asia, Africa, and Latin America. In the same vein, the moral and normative imagination of these poets was already deeply cosmopolitan. Iran, as a result, and as a concept, was always already transnational and cosmopolitan: a focal point of concentric reverberations that extended wider into the world. What ultimately rises as the formative forces of post-modernism in the European context we might therefore see as coterminous with the rise of postcolonialism in the larger global context, when anticolonial nationalism (Nehru, Nasser, or Mosaddegh) is in fact the precise opposite of its European colonizing context. Nationalism around the globe was— as Anthony Smith, among others, has said in his pioneering work *Theories of Nationalism* (1971)—indeed anticolonialism: "Nationalism is really only anticolonialism: so runs the most popular explanation today. At the simplest level, nationalism is seen as a natural response to foreign oppression, i.e. colonialism."[21]

Smith has proceeded to offer "more sophisticated" theories of nationalism as to extend from colonialism to imperialism.[22] But we may equally suggest that anticolonialism also is not merely third-world nationalism. If so, then what that ultimately suggests is that the study of these six poets has been a study of postcolonial poetics, where these poets have been at work to define the contours of a postcolonial person who has survived the parameters of a post-imperial (Qajar) persona deprived of personhood and has been restored to a postcolonial person in possession of an agential subjectness. The historic transition from *ra'iyyat* (the subject of a monarchy) to *shahrvand* (the citizen of a republic) was facilitated by this historic momentum of, first, the Constitutional poetry of Aref and his company, and then the poetic revolution of Nima and his followers.

The result and cumulative effect of these six poets' oeuvre has been the collective thinking of not a generic subject without an abstract nation, as Stefan Jonsson would have said, but a postcolonial nation without racist nationalism, conducive to the formation of a poetically posited subject without implicating it in any political illusions—Nationalism, Socialism, Islamism, or otherwise. From Aref Qazvini to Nima Yushij, we are therefore witnessing the rise of a poetic subconscious of the nation, or a poetic intuition of collective transcendence, where poetry has posited itself as the moral subconscious of the postcolonial nation. At the heart of this conception of the nation is therefore not a political but a poetic unconscious, where the nation is not a narration but an aesthetic transcendence of the sublime and the beautiful, of the just and the judicious. This poetic intuition is more akin to Adorno's famous "immanent" rather than "transcendent" critique of societal formations, internal to the nation rather than external to it. Thus, while in his seminal study *The Political Unconscious* (1981), the late Fredric Jameson has demonstrated how there is a political unconscious at the root of the literary work of art, we might also add that, in the Persian case, there is a poetic subconscious at the root of such political protestations. Not just French literary modernism but the entire European project of colonial modernity was nothing but moral and political fodder for this defiance of a postcolonial national consciousness, which was cosmopolitan at the very heart of its aesthetic imagination. By the grace and power of these poets, the figurative shadow of the Persian Prince hailing from time immemorial yielded to its elemental and formative forces: the poet, the prophet, the rebel, and the pilgrim—all of them coterminous with the fact and figure of the Nimaic revolution at one and the same time. In the work of an entire generation of poets whom Nima envisioned, enabled, empowered, and let loose on a nation, the Persian monarchy and patriarchy as interchangeable archetypes collapsed, and the figure of the poet emerged as the rebel, the prophet, and the pilgrim all at once. The lasting memories of that pivotal moment in the Iranian encounter with colonial modernity will outlast any and all claims that may persist or may follow in the history of the nation thus convened and immortalized.

NOTES

Introduction

1 Nima Yushij, "Ta Sobh-daman/Till the Morning Dawns," in Nima Yushij, *Majmu'eh-ye Kamel Ash'ar-e Nima Yushij/The Complete Collection of Nima Yushij's Poems*, ed. Sirus Tahbaz (Tehran: Negah Publications, 1991), 488–9. All translations from the Persian original of this and all the other poems that I cite are my own.
2 See the seminal work of Walter Mignolo, *The Darker Side of Western Modernity: Global Futures, Decolonial Options* (Durham: Duke University Press, 2011), for the detailed theoretical reasons behind this decolonial critique of European modernity that the world has received solely through the gun barrels of colonial savagery.
3 For a complete and unabashed reduction of the entire phenomenon of Persian New Poetry to French influence, see Amr Taher Ahmed, *La "Révolution littéraire": Étude de l'influence de la poésie francaise sur la modernisation des formes poétiques persanes au début du XXe siecle* (Vienna: Austrian Academy of Sciences Press, 2012). From the revolutionary era of the Constitutional period to the rise of New Poetry, where modernization and Westernization are seen as interchangeable, the author believes that it is entirely indebted to French influence. This Eurocentric—in this case, francophone—imagination, performed in French, of course, is sheer Orientalism on steroids.
4 The most significant body of scholarship on Persian New Poetry has naturally been written in Persian and not in English, French, or any other European language. It is a sad and damning aspect of scholarship in English or other European languages in the troubled field of "Area Studies" that they are astonishingly myopic and almost entirely oblivious to this immense body of rich and path-breaking scholarship by generations of Iranian scholars. A bizarre combination of outright racism, belated and watered-down Orientalism, and documented ignorance is the underlying animus of this scholarly illiteracy. In this study, as in my other works, I therefore seek to remedy this malady and pay particular attention to scholarship written in Persian, mostly by Iranian scholars.
5 I have addressed these enduring and endemic issues in some detail in my book on *Post-Orientalism: Knowledge and Power in a Time of Terror* (London: Routledge, 2009).
6 A classic example of this genre is S. N. Eisenstadt, "Multiple Modernities," *Daedalus* 129, no. 1 (2000): 1–29.
7 For an excellent comparative study, see, for example, Levi Thompson, *Reorienting Modernism in Arabic and Persian Poetry* (Cambridge: Cambridge University Press, 2022). The perspective is still taking the idea of European modernism for granted and seeking to expand and globalize it. Although I disagree with the basic analytical foregrounding, Thompson's discussions of the Iraqi poets Badr Shakir al-Sayyab and Abd al-Wahhab al-Bayati, as well as of the Iranian poets Nima Yushij, Ahmad Shamlou, and Forough Farrokhzad, are exceptionally insightful, and for none of these was the unqualified idea of "modernism" necessary, for such a term robs them all of their poetic

distance from and political angle on the colonial consequences of European capitalist modernity, which had come *at them* violently and not *to them* naturally.

8 Mohammad Reza Shafi'i-Kadkani, *Advar-e She'r-e Farsi: Az Mashrutiyyat ta Soqut-e Saltant/Periods of Persian Poetry: From Constitutionalism to the Collapse of the Monarchy* (Tehran: Sokhan Publications, 2008), 17–18.

9 A related recent study is Farshad Sonboldel's *The Rebellion of Forms in Modern Persian Poetry: Politics of Poetic Experimentation* (London: Bloomsbury Academic, 2024). Despite the superfluous frame of the "modern," Sonboldel's book is a singularly important study where the formal experimentation of an entire generation of poets has been judiciously examined. Particularly insightful is his discussion of such key poets as Mohammad Taqi Bahar, Mirzadeh Eshqi, Abolqasem Lahuti, Mohammad Moqaddam, Zabih Behruz, Shin Partow, Tondar Kia, and Hushang Irani.

10 Jason Bahbak Mohaghegh has underscored the revolutionary dimensions of this poetry in his *Born upon the Dark Spear: Selected Poems of Ahmad Shamlou* (New York: Contra Mundum Press, 2015).

11 Shafi'i-Kadkani, *Periods of Persian Poetry*, 20.

12 Ibid., 34.

13 Ibid., 40.

14 Ibid., 50.

15 Ibid., 58.

16 Ibid., 81.

17 Ibid., 133.

18 Ibid., 141.

19 Ibid., 141–4.

20 Ibid., 133–61.

21 I have detailed this European influence on the canonization of masterpieces of Persian classics in Hamid Dabashi, *Persophilia: Persian Culture on the Global Scene* (Cambridge, MA: Harvard University Press, 2015).

22 I have detailed this argument in my book *Close Up: Iranian Cinema, Past, Present, Future* (London: Verso, 2001).

23 See Hamdi Dabashi, *Masters and Masterpieces of Iranian Cinema* (Washington DC: Mage Publishers, 2007, 2013, 2023).

24 For a detailed study of the travelogue genre of this period, see Hamid Dabashi, *Reversing the Colonial Gaze: Persian Travelers Abroad* (Cambridge: Cambridge University Press, 2019).

25 In his doctoral dissertation, "The Poetics of Commitment in Modern Persian: A Case of Three Revolutionary Poets in Iran" (Berkeley: University of California, 2013), Samad Josef Alavi has offered a detailed reading of the unfolding interface between poetics and politics in the Iran of this era. This dissertation is, in fact, a study of four poets: Sa'id Soltanpour, M. R. Shafi'i-Kadkani, Ahmad Shamlou, and Mohammad Mokhtari. The point of the study is that these four poets exhibit four distinct senses of political commitments in their respective poetry. The dissertation is available at: https://escholarship.org/uc/item/9vn474vw. I had addressed similar issues almost three decades earlier in Hamid Dabashi, "The Poetics of Politics: Commitment in Modern Persian Literature," *Iranian Studies* 18, no. 2/4 (1985): 147–88.

26 To watch Amanda Gorman delivering her poem, see the video at: https://www.youtube.com/watch?v=LZ055ilIiN4. For the full text of the poem, see Amanda Gorman, *The Hill We Climb: An Inaugural Poem for the Country*, with a foreword by Oprah Winfrey (New York: Viking, 2021).

27 Gorman, "The Hill We Climb."
28 Ahmad Shamlou's "Sayeh-ye Kodam Omr/The Shadow of Which Life?" (1965), in Ahmad Shamlou, *Az Mahtabi beh Kucheh: Majmu'eh Maqalat/From the Balcony to the Street: Collection of Essays* (Tehran: Tus Publications, 1975).
29 Ibid., 10–11.
30 Bertolt Brecht, "To Those Who Follow in Our Wake/An die Nachgeborenen," first published in *Svendborger Gedichte* (1939), in *Gesammelte Werke in acht Bänden* (Frankfurt am Main: Suhrkamp, 1967), vol. 4: 722–5. This translation is by Scott Horton (*Harper Magazine*, January 15, 2008, https://harpers.org/2008/01/brecht-to-those-who-follow-in-our-wake/).
31 For a pioneering study of Persian poetry in a larger comparative context—Turkey, Iran, Afghanistan, India, and the Soviet East both classical and contemporary—see Sam Hodgkin, *Persianate Verse and the Poetics of Eastern Internationalism* (Cambridge: Cambridge University Press, 2023).
32 Ahmad Shamlou, "La'nat/Curse" (1956), in Ahmad Shamlou, *Collected Works* (Giessen: Bamdad Verlag, 1988), vol. 1: 172. My translation from the Persian original.
33 I have developed this idea of the "nomadic unknowing subject" on multiple occasions, most recently in "Rethinking the Saqqa-khaneh Art: The Pilgrim as Unknowing Subject," in *Rethinking the Contemporary Art of Iran*, ed. Hamid Keshmirshekan (Milan: Skira Editore, 2023), 29–44.
34 For the most recent scholarly study of Arabic poetics, see Lara Harb, *Arabic Poetics: Aesthetic Experience in Classical Arabic Literature* (Cambridge: Cambridge University Press, 2020). For a critical edition of Tusi's seminal text *Asas al-Iqtibas*, see Muhammad ibn Hasan al-Tusi, *Asas al-Iqtibas*, ed. Modarres Razavi (Tehran: Tehran University Press, 1988).
35 Martin Heidegger, "What Are the Poets for" (1936), in Martin Heidegger, *Poetry, Language, Thought* (New York: Harper Perennial, 1975), 94.
36 Ibid., 115.
37 For more, see Henry Corbin, "Mundus Imaginalis, or the Imaginary and the Imaginal." Originally delivered at the Colloquium on Symbolism in Paris in June 1964, which subsequently appeared in the *Cahiers internationaux de symbolisme* 6 (1964): 3–26. The text is available at: http://www.bahaistudies.net/asma/mundus_imaginalis.pdf. The complete text has been published in Henry Corbin's *magnum opus*, *En Islam iranien: Aspects spirituels et philosophiques* (Paris: Gallimard, 1971), tome IV, livre 7.
38 Sohrab Sepehri, "Niyayesh/Prayer," in Sohrab Sepehri, *Hasht Ketab* (Tehran: Tahuri, 1977), 192–3.
39 A pioneering work in this comparative respect is Rebecca Gould's "The Persian Translation of Arabic Aesthetics: Rādūyānī's Rhetorical Renaissance," *Rhetorica: A Journal of the History of Rhetoric* 33, no. 4 (2016): 339–71. The word and the assumption of "translation" between Arabic and Persian in this study is deeply mistaken, however.
40 An exquisite piece of scholarship in these domains is the recent doctoral dissertation of Catherine Ambler, "Masters of the Distant Meanings: Unity and Multiplicity in the Persian Poesis of Freshness" (Columbia University, 2022). Equally important is the impressive scholarship of Rebecca Ruth Gould, such as her *Writers and Rebels: The Literature of Insurgency in the Caucasus* (New Haven: Yale University Press, 2016).
41 See Dick Davis (trans.), *The Mirror of My Heart: A Thousand Years of Persian Poetry by Women* (Washington DC: Mage, 2019). Equally important is Domenico Ingenito's recent work, *Io parlo dai confini della notte/I Speak from the Edges of the Night* (Milano:

42 See Hamid Dabashi, "Forough Farrokhzad and the Formative Forces of Iranian Culture," in *The World is My Home: A Hamid Dabashi Reader*, eds. Andrew Davison and Himadeep Muppidi (New Brunswick: Transaction Publishers, 2011), 187–214.
43 Dominic Parviz Brookshaw, "Women Poets," in *Literature of the Early Twentieth Century: From the Constitutional Period to Reza Shah, A History of Persian Literature*, Vol. XI, ed. Asghar Seyet-Gohrab (London: I. B. Tauris, 2015), 240–310.
44 See Dabashi, "The Poetics of Politics."
45 Forough Farrokhzad, "Iman Biavarim Beh Aghaz-e Fasl-e Sard/Let Us Believe in the Beginning of the Cold Season," in Forough Farrokhzad, *Iman Biavarim Beh Aghaz-e Fasl-e Sard/Let Us Believe in the Beginning of the Cold Season* (Tehran: Morvarid Publications, 1973), 23–4.
46 Geoffrey Squires has continued to translate other Persian poems, both classical and contemporary. For more details, see https://geoffreysquirespoettranslator.wordpress.com.
47 In an excellent recent study, *Persian Prison Poem: Sovereignty and the Political Imagination* (Edinburgh: Edinburgh University Press, 2021), Rebecca Ruth Gould has paid close attention to how a significant body of poetic evidence showing this fusion of politics and poetry was formed.
48 Esmail Kho'i, "Tarh/Sketch" (1961), in Esmail Kho'i, *Gozideh She'r ha-ye Esma'il Kho'i/Esmail Kho'i's Selected Poems* (Tehran: Sepehr Publications, 1973), 29.
49 In my previous work I have detected and suggested this element in Nima's poetic constitution of the Iranian subject. See Hamid Dabashi, "Nima Yushij and the Constitution of a National Subject," in *The World is My Home: A Hamid Dabashi Reader*, 147–86.
50 Homi Bhabha, "DissemiNation: Time, Narrative and the Margins of the Modern Nation," in Homi Bhabha, *The Location of Culture* (London: Routledge, 1994), 139.
51 Ibid.
52 Mohammad Ali Sepanlu has studied these four poets in his *Chahar Sha'er-e Azadi: Aref, Eshqi, Bahar, Farrokhi Yazdi/Four Poets of Freedom: Aref, Eshqi, Bahar, Farrokhi Yazdi* (Tehran: Negah, 1369).
53 See Partha Chatterjee, *The Nation and Its Fragments: Colonial and Postcolonial History* (Princeton: Princeton University Press, 1993), 5.
54 Sohrab Sepehri, "Va/And," in Sohrab Sepehri, *Hasht Ketab*, 229–30.
55 Alain Badiou, *Being and Event*, trans. Oliver Feltham (New York: Continuum, 1998, 2005), 189.
56 Ernst Cassirer, *An Essay on Man: An Introduction to a Philosophy of Human Nature* (New Haven: Yale University Press, 1944), 52.
57 Farrokhzad, "Iman Biavarim Beh Aghaz-e Fasl-e Sard/Let Us Believe in the Beginning of the Cold Season," 24.

Chapter 1

1 I have detailed this argument in Hamid Dabashi, *The Emperor is Naked: On the Inevitable Demise of the Nation-state* (London: Pluto, 2020).
2 Nima Yushij, "Ay Adam-ha/Ahoy People" (November 1941), in *Majmu'eh-ye Kamel Ash'ar-e Nima Yushij/The Complete Collection of Nima Yushij's Poems*, 301.

3 Mohammad Reza Shafi'i-Kadkani, *Ba Cheraq va Ayeneh: Dar Josteju-ye Risheh-ha-ye Tahavvol-She'r-e Mo'aser Iran/With a Lantern and a Mirror: In Search of the Roots of the Transformation of Contemporary Iranian Poetry* (Tehran: Sokhan, 2011), 17.
4 Ibid., 27.
5 Ibid., 119.
6 Ibid., 139.
7 Ibid., 241.
8 Ibid., 319.
9 Ibid., 593.
10 Ibid., 620.
11 Ibid., 641.
12 Ibid., 672.
13 Ibid., 697.
14 A typical example of this genre specifically on Nima Yushij is Ahmad Karimi-Hakkak and Kamran Talattof (eds.), *Essays on Nima Yushij: Animating Modernism in Persian Poetry* (Leiden: Brill, 2004). These essays, to be sure, are perfectly competent and insightful pieces of writing, but still their framing within "modernism" is entirely compulsive, unnecessary, misleading, and flawed. For a comparison, see a volume of edited essays in Persian: Mojtaba Mas'udi (ed.), *Mitaravad Mahtab/The Moon Shines* (Tehran: Arghanun Publications, 1994). This volume consists of six excellent essays on various aspects of Nima's poetry, including one about the presumed influence of contemporary European poetry on his poetry, and an introduction, with the words "modern" or "modernism" nowhere to be found.
15 A chief proponent of "*moderniyyat*," as he has called it in his writings (all in Persian), is Daryoush Ashuri, mainly in his book *Ma va Moderniyyat/We and Modernity* (Tehran: Sirat Publications, 1997). Ashuri has been singularly leading the cause of positing Iranians, Muslims, and "the Third World" (all the non-White people) all trapped in a backward "tradition" and Europe as the hallmark of civilizing modernity, towards which ahistorical illusion he has an entirely sanguine and submissive position. There are severely critical takes on aspects of "Modern Persian Poetry" by an emerging body of scholarship in Persian, such as the essay by Ali Hosseinpour, a professor of literature at Kashan University: "She'r-e No va She'r-e Hajm-gara-ye Mo'aser Farsi/Contemporary Persian 'New' and 'Volume-Oriented' Poetry," *Journal of the Tabriz University Faculty of Literature* 46, no. 188 (2003): 157–80. Herein, the author has identified and dismissed minor poets coming from the US or Europe and seeking "to modernize" Persian poetry. In this and other similar studies, the words "modern" and "modernity" are, in fact, used in a derogatory and severely critical way for irrelevant poets who failed to understand the nature of the Nimaic revolution or to form any serious front. The enormity of this body of literature in Persian, almost entirely neglected in the field of "Area Studies," is too vast to even catalogue. My point here is simply to give samples of the kinds of critical thinking at work outside the blind-sided purview of Eurocentric scholarship mostly in English and French.
16 Shafi'i-Kadkani, *With a Lantern and a Mirror*, 110–12.
17 In contrast, there exist exquisite studies of Nima's poetry by Afghan and Arab scholars who point to vastly more liberating directions. For example, see Najibullah Qayyum, "Chegunegi Qafiyeh dar She'r-e Nima'i (Sha'eran Iran va Afghanistan)/The Particularity of Rhyme in Nimaic Poetry (Iranian and Afghan Poets)," *Pazhuhesh-ha-ye Novin-e Adabi* 3, no. 2 (2024): 253–75. There is an equally insightful essay by Gohar Alamdari and Afsaneh Moradi, where Nima's poetry is compared with that of the

Iraqi poet Nazik Al-Malaika. See their "Ostureh dar Sh'er-e Nima va Nazik Al-Malaika: Pishgaman-e She'r-e Jadid Parsi va Tazi/Myths in the Poetry of Nima Yushij and Nazik Al-Malaika: Pioneers in New Persian and Arabic Poetry," *Fasl nameh Elmi Pazhuheshi* 17, no. 5 (2011): 53–64.

18 For more on the Persian travelogues of this period, see Hamid Dabashi, *Reversing the Colonial Gaze: Persian Travelers Abroad* (Cambridge: Cambridge University Press, 2019).

19 Shafi'i-Kadkani, *With a Lantern and a Mirror*, 452.

20 Ibid., 453.

21 Nima Yushij, "Ojaq-e Sard/Cold Campfire" (1944), in *Majmu'eh-ye Kamel Ash'ar-e Nima Yushij/The Complete Collection of Nima Yushij's Poems*, 453–4.

22 For a reliable short biography of Nima Yushij in English, see "NIMĀ YUŠIJ," *Encyclopedia Iranica*, https://referenceworks.brill.com/display/entries/EIRO/COM-363895.xml?rskey=kvq3Ew&result=1. Equally useful is Ahmad Karimi-Hakkak, "Nima Yushij: A Life," in *Essays on Nima Yushij: Animating Modernism in Persian Poetry*, eds. Ahmad Karimi-Hakkak and Kamran Talattoff, 11–68. There is also a precious short autobiography of Nima in Sirus Tahbaz (ed.), *Nemuneh-ha-'i az She'r-e Nima/Selections from Nima Yushij's Poetry* (Tehran: Jibi, 1963), 11–15.

23 The significance of Nima Yushij as the founding father of New Poetry is now so solid that a new generation of Iranian scholars has sought to make an academic reputation for themselves by questioning that significance. See, for example, Omid Majd, "Negahi Tazeh beh Jaygah-e Nima dar Sh'er-e No/A New Perspective on Nima's Place in New Poetry," *Bahar-e Adab* 3, no. 2 (2010): 77–94.

24 Years after his father's passing, Nima Yushij's son Sheragim Yushij commenced a cantankerous public feud with Sirus Tahbaz, questioning the latter's qualifications to edit and publish Nima's work. Sheragim Yushij subsequently sold what was left of Nima's manuscripts to the Academy of Persian Language and Literature of the ruling Islamic Republic, in exchange for cash and a house in Tehran, in order to officially entrust his father's home in Yush to the Ministry of Culture and Islamic Guidance. He is, of course, entirely unqualified to judge the painstaking work of Sirus Tahbaz, who, under the supervision of some of the most trusted Iranian literary scholars such as Mohammad Mo'in, has done an admirable job publishing Nima's work. For more details of this sad saga of Nima's son trying to cash in on his father's legacy, see "Chalesh bar Sar Miras-e Nima Yushij/Challenges to Nima Yushij's Legacy," *ISNA* 27 (November 2018), https://www.isna.ir/news/97090502119/چالش-بر-سر-میراث-نیما-یوشیج.

25 Mohammad Mo'in, "Note," in *Majmu'eh-ye Kamel Ash'ar-e Nima Yushij/The Complete Collection of Nima Yushij's Poems*, 7.

26 Ibid., 8.

27 Ibid., 9–11.

28 For a detailed review of these two new volumes, see Azita Moradi et al., "Barresi va Tahlil-e Do Majmu'eh Jadid-e Ash'ar-e Nima Yushij bar Asas-e Teori-ha-ye Ou dar Bareh She'r va Sha'eri/An Examination and Discussion of Two New Collections of Nima Yushij's Poetry Based on his Theories of Poetry and Poetics," *Scholarly Journals Management System* 27, no. 97 (2023), https://journals.atu.ac.ir/article_15143.html.

29 A testimony to his significance even among his contemporaries is evident in that Hossein Samedi has published a whole bibliography of work on Nima in a sizeable volume: *Ketabshenasai Nima Yushij/A Bibliography of Nima Yushij* (Mazandaran: Kanun-e Farhang va Honar Mazandaran, 1990), which consists of both Nima Yushij's own works and those written on his poetry.

30 See Zahra Jan-nesar Ladani and Tohid Teymuri, "She'r-e Bumgara-ye Nima Yushij va William Butler Yeats dar Mobarezeh ba Este'mar/Nativist Poetry of Nima Yushij and William Butler Yeats in the Struggle against Colonialism," *Pazhuhesh-ha-ye Tatbiqi ye Zaban va Adabiyat-e Melal* 2, no. 5 (2016): 31–45.

31 Nima Yushij, "Dar Javar-e Sakhtsar/By Sakhtsar" (1930), in *Majmu'eh-ye Kamel Ash'ar-e Nima Yushij/The Complete Collection of Nima Yushij's Poems*, 157. Sakhtsar is a coastal town in Northern Iran; its name has now been changed to Ramsar.

32 Two young Iranian scholars, Fatemeh Sadat Taheri and Marziyeh Hemmati, have published an excellent study: "Shiveh-ha-ye No-avari dar Monazereh ha ye She'r-e Nima'i/Innovative Methods in Nimaic Poetic Dialogues," *Bustan-e Adab Shiraz University* 14, no. 2 (2022): 167–96. Here they have discussed the dialogical disposition in Nima's poetry through Mikhail Bakhtin's ideas of heteroglossia.

33 Jalal Al-e Ahmad's "Pir Mard Chashm-e ma bud/The Old Man Was Our Eyes," *Arash* 2 (1961): 65–75.

34 For more on Al-e Ahmad, see my recent book on him: Hamid Dabashi, *The Last Muslim Intellectuals: The Life and Legacy of Jalal Al-e Ahmad* (Edinburgh: Edinburgh University Press, 2021).

35 Al-e Ahmad, "Pir Mard Chashm-e ma bud/The Old Man Was Our Eyes," 73.

36 Nima Yushij, "Ay Asheq-e Fesordeh/Oh Sad Lover" (1930), *Majmu'eh-ye Kamel Ash'ar-e Nima Yushij/The Complete Collection of Nima Yushij's Poems*, 241–2.

37 In addition to writing poetry in his native Tabari, Nima also published a number of short stories and novellas in Persian. For a study of these works of fiction, see Ahmad Hosseini Makarem, "Sabk-Shenasi-ye Dastan-ha-ye Nima Yushij/The Styles of Nima Yushij's Stories," *Sabk-Shenasi-ye Nazm va Nasr-e Farsi* 14, no. 68 (2021): 157–71. Nima also tried his hand at writing travelogue. See his "Safar-nameh beh Barforush/Travelogue to Barforush" (1928), in Ali Mir Ansari (ed.), *Asnadi dar bareh-ye Nima Yushij/Some Documents on Nima Yushij* (Tehran: Iran National Archive Organization, 1996), 79–121.

38 Among the earliest attempts at understanding the totality of Nima's poetry is Bahman Sharegh, *Nima va Sh'er-e Parsi/Nima and Persian Poetry* (Tehran: Tahuri, 1971). The short treatise oscillates between the sociological implications and close readings of his poems. The author, however, has a particularly important point in one of his chapters (9–37) on the rise of the poetic self to social and global consciousness. My concern here, however, is something entirely different. I wish to tease out the particular formative forces of Nima's poetic thinking through his own artworld.

39 Taghi Pournamdarian, another senior literary scholar, has also written a major study of Nima's poetry in his *Khaneh-am Abri ast: She'r-e Nima az Sonnat ta Tajaddod/My Home Is a Cloud: Nima's Poetry from Classicism to Innovation* (Tehran: Soroush, 2004). This is an exceptionally rich and insightful formalist reading of Nima's poetry. Again, please note that yet another senior Iranian scholar has no use for the words "modernity" or "modernism." Instead, he has used the classic term "*tajaddod*," which simply means innovation or renovation and has no etymological or conceptional link to modernity or modernism.

40 Nima Yushij, "Hengam keh Geryeh Midahad Saz/When Weeping Melodiously" (1928), in *Majmu'eh-ye Kamel Ash'ar-e Nima Yushij/The Complete Collection of Nima Yushij's Poems*, 454.

41 Nima Yushij, "Mahtab/Moonlight" (1948), in *Majmu'eh-ye Kamel Ash'ar-e Nima Yushij/The Complete Collection of Nima Yushij's Poems*, 444–5.

42 Given the two different ways in which the Persian word "*abri*" can be read—both "cloudy" and "a cloud"—some have read this opening line as "my home is cloudy." I believe the logic of the stanza requires that we read it as "a cloud."

43 Nima Yushij, "Khaneh-am Abri Ast/My Home Is a Cloud" (1952), in *Majmu'eh-ye Kamel Ash'ar-e Nima Yushij/The Complete Collection of Nima Yushij's Poems*, 504–5.
44 There exists an excellent study of Nima's politics through the articulation of individuality and individuation in his poetry. See Manouchehr Tashakkori and Mohammad Hossein Dallal Rahmani, "Barrasi va Naqd-e Fardiyyat va Shay'yyat (Joz'iyyat) dar Sh'er-e Nima Yushij/A Critical Assessment of Individuality and Individuation (Particularization) in the Poetry of Niam Yushij," *Naqd-e Adabi* 6, no. 21 (2013): 63–84. There are, however, two problems with this study: (1) a much too mechanical reading of Karl Mannheim to understand democracy, and (2) a questionable bifurcation that the authors make between the two periods of Nima's poetry as one closer to the Constitution period and the other closer to Reza Shah's period. Be that as it may, this is one of the best studies of the embedded politics of Nima's poetic oeuvre. My reading of Nima's politics here however is embedded in the entirety of his oeuvre, with no particular privilege given to Mannheim's conception of democracy.
45 Nima Yushij, "Morgh-e Amin/The Amen Bird" (1951), in *Majmu'eh-ye Kamel Ash'ar-e Nima Yushij/The Complete Collection of Nima Yushij's Poems*, 491.
46 Ibid.
47 *"Talajan"* is a short bushy tree native to Mazandaran.
48 Nima Yushij, "To-ra man chashm dar raham/I Long for You!" (1968), in *Majmu'eh-ye Kamel Ash'ar-e Nima Yushij/The Complete Collection of Nima Yushij's Poems*, 517.
49 Emmanuel Levinas, *Totality and Infinity: An Essay on Exteriority*, trans. Alphonso Lings (Hingham, MA: Martinus Nijhoff Publishers; Duquesne University Press, 1969).
50 Ibid., 21–2.
51 Ibid., 22–3.
52 For a collective effort to address this (in my judgment incurable) Eurocentrism of Levinas, see Peter Atterton and Matthew Calarco (eds.), *Radicalizing Levinas* (Stony Brook: SUNY Press, 2010), especially Chapter 4 by Robert Eaglestone, "Postcolonial Thought and Levinas's Double Vision," 57–68.
53 Nima Yushij, *Harf-ha-ye Hamsayeh/The Neighbor's Words* (Tehran: Donya Publishers, 1972), 3. All translations from the original Persian of these letters are mine.
54 Ibid., 5.
55 Ibid., 7.
56 For more on Ayn al-Qozat's life and work, see Hamid Dabashi, *Truth and Narrative: The Untimely Thoughts of 'Ayn al-Qudat la-Hamadhani* (London: Routledge, 1999).
57 Yushij, *Harf-ha-ye Hamsayeh/The Neighbor's Words*, 41.
58 Ibid., 52.
59 Ibid., 67.
60 Ibid., 100.
61 Ibid., 123–4.
62 Nima Yushij, *Setareh'i dar Zamin/A Star on Earth* (Tehran: Tus, 1975), 28.
63 Ibid., 36–7.
64 Ibid., 97.
65 Mehdi Akhavan-e Sales, *Ata va Laqa-ye Nima/The Pros and Cons of Nima* (Tehran: Damavand, 1982), 9.
66 Ibid., 68–9.
67 Mehdi Akhavan-e Sales, *Bed'at-ha va Badaye'e Nima/Nima's Innovations and Novelties* (Tehran: Fajr-e Islam, 1989).
68 Nima Yushij, *Donya Khaneh-ye Man Ast/The World Is My Home* (Tehran: Zaman, 1971), 5–7.

69 Ibid., 15.
70 Ibid., 20.
71 Ibid., 34.
72 Ibid., 101.
73 Nima Yushij, *Nameh-ha-ye Nima beh Hemsarash/The Letters of Nima to His Wife*, ed. Sirus Tahbaz (Tehran: Payam Publishers, 1971), 8.
74 Ibid., 8.
75 Ibid., 12–13.
76 Ibid., 16.
77 Ibid., 20.
78 Ibid., 26–7.
79 Ibid., 33.
80 Ibid., 36.
81 Ibid. Laleh-zar is a crowded avenue in Tehran, and it was so particularly during Nima's time.
82 Ibid., 41.
83 Cassirer, *An Essay on Man*, 52–3.
84 Badiou, *Being and Event*, 25.
85 Alain Badiou, *Logics of Worlds: Being and Event, 2*, trans. Alberto Toscano (New York: Continuum, 2006/9), 72–5.
86 Ibid., 73.
87 See "BĀBĀ AFŻAL-AL-DĪN," *Encyclopedia Iranica*, https://iranicaonline.org/articles/baba-afzal-al-din#:~:text=Bābā%20Afżal's%20most%20universally%20recognized,stands%20on%20the%20same%20level.
88 Ibid.
89 Yushij, "Mahtab/Moonlight," 444.

Chapter 2

1 For a short biography of Akhavan-e Sales, see "AKHAVAN-E SALESS, MEHDI," *Encyclopedia Iranica*, https://www.iranicaonline.org/articles/akhavan-e-saless. For a detailed chronology of Akhavan-e Sales' life, see Morteza Kakhi, *Bagh-e Bi-Bargi: Yadnameh Mehdi Akhavan-e Sales/A Leafless Garden: A Festschrift for Mehdi Akhavan-e Sales* (Tehran: A Collection of Publishers, 1991). The most comprehensive study of Akhavan-e Sales' poetry is, of course, in Persian and by Mohammad Hoghughi, *She'r-e Zaman-e Ma: Mehdi Akhavan-e Sales/The Poetry of Our Time: Mehdi Akhavan-e Sales* (Tehran: Negah, 1991). By the early 1960s, Akhavan had been solidly established as a towering poet of his time. The best evidence for this is the publication of his selected poetry: *Behtarin-e Omid/The Best of Omid* (Tehran: [n. p.], 1969).
2 Mehdi Akhavan-e Sales, "Shenasnameh-ye Sha'er/The Identity of the Poet," in *Collected Works*, vol. 1, 7.
3 Ibid., 250–1.
4 Mehdi Akhavan-e Sales, "Qesseh-ye Shahryar-e Shahr-e Sangestan/The Ballad of the Prince of Stoneville" (1960), in *Az in Avesta/From This Avesta*, in *Collected Works* (Tehran: Zemestan Publishers, 2018), vol. 1, 587–8. I have in my own library the precious first editions of all of Akhavan-e Sales' books that I purchased in Tehran and brought with me to New York when I came to the US. For the sake of consistency,

however, I will use, cite, and translate everything I use in this chapter from the critical edition prepared by Akhavan-e Sales' own children. Bahram-e Varjavand is the messianic figure in the Zoroastrian faith. In addition to the overwhelming presence of storytelling in his poetry, Akhavan-e Sales was a master storyteller in prose, too. For a collection of his short stories, see Mehdi Akhavan-e Sales, *Mard-e Jen-Zadeh/The Possessed Man* (Tehran: Tus, 1975). The stories collected in this book were originally published from the 1940s to the 1960s.
5 Mehdi Akhavan-e Sales, "Khan-e Hashtom and Adamak/The Eighth Task and The Little Man" (1968), in *Collected Works*, vol. 1, 852–69.
6 Ibid.
7 Ibid. The last set of names are all heroes from the *Shahnameh*, the Persian Book of Kings.
8 In a poignant essay, "An Shu'ubi-ye Digar/That Other Shu'ubi," Nader Ebrahimi has noted and underlined Akhavan-e Sales' potent anticolonial nationalism. See Kakhi, *Bagh-e Bi-Bargi*, 77–85. This volume contains some of the most insightful essays on the character and poetry of Akhavan-e Sales by the leading literati and public intellectuals of the time, including poetry composed in his honor, and a sample of his own poetry.
9 I have addressed this flawed reading of the idea of "philosophy" as exclusively European in my recent book: Hamid Dabashi, *Where Is Abbas Kiarostami? Toward a Postcolonial Film-Philosophy* (Oakland: University of California Press, 2025).
10 Marie Huber, *Memories of an Impossible Future: Mehdi Akhavān Sāles and the Poetics of Time* (Leiden: Brill, 2016), 1.
11 Ibid., 1–2.
12 I have detailed this alternative world, one among many others, in my book on *The Shahnameh: The Persian Epic as World Literature* (New York: Columbia University Press, 2019).
13 Among other places, see Hamid Dabashi, *Can Non-Europeans Think?* (London: Zed Books, 2015).
14 Huber, *Memories of an Impossible Future*, 6.
15 Ibid., 7.
16 Mehdi Akhavan-e Sales, "Khan-e Hashtom and Adamak/The Eighth Task and The Little Man" (1968), in *Collected Works*, vol. 1, 858.
17 Gholamhossein Youssefi, *Cheshmeh-ye Roshan/The Enlightened Fountain* (Tehran: Elmi, 1990).
18 Eric Hobsbawm and Terence Ranger (eds.), *The Invention of Tradition* (Cambridge: Cambridge University Press, 1983), 1.
19 Ibid., 2.
20 Walter Mignolo, *The Darker Side of Western Modernity: Global Futures, Decolonial Options* (Durham: Duke University Press, 2011), xi–xii.
21 See Hamid Dabashi, "For the Last Time Civilization," *International Sociological Association* 16, no. 3 (2001), https://journals.sagepub.com/doi/abs/10.1177/026858001016003007.
22 Mehdi Akhavan-e Sales, "Akhar-e Shahnameh/The End of the *Shahnameh*" (1957), in *Collected Works*, vol. 1, 512–18.
23 Ibid.
24 Ibid.
25 Mehdi Akhavan-e Sales, "Chavoshi/Pilgrims Ballad," in *Collected Works*, vol. 1, 418.
26 Ibid.
27 Ibid., 419.
28 Ibid.

29 See "BĀBĀ AFŻAL-AL-DĪN," *Encyclopedia Iranica*.
30 Baba Afzal Kashani, "Rah-anjam-nameh/The Book of Ending," in Baba Afzal Kashani, *Musannafat/Collected Works*, eds. Mojtaba Minovi and Yahya Mahdavi (Tehran: Khwarizmi, 1952), 59–60. My translation of the original Persian prose.
31 Mehdi Akhavan-e Sales, "Derakht-e Ma'refat/The Tree of Knowledge" (1985), in *Collected Works*, vol. 2, 1271–3.
32 See Mehdi Akhavan-e Sales, "Mo'akkhareh/Conclusion," in *Az In Avesta/From This Avesta*, in *Collected Works*, vol. 1, 671–787. Akhavan was a master prose stylist and wrote extensively on various issues, most importantly on poetry. A collection of his essays has been edited by Morteza Kakhi, *Harim-e Sayeh-ha Ye Sabz: Majmu'eh Maqalat Mehdi Akhavan-e Sales/The Sanctum of Green Shades: A Collection of Mehdi Akhavan-e Sales' Essays* (Tehran: Zemestan, 1970).
33 In a conversation among Mehdi Akhavan-e Sales, Sirus Tahbaz, Mohammad Reza Shafi'i-Kadkani, and Esmail Kho'i, the *crème de la crème* of the Iranian poets and literati of the time, Akhavan-e Sales downplayed the presence of any Manichean ideas in his poetry, while others among his contemporaries insisted otherwise. He equally ridiculed and dismissed Kho'i's insistence that there were similarities between his poetry and existentialist philosophy. See this extensive interview in *Daftar-ha-ye Zamaneh* (1968): 72–4.
34 See Mehdi Akhavan-e Sales, "Mo'akkhareh/Conclusion," in *Az In Avesta/From This Avesta*, in *Collected Works*, vol. 1, 674–5.
35 Ibid., 681.
36 Ibid., 690.
37 Ibid., 692.
38 Ibid., 758.
39 Mehdi Akhavan-e Sales, "To Ra Ey Kohan Bum-o-Bar Dust Daram/I Love You, oh Ancient Home and Land" (1989), in *Collected Works*, vol. 2, 1292–4.
40 For an account of Jalal al-Din Mirza's life and the significance of this book, see "JALĀL-AL-DIN MIRZĀ," *Encyclopedia Iranica*, https://www.iranicaonline.org/articles/jalal-al-din-mirza.
41 For a detailed account of Mulla Sadra's doctrine in English, see Hamid Fahmy Zarkasyi, "The Philosophy of Mulla Sadra: Being a Summary of His Book *al-Hikmah al-Muta'aliyah fi al-Asfar al-'Aqliyyahal-Arba'ah*," *TSAQAFAH* 5, no. 2 (2009): 325–51.
42 Ibid., 327.
43 Ibid., 332. For more on Mulla Sadra's philosophy in general and this idea of Transubstantial Motion in particular, see also the doctoral dissertation of Mehdi Dehbashi, "Mulla Sadra's Theory of Transubstantial Motion: A Translation and Critical Exposition" (Fordham University, 1981), https://research.library.fordham.edu/dissertations/AAI8111542/.
44 Mehdi Akhavan-e Sales, "Peyvand-ha va Bagh/Grafting and Garden" (1962), in *Collected Works*, vol. 1, 656–7.
45 Ibid., 657.
46 Ibid.
47 Akhavan-e Sales, "Qesseh-ye Shahryar-e Shahr-e Sangestan/The Ballad of the Prince of Stoneville," in *Collected Works*, vol. 1, 585–95.
48 Mehdi Akhavan-e Sales, "Akhar-e Khat/The End of the Line" (1988), in *To Ra Ay Kohan Bum-o-Bar Dust Daram/I Love You, oh Ancient Home and Land*, in *Collected Works*, vol. 2, 1487.
49 Akhavan-e Sales, "Akhar-e Shahnameh/The End of the *Shahnameh*."

Chapter 3

1 Ahmad Shamlou, "Dar Jedal ba Khamushi/Battling Silence" (1984), in Ahmad Shamlou, *Madayh-e bi-Saleh/Thankless Elegies* (Tehran: Zamaneh Publishers, 1999): 45–53. Alef Bamdad was Ahmad Shamlou's pen name. Alef stands for Ahmad, and Bamdad means Dawn. All translations of Shamlou's poems from the Persian originals are mine, as are all the translations of other poets' works I discuss in this book. There are, of course, a good number of volumes of translation of Shamlou's poetry. For a pioneering example, see Ahmad Karimi Hakkak, *An Anthology of Modern Persian Poetry (English and Persian Edition)* (Costa Mesa: Mazda, 1978). For a more recent translation of Shamlou, see Firoozeh Papan-Matin (ed.), *The Love Poems of Ahmad Shamlou* (Bethesda: Ibex, 2005). Meanwhile, Sholeh Wolpe has continued to produce some of the best translations of Shamlou available in English. See https://www.sholehwolpe.com/shamlou. There exist translations of Shamlou in other European languages, such as Ahmad Shamlou, *La Passion de la Recréation: Poésies, choisies et traduites du persan par Media Kashigar Jalal Alavinia* (Paris: Persanes, 2022). For a provocative translation and commentary of Shamlou's poetry, see Jason Bahbak Mohaghegh (trans.), *Ahmad Shamlou: Born upon the Dark Spear* (New York: Contra Mundum, 2015).
2 Ahmad Shamlou, "Sar Cheshmeh/Fountainhead" (1956), in Ahmad Shamlou, *Majmu'eh Ash'ar/Collected Poems* (Giessen: Bamdad Verlag, 1989), vol. 1, 265. I have all of Shamlou's collections of poetry in their original editions in my library, which I began collecting during my undergraduate years in Tehran. However, for consistency I mostly use this collected volume prepared in Germany under Shamlou's own supervision.
3 For a brief and sympathetic review of the major events of Shamlou's life and the highlights of his poetry in English, see the pioneering essay by the late Leonardo P. Alishan, "Ahmad Shamlu: The Rebel Poet in Search of an Audience," *Iranian Studies* 18, no. 2/4 (1985): 375–422. Leonardo P. Alishan (1951–2005), whom I knew and deeply admired, was a poet and scholar of Persian prose and poetry at the University of Utah in Salt Lake City; he tragically died in a fire accident. He knew Shamlou personally, and Shamlou even dedicated one of his poems to him. For a detailed chronology of Shamlou's life, see Javad Mojabi (ed.), *Shenakht-nameh-ye Shamlu/Shamlou Festschrift* (Tehran: Nashr-e Qatreh, 1998), 8–13. This entire festschrift was prepared under Shamlou's own supervision. There exists another, more recent collection of learned essays on Shamlou collected by Sa'id Pour-Azimi (ed.), *Man Bamdadam, Saranjam/I am Bamdad, Finally* (Tehran: Nashr-e No, 2020). Published some two decades after Shamlou's passing, this excellent collection of essays and recollections is the most comprehensive and authoritative critical assessment of his character and poetry.
4 His host on this occasion was Houshang Amir Ahmadi, who at that time served as the director of the Center for Iranian Research and Analysis (CIRA), which had invited him to deliver a keynote lecture at the University of California, Berkeley. There he delivered his very controversial lecture titled "Negarani-ha-ye Man/My Concerns" (1990). For the official text, see Ahmad Shamlou, *Negaran haye man/My Concerns* (Berkeley: CIRA, 1990). During this trip to the US, Shamlou then gave another talk at the University of California, Berkeley, in which he sought to offer a response to his critics. See Ahmad Shamlou, *Mafahim-e Rend va Rendi dar Hafez/Concepts of Rend and Rendi in Hafez* (Berkeley: [n. p.], 1990).
5 Ahmad Shamlou, "Dar in Bon-bast/In this Dead-End" (1979), in *Collected Poems* (Giessen: Bamdad Verlag, 1989), vol. 2, 1120–2.

6 Ahmad Shamlou, "Dar Jedal ba Khamushi/Battling Silence," in Ahmad Shamlou, *Majmu'eh Asar/Collected Works* (Tehran: Zamaneh Publications, 2002), vol. 1, 872–9. Please note that this is a different collection of Shamlou's poetry than the one cited above, published in Iran after his passing, and as a result more complete, for it includes Shamlou's latest poems before his death.
7 Ahmad Shamlou, "Dar Astaneh/At the Threshold," in *Majmu'eh Asar/Collected Works* (Tehran: Zamaneh Publications, 2002), vol. 1, 971–5.
8 Ahmad Shamlou, "Va Hasrati/And a Regret," in *Marsiyeh ha ye Khak/Earthly Elegies* (1969), in *Collected Poems* (Giessen: Bamdad Verlag, 1989), vol. 2, 919–21.
9 For this chronology, I am using the final collection of Shamlou's poems after his passing, collected in *Majmu'eh Asar/Collected Works* (Tehran: Zamaneh Publications, 2002). There exists an extensive body of critical writing on Shamlou's poetry in Persian, some of which have been edited and published in Javad Mojabi, *Shenakht-nameh Shamlou/Shamlou Festschrift*, 179–336.
10 See Taghi Pournamdarian, *Ta'mmoli dar She'r-e Ahmad Shamlou/A Meditation on Ahmad Shamlou's Poetry* (Tarhan: Entesharat-e Aban, 1978).
11 Ibid., 287–315.
12 Ibid., 32–81.
13 Ahmad Shamlou, "Dar Bareh-ye Nima va Digaran/Concerning Nima and Others," in *Ahmad Shamlou: Ketab-e She'r/Ahmad Shamlou: The Book of Poetry*, ed. Hiva Massih (Tehran: Mehra Publications, 2005), 49–50.
14 Ahmad Shamlou, "Bar Sarma-ye Darun/Upon the Cold Inside," in *Collected Poems* (Giessen: Bamdad Verlag, 1989), vol. 2, 1015–16.
15 Ahmad Shamlou, "Marsiyeh/Elegy" (1970), in *Collected Poems* (Giessen: Bamdad Verlag, 1989), vol. 2, 896–8.
16 Ahmad Shamlou, "Shabaneh/Nocturnal," in *Collected Poems* (Giessen: Bamdad Verlag, 1989), vol. 2, 995–7.
17 Ahmad Shamlou, "Oghubat/Punishment" (1970), in *Collected Poems* (Giessen: Bamdad Verlag, 1989), vol. 2, 955–9.
18 See Mahmoud Omidsalar, "Dar bareh Farhang-e Kucheh/Concerning Farhang-e Kucheh," in Mahmoud Omidsalar, *Maqalati dar Bab-e Tarikh, Adab, va Farhang-e Iran/Essays on the History, Literature, and Culture of Iran* (Tehran: Mahmoud Afshar Publications, 2018), 459–93. Compare the balanced dignity of this article with the sensational screed of Bahram Gerami, *Ahmad Shamlou: Dar Pas-e Ayeneh/Ahmad Shamlou: Behind the Mirror* ([n. p.]: Ketab Corporation, 2022). Published by vanity presses and promoted by retrograde neo-con operatives employed by reactionary outfits such as the Hoover Institution, such volumes are published for entirely abusive purposes, seeking in vain to discredit an iconic figure of the Iranian left.
19 See Behrang Nikaeen and Anna Oldfield, "The Azerbaijani Ashiq: Musical Change, Transmission, and the Future of a Bardic Art," *Journal of Folklore Research* 57, no. 3 (2020): 1–26. See also Charlotte F. Albright, *The Azerbaijani Āshiq and His Performance of a Dāstān* (Cambridge: Cambridge University Press, 2022).
20 For more details, see "GŌSĀN," *Encyclopedia Iranica*, https://www.iranicaonline.org/articles/gosan.
21 Ahmad Shamlou, "Fasl-e Digar/Another Season," in *Collected Works* (Giessen: Bamdad Verlag, 1989), vol. 2, 965–8. For a recording, see https://www.youtube.com/watch?app=desktop&v=V45pQnNUtd4.
22 See Ahmad Shamlou (ed.), *Hafez-e Shirazi* (Tehran: Nil Publications, 1957). In his introduction to this edition of Hafez, Shamlou has clearly said that it is not based

on any manuscript but on his estimation of beauty (*ziba'i*) and accuracy (*dorosti*)—meaning his own subjective assessment of such aesthetic factors.
23 Ahmad Shamlou, "Ta Shokoufeh Sorkh-e Yek Pirahan/Until the Red Blossom of a Dress" (1950), in *Collected Poems* (Giessen: Bamdad Verlag, 1989), vol. 2, 35–6.
24 See Hamid Dabashi, *The Persian Prince: The Rise and Resurrection of an Imperial Archetype* (Palo Alto: Stanford University Press, 2023).
25 Ahmad Shamlou, "Ebrahim dar Atash/Abraham in the Fire" (1973), in *Collected Poems* (Giessen: Bamdad Verlag, 1989), vol. 2, 1001–6.
26 Ahmad Shamlou, "Khatabeh Tadfin/The Funeral Elegy," in "Kashefan Forutan-e Shukaran/The Humble Discoverers of the Hemlock," which he dedicated to Che Guevara, in *Collected Poems* (Tehran: Zamaneh Publishers, 2002), 785–6.
27 Ahmad Shamlou, "Pariya/Fairies" (1953), in *Collected Poems* (Giessen: Bamdad Verlag, 1989), vol. 1, 229–39.
28 Ahmad Shamlou, "Dokhtara-ye Naneh Darya/The Daughters of Mother Sea," in *Collected Poems* (Giessen: Bamdad Verlag, 1989), vol. 1, 523–34.
29 Shams al-Din Muhammad Ibn Qais al-Razi, *Al-Mo'jam fi Ma'a'ir Ash'ar al-'Ajam/Compendium on the Principles of Persian Poetry*, ed. Mohammad Qazvini and Modarres Razavi (Tehran: Khavar Publications, 1935), 20–145.
30 Ibid., 146–326.
31 Ibid., 327–48.
32 Ibid., 327–33.
33 Ibid., 333–40.
34 Ibid., 340–7.
35 Ibid., 347–8.
36 Ahmad Shamlou, "Keyfar/Punishment," in *Collected Poems* (Tehran: Zamaneh Publications, 2002), vol. 1, 427–30.
37 For a critical assessment of this temporal aspect of Paul Ricœur's idea, see William C. Dowling, *Ricoeur on Time and Narrative: An Introduction to Temps et récit* (Notre Dame: University of Notre Dame Press, 2011).
38 Ahmad Shamlou, "Marg-e Naseri/The Death of the Nazarene," in *Collected Poems* (Giessen: Bamdad Verlag, 1989), vol. 2, 845–8.
39 Ahmad Shamlou, "Taraneh-ye Tarik/Dark Song," in *Collected Poems* (Giessen: Bamdad Verlag, 1989), 1010–11.

Chapter 4

1 Forough Farrokhzad, "Vahm-e Sabz/Green Apprehension" (1963), in Forough Farrokhzad, *Tavallodi Digar/Another Birth* (Tehran: Morvarid Publications, 1963), 109–14. Again, there are many excellent English translations of Farrokhzad's poems. But in this book I prefer to publish my own translations, based on the first editions of Farrokhzad's published volumes, which I purchased when I was still in Tehran and subsequently brought with me to the US. These are editions published by the poet herself with reputable publishers—including her posthumous volume *Iman Biavarim beh Aghaz-e Fast-e Sard/Let Us Believe in the Commencement of the Cold Season*. The final volume published before her passing was a selection of her poetry, *Gozideh Ash'ar-e Forough Farrokhzad/A Selection of Forough Farrokhzad's Poetry* (Tehran: Morvard Publishers, 1965). I hope to entrust all of these first editions of my personal library to the Rare Book Collection of Columbia University.

2 In her magnificent book *Recite in the Name of the Red Rose: Poetic Sacred Making in Twentieth-Century Iran* (Columbia: The University of South Carolina Press, 2006), Fatemeh Keshavarz has paid exquisite attention to these sacred elements.
3 Hamid Dabashi, "Forough Farrokhzad and the Formative Forces in Iranian Culture," in *Forough Farrokhzad: A Quarter-Century Later*, ed. Michael Craig Hillmann (*Literature East & West* 24, no. 7 [1988]): 7–36.
4 For a brief account of Farrokhzad's life and works, see "FARROKZĀD, FORŪĠ-ZAMĀN," *Encyclopedia Iranica*, https://www.iranicaonline.org/articles/farrokzad-forug-zaman. The entry is fairly reliable in terms of its basic facts and chronology, but otherwise weak and entirely cliché and outdated in its prose and critical analysis. What is noteworthy here is the uncontested superiority of the scholarship written in Persian by Iranian scholars and literati. See, for example, three excellent monographs by Sirus Tahbaz, *Zendegi va Honar-e Forough Farrokhzad: Zani Tanha/The Life and Art of Forough Farrokhzad: A Lonely Woman* (Tehran: Zaryab Publications, 1997); Kamyar Abedi, *Zendegi va She'r-e Forough Farrokhzad: Tanha-tar az Yek Barg/The Life and Poetry of Forough Farrokhzad: Lonelier than a Leaf* (Tehran: Jami Publications, 1998); and M. Azad, *Parishadokht-e She'r: Zendegi va She'r-e Forough Farrokhzad/The Princess of Poetry: The Life and Poetry of Forough Farrokhzad* (Tehran: Sales Publications, 1997). There is simply nothing in English on Farrokhzad's poetry that compares in insight and deep archival work to these volumes.
5 For a translation of this seminal poem, see Forough Farrokhzad, *Let Us Believe in the Beginning of the Cold Season: Selected Poems*, trans. Elizabeth T. Gray Jr. (New York: New Directions, 2022). This is my own translation.
6 For a detailed study of *The House Is Black* (1962), see my chapter on Forough Farrokhzad in Hamid Dabashi, *Masters and Masterpieces of Iranian Cinema* (Washington DC: Mage Publications, 2007), 39–70.
7 For a pioneering study of Farrokhzad's life and poetry, see M. C. Hillmann, *A Lonely Woman: Forough Farrokhzad and Her Poetry* (Washington DC: Three Continents Press, 1985). Equally detailed and insightful is the collection of essays edited by Michael Hillmann in *Forough Farrokhzad: A Quarter Century Later*. The state of critical thinking in Persian literary scholarship has advanced by leaps and bounds since the period that these early works represent. For a more recent encyclopedic entry (2022), see Michael Hillmann, "Furūgh Farrukhzād," *Women Poets Iranica*, https://poets.iranicaonline.org/article/furugh-farrukhzad/. This entry is the most up to date with recent translations and scholarship on Farrokhzad, including of course gossipy rumors about Farrokhzad's personal life, among them tabloid headlines such as that she presumably "underwent rhinoplasty, used heroin, suffered from depression, and attempted suicide on multiple occasions," or that she may have terminated a pregnancy! All of this is an excellent specimen of the state of "Iranian Studies" scholarship. Exceptionally insightful, however, is the collection of essays in Dominic Parviz Brookshaw and Nasrin Rahimieh (eds.), *Forough Farrokhzad Poet of Modern Iran: Iconic Woman and Feminist Pioneer of New Persian Poetry* (London: I. B. Tauris, 2010).
8 Forough Farrokhzad, "Tanha Sedast keh Mimanad/Only the Voice Will Remain," in Forough Farrokhzad, *Iman Biavarim Beh Aghaz-e Fasl-e Sard/Let Us Believe in the Beginning of the Cold Season* (Tehran: Morvarid, 1983), 93–5.
9 One of my most precious possessions in my personal library is the first original edition of a memorial volume published soon after Farrokhzad's passing, Amir Esma'ili and Abolqasem Sedarat (eds.), *Javdaneh Forough Farrokhzad/Immortal Forough Farrokhzad* (Tehran: Marjan Publications, 1966). The volume exudes a sense of mourning by

Farrokhzad's friends, consisting of anecdotal recollections by her family and friends, learned articles by the leading Iranian literati and poets, samples of her poetry and prose, and a short outline of her life. The whole book reads like a public memorial for a recently lost and deeply loved and admired poet. Years later, in 1993, a more detailed volume appeared to update this earlier document. See Behruz Jalali, *Javdaneh Zistan, dar Awj Mandan: Forough Farrokhzad/Eternally to Live, Remaining at the Summit: Forough Farrokhzad* (Tehran: Morvarid Publications, 1993).

10 Farrokhzad's poetry is, of course, located within a larger context of Iranian women poets of this era, for a detailed account of which, see Dominic Parviz Brookshaw, "Women Poets," in *Literature of the Early Twentieth Century from the Constitutional Period to Reza Shah*, Volume V, ed. Ali Asghar Seyed Ghora, in *A History of Persian Literature*, ed. Ehsan Yarshater (London: I. B. Tauris, 2015), 240–310.

11 Forough Farrokhzad, "Tavallod-i Digar/Another Birth," in Forough Farrokhzad, *Tavallod-i Digar/Another Birth* (Tehran: Morvarid Publications, 1963), 156–61. There are countless translations of this famous poem by Farrokhzad. This is my own translation. For a detailed translation of Iranian women poets' works, see Dick Davis (trans.), *The Mirror of My Heart: A Thousand Years of Persian Poetry by Women: A Bilingual Text in English and Persian* (Washington DC: Mage Publishers, 2020).

12 For a detailed study of Farrokhzad's poetic terminologies, see the extraordinary work of Mohammad Abd Ali, *Aseman-e Roshan-e She'r: Vazhegan va Tarkibat-e Ash'ar Forough Farrokhzad/The Clear Sky of Poetry: Words and Compound Constructions in Forough Farrokhzad's Poetry* (Tehran: Fekr-re Ruz, 1998).

13 For the most recent, truly exquisite, translation of Enheduana's *Exultation of Inana*, see *Enheduana: The Complete Poems of the World's First Author*, trans. Sophus Helle (New Haven: Yale University Press, 2023). Equally and eminently readable and relatable is *If Not, Winter: Fragments of Sappho*, trans. Anne Carson (New York: Vintage Canada, 2003). At the time of writing this chapter, I have been teaching these two texts for two consecutive years at Columbia University; thus, they are fresh in my mind as I reread Farrokhzad.

14 Farrokhzad, "Tavallod-i Digar/Another Birth."

15 Baba Afzal Kashani, *Madarej al-Kamal/Stages of Perfection*, in *Musannafat/Collected Works*, 8–9. My translation of the original Persian prose.

16 Farrokhzad, "Tavallod-i Digar/Another Birth."

17 Ibid.

18 Ibid.

19 Ibid.

20 Ibid.

21 Forough Farrokhzad, "Kasi keh Mesl-e Hichkas Nist/Someone Who Is Like No One" (1973), in *Iman Biavarim beh Aghaz-e Fasl-e Sard/Let Us Believe in the Commencement of the Cold Season*, 79–88.

22 Ibid.

23 Ibid.

24 Ibid.

25 Ibid.

26 See Abd al-Razzaq Lahiji, *Gohar Morad/The Desired Jewel*, ed. Samad Movahhed (Tehran: Tahuri, 1985), 305–13.

27 For an excellent critical edition of Farrokhzad's entire oeuvre, see Forugh Farrokhzad, *Io parlo dai confini della notte: Tutte le poesie*, trans. and ed. Domenico Ingenito (Milan: Bompiani, 2023). This is an admirable book by a serious Italian scholar seeking to

document both the Persian originals and their Italian translations. Over the years, another translator, Sholeh Wolpe, has done equally admirable work promoting Farrokhzad's poetry with her own excellent translations. See https://www.sholehwolpe.com/sin-selected-poems-of-forugh-farrokhzad. Of course, Domenico Ingenito's is by no means the first "critical edition" of Farrokhzad's works. More than two decades before this Italian edition and translation, Behruz Jalali had prepared a critical edition of Farrokhzad's collected poems with *Divan-e Ash'ar-e Forough Farrokhzad* (Tehran: Morvarid Publications, 1993). Even though I admire all these excellent publications, I still prefer doing my own translations, based on the original editions of her books of poetry. I am never satisfied with any of these translations because of the moral and imaginative distance of these translations from the Persian originals with which I have a lifelong close acquaintance. When I translate Farrokhzad, I feel her sitting by my side, looking over my shoulder, sometimes approvingly, sometimes disapprovingly, but always happy, gently holding my hands.

28 Farrokhzad was fully aware of her own significance in the constellation of Nimaic poetry. In a volume that she edited and published shortly before her death, she included samples of her own poetry immediately after those of Nima, Shamlou, and Akhavan as the pioneers, to which she then added a number of other, more debatable names, except for Sohrab Sepehri, who also features in this volume. This is among the earliest evidence for the canonization of these six poets by one of their own. She obviously did not include Esmail Kho'i, for he was not among the leading poets of his time yet. He was still in his late twenties, and it would take decades before his significance would ultimately ascend. See Forough Farrokhzad (ed.), *Az Nima ta Ba'd/From Nima Forward*, with the collaboration of Majid Roshangar (Tehran: Morvarid 1967).

29 See Dabashi, *Masters and Masterpieces of Iranian Cinema*, 39–70.

30 Forough Farrokhzad also acted in a short film by Ebrahim Golestan, *Khastegari/Courtship* (1961). The joy of seeing Farrokhzad act in this short film is made bitterly intolerable by the ghastly self-Orientalizing tone of the documentary by Ebrahim Golestan, whose voice-over we can hear when the father of the would-be bride speaks. The American or Canadian accent of the narrator of the documentary in English, by a certain "Professor Frank Jones" and a couple of other Americans or Canadians joining the commentary, is truly obnoxious. To grasp the superior sense of filmmaking in Farrokhzad, one should remember that she made her masterpiece *The House Is Black* almost the same year that Golestan made this supercilious documentary for the benefit of North American anthropological curiosity. To learn more about the film, see https://www.viennale.at/en/film/khestegarsi. To watch the film, see https://www.youtube.com/watch?v=g8arM5jbauE. In addition to Forough Farrokhzad as the sister, we also see Tusi Hae'ri, Ahmad Shamlou's ex-wife, as Hassan's mother. Meanwhile, Parviz Dariush (1923-2001), a gifted translator of major novels, played the role of the bride's father.

31 For a classic example of contemporary Iranian literary scholars paying extensive attention to poetic forms, see Mohammad Reza Shafi'i-Kadkani, *Sovar-e Khayal dar She'r-e Farsi/Imaginative Imageries in Persian Poetry* (Tehran: Agah Publications, 1971). For more recent scholarship on the subject, see Maryam Alijanzadah, "Naqd-e Formalisti-ye She'r-e Forough Farrokhzad/Formalist Criticism of Forough Farrokhzad's Poetry" (PhD diss., Mazandaran University, 2010), https://elmnet.ir/doc/10527579-31581. This dissertation is a fairly representative piece of scholarship, representing a plethora of work written in Persian by Iranian scholars that barely

reaches the attention of the outside world trapped in the English language of the "Iranian Studies" nomenklatura.

32 Forough Farrokhzad, "Gonah/Sin," in Forough Farrokhzad, *Divar/Wall* (Tehran: Amir Kabir, 1956), 11–16.
33 Plato, *The Dialogues of Plato, Volume II: Symposium*, trans. and with commentary by R. E. Allen (New Haven: Yale University Press, 1993), 147, 203c–204c.
34 Forough Farrokhzad, "Asheqaneh/Lovingly," in *Another Birth*, 46–51.
35 For the astonishing range of meaning of the word "*hal*" in Persian, see the respective entry in the *Dehkhoda* encyclopedic dictionary: https://vajehyab.com/dehkhoda/حال.
36 For the range of meanings of "*zaman*," all rooted in the fact that it also means "to die," see the respective entry in *Dehkhoda*, https://vajehyab.com/dehkhoda/زمان.
37 Qotb al-Din Ardeshir al-Ebadi, *Al-Tasfiyyeh fi Ahval al-Mutesavvefeh: Sufi Nameh/ Purification in the Conditions of the Mystics: Sufi Nameh*, ed. Gholamhossein Youssefi (Tehran: Bonyad e Farhang Iran Publications, 1968), 139–59.
38 Ibid., 160–79.
39 Forough Farrokhzad, "Ghorubi Abadi/An Eternal Sunset!" (1963), in *Another Birth*, 78–84.
40 Fredric Jameson, *Inventions of a Present: The Novel in Its Crisis of Globalization* (New York: Verso, 2024), 2–3.
41 Forough Farrokhzad, "Mordab/Swamp," in *Another Birth*, 85–8.
42 I have detailed aspects of these banalities of Area Studies in my *Post-Orientalism: Knowledge and Power in a Time of Terror* (New York: Routledge, 2009).
43 Søren Kierkegaard, *The Sickness unto Death* (1849), in *A Kierkegaard Anthology*, ed. Robert Bretall (New York: The Modern Library, 1946), 363.
44 Farrokhzad, "Iman Biavarim Beh Aghaz-e Fasl-e Sard/Let Us Believe in the Beginning of the Cold Season," 23–43.
45 In *Mirrors of Entrapment and Emancipation: Forugh Farrokhzad and Sylvia Plath* (Leiden: Leiden University Press, 2015), Leila Rahimi Bahmany has zoomed in on the image of the mirror in both poets to offer a detailed study of how "the mirror and the woman have both long been regarded as delusory and guileful, responsible for man's downfall" (Ibid., 12). There are a number of other similar comparative studies of Farrokhzad and Plath, such as Narges Raoufzadeh, Sharzad Mohammad Hosein, and Shiva Zaheri Birgani, "Analysis of Love, Death, Rebirth and Patriarchy in Two Contemporary Poetess Forough Farrokhzad and Sylvia Plath's Selected Poems," *Budapest International Research and Critics Institute Journal* 2, no. 4 (2019): 56–64. See also Mohsen Mohammadpour and Hossein Valizade, "Sylvia Plath's 'Mirror' and Forough Farrokhzad's 'The Bird May Die': Comparative Analysis from a Mystical Perspective," *Advances in Language and Literary Studies* 8, no. 1 (2017): 162–6.
46 Forough Farrokhzad, "Beh Aftab Salami Do-bareh Khaham Dad/I Shall Greet the Sun Again" (1963), in *Another Birth*, 150–1.
47 Forough Farrokhzad, "Delam Bara-ye Baghcheh Misuzad/I Feel Sorry for the Flowerbed" (1963), in *Iman Biavarim Beh Aghaz-e Fasl-e Sard/Let Us Believe in the Beginning of the Cold Season*, 69–78.
48 Forough Farrokhzad, "Ayeh-ha-ye Zamini/Earthly Verses" (1963), in *Another Birth*, 89–96.
49 Forough Farrokhzad, "Ay Marz-e Por Gohar/Oh Most Precious Homeland" (1963), in *Another Birth*, 139–49.

Chapter 5

1. For an autobiographical sketch, see Sohrab Sepehri, *Hanuz dar Safaram/I Am Still Traveling: Unpublished Poems and Prose of Sohrab Sepehri*, ed. Paridokht Sepehri (Tehran: Farzan Ruz Publications, 2001), passim. All translations of Sepehri's prose and poetry from the original Persian are mine.
2. Sohrab Sepehri, "Hamrah/Fellow Traveler" (1961), in Sohrab Sepehri, *Hasht Ketab/Eight Books* (Tehran: Tahuri Publications, 1977), 153. I still have in my personal library the first edition of this seminal collection, published in Tehran when I was an undergraduate student and just before I left Iran for the US!
3. For a detailed sketch of Sepehri's life collected from a variety of sources, see Kamyar Abedi (ed.), *Az Mosahebat-e Aftab: Zendegi va She'r-e Sohrab Sepehri/From a Conversation with Sunshine: The Life and Poetry of Sohrab Sepehri* (Tehran: Nashr-e Sales, 1977), 15–49. This is by far the best and most comprehensive study of Sepehri in any language. Before this book, Mohammad Hoghughi's *Sohrab Sepehri* (Tehran: Negah, 1992) was a pioneering work for understanding Sepehri's oeuvre. Equally insightful is Sirus Shamisa's *Negahi beh Sepehri/A Look at Sepehri* (Tehran: Morvarid, 1991). A few years later, Bahram Meqdadi published his deeply insightful book *Tahlil va Gozideh She'r-e Sohrab Sepehri/Analysis and Selected Poetry of Sohrab Sepehri* (Tehran: Mo'assesseh Farhangi Mo'aser, 1998). All these sources in Persian are by far the best scholarly and critical works on Sepehri in any language.
4. The most comprehensive bibliography of Sepehri's work, and the work on Sepehri and his poetry, has been collected by Karim Emami and Kamyar Abedi in Abedi (ed.), *From a Conversation with Sunshine*, 482–579. There are excellent monographs in Persian on specific volumes of Sepehri, collectively published in his *Hasht Ketab/Eight Books*, such as Azim Mahmoudzadeh Shirazi, *Tafsir-e Hajm e Sabz-e Sohrab Sepehri/An Interpretation of Sepehri's Green Volume* (Tehran: Entesharat-e Neda-ye Farhang, 1998).
5. Sohrab Sepehri, "Seda-ye Pa-ye Ab/The Sound of the Water's Footstep" (1964), in *Hasht Ketab*, 271–99.
6. See "SEPEHRI, Sohrab," *Encyclopedia Iranica*, https://www.iranicaonline.org/articles/sepehri-sohrab. This entry is an excellent English-language account of Sepehri's life and his painting and poetry. The *Encyclopedia Iranica*'s entries on Persian New Poetry are uneven. This one, written by Houman Sarshar, is exceptionally informed and insightful.
7. Sohrab Sepehri, "Dust/Friend," in *Hasht Ketab*, 398–401.
8. For the whole poem, see https://poets.org/poem/journey-magi.
9. See "SEPEHRI, Sohrab," *Encyclopedia Iranica*. In this respect, see also Fatemeh Shariati Rad and Shamsuddin Royanian, "Nature as the Source of Wisdom in Sepehri and Wordsworth's Poetry," *Journal of Arts, Humanities and Social Sciences* 2, no. 4 (2014): 471–4. Available online at: https://www.researchgate.net/publication/264420044_Nature_as_the_Source_of_Wisdom_in_Sepehri_and_Wordsworth's_Poetry.
10. There exists an insightful essay by the late Mohammad Mokhtari (1942–98), "Sohrab Sepehri: Mafhum ya Tasvir/Sohrab Sepehri: Concept or Image," in which he sought to distinguish between these two ideas in Sepehri's poetry. The essay is a pioneering attempt to distinguish between these two seminal tropes in a key poet of his time. In an excellent collection of seminal essays collected, see Hamid Siahpush, *Bagh-e Tanha'i: Yadnameh Sohrab Sepehri/The Garden of Solitude: A Memorial Volume on Sohrab Sepehri* (Tehran: Soheil Publications, 1996), 64–72.
11. Cited in Abedi (ed.), *From a Conversation with Sunshine*, 24. The "Three-Pointed Mountain" (*Kuh-e Seh Dandaneh*) is a mountain near Kashan.

12 Ibid.
13 Sohrab Sepehri, *Otaq-e Abi/The Blue Room*, ed. Parvaneh Sepehri (Tehran: Negah Publications, 1991), 33.
14 Ibid., 47.
15 Ibid., 52.
16 Ibid., 83.
17 Sohrab Sepehri, "Dar Golestaneh/In Golestaneh," in *Hasht Ketab*, 348–51. Golestaneh is a village near Kashan, Sepehri's hometown.
18 Sohrab Sepehri, "Neda-ye Aghaz/The Sound of the Beginning," in *Hasht Ketab*, 392.
19 For the original, see Sohrab Sepehri, "Mosafer/Traveler," in *Hasht Ketab*, 301–28.
20 Hasan Hosseini, *Bidel, Sepehri, va Sabk-e Hendi/Bidel, Sepehri and the Indian Style* (Tehran: Soroush, Publications, 1997), 18–29, has offered an excellent analysis of the metaphor of a journey from the visible to the invisible world, based on a comparative reading of these two poets. Saleh Hosseini has also published a chapter on Sepehri and Bidel in his excellent monograph, *Nilufar-e Khamush/The Silent Water Lily: A Look at Sohrab Sepehri's Poetry* (Tehran: Nilufar Publications, 1996), 131–64.
21 I wish to distinguish between this luminous disposition of the comparative archive that informs Sepehri's poetry and the overwhelming attempt to cast his entire poetry in a mystical or else neo-mystical tradition. For the perhaps best example, see Hojjat Emad, *Jahan-e Matlub-e Sohrab-e Sepehri/The Desired World of Sohrab Sepehri* (Tehran: Behzad Publications, 1997).
22 For the Arabic original of Suhrawardi's story of "Qesseh Qorbat Gharbiyeh/The Ballad of the Occidental Exile," see Henry Corbin (ed. and intro.), *Majmu'eh-ye Musannafat-e Shaykh-e Ishraq/Collected Works of the Martyred Master* (Tehran: Académie Impériale Iranienne Philosophie, 1977), vol. 2, 273–97. For an English translation of the story, see Shahab al-Din Yahya Suhrawardi, "A Tale of Occidental Exile," trans. W. M. Thackston Jr., in *The Mystical and Visionary Treatises of Suhrawardi* (London: Octagon Press, 1982), 100–8. I use the Arabic original. These stories have been identified as "Qesseh-ha-ye Ramzi/Allegorical Stories" in Persian and as "Visionary Recitals" by the eminent French scholar Henry Corbin in French and English. Here I opt to call them "ballads," for I believe this term may make more sense in this context.
23 For a pioneering study of landscape in Sohrab Sepehri's poetry, see the excellent work of Atefeh Akbari Shahmirzadi, "'Where Is the Friend's Home?': New World Landscapes in Sohrab Sepehri's Poetic Geography," *Journal of Postcolonial Literary Inquiry* 6, no. 3 (2019): 313–28. Available at: https://www.cambridge.org/core/journals/cambridge-journal-of-postcolonial-literary-inquiry/article/abs/where-is-the-friends-home-new-world-landscapes-in-sohrab-sepehris-poetic-geography/7D737F2826441594D0F2 1429C9410D69. Equally insightful is Mohammad Hussein Oroskhan and Esmaeil Zohdi's "Sohrab Sepehri's Imaginative Voyage from Negative Romanticism to Positive Romanticism in his Cycles of Poems," *Advances in Language and Literary Studies* 5, no. 6 (2014), https://journals.aiac.org.au/index.php/alls/article/view/595.
24 See Hamid Dabashi, *Reversing the Colonial Gaze: Persian Travelers Abroad* (Cambridge: Cambridge University Press, 2020).
25 In an insightful comparative reading of Sohrab Sepehri and Ahmad Shamlou, *Dar Hasrat-e Parvaz: Hekayat-e Nafs dar She'r-e Shamlu va Sepehri/Longing for Flight: Soul-Searching in the Poetry of Shamlou and Sepehri* (Tehran: Peykan, 1998), 56–82, Peyman Azad has offered an insightful reading of solitude in both of their poetic characters.

26 For a classical study of the probable influence of Persian and Islamic sources on Dante's *Divine Comedy*, see Miguel Asin Palacios, *Islam and the Divine Comedy* (London: Routledge, 1968).

Chapter 6

1 Esmail Kho'i, "Akhavan Jan/My Dearest Akhavan," in Esmail Kho'i, *Pezhvak-e Jansorud-e Del-a'inehgan/The Echo of the Soulful Song of the Mirror-Hearted* (Los Angeles: Ketab Corp., 2000), 152–5. All translations of Kho'i's poems from the Persian original in this chapter are mine.
2 Esmail Kho'i, "Dar Setayesh-e Ahmad e Shamlu/Praising Ahmad Shamlou" (1991), in Esmail Kho'i, *Nahang Dar Sahra/The Whale in the Desert* (Los Angeles: Ketab Corp., 2000), 33–40.
3 For all its unforgiveable sins, BBC Persian has produced a precious documentary on Esmail Kho'i, reviewing his life and poetry. See https://www.youtube.com/watch?v=lsMVrz4Q70E. Jamshid Barzegar, the BBC journalist conducting the interview, is an exceptionally learned and competent interlocutor in this conversation with Kho'i.
4 Ibid. Kho'i shared these early biographical details with Jamshid Barzegar in the BBC interview.
5 Esmail Kho'i, "Az She'r Goftan/On Composing Poetry" (1987), in *Pezhvak-e Jansorud-e Del-a'inehgan/The Echo of the Soulful Song of the Mirror-Hearted*, 9–16.
6 Kho'i himself gave an account of this precious moment when Akhavan publicly declared Kho'i his successor, which occurred on July 18, 1990, in his *Pezhvak-e Jansorud-e Del-a'inehgan/The Echo of the Soulful Song of the Mirror-Hearted*, 150.
7 Esmail Kho'i, *Shenakht-nameh Ardeshir Mohassess/An Introduction to Ardeshir Mohassess* (Tehran: Jibi Publications, 1978), 35. My translation from the Persian original.
8 There are countless studies of poets in exile, among them Louis Martz's *Poet of Exile: A Study of Milton's Poetry* (New Haven: Yale University Press, 1980).
9 Caring and capable translators such as Sholeh Wolpe, in anthologies like *The Forbidden: Poems from Iran and Its Exiles* (East Lansing: Michigan State University Press, 2012), have sought to place the works of exilic poets and the poetry of those who have remained inside Iran to come together and coalesce. This, of course, is a worthy idea, but at the same time has failed to demarcate the existential differences between the works of those who have for better or worse opted to stay inside their homeland and those who have been forced to opt for the precarity of exile. In the same vein is the admirable volume by Christopher Nelson (ed.), *Essential Voices: Poetry of Iran and Its Diaspora*, intro. Kaveh Bassiri (Grinnell: Green Linden Press, 2021).
10 Esmail Kho'i, "Soroud-e Azadi/Song of Freedom" (1978), in Esmail Kho'i, *Siahkal* (London: Shoma Publications and other publishers, 1985), 103–6. This volume consists of selections from seven collections of Kho'i's books of poetry. It was prepared and published in London by student organizations in the UK, Scotland, and Wales, followers of the Organization of People's Fada'is (*Sazeman Cherikha-ye Fada'i Khalq*). The collection was named after the Siahkal uprising of February 8, 1971, a failed but symbolically significant guerrilla attack on the military infrastructure of the Pahlavi regime. For more on the context of this uprising, see Ali Rahnema, *Call to Arms: Iran's Marxist Revolutionaries Formation and Evolution of the Fada'is, 1964–1976* (London: OneWorld Academic, 2021). Kho'i has another equally compelling poem, *Koshtar 67 Beh Bang-e Boland/The Massacre of 1988 in a Loud Voice* (Atlanta: The Kho'i

Foundation, 2005), where he commemorated the notorious mass execution of political prisoners in Iran based on Ayatollah Khomeini's edict.
11 This poem was first published in the periodical *Chashm-andaz/Perspective* (no. 6, Summer 1989). It was originally composed in Borgio Verezzi in 1983 and has been widely read and translated. For both the original and an English translation, see Esmail Kho'i, *Outlandia: Songs of Exile*, selected and trans. Ahmad Karimi Hakkak and Michael C. Beard, intro. Erik Nakjavani (Port Coquitlam: Nik Publishers, 1999), 1–16. My own translation.
12 In his otherwise insightful reading of this poem, Michael Beard has missed the figures of these three women and concentrated only on the grandmother. See Michael Beard, "The Woman in the Train: The Esthetics of Exile in Xu'i's 'Return,'" *Oriente Moderno, Nuova serie, Anno 22* 83, no. 1 (2003, = *La letteratura persiana contemporanea tra novazione e tradizione*): 17–27. For another, equally insightful essay on this poem, as well as its German translation, see Nima Mina, "Esmail Khois Rückkehr nach Borgio Verezzi (Esmail Kho'i's Return to Borgio Verezzi)," *SOAS Research Online* (2007), https://eprints.soas.ac.uk/3864/. There are countless commentaries on this poem in Persian, too—among them one by Majid Nafisy, a prominent exile poet. For his weblog, see https://iroon.com/irtn/blog/17166/اسماعیل-خویی-بازگشت-به-بورجو-ورتزی/.
13 For the text of this letter, see the "Declaration of Iranian Intellectuals and Artists in Defense of Salman Rushdie," signed by Homa Sarshar, Mahshid Amir-Shahi, Ali-Asghar Haj Seyed Javadi, Esmail Kho'i, Nader Nader-Poor, and Parviz Sayyad, *The New York Review of Books*, May 14, 1992, https://www.nybooks.com/articles/1992/05/14/declaration-of-iranian-intellectuals-and-artists-i/.
14 Esmail Kho'i, "Sha'er-e Khalqam, Dahan-e Mihanam/I Am the Poet of the People, the Mouth of the Nation," in Esmail Kho'i, *Sha'er-e Khalqam, Dahan-e Mihanam/I Am the Poet of the People, the Mouth of the Nation* (Los Angeles: Ketab Corp., 1999), 34–9.
15 Esmail Kho'i, "Nuruzaneh/A New Year Song" (1996), in *Sha'er-e Khalqam, Dahan-e Mihanam/I Am the Poet of the People, the Mouth of the Nation*, 67–70.
16 Esmail Kho'i, "Qazal-qasideh-ye Man-ha-ye Man/The Panegyric-lyric of My 'I's," in Esmail Kho'i, *Qazal-qasideh Man-ha-ye Man/The Panegyric-lyric of My 'I's* (Los Angeles: Ketab Corp., 2000), 55–6.
17 Esmail Kho'i, *Gozareh Hezareh/The Millennial Testimony* (Los Angeles: Ketab Corp., 2000), 27–8.
18 Mahmoud Mo'taqedi, *Beh Rasm-e Haghighat va Ziba'i: Zendegi va She'r-e Esmail Kho'i/In the Tradition of Truth and Beauty: The Life and Poetry of Esmail Kho'i* (Tehran: Nashr-e Sales, 2014).
19 See Samsam Kashfi (ed.), *Jan-e Del-e She'r: Negahi beh Chand Sh'er-e Esmail Kho'i/The Heart and Soul of Poetry: A Glance at a Few Poems of Esmail Kho'i* (Atlanta: The Esmail Kho'i Foundation, 2002).
20 Ibid., 13–28. Equally important is Majid Nafisi's learned essay "Masti dar She'r-e Esmail Kho'i/Drunkenness in Esmail Kho'i's Poetry" (January 2002), https://iroon.com/irtn/blog/17158/مستی-در-شعر-اسماعیل-خویی/. This hermeneutic circle became particularly staged soon after Kho'i's death, after the avalanche of obituaries that his friends and comrades wrote celebrating his life. See, for example, Ali Mirfetrus, "Esmail Kho'i Chashm az Jahan Forobast/Esmail Kho'i Passed Away," May 25, 2021, https://mirfetros.com/fa/?p=33211.
21 Ibid., 11.
22 When, for example, Niusha Farrahi (died 1987), a revolutionary activist, committed suicide on September 20, 1987, in protest against human rights abuses in Iran, Kho'i

was expected to compose a poem, which he did not do until much later, with an explanation. See Esmail Kho'i, *Dar Khwabi az Hamareh Hich/In a Slumber of Perpetual Nothingness* (Los Angeles: Kanun Farhangi Nima, 1987), 5–11. For more on Niusha Farrahi's self-immolation, see "Iranian Who Set Himself Afire in Protest Hailed by Exiles as Martyr," *Los Angeles Times*, October 4, 1987, https://www.latimes.com/archives/la-xpm-1987-10-04-me-33060-story.html.

23 For a good sample of this literature, see Esmail Kho'i, *Outlandia: Songs of Exile*. See also Esmail Kho'i, *Edges of Poetry: Selected Poems*, trans. Ahmad Karimi Hakkak and Michael Beard (Santa Monica: Blue Logos, 1995). For another collection, see Esmail Kho'i, *Voice of Exile: A Collection of Poems and Essays* (Atlanta: Omega Publishers, 2002). For an insightful essay on Kho'i based on such sources, see Erik Nakjavani, "Esmail Khoi: The Poet as Observer and Creative Explorer," *Iranian Studies* 44, no. 1 (2011): 77–98, https://www.cambridge.org/core/journals/iranian-studies/article/abs/esmail-khoi-the-poet-as-observer-and-creative-explorer/B8656AB545079E2761EC87910ED14116.

24 See Kofi Anyidoho, *The Word Behind Bars and the Paradox of Exile* (Evanston: Northwestern University Press, 1997). Coming close to this volume is the important essay of Peyman Vahabzadeh, "Space, Identity, and Bilingual Poetry: Rethinking Iranian 'Emigration Poetry,'" *The Literary Review* 40, no. 1 (1996): 42–58. Equally path-breaking was Ahmad Karimi-Hakkak, "From Translation to Appropriation: Poetic Cross-Breeding in Early-Twentieth-Century Iran," *Comparative Literature* 47, no. 1 (1995): 53–78.

25 Esmail Kho'i, "Az Mihan Ancheh dar Chamadan dan Daram/What I Have in My Suitcase from the Homeland," in Esmail Kho'i, *Az Mihan Ancheh dar Chamadan Daram/What I Have in My Suitcase from the Homeland* (Los Angeles: Kanun Farhangi Nima, 1999), 11–20. The reference to "Your lantern you graciously say/Burns there!" is an allusion to a similar phrase that Ahmad Shamlou said when he returned to Iran from abroad.

26 Esmail Kho'i, "Ja'i keh Vatan Shavad/Where We Might Call Homeland" (2016), in Esmail Kho'i, *Dar Barzakh-e Panah-jouyan/In the Purgatory of the Refugees* (London: H&S Media, 2017), 36.

27 Esmail Kho'i, *Yek Tekkeh-am Aseman Abi Beferest/Send Me a Patch of Blue Sky* (London: Aras, 1994), 8.

28 Ibid., 11. This quatrain was composed for Akhavan-e Sales, whose pen name was Omid/Hope.

29 Ibid., 35.

30 Ibid., 50.

31 Ibid., 72.

32 Esmail Kho'i, "Khod-sanji/Self-Appraisal," in *Sha'er-e Khalqam, Dahan-e Mihanam/I Am the Poet of the People, the Mouth of the Nation*, 50–2.

Conclusion

1 Mohammad Hoghughi, *She'r-e No: Az Aghaz ta Emruz, 1301–1350/New Poetry: From the Beginning to Today, 1922–1971* (Tehran: Jibi Publications, 1975).

2 Hamid Zarrinkub, *Cheshm-andaz-e She'r-e No-e Farsi/A Perspective on Persian New Poetry* (Tehran: Tus Publications, 1979).

3 Morteza Kakhi (ed.), *Roshan tar az Khamushi: Bargozideh She'r e Emruz Iran, 1300–1357/Brighter than Silence: An Anthology of the Poetry of Today, 1921–1978* (Tehran: Agah Publishers, 1989).
4 Shams Langerudi, *Tarikh Tahlili She'r-e No/The Analytical History of New Poetry* (Tehran: Nashr-e Markaz, 1991), vol. 3, 450–1.
5 I have dealt with this matter extensively in my *Post-Orientalism: Knowledge and Power in a Time of Terror*.
6 This does not mean that Europeans might not produce some of the most readable translations of this body of poetry, such as Geoffrey Squires, *The New Verse: A Selection of Modern Persian Poetry* (Costa Mesa: Mazda Publishers, 2021).
7 See, for example, Rebecca Ruth Gould and Kayvan Tahmasebian Dehkordi, "The Translational Horizons of Iranian Modernism: Ahmad Shamlu's Canon of the Global South," *Twentieth-Century Literature* 68, no. 1 (2022): 25–52; or "Translating Line Breaks: A View from Persian Poetics," *Comparative Literature* 75, no. 3 (2023): 373–91. For more work by these scholars, see https://eprints.soas.ac.uk/view/people/Tahmasebian_Dehkordi=3AKayvan=3A=3A.html. Peyman Vahabzadeh's most recent book, *The Art of Defiance: Dissident Culture and Militant Resistance in 1970s Iran* (Edinburgh: Edinburgh University Press, 2022), has put his exquisite command of a massive body of cultural evidence to one of the most insightful books of recent years.
8 Amr Ahmad, *La "Révolution littéraire": Étude de l'influence de la poésie française sur la modernisation des formes poétiques persanes au début du XXe siècle* (Vienna: Verlag der Österreichischen Akademie der Wissenschaften, 2012), 31. The original reads: "La modernité poétique en Iran s'inscrit au coeur d'une vague d'occidentalisation qui toucha la littérature dans son ensemble, et plus généralement tous les aspects de la vie politique, économique, sociale et culturelle du pays." Translation mine.
9 A dozen of these filmmakers are the subject of my book *Masters and Masterpieces of Iranian Cinema* (Washington DC: Mage Publications, 2007).
10 Ahmad Shamlou, "Bara-ye Khun va Matik/For Blood and Lipstick" (1950), in *Collected Poems* (Giessen: Bamdad Verlag, 1989), vol. 1, 10–11.
11 I have extensively studied these travelogues in my book *Reversing the Colonial Gaze: Persian Travelers Abroad*.
12 For a pioneering study of this recasting, see Ahmad Karimi-Hakkak, *Recasting Persian Poetry: Scenarios of Poetic Modernity in Iran* (London: OneWorld Publications, 2012). The study is detailed in its attention to major debates in early-twentieth-century Iran, but alas threadbare cliché in its attribution of such changes to the encounter with European modernity.
13 See Richard M. Eaton, "The Persian Cosmopolis," *Oxford Research Encyclopedia of Asian History*, February 23, 2021, https://oxfordre.com/asianhistory/display/10.1093/acrefore/9780190277727.001.0001/acrefore-9780190277727-e-402. Equally detailed and insightful is Richard M. Eaton's other essay on the subject, "The Persian Cosmopolis (900–1900) and the Sanskrit Cosmopolis (400–1400)," in *The Persianate World: Rethinking a Shared Sphere*, eds. Abbas Amanat and Assef Ashraf (= Iran Studies 18): 63–83, https://brill.com/display/book/edcoll/9789004387287/BP000009.xml.
14 See Alexander Jabbari, *The Making of Persianate Modernity: Language and Literary History between Iran and India* (Cambridge: Cambridge University Press, 2023).
15 It is not accidental that the malady of Iranophobia was first diagnosed in Israel by an Israeli scholar. See Haggai Ram, *Iranophobia: The Logic of an Israeli Obsession* (Palo Alto: Stanford University Press, 2009). The original of this book was first published in Hebrew in Israel.

16 Saïd Amir Arjomand, the renowned sociologist who is also a product of the University of Chicago, has continued to use the term in the way in which Marshall Hodgson originally meant it in the title of a journal that Arjomand inaugurated decades ago, entirely devoid of any element of active Iranophobia, which the younger US-based scholars are now spinning in the Bush to Trump America.
17 For a *tour de force* of this storm in the teacup of "Persianate World," see Nile Green (ed.), *The Persianate World: The Frontiers of a Eurasian Lingua Franca* (Berkeley: University of California Press, 2019). Astonishing about this volume is that the overwhelming majority of the chapters (ten out of twelve) are actually about the Persian language and culture in different parts of the world, and the term "Persianate" appears only in two chapters. One of these, Michael Fisher's "Conflicting Meanings of Persianate Culture: An Intimate Example from Colonial India" (225–42), has actually questioned the consistency of the term—and yet the whole book is called "Persianate World!" Noteworthy also is the fact that not a single chapter of this edited volume is about Iran proper. Nothing! Iran is completely erased from the map of the world and dissolved into this vacuous "Persianate world." Iran is not part of the Persianate world! Iran is a satellite hovering somewhere around the moon!
18 See Shuchen Xiang, *Chinese Cosmopolitanism: The History and Philosophy of an Idea* (Princeton: Princeton University Press, 2024).
19 For my extensive study of *adab*, see Hamid Dabashi, *The World of Persian Literary Humanism* (Cambridge, MA: Harvard University Press, 2012).
20 Stefan Jonsson, *Subject without Nation: Robert Musil and the History of Modern Identity* (Durham: Duke University Press, 2000), x.
21 Anthony D. Smith, *Theories of Nationalism* (New York: Harper & Row, 1971), 65.
22 Ibid., 67. Partha Chatterjee has, of course, offered a far more detailed and cogent reading of the link between nationalism and colonialism in his seminal work *The Nation and Its Fragments: Colonial and Postcolonial History*. This new coterie of "Persianate" characters could do well to read some serious work on nationalism.

INDEX

Abraham in the Fire, Ahmad Shamlou 96, 105–6, 114
African-American poetry 14
Afzal, Baba 29–30, 33, 60–1, 79–81, 83, 131
  and Nima Yushij 60–1
  "Stages of Perfection" 120
agent provocateur, Ahmad Shamlou 113–14
"Ahoy People", Nima Yushij 35–6
ahval 133–7, 150
Aida in the Mirror, Ahmad Shamlou 95
Aida, Tree, Dagger, and Memory, Ahmad Shamlou 95
Ajoudani, Mashallah 201
Akhavan-e Sales, Mazdak 63–4
Akhavan-e Sales, Mehdi 63–5
  early life 64
  episteme ending 86–8
  Eurocentric modernity 67–72
  exile 73
  and Ferdowsi 65, 74, 76–7
  homeland 83
  meeting the author 2
  and New Poetry 81–4
  and Nima Yushij 65–7
  and past poets 77–9
  Platonic philosophy 79–81
  tradition and modernity 72–7
  transubstantial motion 84–6
Akhavan-e Sales, Mehdi poems
  Arda Viraf Nameh 78
  End of the Shahnameh, The 74–7, 87
  From This Avesta 81–2
  "Grafting and Garden" 85–6
  I Love You, oh Ancient Home and Land 81–2
  Little Man 66–7
  Pilgrims Ballad 77–9
  The Ballad of the Prince of Stoneville 64–5, 86

The Eighth Task 65–6, 71–2
Tree of Knowledge, The 80–1
Akhavan-e Sales, Zardosht 63–4
al-Adawiyeh, Rabe'eh 119–20, 122–3, 150
al-Din Mirza, Jalal 84
al-Din Yahya Suhrawardi, Shahab 17, 169–71, 183, 201
Al-e Ahmad, Jalal 20
  and Nima Yushij 39–40, 43
  The Old Man Was Our Eyes 42–4
al-Ghazali, Ahmad 56, 72
al-Mu'taz, Ibn 19
al-Qahir al-Jorjani, Abd 19
al-Qozat al-Hamadani, Ayn 53, 56
al-Razzaq Lahiji, Abd 127
alfaz 109
Allied occupation, Iran 7, 95, 187
"Amen Bird, The", Nima Yushij 49–50
Aminpour, Qeysar 10
"And a Regret", Ahmad Shamlou 94–5
Angelou, Maya 3, 12, 143
Another Birth, Forough Farrokhzad 116, 118–23, 127–8
Arda Viraf Nameh, Mehdi Akhavan-e Sales 78
Aristotle 111
  Poetics 16–17
art, Alain Badiou 59
Asheqaneh, Forough Farrokhzad 131–3
ashiq 102
At the Threshold, Ahmad Shamlou 93–4, 96
atmospheric environments 46
atmospheric poems, Nima Yushij 46–9
autochthonous voice 46–7
  Nima Yushij 47–9

Badiou, Alain 59
  and Nima Yushij 59–60
Bahar, Mohammad Taqi 6, 27, 40, 214

Ballad of the Occidental Exile, The, Shihab al-Din Yahya Suhrawardi 169–70, 183, 201
Ballad of the Prince of Stoneville, The, Mehdi Akhavan-e Sales 64–5, 86
Bamdadan, Mazdak 82
Battling Silence, Ahmad Shamlou 89
Being (*budan*) 29, 60–1, 79–80, 119
Beyond the Night of the Contemporaries, Esmail Kho'i 187
Biden, Joe (US President) 11, 13
blank verse 96
Bloody Nightmare of the Awake, The, Esmail Kho'i 188
Blossoming in the Fog, Ahmad Shamlou 96
Blue Room, The, Sohrab Sepehri 160–2
Brecht, Bertolt, *To Those Who Follow in Our Wake* 13–14
budan 29, 60–1, 79–80, 119
By Sakhtsar, Nima Yushij 41

capitalist modernity, Iran 4, 68, 71, 215
Captive, Forough Farrokhzad 116, 127
Cassirer, Ernst 29–31, 33
  on Nima Yushij 58–9
changing worlds, Persian poetry 13–16
Chatterjee, Partha 27
Christianity
  belief 6, 8, 18, 59, 73
  context 121
  eschatology 124
  existentialism 140
  monks 173
Christians
  calendar 5
  existentialism 140
  iconography 8
CIA-MI6 military coup 7, 23, 39, 90, 127, 146, 153, 187
classical prosody 96
Cold Campfire, Nima Yushij 38–9
colonialism
  European 5, 41, 69, 73, 84
  of Iran 37, 70, 112
  postcolonial era 10–12, 34, 76–7, 213–14

Constitutional Revolution
  and Persian poetry 23–6
  poetic emergence 3
  poets 11
contemporary poetry 8
Culture of the Street, The, Ahmad Shamlou 113
Curse, Ahmad Shamlou 14–15

Dabashi, Hamid (author)
  inspiration for book 2–3
  meeting the poets 2–3
Dabashi, Hamid (author) books
  Can Non-Europeans Think? 232
  For the Last Time Civilization 232
  Forough Farrokhzad: A Quarter-Century Later 237
  Masters and Masterpieces of Iranian Cinema 224, 237, 239
  Persophilia: Persian Culture on the Global Scene 224
  Reversing the Colonial Gaze: Persian Travelers Abroad 228, 242
  The Emperor is Naked: On the Inevitable Demise of the Nation-state 226
  The Last Muslim Intellectuals: The Life and Legacy of Jalal Al-e Ahmad 229
  The Persian Prince: The Rise and Resurrection of an Imperial Archetype 236
  The Poetics of Politics 226
  The World is My Home: A Hamid Dabashi Reader 226
  The World of Persian Literary Humanism 247
  Truth and Narrative: The Untimely Thoughts of 'Ayn al-Qudat la-Hamadhani 230
  Where Is Abbas Kiarostami? Toward a Postcolonial Film-Philosophy 232
Dagger on the Plate, Ahmad Shamlou 96
Damghani, Ali Moallem 10
Daneshvar, Simin 42
Dante Alighieri 78, 171, 173, 191
  Divine Comedy 78
Dari poetry 56
Dark Song, Ahmad Shamlou 114

Darwish, Mahmoud 14
Daughters of Mother Sea, The, Ahmad Shamlou 108–9
Davis, Dick 20
Day of Judgment 124
de la Cruz, Sor Juana Inés 119
Death of Color, The, Sohrab Sepehri 153
Death of the Nazarene, The, Ahmad Shamlou 112
Dehkhoda, Ali Akbar 6, 8, 208
Divine Comedy, Dante Alighieri 78
Doust, Sohrab Sepehri 158–9

Earthly Elegies, Ahmad Shamlou 96
Earthly Verses, Forough Farrokhzad 146
East of Sorrow, The, Sohrab Sepehri 153
Eight Books, Sohrab Sepehri 153
Eight Paradises, Amir Khosrow Dehlavi 153
Eighth Task, The, Mehdi Akhavan-e Sales 65–6, 71–2
Elegy, Ahmad Shamlou 98
Eliot, T. S. 3, 159
End of the Shahnameh, The, Mehdi Akhavan-e Sales 74–7, 87
English translators, New Poetry 20–3
Enheduana 119–20, 122–3, 150
episteme
　closure 25, 205–7
　ending 86–8
epistolary poetics, Nima Yushij 52–8
eschatology
　Christian 73, 124
　and Parousia 123–7
　in poems 94, 127, 150
　theories of 52
Eshqi, Mirzadeh 6, 11, 25, 27, 34, 40, 72, 214
Eternal Sunset, An, Forough Farrokhzad 134–7
Eurocentrism, militant 52
Eurocentric modernity Mehdi Akhavan-e Sales 67–72
European colonialism 5, 41, 69, 73, 84
European philosophers 30, 52, 70
European philosophy 68, 71, 187–8
European poetry 14
　influence on New Poetry 36–7

exile 190–4
　and homeland 203–5
　and return 194–6
exilic community, Esmail Kho'i 200–3
existentialism 140

Fairies, Ahmad Shamlou 107–8
Faiz, Faiz Ahmed 14
families, ruling 126
Farrokhzad, Forough 24–5, 115–16
　death of 3
　early works 127–30
　Elegy (Shamlou) 97–8
　here and now sense 133–7
　and homeland 146–50
　life of 116–18
　love 130–3
　as a Muslim woman 123–7
　original works 20
　and other poets 143–6
　and Sohrab Sepehri 157–60
　solitary world of 139–43
　temporal spontaneity 118–23
　transcendence 21, 31
Farrokhzad, Forough poems
　An Eternal Sunset 134–7
　Another Birth 116, 118–23, 127–8
　Asheqaneh 131–3
　Captive 116, 127
　Earthly Verses 146
　Green Apprehension 115–16
　I Feel Sorry for the Flowerbed 144–6
　I Shall Greet the Sun Again 143–4
　Let Us Believe in the Commencement of the Cold Season 212, 31, 116–17, 127–8, 141–3
　Oh Most Precious Homeland 146–50
　Only the Voice Will Remain 117–18
　Rebellion 116, 127–8
　Someone Who Is Like No One Else 124–7
　Swamp 138–9
　The House Is Black 116, 128
　Wall 116, 127, 129–30
Fellow Traveler, Sohrab Sepehri 152
Ferdowsi 34, 83, 173, 190, 217
　and Mehdi Akhavan-e Sales 65, 74, 76–7
　Shahnameh 64, 70, 89–90, 101, 103, 110, 113

Fighting Silence, Ahmad Shamlou 92–3
Finding (*yaftan*) 29, 60–1, 79–80
For Blood and Lipstick, Ahmad Shamlou 213–14
Fountainhead, Ahmad Shamlou 90
Frederic Jameson, *Inventions of a Present* 137–9
free poetry 8
Fresh Air, Ahmad Shamlou 95
From the Sound of the Word of Love, Esmail Kho'i 187
From This Avesta, Mehdi Akhavan-e Sales 81–2
Funeral Elegy, The, Ahmad Shamlou 106–7

Garden of Mirrors, The, Ahmad Shamlou 95, 110–11
Gandhi, Mahatma 82
ghaybat 123–4, 150
ghazal 13, 37, 99
Golestan, Ebrahim 24, 28, 43
    and Esmail Kho'i 191
    and Forough Farrokhzad 116
Gorman, Amanda 23
    The Hill We Climb 11–13
Grafting and Garden, Mehdi Akhavan-e Sales 85–6
Green Apprehension, Forough Farrokhzad 115–16
Green Volume, The, Sohrab Sepehri 153
Guevara, Che 106

hal 133–7, 141, 150–1, 164
Harris, Kamala (US Vice-President) 13
Heidegger, Martin 16–17, 29
Hikmet, Nazým 14
Hill We Climb, The, Amanda Gorman 11–13
Hillmann, Michael 20, 128
Hinduism 159–60, 219
homeland 2, 207–8
    and Forough Farrokhzad 146–50
    idea of nation 219–22
    Iran 25, 63
    Persian Cosmopolis 215–19
    Persian New Poetry 208–12
    poets and politics 212–15

House Is Black, The, Forough Farrokhzad 116, 128
Huber, Marie 67–8, 70
Hughes, Langston 3, 12, 14, 91, 101
Humble Discoverers of Hemlock, The, Ahmad Shamlou 106–7

I Am the Poet of the People, the Mouth of the Nation, Esmail Kho'i 188, 198
[I am sorry] Bi ankeh dideh binad, Ahmad Shamlou 102–3
I Am Still Traveling, Sohrab Sepehri 153
I Feel Sorry for the Flowerbed, Forough Farrokhzad 144–6
I Long for You, Nima Yushij 50–1
I Love You, oh Ancient Home and Land, Mehdi Akhavan-e Sales 81–2
I Shall Greet the Sun Again, Forough Farrokhzad 143–4
I Will Create Another World, Esmail Kho'i 188
In a Dream of the Perpetual Nothing, Esmail Kho'i 188
In this Dead-End, Ahmad Shamlou 91–2
infinity, and totality 52
Inventions of a Present, Frederic Jameson 137–9
Iran
    Allied occupation of 7, 95, 187
    capitalist modernity 4, 68, 71, 215
    CIA-MI6 military coup 7, 23, 39, 90, 127, 146, 153, 187
    colonialism 37, 70, 112
    emergence of 2–3, 27–8
    exile from 3, 13
    hatred of 216–17
    as homeland 25, 63
    life as a woman 118, 123
    as a nation 11, 27–9, 213, 218, 221
    poems 35, 192–3
    postcolonial 10–12, 34, 76–7, 213–14
    ruling families 126
Iran–Iraq War 83, 191
Iranian Communist (Tudeh) Party 35, 39, 42, 50, 95
Irons and Emotions, Ahmad Shamlou 95

Islamic Republic 3, 10
  collapse of 187
  imposition of 23, 83
  poems 199
  poets after 212
Islamism 222
  militant 37, 83, 198
Islamist theocracy, and Persian poetry 192
Islamophobia 123, 196–7, 217
It is Night, Nima Yushij 56

Jameson, Frederic, *Inventions of a Present* 137–9
Jonsson, Stefan 220–22
Judeo-centrism 52
Judeo-Christian concepts 52
Judgment, Day of 124

khalvat 141
Khanlari, Parviz Natel 43
Kho'i, Esmail 183–5
  and Ardeshir Mohassess 190
  episteme closure 25, 205–7
  exile 183–4, 186, 190–4
  exile and homeland 196, 202–5
  exile and return 187, 194–6
  exilic community 200–3
  homeland 191, 195
  Islamophobia 196, 198–9
  politics 196–200
  quatrains 204–5
  revolutionary 185–90
  transcendence 26
Kho'i, Esmail poems
  Beyond the Night of the Contemporaries 187
  From the Sound of the Word of Love 187
  I Am the Poet of the People, the Mouth of the Nation 188, 198
  I Will Create Another World 188
  In a Dream of the Perpetual Nothing 188
  My Heart Will Not Be Late 188
  My Sweet Akhavan 184
  New Year Song, A 198–9
  On Composing Poetry 188–90
  On the Roof of the Whirlwind 187
  Praising Ahmad Shamlou 184–5
  Restless 187
  Return to Borgio Verezzi 194–5
  Self-Appraisal 206
  Sketch 25–6
  Song of Freedom 192–4
  Suddenly 188
  The Bloody Nightmare of the Awake 188
  The Millennial Testimony 188, 199–200
  The Nowhereville of London 192
  The Panegyric-lyric of All My 'I's 199
  Upon the Fast Steed of the Earth 187
  Where We Might Call Homeland 204
Khomeini, Ayatollah 34, 95, 190
khonyagar 102–4
Khosrow Dehlavi, Amir, *Eight Paradises* 153
Khosrow, Naser 79, 81–3, 110, 131, 167, 190, 204–5
Kiarostami, Abbas 10, 13, 213
  cinema 70, 166, 212
Kierkegaard, Søren 121, 140
  Present Age, The 139
  Sickness unto Death, The 140–1
  The Present Age 139
  The Sickness unto Death 140–1

Let Us Believe in the Commencement of the Cold Season, Forough Farrokhzad 21–2, 31, 116–17, 127–8, 141–3
Levinas, Emmanuel 51–2
Life of Dreams, The, Sohrab Sepehri 153
Little Man, Mehdi Akhavan-e Sales 66–7
love
  Badiou 59
  Forough Farrokhzad 130–3
lyricism 46, 50–1

ma'ani 109
Mahmoud Amoli, Mohammad ibn 19
Mani 83
Mazdak 83, 200
militant Eurocentrism 52
militant Islamism 37, 83, 198
Millennial Testimony, The, Esmail Kho'i 188, 199–200
Mirza, Iraj 6, 11, 25, 27, 34, 38, 72, 214

Mo'ayyeri, Rahi 13–14
  Shadow of Life 13
modernism 41
  Persian poetry 19–23
modernization 17–18, 37, 41, 207, 210, 215
  court-sponsored 7
Mohammad Reza Shah 7
Mohassess, Ardeshir, and Esmail Kho'i 190
Mo'in, Mohammad 40
Moments and Forever, Ahmad Shamlou 95
Moonlight, Nima Yushij 47–8, 61
moraqebeh 164
moshahedeh 54
Mulla Sadra Shirazi 25, 29–30, 84, 86–7
Muslims
  faith 154–5, 199–200
  hatred of 197
  mystics 53, 61, 119
  philosophers 69, 81, 84
  women 123–7, 157
My Heart Will Not Be Late, Esmail Kho'i 188
My Home Is a Cloud, Nima Yushij 48–9
My Sweet Akhavan, Esmail Kho'i 184
Myth, Nima Yushij 26

Naderi, Amir 10, 24, 205
naqqali 65–7
nation
  idea of 219–22
  narrative in Persian poetry 26–9
Neighbor's Words, The, Nima Yushij 52–3
New Poetry 4, 8–9, 13–16, 207–9
  English translators 20–3
  European poetry influence 36–7
  homeland 208–12
  and Mehdi Akhavan-e Sales 81–4
  and Nima Yushij 9, 23–5, 33
  in Persian 19–21, 26, 30
  translations of 20–1
New Year Song, A, Esmail Kho'i 198–9
Nimaic episteme 87, 151, 188
Nimaic poetry 15, 25, 60–1, 80, 85, 87, 187
  end of 25, 192
  nations 28
Nimaic prosody 91, 96

Nimaic revolution 59, 110, 188, 205, 222
  Akhavan 95
  Constitutional era 40
  nation 28
  phases 72, 81–2
Nimaic Transubstantial Motion 86
Nocturnal, Ahmad Shamlou 103
Nowhereville of London, The, Esmail Kho'i 192

Oh Most Precious Homeland, Forough Farrokhzad 146–50
Old Man Was Our Eyes, The, Jalal Al-e Ahmad 42–4
On Composing Poetry, Esmail Kho'i 188–90
On the Roof of the Whirlwind, Esmail Kho'i 187
Only the Voice Will Remain, Forough Farrokhzad 117–18
opium 42–3

Pahlavi dynasty 3, 28, 90
Panegyric-lyric of All My 'I's, The, Esmail Kho'i 199
Parousia, and eschatology 123–7
periodization, Persian poetry 9–10
Persian Cosmopolis, homeland 215–
Persian language 23, 40, 44, 79, 82, 107, 215
Persian poetry 1–3
  in a changing world 13–16
  and the Constitutional Revolution 23–6
  contemporary 3–8
  in exile 23
  and Islamist theocracy 192
  modernism 19–23
  nation narrative 26–9
  periodization 9–10
  poetics and politics 10–13, 16–19
  time and narrative 29–31
Persianate world 19, 82, 215–19
philosopher-poets 79, 81, 83, 120
philosophers 81, 130
  Abd al-Razzaq Lahiji 127
  European 30, 52, 70
  György Politzer 186
  Martin Heidegger 16–17, 29

Mulla Sadra Shirazi 25, 84
Naser Khosrow 79, 81–3, 110, 131, 167, 190, 204–5
Paul Ricœur 29, 33, 69, 111
Plato 80–1, 130, 200
Shahab al-Din Yahya Suhrawardi 17, 169–71, 183, 201
Søren Kierkegaard 121, 139–41
philosophy
    European 68, 71, 187–8
    and science 54
Phoenix in the Rain, Ahmad Shamlou 95
Pilgrims Ballad, Mehdi Akhavan-e Sales 77–9
Plath, Sylvia 3, 143
Plato 80–1, 130, 200
Platonic philosophy, Mehidi Akhavan-e Sales 79–81
poet laureate, Ahmad Shamlou 95–101
poet-painter 152–3, 157
poetic events 22–3, 33
    Nima Yushij 58–61
poetic modernity 211
poetic temporality 9, 30, 60, 68
Poetics, Aristotle 16–17
poetics, and politics 10–13, 16–19
poetry
    African-American 14
    European 14, 36–7
poets
    Constitutional Revolution 11
    and homeland politics 212–15
    and Mehdi Akhavan-e Sales 77–9
    sha'er 8, 22, 57–8, 198, 210
political power 49
    Nima Yushij 49–51
politics 210
    Alain Badiou 59
    of defiance 35–6
    Esmail Kho'i 196–200
    Nima Yushij 35–6
    presence 46
Politzer, György 186
Praising Ahmad Shamlou, Esmail Kho'i 184–5
Prayer, Sohrab Sepehri 18
Present Age, The, Søren Kierkegaard 139
Proclamation, Ahmad Shamlou 95

prosody 96, 128
    Nimaic 33–4, 91, 96
Punishment, Ahmad Shamlou 99–101

Qais-e Razi, Shams 19, 109, 128–9
Qajar dynasty 3, 90
qasideh 83, 99, 199
Qazvini, Aref 11, 34, 72, 102, 214, 222
    Constitutional period 6, 11, 25, 27

Rahi Mo'ayyeri, *Shadow of Life* 13
Rebellion, Forough Farrokhzad 116, 127–8
Restless, Esmail Kho'i 187
Return to Borgio Verezzi, Esmail Kho'i 194–5
revolutionary
    Esmail Kho'i 185–90
    Sohrab Sepehri 152–7
revolutionary witness, Ahmad Shamlou 105–13
Reza Shah 7, 28
    abdication 39
rhyme and rhythm, Nima Yushij 52–3
Ricœur, Paul 29, 33, 69, 111
Rieff, Phillip 139
Ruins of the Sunshine, The, Sohrab Sepehri 153

Sabari, Pari 2
Sappho 119–20, 122–3, 150
Sarkisian, Aida, and Ahmad Shamlou 91–2, 95–6, 98–9
science 55, 109, 199
    Alain Badiou 59
    and philosophy 54
selat 99
Self-Appraisal, Esmail Kho'i 206
Sepehri, Sohrab 29, 151–2
    early life 152
    exile in US 24
    and Forough Farrokhzad 157–60
    revolutionary 152–7
    transcendence 18, 164, 175, 177
Sepehri, Sohrab poems
    Doust 158–9
    Eight Books 153
    Fellow Traveler 152
    I Am Still Traveling 153
    Prayer 18

The Blue Room 160–2
The Death of Color 153
The East of Sorrow 153
The Green Volume 153
The Life of Dreams 153
The Ruins of the Sunshine 153
The Sound of the Beginning 163
The Sound of the Water's Footstep 153–7
The Tired Presence of Things 162–4
Traveler 153, 163–81
We Nothing, We the Look 153
Shadow of Life, Rahi Mo'ayyeri 13
sha'er 8, 22, 57, 198, 210
Shafi'i-Kadkani, Mohammad-Reza 19, 129, 188
   capitalist modernity 4
   classical context 21
   Nima Yushij 36–8, 45
   periodization 5–9
Shahnameh
   Ferdowsi 70, 89–90, 101, 103, 110, 113
   Persian names 64
Shamlou, Ahmad 89–90
   agent provocateur 113–14
   and Aida Sarkisian 91–2, 95–6, 98–9
   early life 90–5
   exile 105
   Forough Farrokhzad elegy 97–8
   meeting the author 2
   on Nima Yushij 96–7
   poet laureate 95–101
   revolutionary witness 105–13
   transcendence 214
   troubadour 101–5
Shamlou, Ahmad poems 23 95
   Abraham in the Fire 96, 105–6, 114
   Aida in the Mirror 95
   Aida, Tree, Dagger, and Memory 95
   And a Regret 94–5
   At the Threshold 93–4, 96
   Battling Silence 89
   Blossoming in the Fog 96
   Curse 14–15
   Dagger on the Plate 96
   Dark Song 114
   Earthly Elegies 96
   Elegy 98
   Fairies 107–8

   Fighting Silence 92–3
   For Blood and Lipstick 213–14
   Fountainhead 90
   Fresh Air 95
   [I am sorry] Bi ankeh dideh binad 102–3
   In this Dead-End 91–2
   Irons and Emotions 95
   Moments and Forever 95
   Nocturnal 103
   Phoenix in the Rain 95
   Proclamation 95
   Punishment 99–101
   Short Songs of Exile 96
   Thankless Panegyrics 96
   The Culture of the Street 113
   The Daughters of Mother Sea 108–9
   The Death of the Nazarene 112
   The Funeral Elegy 106–7
   The Garden of Mirrors 95, 110–1
   The Humble Discoverers of Hemlock 106–7
   The Story of Mahan's Restlessness 96
   Until the Red Blossom of a Dress 103–5
   Upon the Cold Inside 97
Shapour, Parviz 116
she'r sepid 103
She'r-e Azad *see* free poetry
She'r-e Emruz *see* contemporary poetry
She'r-e No *see* New Poetry
Short Songs of Exile, Ahmad Shamlou 96
Sickness unto Death, The, Søren Kierkegaard 140–1
Sketch, Esmail Kho'i 25–6
Socialist Jungle Movement of Gilan 39
solitary worlds, Forough Farrokhzad 139–43
Someone Who Is Like No One Else, Forough Farrokhzad 124–7
Song of Freedom, Esmail Kho'i 192–4
Sound of the Beginning, The, Sohrab Sepehri 163
Sound of the Water's Footstep, The, Sohrab Sepehri 153–7
Stages of Perfection, Afzal, Baba 120
Story of Mahan's Restlessness, The, Ahmad Shamlou 96
storytelling 65
Suddenly, Esmail Kho'i 188

Sufism 159
Suhrawardi, Shihab al-Din Yahya, *The Ballad of the Occidental Exile* 169–70, 183, 201
Swamp, Forough Farrokhzad 138–9

Tabari 40, 45
Tahbaz, Sirus 40, 45
tajaddod 72
Tajik poetry 56, 210
Takhti, Gholamreza 66
Taoism 159
temporal spontaneity, Forough Farrokhzad 118–23
temporality 9, 30, 60, 68
Thankless Panegyrics, Ahmad Shamlou 96
Till the Morning Dawns, Nima Yushij 1–2
time and narrative, Persian poetry 29–31
Tired Presence of Things, The, Sohrab Sepehri 162–4
To Those Who Follow in Our Wake, Bertolt Brecht 13–14
totality, and infinity 52
tradition and modernity, Mehdi Akhavan-e Sales 72–7
transcendence 4, 17, 222
  Ahmad Shamlou 214
  Esmail Kho'i 26
  Forough Farrokhzad 21, 31
  Nima Yushij 48, 52
  Sohrab Sepehri 18, 164, 175, 177
transubstantial motion
  Mehdi Akhavan-e Sales 84–6
  Nima Yushij 33
Traveler, Sohrab Sepehri 153, 163–81
Tree of Knowledge, The, Mehdi Akhavan-e Sales 80–1
troubadour, Ahmad Shamlou 101–5
Tudeh Party 35, 39, 42, 50, 55, 95
Twentythree23, Ahmad Shamlou 95

Until the Red Blossom of a Dress, Ahmad Shamlou 103–5
Upon the Cold Inside, Ahmad Shamlou 97
Upon the Fast Steed of the Earth, Esmail Kho'i 187

Virgil 78, 173

Wall, Forough Farrokhzad 116, 127, 129–30
We Nothing, We the Look, Sohrab Sepehri 153
West, the 6, 66
  Christianity in 41
  exile in 183
  modernity 68, 78
  problems from 70, 219
West, the and the East
  homeland 181, 184
  modernity 71–2
  separation of 123, 153, 160–1, 166, 175
Westernization 41, 210–11, 215
When Weeping Melodiously, Nima Yushij 46–7
Where We Might Call Homeland, Esmail Kho'i 204
Willow Song, The, Nima Yushij 44
women's rights 6, 37
wujud 29, 60, 84–5, 164

yaftan 29, 60–1, 79–80
Yazdi, Farrokhi 11
Yushij, Nima 3, 33–6
  and Alan Badiou 59
  and Alieh Khanom Jahangir 39–40, 42
  and Baba Afzal 60–1
  context 36–9
  epistolary poetics 52–8
  and Ernst Cassirer 58–9
  forces of 45–52
  imprisonment 39–40, 43
  and Jalal Al-e Ahmad 43
  letters 53–5
  life of 39–44
  and Mehdi Akhavan-e Sales 65–7
  opium addiction 42–3
  poetic events 58–61
  transcendence 48, 52
Yushij, Nima poems
  Ahoy People 35–6
  By Sakhtsar 41
  Cold Campfire 38–9
  I Long for You 50–1
  It is Night 56
  Moonlight 47–8, 61
  My Home Is a Cloud 48–9
  Myth 26

The Amen Bird 49–50
The Neighbor's Words 52–3
Till the Morning Dawns 1–2
When Weeping Melodiously 46–4
Willow Song, The 44

Zarrinkub, Abdolhossein 19, 21, 80
Zen Buddhism 8, 18, 159–60, 219

Zionists 197
Zoroaster 63, 83
Zoroastrianism
    beliefs 8, 199–200
    deities 82
    icons 65
    texts 78
zuhur 123–4, 150